Practical social work

Published in conjunction with
the British Ass~~~ ~~~~~~~ ~f So~ial Workers

B A S W

Social work is at an important stage in its development. The profession is facing fresh challenges to work flexibly in fast-changing social and organisational environments. New requirements for training are also demanding a more critical and reflective, as well as more highly skilled, approach to practice.

The British Association of Social Workers (www.basw.co.uk) has always been conscious of its role in setting guidelines for practice and in seeking to raise professional standards. The concept of the *Practical Social Work* series was conceived to fulfil a genuine professional need for a carefully planned, coherent series of texts that would stimulate and inform debate, thereby contributing to the development of practitioners' skills and professionalism.

Newly relaunched, the series continues to address the needs of all those who are looking to deepen and refresh their understanding and skills. It is designed for students and busy professionals alike. Each book marries practice issues and challenges with the latest theory and research in a compact and applied format. The authors represent a wide variety of experience both as educators and practitioners. Taken together, the books set a standard in their clarity, relevance and rigour.

A list of new and best-selling titles in this series follows overleaf. A comprehensive list of titles available in the series, and further details about individual books, can be found online at :
www.palgrave.com/socialworkpolicy/basw

Series standing order **ISBN 0–333–80313–2**

You can receive future titles in this series as they are published by placing a standing order. Please contact your bookseller or, in the case of difficulty, contact us at the address below with your name and address, the title of the series and the ISBN quoted above.

Customer Services Department, Macmillan Distribution Ltd, Houndmills, Basingstoke, Hampshire RG21 6XS, England

Practical social work series

New and best-selling titles

Suzy Braye
Michael Preston-Shoot

Practising Social
Work Law

Third edition

palgrave
macmillan

First edition published 1992
Reprinted once
Second edition published 1997
Reprinted eleven times
Third edition published 2010 by
PALGRAVE MACMILLAN

Palgrave Macmillan in the UK is an imprint of Macmillan Publishers Limited, registered in England, company number 785998, of Houndmills, Basingstoke, Hampshire RG21 6XS.

Palgrave Macmillan in the US is a division of St Martin's Press LLC, 175 Fifth Avenue, New York, NY 10010.

Palgrave Macmillan is the global academic imprint of the above companies and has companies and representatives throughout the world.

Palgrave® and Macmillan® are registered trademarks in the United States, the United Kingdom, Europe and other countries

978-0-230-54318-8

This book is printed on paper suitable for recycling and made from fully managed and sustained forest sources. Logging, pulping and manufacturing processes are expected to conform to the environmental regulations of the country of origin.

A catalogue record for this book is available from the British Library.

A catalog record for this book is available from the Library of Congress.

10   9   8   7   6   5   4   3   2
19   18   17   16   15   14   13   12   11   10

Printed in China

Contents

Acknowledgements

Since publication of the second edition we have continued to engage in critical reflection of law and social work practice, and to learn about law as a discipline. We have continued to anticipate and to read legal judgements with as much excitement as social work texts and we remain aware of the less than adequate reporting of law in social work's literature. One of us (SB) has returned from social work management to academe. One of us (MPS) has had to embrace yet another discipline, health, as part of a portfolio of responsibilities. Both of us have continued to enjoy interactions with social workers in training and with practitioners and managers, which have enhanced our thinking and the teaching and learning opportunities we have offered.

On this journey we have continued to benefit from the encouragement and friendship of colleagues, friends and family. Stuart Vernon and Gwyneth Roberts have shared in our enthusiasm for connecting law and social work, and have helped us to develop our thinking about social work law. Colleagues at the University of Sussex and the University of Bedfordshire have been critical friends as we have engaged first in research around teaching, learning and assessment of law in social work education and subsequently in developing social work law resources for social workers in training, practice teachers, practitioners and managers. Enid Levin, Mike Fisher Gavin Nettleton and Colin Paton, at the Social Care Institute for Excellence, have had faith in our research skills and our subject expertise, giving us several opportunities to place our research and development work in the public domain. We are also grateful to SCIE for permission to reproduce the figure and tables in Chapter 3.

We have also benefited from working with experts by experience who have shared honestly and forthrightly their narratives of social work law in action. Their experiences and their vision for lawful and ethical social work practice continue to enrich our teaching and our writing on social work law. We continue to be inspired by their work through the organizations *Parents Fight Back, Disabled Parents Network, Advocacy in Action, Moving on with Learning,* and *Suresearch.*

Catherine Gray, of Palgrave Macmillan, had faith in our project and helped us to clarify our thinking for this third edition. Sadly, Jo Campling did not live to see the third edition commissioned but we remember her support, advocacy and affection with love.

Gywneth, Sue and Stuart, Vic and Linda, Liz and Dick, Nadette and René, Amanda and Courtney, and Imogen and Roger have provided practical and moral support, friendship and love, which have sustained us.

As always, Hannah and Sebastian deserve special mention for their gifts and their love.

Suzy Braye
Michael Preston-Shoot

Table of legal rules

Local Authority Circulars and Letters

Abbreviations

AMHP	Approved Mental Health Professional
CAF	Common Assessment Framework
CAFCASS	Children and Family Court Advisory Support Service
CQC	Care Quality Commission
CRB	Criminal Records Bureau
CSCI	Commission for Social Care Inspection
CST	Care Standards Tribunal
EC	European Community
ECHR	European Convention on Human Rights and Fundamental Freedoms
ECtHR	European Court of Human Rights
EHRC	Equality and Human Rights Commission
FACS	Fair Access to Care Services
GSCC	General Social Care Council
ICS	Integrated Children's System
IMCA	Independent Mental Capacity Advocate
IMHA	Independent Mental Health Advocate
IRO	Independent Reviewing Officer
ISA	Independent Safeguarding Authority
LEA	Local education authority
MAPPA	Multi-Agency Public Protection Arrangements
MHAC	Mental Health Act Commission
MHRT	Mental Health Review Tribunal
NASS	National Asylum Support Service
NHS	National Health Service
NR	Nearest Relative
NSF	National Service Framework
PCT	Primary Care Trust
SAP	Single Assessment Process
SEN	Special Educational Needs
UNCRC	United Nations Convention on the Rights of the Child

Table of cases

Preface to the third edition

Since the publication of the second edition the legal mandate underpinning social work practice has continued to evolve. There have been significant developments in the areas of human rights (Human Rights Act 1998) and discrimination (Race Relations (Amendment) Act 2000; Disability Discrimination Act 2005; Equality Act 2006). There have been major reforms of child care law (Children Act 2004; Adoption and Children Act 2002; Children (Leaving Care) Act 2000) and of youth justice (Crime and Disorder Act 1998; Youth Justice and Criminal Evidence Act 1999). Community care law has continued to develop, both in case law and policy guidance and in statute (Carers and Disabled Children Act 2000; Carers (Equal Opportunities) Act 2004). There are new legal rules surrounding 'vulnerable adults' (Mental Capacity Act 2005) and severe mental distress (Mental Health Act 2007). Finally, the law relating to asylum and immigration continues to tighten, to attract judicial challenge, and to present ethical dilemmas to social workers.

To some degree there has been a shift in values expressed through legal rules. The Civil Partnership Act 2004 gives legal recognition to same-sex partners, although they are still not accorded the actual title and status of marriage (*Wilkinson v Kitzinger and Another* [2006]). The Gender Recognition Act 2004 allows people who have decided to live permanently and fully in their chosen gender to apply for legal recognition of this change. The age of consent for sexual activity has been equalized (Sexual Offences (Amendment) Act 2000). Less positively, asylum seekers are demonized and perceived as a threat. The legal rules continue to minimize their rights and to downplay their motivations for seeking refuge (Roberts and Harris, 2002).

Some of these changes have occasioned sharp debates, such as the degree to which reform of mental health legislation should prioritize public safety or the rights of people with mental distress. The balance between public safety and the due process rights of individuals continues to be contested, especially in respect of people suspected of terrorism, those diagnosed with personality disorders, and those convicted of serious offences. The same may be said of separated parents' rights in respect of contact with their children, where domestic oppression not infrequently lies behind disputes and hostility. The Children and Adoption Act 2006 has created new powers to enforce contact and it remains to be seen whether its provisions will, in some cases, destabilize the care provided by the resident parent and thereby jeopardize the best interests of the child. Debates about the balance to be struck between victims, communities and offenders, coupled with social policy preoccupations with individual responsibility, risk and dangerousness, and disillusionment with penal and welfare agencies, are played out in every criminal justice reform proposal.

Paradoxically, however, although social policy and the legal rules reflective of it appear indifferent or hostile towards the needs of some groups, government has also endorsed the international definition of social work (IASSW, 2001) which, in endorsing social change, resonates with social work's concern with inequality, injustice and oppression. Social workers must challenge those situations that put children and adults at risk. These include institutionalized discrimination, and deprivation of human and civil rights, alongside familial abuse and neglect, and behaviours which place them or others at risk (GSCC, 2008). Moreover, the Human Rights Act 1998, and its incorporation of the European Convention on Human Rights and Fundamental Freedoms (ECHR) into UK law, also strengthens the procedural rights available to citizens in respect of the use of power and authority by public organizations. Nonetheless, despite these changes and complexities, one feature remains constant, namely that some vulnerable people are still being denied the social care assistance that they need within a welfare system that is structured in the main around duties on public authorities rather than rights for individuals in respect of support and services.

Also since publication of the second edition, the discipline of social work law has been the focus of continued theory-building, with the twin aims of analyzing, defining and describing the nature, extent and complexities of the relationship between law and social work, and of providing a framework for legal, ethical and humane practice. This has crystallized around three distinct components. Firstly, the legal powers and duties, contained in statute, secondary legislation, policy and practice guidance, and case law, provide social workers with a mandate to practise. Secondly, social work values and knowledge shape and are influenced by these powers and duties, through such principles as anti-discriminatory practice, partnership, self-determination and proportional intervention. This interactive relationship both creates dilemmas in professional practice and provides one framework for their potential resolution. Thirdly, practice is held accountable through administrative law, whereby organizations are subject to scrutiny and control by the courts, non-judicial bodies such as the Local Commissioner for Administration (Ombudsman), and Care Council codes of conduct (GSCC, 2002; Braye and Preston-Shoot, 1999; Preston-Shoot et al, 1998a, 2001). This tripartite framework rests on the belief that each day's social work requires not only a good technical knowledge of the law and ability to apply it to situations encountered in practice but also a sound awareness of the ethical and moral dimensions involved when using legal powers and duties, and a critical understanding of the role of law and other forms of knowledge in promoting human rights and social justice.

This theory-building has also advanced the view presented in the second edition, and reiterated here, that practising social work law must involve not only those powers and duties that social workers implement directly, known as social work law. It must also involve those mandates, collectively known as social welfare law, with which they must be familiar when working with service users and carers, to whom we often refer here as 'experts by experience'. This breadth of relevant legal knowledge has also been strongly emphasized by experts by experience (Braye and Preston-Shoot, 2006a). Accordingly, the law relating to human rights, discrimination, homelessness, divorce, domestic oppression and special educational needs is included.

In addition to this analysis of the interface between law and social work practice, focus has been turned on teaching, learning and assessment of law in social work education. There has been a knowledge review (Braye and Preston-Shoot et al., 2005), comprising a systematic review of the literature and a survey of law teaching on social work degree programmes, its importance derived from the continued centrality of this subject in the rules and requirements for social work training (DH, 2000a). It is now also possible to link explicitly knowledge of the law to the skills and knowledge identified by the national occupational standards (TOPSS, 2002) and the social work benchmark statement (QAA, 2008). The knowledge review has been followed by publication of a resource guide (Braye and Preston-Shoot, 2006a) and e-learning resources (Braye and Preston-Shoot, 2007), designed to enrich learning within qualifying and post-qualifying education.

Social work practice has continued to be the site of major change. Divisions between children's and adults' services have increasingly fragmented social work when, as experts by experience continue to attest, social care needs do not come in neat boxes but rather straddle attempts at discrete organizational separations. Disabled parents and young disabled people approaching transition from adolescence to adulthood are two cases in point. These divisions have been accompanied more recently by closer alignments between social care and health, housing and education. The Health Act 1999, the Health and Social Care Act 2001, and the Children Act 2004 have been the driving forces towards greater co-ordination between at least some professional groupings. It remains to be seen how far legislative direction alone will address the distorted, disrupted and/ or damaged relationships among agency and professional groups, which inquiries into mental health, community care and child care tragedies have highlighted (Reder et al., 1993; Sheppard, 1996; Reder and Duncan, 1999; Laming, 2003). A cautionary tale (Utting, 1996) has been the limited effect of legislation on the objectives for community care due to levels of investment and organizational configurations.

Increasingly, social policy is emphasizing the outcomes on which welfare activity must be focused. For young people (DfES, 2004a) this involves a move from identifying need, safeguarding and promoting the welfare of children at risk (Children Act 1989), to promoting the well-being of all children, active intervention and prevention, and integrated service provision (Children Act 2004). All agencies should be focused on maximizing young people's physical and mental health, their emotional, social and economic well-being, take-up of education, training and recreation, and involvement in society, whilst also protecting them from harm and neglect. For adults the focus is on promoting a wider range of services in the community, providing better support for ongoing complex needs, making care more responsive and accessible, maximizing independence and well-being, and placing people in control of person-centred provision, all key features of the personalization agenda (DH, 2006a). These themes are reiterated in the vision for the workforce profile in 2020 (DH/DfES, 2006), which also emphasizes the need to rethink agency and practitioner roles, relationships and responsibilities, and envisages different ways of commissioning and delivering services. However, councils with social services responsibilities remain resource-constrained, such that people's situations can be left to deteriorate until their needs become critical, and organized around traditional structures and processes. The resource base and the legal rules remain focused on care rather than support to enable people to engage in active citizenship. Moreover, the care given can mean enforced institutionalization because of the cost of meeting needs in the community.

This reconfiguration of the practice landscape is part of the modernization agenda (DH, 1998), with its emphasis on raising standards, improving protection, and enhancing accountability. It has been accompanied by a more positive perspective from government on the importance of social work, with the determination to raise the profession's standing and profile evident particularly in the introduction of the social work degree and a renewed emphasis on evidence for practice. The emphasis on standards is reflected in the Care Standards Act 2000, with registration of social (care) workers, protected title for social work, and publication of codes of conduct (GSCC, 2002) and national service frameworks. The emphasis on protection may be seen in the Public Interest Disclosure Act 1998, which seeks to give employees protection when they disclose unlawful actions within organizations, and in the Safeguarding Vulnerable Groups Act 2006, which requires closer monitoring of staff recruitment. Provisions in the Children Act 2004 for registration and monitoring of private fostering and childminding have a similar inspiration. The emphasis on quality may be seen in the best value provisions within the Local Government Act 1999, in the creation by the Care Standards Act 2000 of regulatory councils and the Social Care Institute for Excellence (SCIE), and in the framework for performance assessment and inspection. The emphasis on accountability is perhaps most clearly seen in the Human Rights Act 1998, which has swept away the immunity of public organizations from claims for damages arising from how statutory duties have been implemented because of the rights to a fair hearing and to an effective remedy contained within the ECHR.

These changes to the balance of power between practitioners and their employing organizations, and between service users and public authorities, may be welcome. However, they may prove insufficient alone to ensure lawful and ethical practice (Preston-Shoot, 2001a, 2008), given the under-funded position of many councils, the evidence from judicial reviews of restrictive assessments, inappropriate care planning and failure to adhere to the legal rules, and the levels of confidence and disillusionment amongst social workers. Thus, when declaring a care plan for a disabled young person unlawful, one judge compared a local authority to a computer system in which a virus had come to infect decision-making (*R (CD) (a child by her litigation friend VD) v Isle of Anglesey CC* [2004]). Indeed, the use of case law in this book, to demonstrate the sometimes positive contribution that judicial decision-making can make to effective and ethical social work practice, begs the question of whether social workers have been challenging their own managers, drawing on legal literacy as well as evidence from research, theory, practice wisdom and the narratives of experts by experience. At stake are people's human rights, quality of life and citizenship. Moreover, the accountability framework remains incomplete in terms of what is protected within social work's title and the absence of automatic referral to the regulatory council when there is a finding of unethical conduct. There remains a muddle in practice between accountability to professional ethics, the code of conduct and the employer, whilst sanctions against individual social workers in terms of their registration are much stronger than those against an employer who acts unlawfully and/or unethically. Finally, whilst there are many excellent social (care) workers, there are also incidents of neglect and mistreatment, which complaints and inspection procedures do not always detect or rectify (Wellard, 1999; Flynn, 2004; Valios, 2006).

To help social workers navigate this complex practice terrain, some chapters from the second edition have been retained but substantially revised whilst the material in others has been integrated. In this edition there is an enhanced discussion of case studies and the law *on* social work practice in order to reflect and respond to real pressures within social workers' lived experience of practice and since knowledge is retained and promoted when couched in a framework directly relevant to everyday practice.

The book's core orientation and distinctive contribution, however, has not changed. It presents contextualized substantive legal knowledge through the use of case studies, which remain at the core of the book and achieve three important purposes. Firstly, they mirror how social work practitioners encounter and use the law in their practice and model the inductive thinking necessary in that context. Secondly, they make explicit the links and connections between areas of law. Thirdly, they demonstrate how to approach the application of legal knowledge in a casework context. Besides this interlinking of law with practice knowledge and skills, additionally the book presents a critical and theorized analysis of the relationship between law and social work, and offers a critical perspective on the discipline of social work law through analysis of practice dilemmas, and the knowledge, skills and processes for the application of the legal rules in social work practice. It places a significant focus on legal rules for *how* social workers conduct their practice, as well as the content of *what* they do, having been informed by substantial discussions with experts by experience, social workers in training, practitioners and managers, in which key questions have featured routinely. Some questions have related to currency of knowledge about the content of legal rules in the context of limited opportunities for practitioners to update their knowledge. The interface between child care and community care law, in respect of disabled parents and young people facing transition and/or leaving care, has been prominent here, as have the impact of the Human Rights Act 1998 and concerns about court skills. Some questions have focused on the practice context, including how the health and safety needs of staff may be balanced with duties of care towards service users, and how managers perceived as implementing resource-led decisions about care packages, assessments, and placements may be challenged.

The book is intended to promote social workers' confidence, knowledge and skills in recognizing, locating and articulating legal issues to managers and experts by experience, and using the law to inform practice standards and to deliver positive outcomes for service users and their carers. There are, of course, few right answers in social work. There is no substitute for finely tuned judgements; no remedy for the inevitability of risk. However, this book provides a rounded model as a solid foundation for practice.

A note on terminology

The phrase 'experts by experience' refers to service users and carers and is a term chosen by them. It acknowledges that personal experience is a source of knowledge about the impact and outcomes of professional practice. It reflects the changing nature of the relationship between service users, educators and practitioners. Service users increasingly are seen as experts on defining their own situation, choosing from a range of intervention options, and commenting on the effects of policy and practice, as well as change agents through involvement in service commissioning, delivery, monitoring and evaluation, and participation in the selection, teaching and assessment of social workers in training.

A note on legal frameworks

Except where specifically stated to apply to all four nations in the UK, the legal rules referred to apply to England. However, the conceptual analysis of practising social work law has broader applicability and will assist students and qualified practitioners in other jurisdictions to understand and implement their legal powers and duties.

A note on the book's structure

Chapter 1 reviews the research evidence relating to the law in action in social work, and how far the outcomes of social work intervention correspond to legislative intention. Chapters 2 and 3 explore the relationship between law and social work, and how values, rights and diverse sources of knowledge might help social work practitioners and students understand and navigate the dilemmas and choices they will encounter. Chapters 4 and 5 use case studies to identify, apply and critique relevant legal rules. Chapters 6 and 7 take key stages of planning and providing social work services, identifying and critically reviewing the content and application of the legal rules *on* practice. Chapter 8, finally, explores core social work skills and how social work students and practitioners, drawing on their values and knowledge-base, can practise social work law confidently.

1 | Towards practising social work law

Social workers in training and experienced practitioners alike often appear apprehensive and lacking in confidence about working in the legal arena (Braye and Preston-Shoot et al., 2005). They perceive social work practice, experience, training and evidence to have limited credibility compared with that of other professional groups (Preston-Shoot et al., 1998b), whilst they are also concerned about the complex jargon and high volume of factual detail to be grasped. Others may struggle owing to limited opportunities to develop and update their knowledge and skills for interacting in the legal arena. Indeed, ignorance of, or uncertainty about, the legal rules features in inquiries into mental health tragedies (Sheppard, 1996) and in research on direct payments (Glasby and Littlechild, 2002) and on child protection (Hunt and Macleod, 1998). Alternatively, social workers may be disappointed when the clear boundaries they expect from the legal rules are not apparent. Some may question the very idea of law being part of social work.

Research has also found that teams are sometimes not up to date with changes to the legal rules. Performance targets may matter more to managers than legal challenges to unlawful practice, with practice being driven and distorted by an organizational focus on agency procedures, such that the law becomes less visible (Braye et al., 2007). The role of the organization is influential in determining the extent to which law is seen as a significant feature of practice. Competence depends not just on practitioners taking responsibility for their continuing professional development but also on organizational competence (Preston-Shoot, 2000a) in providing regular legal updates and clear information that is not mediated through agency interpretation (Braye and Preston-Shoot, 2006a). This should be coupled with supervision and debriefing to help practitioners manage the anxiety, ambiguity and pressure which accompany the legal mandate, and to learn from experience.

By contrast, experts by experience expect social workers to have up-to-date legal knowledge and to be technically competent in its use (Barnes,

1

2002; Braye and Preston-Shoot et al., 2005). However, they also expect practitioners to be *critically* competent. Critical thinking here refers to being able to articulate legal knowledge, debate the relationship between law and professional practice, share ethical dilemmas and options for their resolution, and explain their decision-making. It includes a commitment to tackling discrimination and oppression alongside individual need, responding to the impact of the law on people's lives, and taking action when the law disadvantages particular social groups.

How well do social workers in training and experienced practitioners measure up against these expressed standards? The picture is variable. Practice teachers appear daunted by their responsibility for teaching and assessing social work law and express reservations about their own legal competence (Preston-Shoot et al., 1997; Braye and Preston-Shoot et al., 2005; Braye et al., 2007). Marsh and Triseliotis (1996) reported a lack of confidence among newly qualified practitioners. Barnes (2002) found that most students were competent when answering questions about the law but that carers considered social workers to be ill-equipped with legal skills. Another survey (Willis, 2002) found respondents critical of management support and of their lack of training, for example on court skills and legal proceedings, which created difficulties when working with lawyers. Half of the students in another project recognized that complying with legal rules was a key task but believed that they did not have sufficient knowledge of relevant legislation (Mathias-Williams and Thomas, 2002). More positively, social workers in training are increasingly ranking their law teaching as good and relevant (Ball et al., 1995; Marsh and Triseliotis, 1996; Lyons and Manion, 2004).

Crucially, then, what is written and taught about social work must leave practitioners certain in relation to 'knowing what' and 'knowing how'. It must also enable them to question the roles prescribed for them in law and to debate how legislation defines problems and solutions. Finally, it must provide understanding of the relationship between law and practice, and facilitate confidence in responding as that interface changes and develops.

The contested relationship between law and social work

There is long-standing concern about apparent deficiencies in social workers' knowledge and use of legislation, and their unease when acting as statutory agents (Ball et al., 1988). During the 1980s reports into child abuse tragedies criticized the failure of practitioners to identify and observe their legal duties, and to use positively their available legal powers (DHSS, 1982; Blom-Cooper, 1985; London Borough of

Greenwich, 1987). They suggested that social workers disliked an authoritarian role and the use of legal intervention. By contrast, other reports criticized social workers for being over-zealous and ill-advised in their use of the law, and found that using statutory controls can be counter-productive to risk management and decision-making in child care (DHSS, 1985; Butler-Sloss, 1988). The paradox was stark: social workers appear damned if they act and damned if they do not act.

This paradox has continued, with social workers criticized (DH, 1995) for focusing more on child abuse and child protection than on the support needs of children and families, without examining the context which had created this situation. This research advocated an increased emphasis on preventive services without indicating how an apparent preoccupation with abuse was to be modified, thereby failing to address the roots of the paradox in the legal mandate and its relationship with social work. Similarly, Hunt and Macleod (1998) found evidence of social workers refocusing risk assessment and supporting families through partnership but concluded that some cases enter the court system too early and others too late. The paradox or dilemma is further reinforced by the Laming Report (2003) appearing to require social workers to adopt a more suspicious approach towards families, which could risk alienating them and jeopardize preventive and collaborative work (Sinclair and Corden, 2005).

Policy pronouncements envisage more support to enable older people to live independently, with high quality, flexible services designed to promote personal dignity, respond to individual need, and afford people greater control over their lives (DH, 2006a). Similarly, excellence is defined as better access to services, improved well-being and enhanced quality (DH/DfES, 2006). Whilst this is acknowledged as requiring a fundamental change in service provision, changes in the legal mandate have yet to follow to ensure more user-focused services.

The paradox is reflected in ambivalence about social workers' authority within the legal rules. Only qualified social workers can become independent reviewing officers, monitoring how local authorities implement plans for looked after children (Adoption and Children Act 2002), and they have a lead role in core assessments to safeguard and protect young people (DfES, 2006a). However, social work has lost its pre-eminence in decision-making on admissions to psychiatric hospital or guardianship (Mental Health Act 2007), with the newer role of approved mental health professional also pivotal to best interests assessments (Mental Capacity Act 2005).

Another discourse also identifies implementation failure in front-line practice but attributes it to lack of clarity about managerial responsibility and accountability, procedural and practice failure, assessment of eligibility rather than need, harm and risk, and inadequate information exchange between agencies (Laming, 2003). Rather than the relationship between law and social work being seen as problematic, personal failures (unprofessional performance) and systemic problems (organizational malaise) are highlighted. Changes to the law (Children Act 2004) seek to create legal underpinning for a procedural system for sharing information and monitoring children, whilst leaving unaltered other aspects of the interface between law and social work. Sinclair and Corden (2005) argue, indeed, that the belief that children's safety will be enhanced through information collation and procedures is based on presupposition not fact.

The prescribed remedies for this 'malaise' differ fundamentally. The inquiry into the death of Jasmine Beckford (Blom-Cooper, 1985) argued that social work can only be defined in terms of the functions required of its practitioners by their employing agencies operating within a statutory framework. Here the law is seen as social work's core mandate, the pivot for practice, legal knowledge as offering direction in an uncertain and confusing world, as if it is somehow obvious when and how practitioners must act. What is required, therefore, is a higher degree of proven competence in relation to statutory duties, and an ability to interpret and exercise those duties in a technically correct way (Blom-Cooper, 1985). This legalistic model is reflected in *The Law Report* (Ball et al., 1988) which allocates legal knowledge the central position in social work. It is seen in the faith placed in the legal rules to shape aspects of practice such as interagency working (Laming, 2003; Children Act 2004; DfES, 2006a) without apparent questioning of their feasibility and impact on necessary relationships with families (Sinclair and Corden, 2005).

An alternative pivot for practice was offered by Stevenson (1988): an ethical duty of care. Here the law is but one framework, alongside key social work values and skills, including user self-determination, professional judgement, assessment and working for individual and social change. Law may be an obstacle to values-based and research-informed practice, work with asylum-seekers being one example (Humphries, 2004), even if there are other instances where principles codified in the legal rules correspond closely to social work values (Preston-Shoot et al., 2001). The belief that law alone is insufficient also has government endorsement: the assessment of young people and their families requires professional skill and judgement in addition to legal regulations and guidance (DH, 1989a, 2000b; GSCC, 2008). Rather than an ideology of legalism, emphasizing the pre-eminence of law in defining social work, a close fit between the law and appropriate courses of action is not assumed. The law is seen only as one resource, ambiguous, open to interpretation, and not always effective.

These two positions, arguably, over-simplify everyday practice. Periodically, practitioners will encounter situations where law and values – two mandates for professional activity – collide. Routinely practitioners will encounter dilemmas and competing imperatives, such as care vs control, needs vs resources, welfare vs justice, individual vs society, or rights vs risks. There will be questions of how to respond when social policies neglect people's basic needs and social rights. There will be tensions to be negotiated between helping individuals and acting for society, between enforcing people's rights, affording them protection and securing social control. There will be cases where it is unclear what constitutes high or unacceptable risk, or which cluster of factors indicate action, or whether or not possible outcomes of intervention are to be preferred. Resolution requires professional analysis, judgement and problem solving (Braye and Preston-Shoot, 1990), assessment skills informed by values, knowledge, practice wisdom and the perspectives of experts by experience, and a delicate balance between law and ethics in a framework of professional accountability (Braye and Preston-Shoot, 2006b). When and how to intervene will not always be obvious. Equally appropriate but different orientations towards a situation will lead workers to prioritize agency procedures, people's needs, people's rights, or the avoidance of risk (Braye and Preston-Shoot, 2007). Neither the law nor social work values, alone, will enable practitioners to decide what they ought to do. Even where a mandate can be identified, and a situation falls on the 'right' side of it, permitted or mandated action may not be the 'right thing to do'.

Questioning law

Legal rules have been used to drive forward the modernization of social services (DH, 1998). The Public Interest Disclosure Act 1998 and the Care Standards Act 2000 address the objective of protecting service users from poor practice. Their provisions for whistleblowing and registration change the balance of power between social workers and their employers. The Community Care (Direct Payments) Act 1996, as extended by the Health and Social Care Act 2001, responds to the objective of prioritizing responsiveness, flexibility, choice and independence in meeting need. The Health Act 1999, the Health and Social Care Act 2001 and the Children Act 2004 tackle co-ordination between services and agencies, whilst the objective of securing greater consistency between services underpins *Fair Access to Care Services* guidance (DH, 2002b), the framework for assessing children in need (DH, 2000b) and the national service frameworks (e.g. DH, 1999b, 2001b).

However, an exclusively legalistic model, where the law is elevated to become the main form of admissible knowledge, is inadequate for the complexities social workers face. It may be challenged for creating an impression that the law offers a clear map for welfare practice when, in fact, it provides a series of maps within statute, regulations, guidance and court decisions, regularly redrawn, sometimes inconsistent, and variable in detail and prescription (Braye and Preston-Shoot, 2006b). For example, youth justice legislation has created six youth justice systems rather than one coherent approach (Preston-Shoot and Vernon, 2002). Therefore, the law is neither simple nor unproblematic to apply. Nor can it be assumed that if the legal mandate is known and followed practitioners will provide appropriate types and levels of intervention. Social workers operate with legal clauses which are discretionary, open to interpretation, and within which what is included and excluded will be a matter of contested judgement. For instance, the House of Lords has returned split decisions in respect of the balance of probability to be shown in cases of likelihood of significant harm (*Re H and R (Child Sexual Abuse: Standard of Proof)* [1996]), and whether private residential care homes are providing a public function within the meaning of the Human Rights Act 1998 (*YL (by her Litigation Friend the Official Solicitor) v Birmingham City Council* [2007]). Moreover, both inquiries (Ritchie et al., 1994) and judges (*R v Gloucestershire County Council, ex parte RADAR* [1996]; *R (Coughlan) v North and East Devon Health Authority* [1999]; *R (Grogan) v Bexley NHS Care Trust and South East London Strategic Health Authority and Secretary of State for Health* [2006]) have criticized Department of Health guidance for being difficult to understand and couched in unhelpful jargon.

This critique extends to challenging how social issues are addressed within legal rules. Humphries (2004) argues that social workers are complicit in implementing degrading and inhumane social policies with respect to asylum and immigration. The evolution of youth justice systems and the frequency of legislative reform betrays the anxiety generated by questions of crime control and the limited reflection on the ethics, evidence for and efficacy of statutory change (Preston-Shoot and Vernon, 2002). Continued faith is invested in legal rules promoting contact between children and parents (Children and Adoption Act 2006) when creative work and resources are more likely than legal interventions to overcome difficulties in contact relationships (Trinder et al., 2002). Some enactments, such as the Children Act 2004, recognize the need to address the full range of variables impacting on raising children; others, such as parenting orders (Crime and Disorder Act 1998), hold parents alone responsible for controlling children's behaviour (Henricson, 2003). Guidance has been lacking on the potential conflict of interest for a local authority holding parental responsibility (Children Act 1989) but whilst also applying for an anti-social behaviour order (Crime and Disorder Act 1998) (*R(M) v Sheffield Magistrates Court* [2004]), and how councils with social services responsibilities should meet their duties both in respect of child protection (Children Act 1989) *and* the widening responsibilities for prevention and well-being (Children Act 2004). Some legislation (Disabled Persons (Services, Consultation and Representation) Act 1986, Children Act 1989) incorporates themes of empowerment and partnership, and is enabling in the sense that individuals may participate in assessment and service design. Some statutes (Human Rights Act 1998, Mental Capacity Act 2005) promote such social work values as self-determination, respect for persons, and openness. Others, however, promote dominant societal values and discriminate against groups of people, effectively denying humanity and embodying value judgements about their behaviour, choices, needs and goals. This presents a challenge to social workers committed to anti-oppressive practice and to changing structures which oppress social groups.

Some commentators (for example, Millar and Corby, 2006; Platt, 2006) have argued that the law, reflected through court orders and assessment frameworks, can assist social work's purposes, for example by helping to improve interagency collaboration, record keeping and the quality of decision-making, and by facilitating therapeutic benefits for children and improved social work relationships with parents. Examples are highlighted where the law supports social work values and purposes (Preston-Shoot et al., 2001), the Race Relations (Amendment) Act 2000 and the Disability Discrimination Act 2005, for instance, offering opportunities to public authorities to address collective concerns. The Human Rights Act 1998 offers opportunities to hold local authorities accountable for their practice. Courts have provided redress for service users by using:

- the right to private and family life to criticize failures in service provision (*R (Bernard and Another) v Enfield LBC* [2002]) or closure of residential care homes (*R (Phillips) v Walsall MBC* [2002]);
- the right to liberty to ensure that people's detention in psychiatric hospital is no longer than necessary (*R (KB and Others) v MHRT and Another* [2002]);
- the right to a fair hearing to criticize local authority consultation procedures on closure of residential homes (*R (Madden) v Bury MBC*

[2002]) and administration of reviews for looked after children (*Barrett v Enfield LBC* [1999]);

- the concept of proportionality to limit the use of without notice emergency applications in care proceedings (*Haringey LBC v C (a child), E and Another (intervening)* [2004]) and to monitor the threshold between supervision and care orders (*Re O (A Child) (Supervision Order)* [2001]);
- the requirement on public authorities to promote European Convention on Human Rights (ECHR) rights to hold them accountable for negligence (*W and Others v Essex CC and Another* [2000]);
- the right to live free of inhuman and degrading treatment to challenge the denial of support to destitute asylum-seekers (*R (Limbuela and others) v Secretary of State for the Home Department* [2006]).

Others (see King and Trowell, 1992; Utting, 1996; Garrett, 2003; Humphries, 2004) have argued that reliance on the law fails to address the problems people face and may, indeed, exacerbate them. By naming, as individual and/or family problems, issues which originate in social problems such as poverty, exclusion and unemployment, and by enforcing policies which dehumanize people, social work risks colluding with oppression. From this viewpoint welfare interventions are a deception and diversion from moral and political questions, masking deprivation, disadvantage and the damage done by inequitable social structures and discriminatory social policies. Increasing reliance on prescription and regulation reduces the discretion necessary for effective social work.

This critical line of argument points to the weakness of the legal rules in preventing institutional abuses and unlawful agency practice (Preston-Shoot, 2000b, 2001a). Social workers' legal options to protect older, abused people remain restricted, notwithstanding the release of policy guidance which requires an interagency framework (DH, 2000a) and legal reform that extends protections available for vulnerable adults (Mental Capacity Act 2005). Victims of domestic violence do not find the law effective if their abusers fail to observe legal injunctions. Legislating to promote interagency co-operation has not of its own accord made it happen. It remains difficult for mental health services to align levels within the health-led *Care Programme Approach* (CPA) to those in *Fair Access to Care Services* (FACS) (DH, 2002b; Cestari et al., 2006). Government commitment to personalization of services is enabled in social care through direct payments, but not within health provision. Additionally, in England health care remains free at the delivery point but charges are levied for social care (Kestenbaum, 1999; Glasby, 2003). The courts have had to intervene to mediate between agencies, for instance in relation to housing children in need and their families (*R v Northavon District Council, ex parte Smith* [1994]) and providing services to families who may just have moved (*R (Stewart) v Wandsworth LBC, Hammersmith and Fulham LBC and Lambeth LBC* [2001]; *R(M) v Barking and Dagenham LBC and Westminster CC (interested party)* [2003]). Despite legislative reform to improve interagency co-operation (Health Act 1999; Health and Social Care Act 2001; Children Act 2004), the barriers to collaboration remain. They include resource levels, differing status accorded to knowledge and expertise, lack of role clarity and the splitting of people's needs (Lymbery, 2006), stereotyping and competitiveness, attitudinal and value differences, for example around medical and social models of disability (Hudson and Henwood, 2002), and separate training. These have to be addressed by managers in the respective services. Collaboration will not be realized without discussion of values, power, objectives, expertise, knowledge, attitudes to information exchange, and structures.

Community care law does not guarantee even limited government objectives on need and choice. Despite the duty to offer direct payments (Health and Social Care Act 2001) service users are still reporting that they are not being told about them (Leece and Leece, 2006). The policy vision may be personalization but financial ceilings set on community care packages restrict choice (Kestenbaum, 1999) and may not be set aside by judicial review. In one case a decision to move an older person from residential to nursing care was quashed when the service user could have remained there, as she and her family wished, providing resources were made available (*R (Goldsmith) v Wandsworth LBC* [2004]). Here the authority had not considered available assessments, proportionality or the right to private and family life (article 8, ECHR). However, in *R v Lancashire CC, ex parte Ingham and Whalley* [1995], the authority was entitled to consider the cost of alternative forms of provision to meet assessed need. Assessment is not user-led and there is no right to self-assessment, to refuse residential care in favour of community care, or care packages that are portable across local authority borders. Needs assessment remains targeted at those with greatest need (Richards, 2000). Some judicial review decisions have upheld policy guidance regarding choice of residential care (*R v Avon CC, ex parte Hazell* [1995]) and scope of needs assessment (*R v Avon CC, ex parte Hazell* [1995] and *R(T) v Richmond LBC* [2001]), and the requirement that services provided must have a reasonable chance of meeting the need identified rather than being solely resource-led (*R v Staffordshire CC, ex parte Farley* [1997]). However, others (for instance *R v Gloucestershire County Council, ex parte Mahfood and others* [1995]; *R v Wandsworth LBC., ex parte Beckwith* [1996]) have appeared to be limited in challenging a government policy which purports to endorse needs-led services but actually undermines people's rights to satisfaction of their needs through the emphasis on resources. Unsurprisingly, policy and practice have been challenged for a meanness of spirit, prejudice, indifference and poverty of provision (Utting, 1996).

In child care the legal system, instead of promoting children's welfare, can lose it amidst rules of evidence, court-room procedures, adversarial tactics and binary decision-making (King and Trowell, 1992). The Children Act 2004 fails to protect children completely from physical violence through corporal punishment, despite a ruling in the European Court of Human Rights (ECtHR) that this represented inhuman and degrading treatment (*A v UK* [1998]). The United Nations continues to allege that the best interests of children, as enshrined in its *Convention on the Rights of the Child* (UNCRC), are not reflected in United Kingdom law relating to the age of criminal responsibility and the detention of young people (Baglietto, 2005). Meanwhile courts have had to assert that every child really should matter by ruling that children in custody are children in need (*R (Howard League for Penal Reform) v Secretary of State for the Home Department and the Department of Health (interested party)* [2003]), and that young people must be tried in settings capable of determining their best interests and those of the community, and of facilitating their understanding of the proceedings (*T v UK* [1999]; *SC v UK* [2004]).

Questioning practice

The modernization agenda (DH, 1998) is built upon a critique of practice for being inflexible and of insufficient quality. Provision was to be transformed by breaking down organizational barriers and promoting people's welfare, for instance through delivering earlier or timely intervention to counteract the causes of social exclusion and promote well-being. However, local authority responses to guidelines on assessment and intervention regarding older-age abuse have been variable (Preston-Shoot and Wigley, 2002). Ellis (2004) and Postle (2007) found variable awareness of and attitudes towards human rights provisions. The take-up of direct payments has been patchy (Glendinning et al., 2004; Leece and Leece, 2006), partly because of social workers' attitudes and work pressures (Bainbridge and Ricketts, 2003; Clark et al., 2004), despite the evidence of considerable benefits for service users, including enhanced flexibility, choice, independence, personalization of care and continuity of support. FACS (DH, 2002b) has not widened the availability of support services for older people with low-intensity needs, because resource concerns continue to dominate practice (Tanner, 2003), nor brought together the assessment of mental health and social care needs (Cestari et al., 2006). There is some evidence that implementation of this policy guidance has been haphazard, with variations in how practitioners actually determine eligibility for assessment (Davis et al., 1998; Cestari et al., 2006; Charles and Manthorpe, 2007).

Few disabled asylum-seekers are receiving any proper assessment of their needs (Roberts and Harris, 2002). Carers feel that they have to fight for assessment and service provision for those they are caring for, and for themselves (Robinson and Williams, 2002). Access to services for black and minority ethnic group older people and disabled people remains problematic because of language and trust issues, knowledge of what is available, and provider attitudes and practices (Vernon, 2002; Bainbridge and Ricketts, 2003; Butt and O'Neil, 2004). Strategic planning within councils and with NHS partners has improved, together with the involvement of experts by experience in service reviews. However, care plans for older people and learning disabled people remain service-led (Bainbridge and Ricketts, 2003; Fyson et al., 2004; Lloyd, 2006).

In child care, serious case reviews (Sinclair and Bullock, 2002) point to limited interagency co-operation between children's and adult services, poor communication and recording, insufficient attention to what children, friends and neighbours say, and inadequate attention to case chronology. Disabled children and young people from black and minority ethnic groups remain over-represented in the care population (DfES, 2007). Authorities vary in their use of preventive services and adoption placements due to the availability of staffing and resources, and their approach to risk (Dickens et al., 2007).

Disabled parents report high levels of unmet need. This appears to be due to (Goodinge, 2000; Wates, 2002; Morris, 2003):

- a lack of co-ordination between child and adult services;
- confusion about the entitlement of disabled parents to parenting support services through community care legislation;
- shortcomings in assessment;
- stereotypical assumptions about disabled people as parents, leading to unnecessary removal of children from their care.

Some commentators point to the detrimental effect on social work of its close proximity to law and to government. Trust in its professional judgement and faith in its use of discretion have been curbed by regulations, national standards, inspection and dependence on judicial decision-making (Valentine, 1994; Lymbery, 1998; Jones, 2001), not all of which facilitate sensitive, flexible and informed practice. The panoply of the legal rules is seen as contributing to routinized, proceduralized or mechanistic assessment and service provision (Richards, 2000; Jones, 2001) and to the commodification of care and to managerialist-technicist practice that undermines professional judgement and advocacy for service users (Harlow, 2003). Manktelow and Lewis (2005) argue that law compromises social work's professional autonomy. In community care, Rummery and Glendinning (1999) pinpoint how bureaucratic and procedural processes, supported by policy guidance on eligibility criteria (DH, 2002b), are influencing access to and levels of provision, and thereby compromising people's legal rights. Richards (2000) found that services for older people became less personalized, responding to perceived problems and with agency preferred solutions, leaving service users powerless to influence the decision-making process.

Moreover, it cannot be assumed that the powers and duties expressed through statute and policy guidance are accurately reflected or interpreted in agency procedures and performance. Local authorities have been criticized in judicial review for lacking compassion and humanity (*R (A & B by their litigation friends X & Y) v East Sussex CC and the Disability Rights Commission (interested party) (no 2)* [2003]), for a disgraceful departure from good practice which ignored people's feelings and rights (*Re F (A Child)* [2008]) and for illegality and irrationality when assessing need or reviewing care plans (*P v Newham LBC* [2004]; *R (LH and MH) v Lambeth LBC* [2006]) (Preston-Shoot, 2001a, 2008). There is evidence of local authorities attempting to sidestep their duties towards young people leaving care or detention (*R(S) v Sutton LBC* [2007]; *R (Behre and Others) v Hillingdon LBC* [2003]), and of implementing policies which were inflexible and contrary to the welfare of a child (*R (L and Others) v Manchester City Council* [2002]; *R (CD by her litigation friend VD) v Isle of Anglesey CC* [2004]). Ombudsman decisions (LGO, 2007) and judicial review cases demonstrate how agencies are failing to assess need in a structured way (*R v Birmingham CC, ex parte Killigrew* [2000]), to interpret law and guidance accurately (*R v Avon County Council, ex parte Hazell* [1995]; *R v Islington LBC, ex parte Rixon* [1996]), to provide sufficient assistance and help within a reasonable time period (*R (Bernard) v Enfield LBC* [2002]), to conduct regular reviews or to provide written plans, to report deficits in service provision, to consult with users and carers and to take their views fully into account, and to manage complaints procedures fairly. In *R (Goldsmith) v Wandsworth LBC* [2004], decision-making was seriously defective as the council had prejudged the situation, failed to reassess, ignored policy guidance and not listened to either the service user or the carer.

These cases provide graphic evidence of how professional practice can be compromised by organizational accountability (Wells, 1997), wherein procedures are elevated regardless of their appropriateness and ethical responsibility becomes undermined.

Practitioners report frustration with increasing bureaucracy, which devalues compassion and decreases the time spent with service users. They reveal stress from lack of control over their work, aggressive managerialism, pressures to conform, bullying and harassment (Syrett et al., 1997; Balloch et al., 1999; Jones, 2001). Students witness manipulation of workers, hopelessness, disillusionment and distortion of actual practice in official reports (Preston-Shoot, 2003a; Braye et al., 2007). Approved Social Workers have reported increased stress and determination to leave statutory social work as a result of their Mental Health Act 1983 duties (Evans et al., 2005), whilst child care practitioners found rigid assessment timeframes (as specified in guidance, DH, 2000b) stressful (Postle, 2007). The Audit Commission (2002) found staff to be exiting the public sector, overwhelmed by bureaucracy and government targets, feeling undervalued and demotivated by unmanageable workloads. Good practice relating to supervision, induction, and matching work allocation to levels of experience is ignored (Marsh and Triseliotis, 1996).

Experts by experience have voiced similar concerns about the lack of time spent with practitioners, inflexible and unreliable provision, poor practice standards, and quality dominated by bureaucratic and financial considerations (Preston-Shoot, 2003a; Braye and Preston-Shoot, 2007). They have identified serious shortcomings in the protection of vulnerable people against abuse and in the administration of complaints procedures (Flynn, 2004). They have strongly challenged artificial divisions between nursing care and social care (Goldsmith, 2005), and between children's services and adult social care for disabled parents (Wates, 2002), highlighting the increased distress, fear and vulnerability that results. They have also identified instances where the legal rules have been manipulated, abused or wrongly interpreted (Braye and Preston-Shoot, 2006a), namely:

- Social workers exploiting people's lack of knowledge to deny them access to assessment, services (such as direct payments) and complaints procedures;
- Managers providing misleading advice and direction about when and how an agency can balance resource considerations against need, or about what particular legislation mandates, requires or enables;
- An agency's refusal to listen to another's concerns about risk to a young person or adult;

- Agencies failing to connect child care with adult services legislation in respect of disabled parents;
- Agencies setting down blanket policies and practitioners uncertain whether and how these can be challenged;
- Uncertainty about what information can be shared and with whom, for instance about sex offenders or people who have been investigated but not prosecuted.

Questioning resources

Despite policy pronouncements about modernization, many people's long-term care needs are not being met, either because of non-provision or inappropriate provision. The imposition on local authorities of tight financial controls has become a dominant theme in health and welfare provision. Managers and practitioners are concerned about the impact of resource constraint on caseloads, time spent with service users, and their ability to meet the needs presented to them (Balloch et al., 1999).

In community care, researchers still point to principles of quality, choice and needs-led assessments becoming secondary to concerns about resource constraints and controlling demand through rationing assessment and restricting services (Tanner, 1998; Richards, 2000; Lloyd, 2006). Wistow (2005) is blunt in his assessment that resources do not match the policy ambitions of early intervention, promoting social inclusion and well-being, and personalization. How care management is being interpreted and eligibility criteria implemented is threatening good practice (Syrett et al., 1997), including the effective use of resources by providing low-intensity support to prevent crises (Clark et al., 1998) and responding to the perspectives of experts by experience (Richards, 2000; Lloyd, 2006). Poor practice, including stereotypical assumptions about carers (Robinson and Williams, 2002) and older people (Davis et al., 1998), becomes more likely as the conduct and performance of staff is affected by the effects of chronic underfunding of community care (Brand, 1999).

Similarly, mental health assessments are being undermined by reductions in resources (Wells, 1997; Stanley, 1999). Thresholds for receiving mental health services have become so high that people are not securing access to much-needed services, with the impact of resource shortage seen in the mismatch between what is needed and what is provided, and in the appropriateness of the initial discharge, of the subsequent placement, and of follow-up support services (Sheppard, 1996; Pilgrim et al., 1997; Warner et al., 1997). People are being left to deteriorate in situations that increase their vulnerability, their rights to equality and participation denied. Unsurprisingly, there is evidence of staff inflating levels of need to ensure that people receive services (Cestari et al., 2006; Charles and Manthorpe, 2007).

The Community Care (Delayed Discharges etc) Act 2003 has been criticized for putting financial priorities ahead of patients' needs and for prioritizing those in hospital ahead of those in the community. Kenny (2004) argues that the Act may reduce the time older people spend in hospital but increase the likelihood of some returning quickly, and some entering residential care inappropriately, underscoring the fragility and understaffing of intensive domiciliary care services (Glendinning et al., 2004). Lymbery (2006) argues that the Act fails to address the complexity of discharge planning, including the separation of health and social care funding streams, and the impact of factors beyond the control of social services.

Laming (2003) found services for children and families underfunded. He was strongly critical of managers and practitioners who limit access to services and adopt mechanisms to reduce demand, pointing out that the use of eligibility criteria to restrict access is not found in legislation or guidance. Only after assessment can criteria be justified to determine the suitability of the referral, the degree of risk, and the urgency of response. In line with other commentators (Blaug, 1995; Lymbery, 1998) who have demonstrated how encounters between social workers and service users have become distorted by eligibility criteria, the purchase/provider split, and the erosion of professional values and decision-making autonomy, Laming (2003) argues that the system has become distorted. Rather than a creative response to children's needs, evidence continues to indicate that:

- Delay has not been reduced in care proceedings (McKeigue and Beckett, 2004; Selwyn et al., 2006);
- Children in need are not being assessed within timescales laid down by government, partly due to staffing resources (Millar and Corby, 2006; Platt, 2006);
- Children are being inappropriately placed in residential care, with local authorities failing to take account of the suitability of a placement to the needs of the young person to be placed (Horwath, 2000), as required by guidance (DH, 1991a);
- The development of information-sharing and assessment systems to protect vulnerable children is delayed by insufficient resources and poor communication (Hunter, 2004), with practitioners also concerned about their mechanical and complex nature (Bell et al., 2007);

- Disabled children, privately fostered children, and unaccompanied asylum-seeking young people are not receiving the full protection of the Children Act 1989. Evidence points to delayed decision-making and reviews, children not being consulted about their wishes and feelings, failures to consider them as children in need, inadequate support for kinship carers, and parents not being assisted to attend reviews (Abbott et al., 2001; Morris, J., 2005);
- The quality of services for children in need is adversely affected by resource constraints (Colton et al., 1995; Reder and Duncan, 2004; Morris, K., 2005), with attention consequently focused on children at risk of abuse and neglect, at the expense of preventive work more generally, for instance with black and minority ethnic children (Ahmed, 2005), which might reduce the need for statutory intervention;
- Inexperienced practitioners are dealing with difficult situations alone, working with unreasonable workloads in unsupportive contexts, the consequences of which include the neglect of important issues in assessment and intervention, and a failure to engage significant people (DH, 1995; Laming, 2003; Reder and Duncan, 2004);
- The effectiveness of child protection services is adversely affected by resource constraints (Laming, 2003);
- Kinship carers feel isolated and want more financial and social work support (Broad et al., 2001);
- Pathway planning (Children (Leaving Care) Act 2000) for young people leaving care, including unaccompanied asylum-seekers, is very patchy, with evidence both of good outcomes in respect of education and of incomplete needs assessments, inappropriate patterns of support, premature discharge, failure to provide pathways plans and personal advisers as required by the Act, and young people experiencing loneliness and isolation (Coles et al., 2004; Broad, 2005; Harris and Broad, 2005; DfES, 2007).

This picture indicates the necessity of rethinking funding arrangements. Government has acknowledged that services have been underfunded (DH, 1998) and that effective safeguarding and quality social care will require that funding issues are addressed (DH/DfES, 2006). However, the legal framework has not been changed. Thus, judicial review decisions in community care have found that local authorities may consider their resource position when setting and reviewing eligibility criteria, and when deciding how to meet with services those needs which they are prepared to accept fall within their statutory duties (*R v Gloucestershire County Council, ex parte Mahfood and others* [1995]; *R v Lancashire County Council, ex parte RADAR and another* [1996]), although any services provided must have a reasonable chance of meeting identified needs (*R v Staffordshire CC, ex parte Farley* [1997]). This undermines the emphasis elsewhere in guidance on needs-led services and choice and encourages slippage from needs-led into service-led provision. In children's services, the renewed emphasis on prevention (DH, 1995) and well-being (DfES, 2004a) has not been followed by either guidance or resources to assist practitioners and managers with how these imperatives are to be balanced against the child protection mandate.

Law-informed practice

How then should social workers practise within and interact with the law and legal system which can discriminate against or fail to protect people? How should they intervene in the context of an unequal society where the law is made by, and frequently benefits, those with social, economic and political power? How might social workers challenge narrow definitions of need and the influence of resource considerations in policy development, whereby practice becomes service-led and residual rather than oriented around considerations of quality of life? Once again social workers, now with a mandate and responsibility to highlight resource and operational difficulties that might affect the delivery of safe and effective care (GSCC, 2002), are faced with both implementing and challenging the law. Much of the remainder of this book is concerned with providing answers to these fundamental questions.

Why another book on the law and social work? Previous publications reflect the polarities discussed above. Some are oriented towards technical competence and therefore provide detailed descriptions of the legislation (see Brayne and Carr, 2008; Brammer, 2007) but downplay a critical framework within which to locate the law and the integration of case studies with the legal commentary. This is less likely to make legal knowledge appear relevant and endure (Braye and Preston-Shoot, 1990). Moreover it promotes the assumption that application of the law in social work practice is unproblematic when, in fact, practice often highlights the difficulty of knowing with any certainty when to intervene.

Other writers (see King and Trowell, 1992; Humphries, 1997; Garrett, 2003) provide a critical analysis of the values and ideologies underpinning legislation. This analysis pinpoints the inadequacies of the law as it affects and defines the needs of users of welfare services. Humphries (1997), for example, argues that law and social work represent a regulatory, normalizing discourse, which polices individuals at risk and engages in surveillance whilst minimizing people's abilities to secure rights or counter discrimination. However these writers are less informative on where and how social workers should intervene, on the skills necessary for anti-discriminatory practice, for making empowerment work in a statutory context, and for challenging the social and economic consequences of attitudes, policies and structures. They downplay the potential for change offered by judicial review, anti-discriminatory and human rights legislation, and good practice standards codified in policy guidance to curb managerialism and policy-making when they risk compromising people's welfare (Dickens, 2008). Moreover the law tends to be presented in discrete areas when the reverse is the more usual practice reality: a breadth of knowledge, legal and otherwise, is required by social workers for effective practice.

Thus a broader focus is required, addressing contemporary social work issues, practice dilemmas and anxiety. It must promote confidence and competence in both knowledge of the law and skills in identifying its relevance to practice. It must therefore connect theory and practice by providing critical frameworks in which to experience, make sense of and resolve dilemmas of application, and by describing skills and principles for positive, effective intervention. It must encourage practitioners to move beyond narrowly defined agency functions of interpreting and implementing legislation based on dominant social values towards debating issues of crucial importance. These include all forms of discrimination and structural oppression, pervasive social constructions of older age, class, disability, sexuality, race and gender, and the principles and skills of anti-discriminatory practice and social action which follow.

This broader focus for social work law comprises eight components. Firstly, the law relating to specific user groups is essential knowledge for effective social work practice. It provides a degree of confidence by clarifying the rights, duties and powers of those involved and the circumstances in which these may be invoked. However, practice-relevant knowledge extends further than the ability to quote Acts of Parliament. Factual legal knowledge of primary and secondary legislation, policy and practice guidance, and case law, whilst important, is only part of the story. Surrounding its application the dynamics of the encounter between practitioner and user are such that legal knowledge alone will not guarantee that practitioners feel confident or intervene appropriately. Many situations are unpredictable and decisions will require skilled judgement (GSCC, 2008). A second requirement, therefore, is knowledge of, and skills in managing, the processes which occur. Social workers encounter frightening and horrifying behaviour, and frequently work where violence is explicitly or implicitly threatened, and for which they cannot usually be granted anonymity when giving evidence (*Re W (Children: Care Proceedings: Witness Anonymity)* [2002]). They inherit an ambiguous mandate which requires certainty before action but the minimum of risk and time delay. Continuing emphasis on the importance of the family can promote over-optimism about the care available therein, which contrasts with the pessimism which follows from recognition of the frequent abuse of power in familial relationships. The dynamics of the helping encounter and the anxiety created by the work can lead social workers to downplay the legal authority vested in them or to simplistic directive authoritarianism to control the dynamics and minimize stress. The result can be inappropriate investigative measures or removal into care, or delayed rehabilitation – measures to minimize risk-taking, when risk may be justified but carries the possibility of an adverse outcome. If these 'forces' are not understood, and that understanding integrated into practice guidelines and supervision, work is more likely to become purposeless, stuck and ineffective.

This extension beyond legal knowledge also applies to the third requirement: knowledge which transcends specific groups. Clearly social workers must possess knowledge of the law which affects their work with users, such as knowledge when rights may be overruled, and procedures for obtaining evidence. However, the timing and mode of intervention demands a practice rationale as well as a legal rationale. Knowledge from social sciences and from social work theory and practice is required too. This knowledge may relate to specific user groups or transcend them. Knowledge of internalized oppression, triangular relationships and defence mechanisms will help to explain the position and needs of victims in abusive relationships. Indicators for managing the children in need/child protection threshold and for rehabilitation of abused children have been developed (DH, 2000b). These inform practice and give meaning to such legal concepts as 'welfare of the child' and 'significant harm'. So too does knowledge of human growth and development and of indicators of risk of abuse or family breakdown.

The law deals mainly with individuals and with presenting problems or symptoms rather than with the structures, relationships and systems which impact on individuals. Systems theories alert us, however, to a circular view of causation which emphasizes the interaction between individual difficulties and internal processes, such as historical experiences, and/or social difficulties and issues, such as class, poverty and structural oppression. Whilst legal measures promote an individual focus, more effective or durable change follows from a person-in-situation focus where both the individual and social dimensions of problems are addressed, where the whole context, rather than just one, individual, part of it is confronted. The limited effectiveness of race and sex discrimination legislation, and the failure of initiatives to curb child abuse or crime, and of measures to reduce poverty, are the result of just such a failure to look beyond the individual to the environment, and to the impact of each on the other.

Fourthly, social workers must understand legal processes and procedures. This includes familiarity with court structures, rules of evidence and limits to confidentiality, and an understanding from administrative law of the standards required when exercising authority. However, it also requires a critical appreciation of the dilemmas inherent in legal processes, such as the rights of victims in giving evidence versus the rights of the accused. Practitioners should challenge assumptions about the neutrality and impartiality of the law, and work to improve the current position of social work *vis-à-vis* other professions within the legal system. Medical and psychiatric evidence has higher status (*Re R (a minor) (disclosure of privileged material)* [1993]; *B v B (Procedure: Alleged Sexual Abuse)* [1994]), yet this evidence is also open to contradictory opinion. Nor is there any evidence to indicate that doctors or lawyers are any more likely to avoid errors of judgement, or to collect evidence more effectively, or to interpret the 'truth' of a situation more accurately. Rather, different professions are judged by different assumptions and standards.

This relates to the fifth component, understanding of the relationship between the law and social work. This understanding operates at two levels. The macro level involves not only identifying the practice relevance of the law but also the ways in which the law contributes to or exacerbates social work's practice dilemmas, role conflict, uncertainty and ambiguity. This requires analysis of the law as a social construct, reflecting dominant (sometimes discriminatory) assumptions about, for instance, the role of women, appropriate needs, ageing, rights and responsibilities of parents, and disability. This understanding must incorporate the concept of conflicting imperatives which are the outcome of compromise and conflicts between value systems and which result in contradictory expectations of welfare services. From understanding of the relationship between law, social work and society practitioners must develop strategies for change at individual and social levels which give life to principles of empowerment, advocacy and anti-discriminatory practice.

The micro level relates to the ethical questions and value and practice dilemmas which the law poses for each practitioner. Each must determine where they stand on the law and anti-discriminatory values, on rights versus risks, on welfare versus justice, and on political action concerning resources and working within agency constraints. These issues must be faced if practitioners are to manage the personal experience of work and be effective rather than inconsistent, defensive and/or dangerous.

The sixth component is the development of a decision-making framework. This must integrate legal and other forms of knowledge to formulate what may or must be done in any given situation, why, when and how. Such a framework provides a considered rationale to guide action and to minimize error, and to meet the standards for using authority laid down by administrative law (Braye and Preston-Shoot, 1999).

A decision-making framework is only as good, however, as the competence of practitioners in relevant skills and social work roles – the seventh and eighth essential components of a model for effective practice in social work law. The relevant skills include legal skills – collecting and giving evidence; applying the law where those to whom it is applied may wish to reject it – and practice skills in removing a child on an emergency protection order, in applying for compulsory admission to psychiatric hospital, or in encouraging but not coercing an older person to accept domiciliary services or residential care. They also include generic social work skills (GSCC, 2002; QAA, 2008): information gathering, formulating assessments, intervening on the basis of assessment and evaluating that intervention, recording and report writing, working in partnership with professionals and service users, transferring learning from one context to another, and advising people how to make complaints.

The importance of social work roles extends beyond legal roles, such as using powers and duties to protect people from abuse, to promote their rights or to assist decision-making when they are unable to exercise capacity or provide informed consent (GSCC, 2002, 2008). Broader roles express the profession's commitment to anti-discriminatory practice by means of social action, advocacy and empowerment, including supporting choice and promoting equality of opportunity, and building relationships through which to seek resolution of complex family and social situations (QAA, 2008). These roles focus on individual and community realization, political awareness and action, and on social change, and may involve challenging agency policies and procedures. Continued credibility will require that social workers, individually and collectively, implement strategies which make empowerment and anti-discriminatory practice a reality in the statutory context. This includes a political awareness which connects the individual and the social, and raises consciousness about the law, about unmet needs, about inadequate resources and structural inequalities and promotes that understanding of social work's mandate.

Conclusion

This book aims to develop the subject of social work law and to empower social workers in their practice. Specifically it aims to provide a critical understanding and appraisal of social work law, including its provisions, efficacy and the values it upholds. This will provide practitioners with one foundation stone: knowing 'what'. It also aims to provide a practical text which will illuminate the relevance and application of the law to social work situations. This is the second foundation stone: knowing 'why'. Finally it aims to connect the law with social work practice principles and skills in order that practice is informed and rigorous, credible and coherent. It is inspired by the anxieties and difficulties faced by practitioners and addresses these by providing conceptual frameworks with which to make sense of and work through them. This is the third foundation stone: knowing 'how' and 'when'.

---

putting it into practice

Reflect on these questions and discuss your ideas with others if you have the opportunity:

● What is the law for?

● How does law affect the lives of the people with whom social workers work?

● What are your fears and hopes about working with the law?

● What experiences have you had of the law in action and what did you learn?

Further reading

Braye S. and Preston-Shoot, M. (2006) 'The role of law in welfare reform: critical perspectives on the relationship between law and social work practice', *International Journal of Social Welfare*, 15, 19–26. This paper considers the complex relationships between law, welfare policy and social work practice, exploring the role legal frameworks might play in achieving welfare policy and professional practice goals.

Kennedy, R. with Richards, J. (2007) *Integrating Human Service Law and Practice*, 2nd edn. Melbourne: Oxford University Press. This book provides an Australian perspective on the relationship between law and social work.

Madden, R. (2003) *Essential Law for Social Workers*. New York: Columbia University Press. This book provides a perspective from the United States of America on legal knowledge and legal processes relating to social work.

2 | Social work law: critical perspectives

In debates about the relationship between social work and the law, law is often presented as a given fact, a clear set of rules of self-evident and unquestionable integrity, which need only to be negotiated with technical skill for helpful solutions to emerge. This chapter challenges this view of the law as firm ground, and likens it more realistically to shifting sand, the reflection of dominant ideologies, attitudes and values which themselves change and develop over time in response to complex political pressures.

Key events, such as the death of a child, often crystallize public and political opinion and lead to far-reaching legal and policy reforms. The death of Victoria Climbié is one such tragic occurrence, and, much like the earlier report of the enquiry into the death of Maria Colwell (DHSS, 1974), the subsequent report into the contributory failures (Laming, 2003) set in motion root-and-branch changes to the organization and delivery of services to safeguard children.

Societal values influence what legislation is enacted, and how sanctions for non-observance are imposed. Concerns about anti-social behaviour, particularly by young people, for example, have been translated by successive governments into a raft of measures in the criminal justice system. Similarly, powerful legislation regulates family relationships and protects children, but until relatively recently there have been no statutory rules for the protection of adults vulnerable through age or disability.

Values also influence how legislation is interpreted, and how professionals act within the legal mandates for intervention. Complex moral questions in practice confront individual workers with the values embedded within the available legislation, professional culture and personal belief systems. Decisions will reflect not only public concerns and priorities but also private attitudes and values. The daily interpretation of the law, the 'law in practice', is far from being a value-free activity and cannot be negotiated by reference merely to technical knowledge. Critical appraisal of the assumptions and potential effects of the law is essential.

Only through such an appraisal can understanding become the foundation for applying the law in practice, understanding based on awareness of the law's underlying social functions and of the influence of values on practice.

This chapter will explore three sets of issues that underpin a critical perspective on the law–social work relationship: the functions of law in society, value assumptions in law, and myths about the law.

The functions of law in society

The purposes that law fulfils in society are multiple, and at times contradictory. Some major themes may be identified.

Regulation of power structures

The law can act to preserve the status quo within society's power structures, often promoting the interests of powerful and dominant groups. Whilst predicated upon the rhetoric of freedom, justice and equality, the law has sometimes colluded with inequalities between women and men, black people and white people, disabled and non-disabled people, young and old. Only in the early years of the 21st century has anti-discrimination legislation extended its reach to encompass religion, sexuality and age, and to require proactive implementation of duties on race, disability and gender equality.

Whilst powerful and dominant groups are over-represented in the law-making machinery of both parliament and the judiciary, disadvantaged and less powerful groups are over-represented in coerced interventions as a result of how law is applied in practice. An overview of research evidence from the mental health field (Sashidharan, 2003), for example, shows an enduring over-emphasis on institutional and coercive models of care for members of black and minority ethnic groups, failing to reassure that much has changed since earlier analyses of psychiatry, social work and law engaged in institutional racism (Francis et al., 1989; Sashidharan, 1989). In children's services, there is ongoing evidence that compared to the general child population, children of African/Caribbean and mixed parentage are over-represented in child protection services and in the care system (Barn, 2006). The problem here may be less the legal rules, which social workers can use to challenge decisions that ignore a child's cultural needs (Allain, 2007), than workload, resource and organizational pressures which encourage narrow responses according to administrative category rather than need (Sinclair and Corden, 2005).

Services for older people remain organized around ageist assumptions (Richards, 2000), needs seen as routine and capable of being met by a limited range of services and unqualified staff. Values and policy goals of choice, independence and personalization remain vulnerable to resource control and are inadequately emphasized in the legal rules (Tanner, 2005; Wistow, 2005).

Rarely does law enshrine individual rights, and even where interests are to some extent protected, rights may cede to those of more powerful parties. The Family Law Act 1996 for example, in codifying the general principle of removing or diminishing risk of violence to either marriage partner, and to their children, qualifies this by stating that this should be only so far as reasonably practicable. The child's welfare is not paramount when a court is determining whether or not to make an occupation order specifying who may occupy the home (s.33(6)). Rather, courts must also consider the housing needs of all the parties involved, their financial resources, the conduct of the parties, and the effect an order would have on them. However, sch.6 of the Act amends the Children Act 1989 (CA 1989) by providing courts with the power to include an exclusion requirement, with powers of arrest, when making an interim care order or an emergency protection order, thus potentially preserving the child's right to occupation of the family home.

Choudhry and Herring (2006) consider that the law's traditional difficulty in responding to domestic violence is in part attributable to the complexity of the power dynamics associated with the issue. 'A legal response alone cannot seek to combat the patriarchal power, social forces, cultural assumptions, personal characteristics and learned behaviour that accounts for much domestic violence' (p. 96). They argue that human rights, notably those available under articles 3 and 8 of the ECHR, provide a powerful vehicle for more proactive approaches under both criminal and civil law.

The Human Rights Act 1998, incorporating the ECHR into the UK legal framework, has introduced important principles, such as proportionality and the duty to positively promote ECHR rights, to decisions on how the law is applied. Whilst the rights protected are civil and political rather than social and economic, the Convention principles provide some rebalancing of power, and have been used extensively to argue that rights have been breached in social work decision-making. For example, failure to protect children from serious abuse may be in breach of their rights under article 3 of the ECHR to protection from inhuman and degrading treatment (*Z v UK* [2001]). It is not just social work that falls foul of such tests. The government's treatment of asylum seekers (*R (Limbuela and others v Secretary of State for the Home Department* [2006]) and of corporal punishment (*A v UK* [1998]) has been judged to breach article 3 also. Overriding parental objections to treatment of a severely disabled child without first obtaining court authority was found to breach article 8 (*Glass v UK* [2005]). The right to private and family life requires very careful use of 'without notice' Emergency Protection Orders (s.44, CA 1989) (*Haringey LBC v C (a child), E and Another Intervening* [2004]) and care for disabled people to be provided at home when possible (*R (Gunter) v SW Staffordshire PCT* [2006]). Nonetheless, gate-keeping access to services continues to impact on people's citizenship and social rights (Rummery and Glendinning, 1999), with the legal rules some considerable distance from facilitating a rights-based approach to meeting needs.

Social engineering

The law undertakes a social control function, establishing norms of behaviour, proscribing and prescribing certain lifestyles. It dictates who may marry, a form of partnership available only to heterosexual male/ female couples. The Civil Partnership Act 2004 provides for legal partnership between couples of the same sex, responding to changing social norms and pressure to provide an avenue for expression of commitments that could not be legally incorporated within marriage. However, this partnership option is not open to heterosexual couples. Although people who have had gender reassignment surgery may now obtain a birth certificate in their reassigned sex, and may thus marry (Gender Recognition Act 2004), Chau and Herring (2002) challenge the more fundamental assumptions in law that a person must be either male or female, arguing that this is at odds with changes in medical and social practices which support self selection of a broader range of sexual identities, which should be recognized in law. Whilst Murphy's objection (2002) that same-sex relationships lag far behind heterosexual partnerships in terms of the hierarchy of legal recognition has in part been overcome by the Civil Partnership Act 2004, his general point about the slow pace of change and the UK's need to respond to more proactive legal provision elsewhere, such as that permitting same-sex marriage, remains pertinent.

Law regulates who may have children, by allowing for sterilization without consent (*F v West Berkshire Health Authority* [1989]; Mental Capacity Act 2005 (MCA 2005)) and by promoting a norm of heterosexual parenthood involving two parents. Lesbianism has long been recognized as a factor reversing the common bias in favour of women in disputes over children's residence during divorce, although lesbian couples have been successful in gaining joint residence orders (s.8, CA 1989) (*Re C (A Minor) (Residence Order: Lesbian Co-parents)* [1994]). Sagar and Hitchings (2007) point out that the emphasis placed by the House of Lords on the uniqueness of the biological connection as a significant factor in residence disputes between biological and non-biological parents (*Re G (Children) (Residence: Same-sex Partner)* [2006]) fails to heed the complex reality of modern parenting practices. Equally, the judgement reinforces and evidences the ongoing difficulties non-biological lesbian parents face in securing recognition and acceptance of their role.

The requirement that fertility clinics must consider the need for any future child to have a father before deciding to offer a woman treatment (Human Fertilisation and Embryology Act 1990) has only just been repealed (s. 117, Human Fertilisation and Embryology Act 2008).The requirement in the 1990 Act that both parents consent to implantation of an embryo, upheld by the ECtHR (*Evans v UK* [2007]), can effectively curtail an individual's pursuit of parenthood through this means. Legal rules continue to determine who may exercise parental responsibility (s.2, CA 1989). The Adoption and Children Act 2002 (ACA 2002), reflecting an evolving understanding of article 8 (ECHR) rights, has given unmarried fathers another means of acquiring parental responsibility (s.111), and has enabled step-parents also to acquire it (s.112). However, a distinction continues to be drawn in law between married and unmarried fathers in terms of the automatic attribution of parental responsibility and the power of the courts to remove it other than through adoption.

Ongoing concern about the experiences of and outcomes for children in public care (for example, Waterhouse, 2000) has fuelled drives for family-based care. The government has strongly promoted adoption as a solution to the needs of children in care, providing national standards (DH, 2001a) and new legislation in the ACA 2002. The emphasis on adoption as the solution of choice, repeated in the Green Paper *Care Matters* (DfES, 2006d), remains impervious to evidence of tensions between the goals of replicating family life and providing reparative parenting (Luckock and Hart, 2005) and to grave misgivings by social workers about the imposition of targets and timescales (Sagar and Hitchings, 2007). Researchers (Morris, 2003), disabled parents (Crawshaw and Wates, 2005) and judges (*Re O (a minor) (custody: adoption)* [1992]; *Re G and A (Care Order: Freeing Order: Parents with a Learning Disability)* [2006]) have cautioned against ignoring the rights of parents and children, concerned about levels of discrimination in practice not justified by law when balancing what substitute families might offer against the care that birth parents can provide. They observe that parenting with support, and reuniting looked after children with their families wherever possible, are core components of the CA 1989. Obligations under the Disability Discrimination Act 1995 should not mean that higher parenting standards, influenced by stereotypes and assumptions, are expected of disabled parents.

Smith (2005), noting that adoption practice commonly now incorporates some ongoing contact between adopted children and their birth families, considers the role of law in regulating this contact. She notes the explicit recognition of post-adoption contact in the ACA 2002, but cautions against blanket assumptions of its benefits in the absence of convincing and robust research evidence. She proposes an alternative approach based on trust, which is better equipped than are legal rules to engage personal responsibility and promote the co-operation and negotiation that make post-adoption contact viable. The issue of contact, and the balance to be struck between law and trust, also feature in separated families. Wyld and Mendoza (1998) argue that courts are insufficiently sensitive to younger children's wishes and feelings regarding contact, and address short-term difficulties in ways that can be damaging in the longer term. Nonetheless, judges remain concerned about persistent opposition to contact between non-resident parents and their children (*Re S (Children: Uncooperative mothers)* [2004]), even where there is a history of domestic violence (*A v N* [1997]), with use of custodial orders as a last resort for persistent refusal to comply with court orders (*Re S (a child) (contact dispute: committal)* [2004]). The Children and Adoption Act 2006 has added to court powers to enforce contact orders (s.8, CA 1989), giving access to a range of orders designed to facilitate ongoing contact.

Solutions to social problems

The law provides for society's response to social problems. Solutions, however, often appear to be based on an assumption that the problems are caused by individuals deviating from a pre-given norm of behaviour or failing to be bound by commonly accepted constraints. The moral panic aroused by deviance is calmed by the existence of measures to cure or contain individual pathology.

Legislation is often at the mercy of public and political opinion and definition of social problems. The Mental Health Act 1983 (MHA 1983) enabled madness to be contained behind locked doors, providing the 'machinery for the suppression of unusual, eccentric or inconvenient behaviour' (Hoggett, 1990). After long debate, amendments to the legislation through the Mental Health Act 2007 (MHA 2007) allow for compliance with treatment to be imposed even in community settings, and for the criteria for detention to be widened to allow detention even of people who may not be treatable. In viewing non-compliance with treatment as grounds for loss of liberty (as opposed to a rational decision), the Act has prioritized public feelings of safety over an individual's experiences of their mental distress. Child maltreatment is well recognized as a phenomenon that requires a legal response, yet the protection of vulnerable adults remains ill-recognized in statute, with no statutory duty to assess or power to intervene where an individual retains decision-making capacity. Williams (2002) advances a strong argument for a new public law in this area.

The level of feeling about the 'social problem' of youth crime has arguably reached the scale of a moral panic. Young people are increasingly highlighted in policy as troublesome rather than troubled, and pervasively regarded, even demonized, as risky (Preston-Shoot and Vernon, 2002; Sharland, 2006). There has been a significant shift from youth justice to youth offending, the care agenda hijacked by concerns about control, and all offenders seen by definition as undeserving (Goldson, 2002). Following the removal of custody as a sentencing option for young people under 15 by the Criminal Justice Act 1991, it took only three years and a few high-profile young criminals, together with government anxiety about votes, to produce children's prisons in the form of secure training centres (Criminal Justice and Public Order Act 1994). Subsequently, as Goldson (2002) identifies, the Crime and Disorder Act 1998, the Youth Justice and Criminal Evidence Act 1999, the Powers of Criminal Courts (Sentencing) Act 2000, the Criminal Justice and Court Services Act 2000, the Criminal Justice and Police Act 2001, the Criminal Justice Act 2003 and the Anti-Social Behaviour Act 2003 have each introduced new punitive measures.

The legal mandate to professionals to deal with social problems is, however, inconsistent. If professionals assume too much autonomy of interpretation, or take things too far, they may come to be seen as part of the problem rather than the solution. Over-zealous use by professionals of powers to remove children from their parents was as influential on the ultimate shape of the CA 1989, as was failure in other circumstances to intervene in families' lives to protect children. The perception that local authorities were not exercising their power to offer direct payments in community care resulted in the power being replaced by a duty (Health and Social Care Act 2001). Thus the shaping of professional activity is an allied function of the law in the field of social problem-solving. Legislation confirms and legitimizes professional power by providing the mandate or permission to act, and similarly provides standards and limitations which must be observed.

Shaping attitudes and behaviours

The law takes a proactive role in shaping attitudes and behaviours, although its scope can be limited and the development of a robust legal framework has taken considerable time. Prohibitions on direct and indirect discrimination in the Race Relations Act 1976 and Sex Discrimination Act 1975 (amended 1986), and the provisions of the Equal Pay Act 1970 (amended 1983), were criticized for their provision of only individual remedies rather than class actions to benefit greater numbers of people. Individualized remedies have often been ineffective. Racism and sexism remain features of the workplace (Balloch et al., 1999) and of services for young carers, older people and people with mental distress from minority communities (Boneham et al., 1997; Jones et al., 2002; Butt and O'Neil, 2004). The Race Relations (Amendment) Act 2000 has considerably extended the scope of legislation to tackle institutionalized racism as a result of the enquiry into the death of Stephen Lawrence (MacPherson, 1999) and the framework has been further strengthened by the Race Relations Act 1976 (Amendment) Regulations 2003, outlawing discrimination on grounds of race or ethnic origin in employment, vocational training, goods and services, social protection, education and housing; offering protection from harassment; and broadening the scope of indirect discrimination. Equally the Employment Equality (Sex Discrimination) Regulations 2005 have strengthened the legislation on sex discrimination in the workplace in relation to protection from harassment/sexual harassment and discrimination on the grounds of pregnancy and maternity leave.

After years of parliamentary reluctance, Disability Discrimination Acts in 1995 and 2005 finally addressed discrimination against disabled people, placing proactive duties on public authorities to promote equality of opportunity and to eliminate unlawful discrimination and harassment. The Equality Act 2006 goes further by laying a broad equality duty, covering race, gender and disability, on all public authorities. Evidence of impact is more equivocal. Disabled parents, for example, encounter pejorative attitudes and misunderstanding of how disability affects families and lifestyles (Goodinge, 2000; Crawshaw and Wates, 2005). The needs of learning disabled people and those with mental distress are underrepresented in direct payment provision (Leece, 2007).

Legislation which prohibits discrimination on grounds of sexuality, age or (other than in Northern Ireland) religion has been even longer in the making. The Employment Equality (Sexual Orientation) Regulations 2003 and the Employment Equality (Religion or Belief) Regulations 2003, introduced to comply with EU directives, offer protection from direct and indirect discrimination, harassment and victimization in employment on grounds of sexual orientation/religion or belief (perceived or actual). The Equality Act 2006 extends protection to outlaw discrimination on these grounds in the provision of goods, facilities and services. Only in 2006, again driven by Europe, was age discrimination in employment proscribed by the Employment Equality (Age) Regulations 2006. However, employers can still retire people with notice and reject applications for employment when people are within six months of the retirement age. Older people are still not protected against discrimination in the provision of goods and services, despite evidence that managers are unable to identify discriminatory practices involving older people and uncertain, therefore, about how to tackle it (Postle et al., 2005; Lloyd, 2006). Although the National Service Framework for older people (DH, 2001b) includes the objective of rooting out age discrimination, unlike policy guidance and regulations the framework and its standards are not enforceable.

Arguably the law in its piecemeal fashion has responded to developments of tolerance in public opinion, reflected for instance in the repeal by s.127, Local Government Act 2003, of the ban in s.28, Local Government Act 1988, on promoting homosexual relationships as acceptable family arrangements. It is also clear that the legal framework on inequalities has a key role to play in providing a benchmark for wider practices, such as giving meaning to the principle within s.8, MHA 2007 that practice should respect diversity. A claim, for example, that a local authority had acted unlawfully in restricting eligibility for community care services to those with critical needs under the FACS framework (DH, 2002b) was upheld in part as a result of the local authority's non-compliance with the disability equality duty in s.49A of the DDA 1995 (*R (Chavda) v Harrow LBC* [2007]). Courts have also struck down legal rules. Section 185(4) HA 1996 was deemed incompatible with articles 8 and 14 of the ECHR because it discriminated between parents subject to immigration controls and other families (*R (Morris) v Westminster CC* [2004]). Rules within s.19 of the AI(TC)A 2004 were deemed unlawful because they required people subject to immigration control to obtain permission for non-Anglican but not Anglican marriage, contravening articles 12 and 14 of the Convention (*R (Baiai and others v Secretary of State for the Home Department)* [2006]).

Ideology

The law can also function as a tool for furthering ideology. It is one means whereby beliefs about how society should be run may be turned into action. The gradual and growing trend of marketization in welfare during the 1980s, resulting in the NHS and Community Care Act 1990 (NHSCCA 1990), brought fundamental changes to the health and welfare economy, based on strong belief in the economic rationality of the market place. The local government monopoly of welfare service provision was dismantled in favour of a mixed market in which 'customers' (or professionals purchasing on their behalf) select services from a range of diverse providers who are in competition for their business. The growing emphasis on the power of consumers exercising choice within a welfare market place was instrumental in securing a broad, if uneasy, consensus between those with more divergent underlying interests – between politicians, professionals and service users – allowing the reforms to be framed both as enabling people to achieve maximum autonomy and independence, and as ensuring cost-effectiveness and value for money in spending from the public purse (Braye and Preston-Shoot, 1995). Vidler and Clarke (2005) trace how the ideology of consumerism has subsequently become the organizing principle for reform of public services under New Labour, driven by a conception of the modern world as dominated by the practices and experiences of a consumer culture, underpinned by public choice theory. Recent developments in health and social care policy (DH, 2005a, 2006a) articulate a vision of informed choice and control over services as the pathway to independence (Baxter et al., 2008), again with legislation (Health and Social Care Act 2001) used to create leverage with those responsible for implementing the vision by turning into a duty the previous power to offer direct payments.

Penna (2005) argues that welfare programmes are technologies of governance through which visions of the 'good society' are steered, rooted in normative perceptions of what constitutes desirable social development and therefore a site of constant struggle over whose visions and interests are to be realized. She mounts a strong critique of the CA 2004 provision for a national children's database, introduced under the guise of finding solutions to technical problems of information-sharing to safeguard children, but, she argues, more properly seen as part of a strategic political project of citizen surveillance with huge implications for civil liberties and human rights.

The youth justice field also provides a prime example of the use of law to pursue ideological goals. Hollingsworth (2007) explores the conceptual underpinning for the matrix of powers available to the courts to instil parental responsibility. In a system of dual responsibility and concurrent liability, youth crime contrasts with the more usual notion of responsibility gradually shifting away from parents towards children as they move towards adulthood. Whilst conceding that the responsibility allocated to parents is conceptually distinct from that allocated to the child, being more related to the parent's assumed role in failing to prevent the child from offending, she argues that the notion of parental responsibility is thereby misused as a mask to control and police children's activities rather than support their development. She concludes that the criminal justice sphere is used inappropriately to coerce or encourage certain types of parenting, concurring with others (Day Sclater and Piper, 2000) that law is being misused as part of a normative project to re-moralize the family and mould images of 'good' parenting.

The common thread which unifies these functions of law in society is its emphasis upon individual solutions for individual problems. The law in effect colludes with an avoidance of the deeper underlying problems inherent in society's structures and institutions. Thus, whilst the CA 1989 provides for the support and protection of individual children, it does not tackle the underlying structural causes of impaired health and development. Economic and social relationships, as foundations for families, are presented uncritically (Garrett, 2003) in the Act's accompanying assessment frameworks (DH, 2000b). Hollingsworth (2007) notes that the youth justice system, in embodying the notion of parental responsibility for children's criminal behaviour, unduly prioritizes one potential factor over others such as poverty and social exclusion, for which there is equal, if not more compelling, evidence. Provision for older and disabled people to manage individualized budgets (DH, 2006a) does little to address the chronic under-funding of adult social care, or the environmental constraints to older people's independence. The legal framework for social work intervention provides much more overtly for individual responses than for more broadly based social change.

Value assumptions in the law

The functions that welfare law fulfils are underpinned by values and assumptions about people, relationships and their place in society. These assumptions are pervasive and influential on both the letter of the law and its interpretation at an individual level. Three will be explored here – images of competence, images of worth, and images of difference.

Images of capacity

The law assumes that people are rational and able to take responsibility for running their own lives and making their own decisions, even if those decisions are risky or unwise. These assumptions are reflected in the five statutory principles set out in the MCA 2005. Keywood (2003) points to the concept of consent as a marker for the law's recognition of the pre-eminence of autonomy as the 'appropriate moral foundation for individual agency and responsibility' (p. 358). The right to give or with-hold consent, and thus exercise autonomy, however, is curtailed for many of those in contact with social workers, and whose consent, or refusal, can be overruled. Social workers and other professionals are empowered in law to question capacity, making decisions on serious matters about intervention, detention and treatment that prioritize others' views about what should happen in given circumstances.

A diagnosis of mental disorder is a major disqualifier. Under the MHA 1983, MHA 2007 and MCA 2005, there exists a complex statu-tory regime for the deprivation of liberty and treatment without consent, either where capacity to consent is lacking or where consent is withheld. In many instances, predictive professional opinion of harm, either to the individual or to others, provides sufficient grounds for these powers to be used. In others it is sufficient that the proposed intervention is in the individual's best interests. The power to make substitute decisions using the 'best interest' principle, where welfare is the paramount considera-tion, first established in *Re F (mental patient: sterilisation)* [1990], has gradually been extended by judicial interpretation from matters of medi-cal treatment to matters of general welfare (Dunn et al., 2007), including where someone might live and who might provide care or have contact (*Re F (Adult Patient)* [2000]; *Newham LBC v BS and S* [2004]). It is now codified as a universal mechanism for decision-making, regardless of context, in the MCA 2005.

The MHA 2007 controversially broadens the range of people who may be detained in certain circumstances and extends powers of compul-sory treatment beyond the confines of hospital. Despite some acknowl-edgement of patients' rights to self determination, the overall emphasis is on paternalism, public protection and risk management (Fennell, 2007). However, the law remains curiously reticent about defining either the clinical or behavioural characteristics that warrant such intervention, arguably more so since the revision and simplification of definitions that took place under the 2007 Act, in which the qualifying condition – mental disorder – is inclusively defined as 'any disorder or disability of mind'. Arguably it remains the case that 'the law pays too little attention to the precise mental qualities which add up to disqualification from the right to make a choice about treatment' (Hoggett, 1990).

In stark contrast there are very few powers to overrule the will of a physically ill person, although those that exist in s.47, NAA 1948, to remove someone from their home on grounds of threat to public health, are sweeping. It is notable that the British Association of Social Workers has for many years expected its members to avoid the use of compulsion to address the severe self-neglect of people who are competent, because of concerns about the ethics of pursuing interventions where outcomes are seen to be so damaging for those involved.

Images of capacity also affect how law is used to intervene in the broader arena of people's lives, beyond that of their own care or treatment. A review of international evidence demonstrates that safeguarding authorities and courts respond still to stereotypical beliefs about the parenting capacity of people with intellectual disability rather than to each parent's individual abilities and their unique circumstances. Parents with intellectual disability suffer disadvantage and discrimination owing to prejudicial beliefs about, first, the risks to which they expose their children and, second, the irremediability of parenting deficiencies (McConnell and Llewellyn, 2002).

A further major factor in images of capacity is the concept of childhood. Absolute adult authority has become a battle ground between competing perspectives on the decision-making capacity of children. A major turning point was the judgement in *Gillick v West Norfolk and Wisbech Area Health Authority* [1986], which stated: 'parental right yields to the child's right to make his [*sic*] own decisions when he reaches sufficient understanding and intelligence to be capable of making up his mind on the matter requiring decision'. A parallel shift of thinking about parental status was hastened by the same judgement: 'parental rights to control a child do not exist for the benefit of the parent. They exist for the benefit of the child and are justified only insofar as they enable the parent to perform his [*sic*] duties towards the child'.

The dual emphasis on parental responsibility and children's views finds legislative expression in the CA 1989. The s.1 checklist of circumstances to which a court must have regard in determining a child's welfare is headed by the ascertainable wishes and feelings of the child. The Act allows a young person of sufficient age and understanding to make an informed decision, to refuse examinations and assessment (ss.38(6), 43(8) and 44(7)), and to refuse psychiatric and medical treatment (sch.3). Moreover the Act allows children, but only with the court's permission, to seek an order about the future and, in the event of disagreements with the Children's Guardian, to directly instruct a solicitor to represent them (DH, 1989b). Under s.53, CA 2004, children's wishes and feelings must also be ascertained and given due consideration when providing services to children in need or implementing the duty to investigate (ss.17 and 47, CA 1989), although due consideration of a child's wishes does not impose an obligation to act on them (*R (Twomey) v Calderdale MBC* [2005]).

Change overall has been slow, with dominant images of children's competence remaining those expressed in *S (A Minor) (Independent Representation)* [1993]:

> The reason why the law is particularly solicitous in protecting the interests of children is because they are liable to be vulnerable and impressionable, lacking maturity…, lacking insight…, lacking experience…

Other judgements too have recaptured some of the adult authority ground eroded by *Gillick*. In *Re R* [1991], the Appeal Court overruled a 15-year-old's lucid withdrawal of consent to anti-psychotic drug treatment, indicating that refusal by a 'Gillick competent' child could be overruled by someone with parental responsibility. In *Re W* [1992] the Appeal Court ruled that legislation distinguishes between a minor's right to consent and their right to refuse, establishing that a competent minor's refusal could be overruled by someone with parental responsibility. In addition a court may overrule either consent or refusal on the part of a minor.

During the early 2000s children's competence was viewed more progressively, with significant developments in children's right to voice opinions supported by advocacy services (s.119, ACA 2002). Both Article 8 (ECHR) and Article 12 (UNCRC) have been used to give significant recognition to children's participatory rights (Boylan and Braye, 2006), with courts increasingly recognizing children's autonomy which 'requires … that the right to freedom of expression and participation in family life outweighs the paternalistic judgement of welfare' (*Mabon v Mabon and others* [2005]) Sawyer (2006), however, argues that children as seen through the lens of family law are potentially denied legal rights through their perceived dependence on the notion of family, and that an alternative perspective of children as social actors more appropriately recognizes their potential legal personality, albeit one that accommodates their youth. She challenges the received wisdom of a late 20th century legal liberation that recognized both children's rights and children's interests, and argues that children's identity remains conflated with that of their parents within the family law paradigm and that childhood is thereby obscured and pathologized.

Images of worth

Much welfare legislation contains expressions, if not definitions, of the concept of 'need' and reflects societal assumptions about deserving and undeserving sectors of the population. Section 21, NAA 1948, provides for accommodation for people '*in need* of care and attention'; s.1, CSDPA 1970, requires local authorities to identify *the needs* of certain groups of people; NHSCCA 1990 imposes a duty to assess *need* for community care services; and s.17 of CA 1989 refers to '*children in need*' (our italics). In a society which promotes a self-help, enterprise culture, valuing responsibility and the ability to provide for oneself, to be publicly identified as 'needy' has an inevitably stigmatizing effect. To be chosen for state intervention somehow lowers citizenship's status, confirming the neediness as some form of personal pathology. Whether the state's response to the pathology is punitive or benevolent depends both upon the legislative framework and upon personal and professional ideologies. Nonetheless social workers implementing the legal framework must practise in a context where their very existence can be seen as implying personal failure on the part of the individuals who are the focus of their attention.

The problem is compounded where people 'in need' are seen to have contributed to their own neediness. Within the Housing Act 1996, for example, those who attain the status of having 'priority need' as a result of vulnerability may fall foul of the same Act's provision on 'intentional homelessness', whereby a housing authority has more limited duties to someone who has contributed to their own housing need. Thus a person whose mental health problems lead to them leaving or losing their accommodation may forfeit their entitlement to priority need and slip through the net (Glover-Thomas, 2007). Additionally several groups remain excluded from direct payments, including homeless people and service users recovering from drugs and alcohol (Leece, 2007).

Immigration and asylum legislation and policy remain among the most controversial arenas of law to affect social work practice, both prescribing and proscribing responses to need. The Nationality, Immigration and Asylum Act 2002 restricts entitlement to support and accommodation where claims have not been made as soon as reasonably practicable after arrival in the UK. The Asylum and Immigration (Treatment of Claimants etc) Act 2004 allows withdrawal of publicly funded welfare support from failed asylum seekers and their families who have failed to leave the UK, and includes (s.9) provision for children of destitute failed asylum seekers to be removed under the CA 1989 (although the Immigration, Asylum and Nationality Act 2006 (s.44) confers a power on the Secretary of State to order that s.9 ceases to have effect). McDonald and Billings (2007) note that, whilst the view of asylum seekers as welfare seekers has become deeply entrenched in public discourse since the early 1990s, government policies designed to restrict and contain responses to their needs have attracted significant judicial censure (for example, *R (Limbuela and others) v Secretary of State for the Home Department* [2005]).

Images of difference

The law struggles to respond to the individual, institutional and cultural manifestations of racism, sexism and disablism which interact to perpetuate oppression experienced by many of those with whom social workers work.

At one level, the law appears benign: the Sex Discrimination Act 1975, the Race Relations Act 1976, extended by the Race Relations (Amendment) Act 2000, the Disability Discrimination Acts 1995 and 2005, and the Equality Act 2006 make direct and indirect discrimination on grounds of race, sex and disability unlawful in a range of situations – employment, education, the provision of goods, services and facilities. Subsequent statute and regulations (outlined in the section on shaping attitudes and behaviours (p. 31)) considerably extend the reach of legal rules to include experiences relating to age, sexuality and religion.

However these developments must be matched against the existence of legislation controlling immigration, nationality, access to income support and welfare benefits, all of which have the effect of imposing constraints upon the freedom of movement, citizenship status, opportunities and eligibility of black people. Indeed, it has long been argued that the very existence of the race relations legislation is only possible politically in a context of strict immigration controls (Layton-Henry, 1984). It is also necessary to consider how effectively the legislation operates in practice. The Race Relations Act has not substantially changed the employment profile of black people, and services are still dominated by white norms. Major problems exist around enforcement, which is left to individual complainants who have to prove discrimination, with all the attendant problems of evidence, rather than employers demonstrating an absence of discrimination. It remains to be seen whether the enforcement of the race equality duty (Equality Act 2006) will make a difference.

Within the field of welfare law there are inconsistencies in the profile held by issues of race. The NHSCCA 1990 and the patchwork of legislation on services to adults are silent on the issue and minority groups are not well served (Wistow, 2005). The MHA 2007 (s.8) requires any subsequent code of practice to address respect for diversity but the equality agenda remains marginalized despite disparities and inequalities in risk of compulsory admission and in experiences of services (Sashidharan, 2003). By contrast, the CA 1989 takes a proactive stance to bring consideration of race, language, religion and culture into decision-making about children. Brophy (2008), however, points to a number of concerns relating to how race, ethnicity, culture, and religious and linguistic diversity have informed legal and welfare policy, notably whether black children are over-represented in the population of children in state care and whether Eurocentric models of parenting are imposed on families. She identifies a gulf between legal discourse and understandings derived from cultural anthropology and sociology, which have been keener to explore cultural contexts to parenting, but without reference to notions of risk or thresholds of harm. Her research found good descriptive information about race, culture, language and religion in documents prepared for courts, but much less substantive information about the significance of those issues for the child or family in question. Experts' reports were variable in content, dependent upon both the discipline of the expert and the ethnic group of the child. Whilst there was no evidence that cases turned on questions of culture or religion, parents' experiences of court proceedings did include examples of disrespectful or insensitive comments.

The legal framework for responses to domestic violence provides an example of institutionalized collusion with women's subordination and rich evidence of how women are viewed within the law. It was only under s.142(2), CJPOA 1994, that statute, following a House of Lords judgement (*R v R* [1991]), withdrew the right of a man to rape his wife. Domestic violence has commonly not been classed as a crime, yet the remedies available to women under civil law have failed to provide adequate solutions. Musgrove and Groves (2007) argue that criminal and civil legislation aimed at supporting and protecting those experiencing domestic violence has been piecemeal, unclear and inadequate. They draw attention to the significance of the Family Law Act 1996 (FLA 1996) in giving legal recognition to the multifaceted nature of violence, to include physical, sexual and psychological, and note that the Domestic Violence, Crime and Victims Act 2004 further assists access to support and protection. Assault on an intimate partner is now an arrestable offence, and the FLA 1996 is extended to give cohabiting and same-sex partners, and non-cohabiting partners who have a relationship of significant duration, access to non-molestation and occupation orders. But they argue that it still misses the wider reality of the lives of women experiencing domestic violence, failing to recognize links with suicide and to allay fears of racism and inconsistency in police responses amongst women from black and minority ethnic communities, who continue to fear and experience racism.

Of equally serious concern are the power dynamics of gender and age within families. The links between men's violence to women and their abuse of children were slow to be recognized. The CA 1989 contributed to the difficulty of promoting safe and appropriate responses to male violence by its assumption that children's interests are served by retaining contact with men who have abused their mothers (Harne and Radford,

1994). Section 52, FLA 1996, has amended the CA 1989 to allow courts to attach exclusion requirements to Emergency Protection Orders and Interim Care Orders so that a suspected abuser rather than the child can be removed from a home. Section 120, ACA 2002, has amended the CA 1989 to insert seeing or hearing ill-treatment within the definition of harm. These amendments have heightened recognition of violence. However, provision of domestic violence services in statutory and voluntary sectors is patchy (Humphreys et al., 2000). Meanwhile judicial attitudes to enforcing contact vary, sometimes highlighting the need to protect the well-being of the child's primary carer and considering the conduct of both adult parties towards each other and the child (*Re L (a child) (contact: domestic violence)* [2000]; *Re II (Contact order)* [2002]), sometimes calling for wider powers of enforcement (*V v V (Children) (Contact: Implacable Hostility)* [2004], to which the Children and Adoption Act 2006 has responded.

Community care policy, originally reflecting a reliance on the continued availability of cheap or free women's labour (Grimwood and Popplestone, 1993), continues to be predicated upon the significant involvement of unpaid carers who, in respect of carers under 65 and those providing personal care, are more likely to be women than men (ONS, 2002). The economic value of their contribution has been quantified as over four times the annual amount spent on adults' and children's social care (Buckner and Yeandle, 2007). Elsewhere decision-making using FACS guidance (DH, 2002b) has proven very variable. Women especially appear to receive poorer access to, and lower levels of, provision (Cestari et al., 2006). Leece and Leece (2006) found some evidence that working-class service users are less likely to be offered direct payments.

In relation to disability, historically welfare legislation has provided for services to address problems experienced as a result of disability rather than to promote change through addressing the interaction between society and disabled people, and the social and economic factors which create and exacerbate disability. The definition of disability used in legislation (s.29, NAA 1948) reinforces this perspective, promoting a predominantly medical, individualized view related to impairment. The Chronically Sick and Disabled Persons Act 1970 and the Disabled Persons Act 1986 are concerned with numbers, assessment of individual need and with care, adjustment and rehabilitation. The emphasis is upon what people with disabilities can or cannot do through their impairment rather than upon inequality of opportunity and what they are prevented from doing through a hostile environment. Local authorities have considerable discretion, being required to provide services *where satisfied that it is necessary to do so* in order to meet the needs of a disabled person.

Key aspects of the 1986 Act concerned with advocacy, assessment and representation have never been implemented, yet these would move legislation away from an individual dependency and medical model towards a focus upon empowerment and partnership in decision-making. This omission has been partially remedied by the advocacy provisions within the MCA 2005 and the MHA 2007.

The Disability Discrimination Acts 1995 and 2005 take a more proactive stance to addressing barriers to disability equality in the environment, whilst stopping short of promoting a social model of disability – an understanding of disability not as an individual problem but as one concerned with the disabling effects of institutional and social environments upon impaired individuals and with the impact of prejudicial attitudes. Without a stronger focus on the structural position of disabled people, protective legislation requires that an individual has to identify and associate herself with a stigmatized state in order to gain protection.

Whilst the issues relating to difference have been separated for exploration, they interact and impact together to create overlapping layers of discrimination. Thus women's oppression within the law is powerfully mediated by race; the images underlying law in the field of disability will operate differentially for women and men. In a social system where the validated and respected norms are white, non-disabled, male, competent and responsible, negative images of deviations from these norms are powerful influences, both within the law itself and in the decision-making of those who implement it.

Myths about law

It is not uncommon for social workers to view law as somehow different from other aspects of their core knowledge base, approaching it with a mixture of apprehension and relief – a mix of emotions based on the assumption that the rules are difficult to understand whilst providing distinct boundaries in the midst of other aspects of knowledge that are cast in shades of grey (Braye and Preston-Shoot et al., 2005). Such assumptions can reflect myths, or false beliefs, about the law which constrain social work's relationship with its legal context.

The myth of clarity

It is commonly assumed that the law provides clarity about what can or should be done, when and how. Yet the rules lack precision, referring for example to 'mental disorder *of a nature or degree which warrants the detention of the patient in a hospital...*' (MHA 1983), '*a substantial amount of care on a regular basis*' (CRSA 1995), '*grave chronic disease*' and '*proper care and attention*' (NAA 1948). Such phrases are neither clear nor uncontested, leaving much to the exercise of professional judgement.

Legal rules in the CA 1989 refer to '*reasonable steps* ... to prevent children ... suffering ill-treatment or neglect'; '*a reasonable standard of health and development*'; care that '*it would be reasonable to expect a parent to give*'. Yet the whole notion of reasonableness is open to contest, interpretation and debate. One key feature in the legal rules for safeguarding children is the notion of '*significant harm*' and its likelihood. Guidance (DfES, 2006a) has noted the absence of absolute criteria for defining significant harm. It may revolve around severity or duration, a single occasion or a compilation of events which impact on a child's physical and psychological development. Guidance lists what it is necessary to consider but is silent, as is the CA 1989 itself, on how social workers are to determine its likelihood. What likely risks are unacceptable? Case law (*Re H and R (Minors) (Child Abuse: Threshold Conditions)* [1996]; *Re T (Children)* [2004]) has clarified that 'likely' should be interpreted as 'more likely than not', a real possibility which cannot sensibly be ignored. However, such decisions will remain contentious and fraught with uncertainty. Indeed, the requirement that likelihood requires more than suspicion but a balance of probabilities determined by facts capable of proof may increase the difficulty of protecting some children from abuse.

Courts have had to determine that s.31(2)(a)(b) – the threshold for making a care order – is a two-stage test and that the words 'is suffering' (s.31(2)(a)), for which the standard of proof is the balance of probabilities, relate to the period immediately before the process of protecting a child is first put into motion by, for instance, an emergency protection order (*Re M (A Minor) (Care Order: Threshold Conditions)* [1994]; *Re G (Care Proceedings: Threshold Conditions)* [2001]). However, evidence-gathering continues and new evidence may be used to show what the situation was when decisions were first made to protect the child.

Similar ambiguities arise in s.31(10). What is '*a similar child*' with whom a child, who may have suffered significant harm to their health and development, may be compared? The guidance given (DH, 1989b) fails to add clarity, referring to a similar child as one with similar attributes and needs. How are these to be determined? Variations between authorities in the number of children whose safety is monitored, and in how categories for registration are used, point to different interpretations of what is abuse and, if all harm is significant, of when state intervention is required. Such inexplicitness in the safeguarding children arena creates stress and uncertainty about whether, how and when to act, and allows subjective values, for example about appropriate parental behaviour, to influence judgements.

Courts have had to intervene to give clarity, ruling for example that the no-order principle (s.1(5), CA 1989) does not create a presumption one way or another (*Re G (Children) (Residence: Making of Order)* [2005]) and that harm *attributable to* the care given to the child (s.31(2)(b)) does not require proof that the harm suffered was due to a failure by one or more identified individuals before making a care order (*Lancashire County Council v Barlow and Another* [2000]).

Lack of clarity arises also from the task facing social workers. The law presents people as homogeneous groups – 'children in need', 'carers', 'disabled people' – but such terms merely define target groups, categories of people who may trigger the exercise of power and duties. Social workers must act as interpreters, individualizing the rules, appraising whether legal rules apply to specific cases. In this gate-keeping and decision-making task the absence of predictive variables creates additional ambiguity and stress. For instance, there is no agreed definition of what is 'good enough child care' or when harm is such as to warrant removal of the child. Whilst key outcomes for all children have been identified (DfES, 2004a) the thresholds for intervention remain a matter of judgement. Prediction is characterized by uncertainty. Whilst specific factors may suggest dangerousness and risk, they can never be conclusive. Checklists alone are insufficient evidence for action, yet there is no legal basis for acting on best guesses, or for statutory intervention 'just in case'.

A particular cause for confusion is the term 'need'. The CA 1989 defines children in need (s.17) loosely, referring to health or development that is not achieving a reasonable standard, or is being impaired. There has been resulting widespread variation in interpretation by local authorities (Colton et al., 1995). In the statutory rules for services to adults, need is not defined at all, despite being the springboard for a duty on local authorities to provide services. Nor do policy and practice guidance assist in establishing clarity. Guidance on community care assessment (DH, 1990, 1991b) uses the concept of need as shorthand for what would be required in order to provide an acceptable level of social independence or quality of life, setting these out in a range of categories such as personal and health care, accommodation and leisure, and dignity and fulfilment, but leaves it to the authority to define what is acceptable. Much debate within case law has turned on questions of whether need is understood as an absolute or a relative concept (for example, *R v Gloucestershire CC, ex parte Barry* [1997]). FACS guidance (DH, 2002b) makes the difference between 'presenting need' and 'eligible need' central to decision-making on what services will be provided to individuals, but again definition is unclear – an eligible need appears to be one that falls above the threshold of risk to independence (critical, substantial, moderate or low risk) at which the local authority has determined services will be provided, thus linking need inexorably with resources. The lack of clarity on need is made more complex by the notion of 'unmet need' which, as Clements and Thompson (2007) point out, consists both of presenting needs that are not assessed as eligible needs and eligible needs which cannot be met.

Legal rules also lack clarity because they do not prioritize objectives. In community care guidance, for instance, using available resources in the most effective way to meet individual needs is juxtaposed without comment with individual choice and restoring independence (DH, 1990); proper assessment of need alongside deciding provision levels according to what is affordable. The MHA 2007 juxtaposes respect for diversity and effectiveness of treatment with the efficient use of resources; patient well-being and safety with public safety.

One danger with ambiguity around key concepts is that interpretations are coloured by organizational imperatives, such as the need to economize on expenditure, or make use of available services, rather than more rounded considerations of effective intervention. Thus 'needs' risk becoming confused with 'services' or 'resources', a practice which has led to decisions being successfully challenged (Clements and Thompson, 2007), for example in cases involving community care assessment (*R v Berkshire CC, ex parte P* [1998]), payments to kinship carers (*R (L and Others) v Manchester City Council* [2002]) and respite care plans for disabled children (*R (CD) v Isle of Anglesey CC* [2004]). Another danger is buck-passing or boundary disputes. Examples are disputes about housing young people in need (*R v Northavon DC, ex parte Smith* [1994]), funding continuing care (*R (Grogan) v Bexley NHS Care Trust* [2006]), or supporting families who have moved areas in order to escape domestic violence (*R (Stewart) v Wandsworth LBC, Hammersmith and Fulham LBC and Lambeth LBC* [2001]). A variant is duplication. Young carers, for instance, may qualify for assessment and services under three separate provisions (s.17, CA 1989; s.8, DPA 1986; Carers (Recognition and Services) Act 1995) but may find, partly as a result of administrative divisions in departments, that services are not co-ordinated and that the different obligations arising from different statutes are not appreciated or met (*R v Bexley LBC, ex parte B* [2000]).

The myth of helpfulness

The law is often seen as a means of amending the balance of power between different parties, supporting people to seek entitlements or redress. However the extent to which the law is (or is designed to be) helpful varies; the extent to which it can (and is designed to) challenge inequalities is questionable and in many respects the law does not provide a continuing or complete framework for welfare.

Not infrequently duties are couched in such a way as to enable agencies providing services to behave in restrictive rather than enabling ways towards service users. Both the CA 1989 and the NHSCCA 1990, whilst laying various duties on local authorities, allow councils to perform these duties as they consider appropriate. Put another way, the law allows considerable discretion in how powers are exercised and duties interpreted. For example, duties in respect of children in need allow local authorities to determine what is reasonable or appropriate. The evidence suggests that these duties, and the quality of such services, are highly vulnerable to resource constraints, such that need and vulnerability to abuse may go unrecognized (Colton et al., 1995; Morris, K., 2005). Duties to offer advice, assistance and befriending to young people who have been looked after by local authorities were strengthened by the Children (Leaving Care) Act 2000, but doubts continue about how financially hard-pressed authorities interpret them (Harris and Broad, 2005; *R (M) v Hammersmith and Fulham LBC* [2008]).

Similarly s.117, MHA 1983, which places a duty on Health and Local Authorities to provide aftercare services until satisfied that an individual no longer needs such services, is open to widely varying practice. The CPA, introduced in 1990 to ensure collaboration between health and local authorities in planning and providing for the social care needs of people referred to specialist psychiatric services, has for many years existing alongside, yet been poorly co-ordinated with, a parallel system of community care management. Reviews have noted inconsistency in implementation, variable standards, a lack of attention to wider social care needs (DH, 2006b) and failure to put people first or involve them in decisions about their care and medication (CHAI, 2007).

Aspects of the law are experienced by some as personally unhelpful. Survivors of psychiatric treatment would question the good intentions which doctors use to justify professional intervention and deprivation of liberty, seeing in the rhetoric of protection a harmful paternalism. There remains a narrow approach to mental distress and a lack of attention to human rights and autonomy (Walton, 2000). Evidence of abuses in residential care and supported living continue to raise doubts about the extent to which human and legal rights are respected (CHAI, 2006). Carers are critical of poor quality information, insensitive assessment procedures, delays and unreliable service provision (Robinson and Williams, 2002). Groups such as disabled parents find their needs are not well catered for by a legal and policy framework that is fragmented and challenging to negotiate (Goodinge, 2000). Disabled children experience a mismatch between demand and the type and level of services available, with provision likened to a lottery and a maze, which provides too little, too late (Audit Commission, 2003). Direct payments may have contributed to inequity (Leece, 2002), with those receiving them able to purchase provision, such as cleaning, which is denied to other service users. Indeed, eligibility criteria guidance (DH, 2002b) has done little to widen access to support services for people with low intensity needs and, therefore, to enhance citizenship (Tanner, 2003). Only in very recent years has anti-discrimination legislation broadened its reach to include discrimination on grounds of disability, sexuality and age, and in relation to the last of these there remain significant gaps in the legal fabric.

One core concern for social work is the focus placed by law on 'presenting problems', on individuals and families, rather than upon social and organizational systems, leading to a narrowing of focus and failure to address underlying relationships between systems which promote or maintain inequality and disadvantage. Even where demonstration projects make significant impact for individual disabled children, for example, there remains a failure to focus on societal barriers to inclusion (Barnes et al., 2006).

Concern exists too about the helpfulness of law in enforcement of rights and redress against the way local authorities interpret their duties. Complaints procedures, mandated by both the CA 1989 and the NHSCCA 1990, are not necessarily an adequate safeguard. They provide relatively limited post-hoc redress rather than proactive avenues for empowering service users to challenging decision-making (Braye and Preston-Shoot, 1999). Flynn (2004) describes one example of how ungenerous and misleading views were attributed to a service user and carer, and a complaints process managed without compassion. Evidence of difficulties faced by young people in making their voices heard through complaints led to the requirement (ACA 2002) for children and young people to have access to advocacy provision when making a complaint, but there is evidence that proceduralization and standardization of advocacy services constrains their helpfulness as perceived by young people themselves (Boylan and Braye, 2006). In this context it is noteworthy that the Children's Commissioner in England (Children Act 2004) has the function of promoting awareness of children's views and interests, rather than advancing and protecting their rights (s.2), has no statutory obligation to have regard for the UNCRC, cannot investigate individual cases (s.1(7)), and is not independent of government when determining whether to hold an inquiry (s.3(3)).

Whilst service users may seek leave for judicial review once complaints procedures are exhausted, this focuses not on the facts or merits of the situation but on whether the local authority has approached its decisions correctly – whether there have been errors in law or procedures, and whether the decision is irrational given current law, procedures and considerations relevant to the case. Similarly the Secretary of State may only intervene, using the default powers in s.7, LASSA 1970, if satisfied that a local authority has acted irrationally and manifestly failed to discharge its duty.

The myth of neutrality

The assumption that everyone is equal before the law is challenged by evidence that the law predominantly reflects rather than challenges power relationships. Inequalities are embedded both within law and within law in practice.

Poverty, racism, poor housing and unemployment, for example, as determinants of children's experiences do not receive statutory recognition – responsibility for reasonable standards of care rests individually with parents. Whilst family environment forms a significant element of the framework for assessing children (DH, 2000b), adverse environmental circumstances will not necessarily be relevant in judgements about what it is reasonable to expect of *this* parent and whether the threshold of significant harm has been crossed (s.31, CA 1989). The test is what *a r*easonable parent would do. Failure is personalized and individual change sought regardless of structural inequalities and limited resources.

Until its repeal in 2003, the Local Government Act 1988 made it unlawful to teach that homosexuality provided an acceptable form of family life, and whilst no prosecutions were made under this prohibition, it represented a powerful statement of bias and inequality on grounds of sexuality.

In relation to mental health services, there is powerful evidence of ongoing racial discrimination (Sashidharan, 2003), and of biased decision-making under the MHA 1983 regarding the assumed dangers posed by mentally disordered black people.

The myth of substantial powers of control

A further assumption about law is that it provides social work practitioners with substantial powers of control. This view has developed partly through the public focus on the profession's role in protecting children. Concern to regulate and restrict the exercise of professional power was one reforming motive behind the CA 1989, and whilst decisions to remove children from their parents are made in an interdisciplinary context, there has been more suspicion and blame of social work in the public arena than of other professions in the welfare field.

Whilst it is undeniable that social workers do have powers to intervene in people's lives, coercive powers are much less a feature of the legal framework than is commonly assumed and are not always backed by the power to implement interventions against the will of the individual. It is only following the MHA 2007 amendments that someone subject to guardianship (s.7, MHA 1983) can be conveyed by force to their place of residence. The provision of residential, day and domiciliary services under the National Assistance Act 1948 is only enforceable if service users consent, regardless of their circumstances. Under the CA 1989 there are numerous checks and balances to the social work role, not least in the form of parental powers and responsibilities, and the court's role in decision-making.

Only in the mental health field do individual social workers, as AMHPs, have a direct decision-making mandate within the law. In all other arenas they act under the delegated authority of their employer. Thus most social work intervention takes place within the framework of broad, permissive legal rules about the provision of 'social work services' (for example, to disabled people under s.29, NAA 1948, to children and their families under sch.2 CA 1989). Much of what is achieved and valued by service users and carers lies within the context of these supportive and engaged relationships rather than coercive frameworks.

The myth of good and right solutions

Chairing the enquiry into the death of Jasmine Beckford, Blom-Cooper (1985) famously claimed that all would have been well if only social workers had obeyed the legal rules, yet there are key questions about the helpfulness and coherence of available guidance, the relevance of an adversarial legal system, appropriate and achievable standards of evidence, and the conditions required for practitioners to protect children.

Equally questions must be raised about the context provided for social workers to exercise authority and the extent to which social work practice is shaped and compromised by its organizational environment, in agencies themselves severely compromised by financial constraint. As Sinclair and Corden (2005) comment, when reviewing Lord Laming's recommendations (2003), social workers practise under pressure, with little supervision, often in uncaring agencies, with consequent impact on professional standards and core tasks. Despite government rhetoric, the increased responsibilities accompanying legislation are often not adequately resourced. The differing attitudes and resource positions of each local authority produce a lack of consistency and wide variations in practice, for instance on care plans and reviews for disabled children (Morris, J., 2005), even where legislation imposes positive duties.

Social work values, knowledge and skills must be re-emphasized, enhanced by and applied in accordance with legal rules certainly, but in many respects independently of them and drawing equally upon commitment to professional morality, the application of research and theory to help understand and support the complexities of people's lives, skills in maintaining relationships, and in releasing the power, expertise and personal authority held by users. At the same time, social work must not allow its power to be overstated or its skills overplayed through mythical belief in the 'correct assessment' and the power of 'evidence-based intervention'. Neither the law nor social work skills can guarantee outcomes, such is the impossibility of controlling all the features and variables that affect safety and well-being. Law and social work bring different strengths, weaknesses and qualities to the practice arena. Both are needed in a balanced relationship.

---

putting it into practice

Reflect on these questions and discuss your ideas with others if you have the opportunity:

● What would you consider to be the 'nature or degree' of mental disorder (s.2, Mental Health Act 1983) that would warrant compulsory admission to hospital?

● What would you consider to be 'a reasonable standard of health and development' (s17(10)(a), Children Act 1989) for a child; how would you define 'care that it would be reasonable to expect a parent to give' (s31(2)(b)(i), Children Act 1989)?

● Should the law be used to challenge discrimination? Can it promote equality?

● Should the law confer social and economic rights as well as the civil and political rights enshrined in the European Convention on Human Rights?

Further reading

Anleu, S. (2000) *Law and Social Change*. London: Sage. This book considers the social conditions in which law emerges, the values and world views it incorporates and the extent to which law can be a resource for social change.

Clements, L. and Thomas, P. (2005) *Human Rights Act: A Success Story? Journal of Law & Society Special Issue*. The papers in this volume explore the early implementation of the Human Rights Act 1998 and assess its impact and potential.

Jordan, B. (2008) *Welfare and Well-Being: Social Value in Public Policy*. Bristol: The Policy Press. This text explores the social value of well-being, and the implications of such a perspective for public policy.

3 | Beyond dilemmas to decisions

This chapter will continue the critique of the relationship between law and social work by exploring conflicting imperatives and practice dilemmas which daily confront practitioners and managers. Two dilemmas are particularly pertinent here: when an individual's right to make his or her own decision potentially conflicts with the social worker's duty to ensure that no harm befalls that person or others, and when the rights of different parties have to be balanced against responsibility to society and welfare agencies. The chapter will then consider decision-making because social workers intervene in situations where diverse constructions of people's needs and rights, and interpretations of legal and ethical approaches, demand attention.

Conflicting imperatives and practice dilemmas

How should practitioners work with disturbing and disturbed people in the context of contradictory public attitudes about intrusions to privacy and failures of protection? How should they manage the tension between an individual's self-determination and calls to minimize and manage risk? How might they promote appropriate standards of care in the context of constraints on public expenditure which raise doubt about whether social welfare organizations can fully implement statutory duties? The complexity of the law's functions in society results in a number of contradictory and contested principles which are embedded within the legal framework and must be negotiated in practice. In addition, in negotiating the legal territory social workers are for the most part acting with delegated power, held as a result of their employment status in an organization which holds the legal mandate, yet must obey other imperatives such as public expenditure constraint and codes of conduct. Increasingly, too, responsibility for interventions is shared with other professions and agencies, requiring complex power and relationship dynamics to be negotiated. Public expectations of the profession are high but, equally, professional codes of conduct entail accountability to the people who use or receive services. Their partnership in decision-making is a further key imperative, even where the purpose or legitimacy of intervention is contested.

In working within the legal framework, social workers must negotiate two key questions. The first is how far can the state intervene in the lives of its citizens? The second is how are decisions about intervention to be made? The challenges embedded in these two key questions mean that social workers encounter a number of conflicting imperatives and practice dilemmas. Here there are no easy or obvious right or ideal answers, because the advantages and drawbacks of each potential course (including taking no action) are equally weighted, or bring different harms and benefits. These two key questions will be explored in turn.

How far can the state intervene in the lives of its citizens?

Statutory duties and powers embody widely differing intentions. Legislation may be prescriptive or proscriptive, preventive or curative, proactive or reactive. The legal mandate may frame intervention to promote rights or to minimize risks, to protect individuals or to protect others from them, to enforce compliance or establish mechanisms for self-expression and choice.

The overarching question here is to what extent, when and how should the state (in the form of government, whether central or local, or through its agents) intervene in the lives of its citizens? The principle of autonomy, in the sense of freedom from interference, is long established in UK law, and is reiterated in article 5 (right to liberty and security of the person) and article 8 (right to respect for private and family life) of the ECHR. In the sense of implying freedom to make decisions it is reiterated in the principles underpinning the MCA 2005. Equally, however, the state has a 'duty of care' towards its citizens, both to protect them from harm (*Z v UK* [2001]; *Keenan v UK* [2001]) and to take positive action to promote their Convention rights. There are limits to individual autonomy, and the legal framework sets out a range of ways in which state 'interference' is legitimate. Article 5 and article 8 rights may be qualified or limited as long as any restriction is proportionate and according to law. The provision of services to older people who have their needs for support assessed under the NHSCCA 1990 is one example; the provision of family support services under the CA 1989 to promote good outcomes for children is another. Taking this one step further, the law makes provision for individual autonomy to be compulsorily curtailed, usually with the purpose of protecting either the individual or others in their immediate environment. Duties under the MHA 1983 to effect compulsory admission to hospital or compliance with treatment, and under the CA 1989 to investigate significant harm to children and powers to remove a child from an abusive situation, are examples.

The CA 1989 in fact neatly encapsulates the conflict between autonomy and intervention. It was the product of strong criticism of failures to protect children (Blom-Cooper, 1985; London Borough of Greenwich, 1987) counter-balanced by outcry at over-zealous attempts to exercise the child protection role (Butler-Sloss, 1988). The polarization in this debate continues with some advocating intervention by the state to protect children from their parents or care-givers (Laming, 2003) and others warning of the risks of jeopardizing prevention and alienating parents (Sinclair and Corden, 2005). Children's rights could be used to justify either position – either that they have a right to family integrity, or that they have a right to protection. The Act attempted both to clarify and to widen the grounds for protection, by providing for situations where harm is anticipated but has not occurred, whilst emphasizing the role of parents through the concept of responsibility and enhancing the protection of family integrity.

Early claims that the legislative emphasis on partnership with families to provide family support services was achieving its purpose proved premature as evidence accrued that local authorities placed too much emphasis on intervention to protect children from abuse at the expense of broader family support measures (Audit Commission, 1994; DH, 1995). Smith (2002) challenges the government rhetoric relating to the integration of safeguarding agendas with broader notions of children's welfare, explicit in the Assessment Framework (DH, 2000b), claiming that the focus of attention remains predominantly upon small areas of risk, in an individualized and reactive manner. More recently, continued universalizing trends under the CA 2004 for improvement to outcomes for all children have shifted the pendulum in the opposite direction, raising concerns that the needs of the most vulnerable children do not receive an appropriately proactive response. At the heart here are the ambivalence and tensions identified by Luckock (2008) between competing broader family policy concerns of preserving the integrity and autonomy of the social unit of the family versus securing optimal outcomes for children as future independent citizens.

This tension between autonomy and protection is equally evident in the treatment of mentally disordered people, who may be compulsorily admitted to psychiatric hospital in the interests of their own health or safety or with a view to protection of others. Thus autonomy is respected only insofar as it produces outcomes that remain on the socially tolerated side of acceptable. The dilemma for social work, as always, is to determine the point at which the balance should swing from self-determination to protective intervention. A further complication lies in the possibility that imposed intervention in the short term may have as its ultimate goal the enhancement of longer-term autonomy. Thus a person may be admitted to guardianship under the MHA 1983, an imposed protective relationship, in order to provide a supportive framework for the learning and development that can lead to future independence.

Different aspects of the legal framework may give expressions to differing and not always complementary principles in relation to intervention. Bartlett (2003) explores the potential for significant overlap between the provisions of the anticipated mental health and mental capacity statutes, expressing concern that for those who fall within the jurisdiction of both, the safeguards afforded by one may be cancelled by resort to the other. So, for example, advance decisions to refuse medical treatment prospectively made under the MCA 2005 could be overruled by provision for compulsory treatment in the MHA 2007. He, like Fennell (2007), points to a conflict in the essential philosophies of the two developments, locating them within their political context. The former stems primarily from an ethos of support for family and other carers, and a regard to individual autonomy, whilst the intrusive nature of the latter reflects a culture of apprehension and moral panic. Equally, Laing (2003) identifies the tension between patient-focused mental capacity legislation and the greater protectionism apparent in mental health reforms.

The tensions between autonomy of the individual and the state's duty towards its citizens are no better illustrated than in the field of adult protection. The role of law is central to this debate, and Williams (2002) advances a strong argument for a new public law. He identifies how human rights can be used to support claims that a more robust legal framework for the protection of vulnerable adults is necessary, including power to intervene when a victim refuses help and the right to protection from inhuman and degrading treatment (article 3, ECHR) outweighs the right to respect for private and family life (article 8, ECHR), or even where intervention can be seen as necessary in pursuit of article 8 rights. However, using any legal rules must be accompanied by moral reasoning, because deciding whether or how to intervene, where a competent victim of adult abuse is refusing assistance, raises clear ethical issues (Preston-Shoot, 2001b). How do practitioners construct self-determination and balance *welfare* with *justice* perspectives? How do they balance the imperative of doing good with that of avoiding harm? To what degree does adherence to an ethical paradigm, whether Kantian, Utilitarian or Feminist, shape how options and outcomes are perceived?

Exploration of the circumstances in which state intervention can be legitimized, autonomy possibly curtailed and self-determination compromised, reveals a number of further challenges for practitioners.

Duty v power

The legal framework constructs its mandates as either duties or powers – duties *must* be carried out, powers *may* be used. Both require the exercise of professional judgement – to determine whether the situation meets the criteria or grounds on which a particular action must or may be carried out. A problem for social workers is that much of the legal framework for promoting welfare is expressed as powers or discretionary duties, and in exercising discretion as to whether they should be used, additional considerations can enter the equation. Thus powers may not be used because of financial constraints – the provision of community care services to older people, for example, is in many areas restricted to those at only the very highest levels of need (Richards, 2000; Tanner, 2003). Alternatively, how powers and duties are implemented, and care provided in the shape of community care, supported housing or residential care, may be shaped by resources (*R v Lancashire County Council, ex parte Ingham and Whalley* [1995]; *R (Rodriguez-Bannister) v Somerset Partnership NHS and Social Care Trust* [2004]). Even duties may be limited. Schedule 2, CA 1989, for example, endorses a restrictive approach to need. The services described therein may help individual children to remain with their families but will not address the poverty, racism, poor housing or unemployment which can undermine parenting capacity. Or duties may be implemented in restricted ways. Since the Carers (Recognition and Services) Act 1995, for example, local authorities undertaking community care assessments in situations where a carer was involved had a duty to assess the carer's willingness and ability to continue in this role. However, failures to implement this duty necessitated further legislation (Carers (Equal Opportunities) Act 2004) to require authorities to inform carers of their right to an assessment.

Care v control

Intervention can be warranted either to provide care and protection or to control a person's behaviour. Determining the balance between the two can present dilemmas for practitioners. Much debated, for example, is the balance to be struck for young people who engage in criminal behaviour, their status in the justice system potentially overriding their status as children in need. Social workers inevitably have to make judgements about what potential harms reside in any given situation, and reach a decision about the timing of intervention, whilst knowing that such intervention may compromise a young person's need for 'care'. Equally, the testimony of people with mental health problems about the negative effects of hospitalization has to be taken into account when making decisions about the necessity for hospital admission. As Hale (2003) has commented:

> Mental health law is a perpetual struggle to reconcile three overlapping but often competing goals: protecting the public, obtaining access to the services people need, and safeguarding the users' civil and human rights. (p. iii)

Again, practitioners must weigh competing principles in the balance.

Welfare v justice

The law provides for interventions that are made either in the interests of an individual's welfare or for purposes of securing a 'just' outcome, as when an offender is called to account for criminal behaviour and pays an appropriate penalty. Just occasionally intervention may be both beneficial and fair. The conflict between the two imperatives has been widely recognized in the field of youth justice where policy developments have increasingly separated the two strands, fuelled by public concern about youth crime. Young offenders are now placed squarely in the criminal justice arena. Legislation from the Crime and Disorder Act 1998 onwards ranges across intervention and prevention, restorative justice, surveillance, and managerialist and punitive initiatives. Through measures such as anti-social behaviour orders and youth offender contracts, the focus is on public safety and on individuals and communities as victims and in need of protection (Preston-Shoot and Vernon, 2002). This makes welfare arguments for provision to address their needs as children even more difficult to sustain.

In the mental health arena, the MHA 1983 was the result of strong lobbying to enhance the civil liberties of people with mental disorder, but allows welfare to override these, compulsory detention and treatment being possible in the interests of health or safety or the protection of others. More recently, the MHA 2007 has extended the 'welfare' net, making it possible to detain individuals previously excluded from the remit of the 1983 Act, on evidence that relies on predictive risk of harm, i.e. before any actions that would require the individual to be brought to justice.

The conflict crystallizes again in the field of child protection, where the requirement to promote the child's welfare conflicts with the parent's right to the justice of a fair trial, and in debates about the treatment or punishment of abusers. In situations where welfare considerations and criminal proceedings are both implicated, such as where a child has been abused and an alleged abuser is awaiting trial, practitioners face the dilemma of needing to facilitate recovery of the abused child without compromising the provision of evidence. Here practitioners must follow available guidance (CPS, 2001; Home Office, 2001), avoiding leading and repeated questions and prompting in interviews, and recognizing that therapeutic interviews are unsuitable for use as part of criminal proceedings (*Re D (Child Abuse: Interviews)* [1998]). Social workers and the police should share information to enable joint consideration of how to proceed in the best interests of the child and to safeguard children more generally (DfES, 2006b). The Youth Justice and Criminal Evidence Act 1999 contains a number of measures, including video-recording of evidence in chief and of cross-examination (s.27), which may reduce the delay in providing therapeutic support for a child. Guidance now also confirms that the best interests of the child are paramount (CPS, 2001). When deciding whether and how therapeutic help is given, social workers must consult the Crown Prosecution Service and the police so that roles are clear and consideration given to the likely impact on any prosecution (Home Office, 2001). Practice should be geared to enabling children who need therapy to receive it at an appropriate time, taking into account the implications for the criminal trial.

Individual v contextual factors

This is a familiar balancing act: between older or disabled people and their carers; between children and parents; between mentally disordered people and their families or communities. Practitioners may be aware that an individual's chosen or preferred solution is not sustainable within their family or community context. A child's wish to remain at home, and the interests that this would serve for them (such as maintaining attachments and networks), may be compromised because their safety cannot be secured in that environment. An older person's wish to remain independent of care services may be compromised by the impact of continued care-giving on their family carers. The living environment of a learning disabled adult may be disrupted by the ill-health of an ageing parent who cares for them. Determining how to intervene in situations where competing rights, interests and wishes must be balanced creates complex challenges – whose needs to prioritize and how can a balance be struck between them in securing necessary yet unwelcome resolutions? Besson (2007) makes the point that human rights enforcement is largely about resolving conflicts of rights and interests.

> Human rights protect fundamental interests and values, which are necessarily plural and hence may conflict with each other. (p. 146)

This requires a concrete balancing of interests, and abstract rules or hierarchies of rights are rarely helpful, even where they exist, as they cannot determine between rights of equal weight, or conflicts that are case specific. Sometimes guidance gives an indication of how the balance is to be struck. For example, in community care, guidance acknowledges that those involved may have different perceptions and elevates the service user's views above those of carers and care agencies when there is disagreement. However, whilst a service user's views concerning the definition of need should carry most weight (DH, 1991c), even when placed alongside those of professionals, the assessing practitioner holds decision-making power.

Needs v rights

The legal framework has traditionally been more strongly oriented towards the concept of 'needs' than that of 'rights'. Service users and carers have few statutory rights in welfare law, although it might be argued that the few absolute duties that exist do in fact confer some limited rights on those to whom they are owed. Rare examples are the duty to undertake carers' assessments (s.1, C(RS)A 1995) and the s.4 DP(SCR)A 1986 duty to decide whether the needs of the disabled person call for the provision of services under the CSDPA 1970. Such rights to assessment are not automatically linked to any rights to services, however, and are predominantly focused on establishing 'need', the meeting of which is discretionary. For non-disabled people, even eligibility for assessment is discretionary under s.47, NHSCCA 1990. Whilst not dependent on the physical availability of services, the duty to assess arises where the local authority has a legal power to provide community care to an individual and decides that assessment is necessary and appropriate (*R v Berkshire CC, ex parte P* [1998]; *R v Bristol CC, ex parte Penfold* [1998]). Even if assessment takes place, a further threshold must be reached before provision is made, thus services are provided not because people have an active right as citizens, but because an individual need conferring eligibility has been recognized.

Similarly in children's services there is no individual enforceable right to services. A court cannot, for instance, make a specific issues order (s.8, CA 1989) to compel a local authority to provide services to a child or family (*Re J (a minor: specific issue order)* [1995]). Section 17, CA 1989, is a general duty towards children in need, a statement of general principle, and not a duty to an individual child (*R (G) v Barnet LBC* [2003] and *R (W) v Lambeth LBC* [2003]).

The concept of need in itself is complex; methods of identifying and defining it have differing implications for intervention and provision. There is tension, for instance, between need as an expression of individual incompleteness and need as an expression of structural inequality. The dominant medical model of welfare, where need is seen to arise from individual pathology, informs much of the legal framework which allows for individual but not group provision and leaves hierarchical power structures intact. Economy rationality is a major influence – needs-led assessments are required but then compromised by what resources can be provided. In guidance (DH, 1989c), key concepts such as the 'careful assessment of need' are juxtaposed with the 'aim to ensure that all available resources are put to best use'. 'Assessment should not focus only on the user's suitability for an existing resource' but 'decisions on service provision will have to take account of what is available and affordable'. Subsequent guidance (DH, 1990) goes one stage further: assessors (of need) should have available to them information about the cost of services 'to assist them in arriving at cost-effective proposals'.

A similar juxtaposition can be found in s.8, MHA 2007. Regard must be had to the efficient use of resources and the equitable distribution of services alongside patient well-being and safety, respect for diversity, the wishes and feelings of patients and the views of carers.

The law has traditionally endorsed this position. Where local authority decisions have been challenged through judicial review, courts have been wary of intervening in decisions about priorities in the allocation of public funds, and reluctant to overturn the exercise of discretion by local authorities in pursuit of their duties unless such exercise has clearly been unreasonable. In relation to eligibility for medical treatment, for example, the Appeal Court ruled that it was not for the court to overrule a health authority's decision over the non-allocation of funding to treatment for a particular child (*R v Cambridge Health Authority, ex parte B* [1995]). An influential judgement (*R v Gloucestershire County Council and Another, ex parte Barry* [1997]) determined that need cannot be determined without some reference to the cost of meeting it. However, decision-making must follow policy guidance and care plans which are mainly or solely resource-driven, such that they cannot meet the needs identified, will be overruled (*R v Staffordshire CC, ex parte Farley* [1997]; *R v Birmingham CC, ex parte Killigrew* [2000]). These contradictions are increasingly being referred to courts for resolution, and here more recent developments in the legal framework have brought about a shift in the needs/rights pendulum.

The Human Rights Act 1998, in incorporating the ECHR into the domestic legal framework, has arguably given rise to the development of a more rights-based discourse in judgements relating to welfare service provision. The ratification in 1991 of the UNCRC provided a further rights-oriented imperative. The Convention sets out standards for children's welfare and civil rights in four broad areas – survival, development, protection and participation. Whilst in itself it has no legal authority, progress in its observance is monitored by the UN Committee on the Rights of the Child and the Convention is frequently quoted in judgements alongside the ECHR as providing core principles to be observed in decision-making (for example *Mabon v Mabon and Others* [2005]; *R (CD) v Isle of Anglesey County Council* [2004]).

Lyon (2007), however, questions the effectiveness of the focus on UNCRC as a vehicle of promoting change for children, noting that whilst it acts as an aspirational gold standard and audit tool against which to measure the practice of those expected to comply with its requirements, it confers no legally enforceable rights. She provides evidence to suggest that it is, instead, cases relying on children's rights under the ECHR that have had the most significant impact on the legal framework. Added force to this critique comes with the recognition that UN criticism of the UK government's observance of the UNCRC in respect of asylum, physical chastisement by parents and the age of criminal responsibility has had little effect.

In contrast Harris-Short (2008) points out that whilst article 8 rights are engaged throughout the adoption process, and in relation to all parties, the ACA 2002 falls short of what would be required of a rights-based analysis. Notably she contends that the emphasis on securing permanence and avoiding drift compromises the prospect of birth family reunion; that the incorporation of the paramountcy principle, alongside powers to dispense with parental consent, risks disregard of the rights and interests of birth parents. Most tellingly she exposes weaknesses in the mandates for post-adoption support, with a failure to shift the culture from one of autonomy for the adoptive family and non-intervention by the state. Masson (2008) also comments that the UK emphasis on adoption from care arguably runs counter to the ECtHR view that the ambition of state care should be reintegration of the family. These concerns are reinforced by the Appeal Court judgement in *Re F(A Child)* [2008], with the local authority strongly criticized on ethical grounds for proceeding with an adoption placement after the birth father had registered an intention to seek leave to apply for a revocation of a placement order (s.24, ACA 2002).

The common thread running through the dilemmas identified above is that of welfare, or 'best interests' as the mediator in questions of intervention by the state in the lives of its citizens. Where an individual lacks capacity to make a decision for themselves, as a result of immaturity or impairment, then professionals and other decision-makers must act in the best interest of that person's welfare. However, this in itself is a complex and contested concept.

Dunn et al. (2007), considering the provisions of the MCA 2005, note that the best interests checklist attempts to balance objective and subjective approaches (the former applying objective criteria for determining 'best' outcomes, with the latter being more akin to a substitute judgement approach based on what a given individual would be likely to choose if able to do so, in the light of his or her individual beliefs, values and past decisions). However, they argue that emotive and controversial ethical dilemmas are likely to remain, particularly in relation to decisions involving family and social networks where consensus might be difficult to achieve and the interests of others are affected by the decision in hand. Equally, in cases where the individual has never had capacity, and therefore substitute judgement approaches are more difficult to achieve, decisions remain prey to institutionalized societal stereotypes about disabled people.

Similarly, other researchers have cautioned against too readily dismissing people's capacity to express clear preferences or to manage direct payments, and have noted wide variations in the opportunities given to people with dementia and to learning disabled people to make everyday choices (Stalker et al., 1999; Hasler, 2003; Bewley and McCulloch, 2004).

Herring (2005) evaluates criticisms of the welfare principle in relation to decisions about children, considering concerns that it is unpredictable when applied in the inevitable conditions of extreme uncertainty that pertain in children's cases, that it conflicts with the notion of children's rights and that it prioritizes children's interests over the interests of others. Whilst recognizing the justification for some of the criticisms, he nonetheless argues in favour of indeterminacy and discretion in interpretation, on the grounds that rules must be flexible and responsive to the diversity of family structures and practices. He points to strong attempts made by judges to ensure that, in the context of wide interpretive discretion, personal values and assumptions do not sway decisions, and to the unifying nature of a general principle with which even the most warring parties must agree. He notes that the theoretical distinction between welfare and children's rights is in many respects less stark in practice, and that both inform the other in reaching conclusions that are respectful and inclusive of children's perspectives and maximize both their present and future well-being. Equally, he argues for an interpretation of welfare that takes account of the rights and interests of others, proposing the concept of 'relationship-based welfare' as a means of recognizing that children's interests must be seen in the context of their relationships with their carers, whose rights and interests must therefore also be considered.

How are decisions about intervention to be made?

Identifying that there are indeed circumstances in which state intervention to support citizens or even to curtail freedom is mandated raises the second key question of how decisions about such intervention are to be made. Exploration of this question similarly reveals a number of practice dilemmas for practitioners.

Professional autonomy v employer direction

This dilemma is located in the relationship between professional practitioners and their employers. Social workers draw predominantly on delegated authority, a concept that places constraints on their autonomy in decision-making about interventions. Where the employer is a council with social services responsibility, it is the council itself that holds the power to determine its interpretation of the legal rules, to decide eligibility for its services and to provide guidance for its employees. Similarly, where the employer is an independent agency but providing services through public funds, it will be operating under the terms of a contract with the funding agency which itself holds the legal accountability for commissioning the service.

The role of resources can be significant in the decisions made within both commissioning and providing agencies, with interpretation of legal rules driven by resource constraints and economic rationality (Braye et al., 2007). Marsh and Triseliotis (1996) report that social workers fear that they are unable to retain social work values when faced with pressures to conform to more budget-led approaches to decision-making. Masson (2008) contends that local authorities act only reluctantly as corporate parents. She notes features such as delay in seeking care orders, placing reliance instead on ss.17 and 20 (CA 1989), premature discharge from care, and heightened emphasis on placement for adoption as evidence of reluctance. Authorities are seen to lack confidence in their provision, and the resources to effect improvements in the context of rising demand and costs.

Consequently, since legal rules are interpreted and translated into agency procedures by managers, social workers must attend, if they are to practise lawfully, not just to the law in theory – how legislators have framed the legal rules – but to the law 'in between' (Jenness and Grattet, 2005) its origins and practice – how local policy-makers have understood their obligations. An audit of an employer's procedures and instructions may well uncover inaccurate interpretations of the legal rules, which should not therefore be followed (Preston-Shoot, 2000b). For example, it will expose the degree to which an agency's approach to practice and to procedures positively promotes ECHR rights and integrates Convention principles of proportionality and equality of arms (McDonald, 2001).

Key dilemmas can arise here in relation to who makes the decision, and what factors are weighed in the balance in making decisions. How can social workers – employees of an impersonal agency which retains significant powers of judgement, decision-making and control of service delivery – balance their accountability to their employer and observe agency guidelines whilst at the same time expressing accountability to service users and carers whose needs may require challenges to agency policy?

The introduction by the Care Councils in the UK of professional Codes of Practice (GSCC, 2002) has considerably strengthened registered social workers in articulating the standards that must be maintained. Partly this is because breach is a disciplinary matter. However, it is also because duties arising from such codes are promises made directly to employers and to service users, which must therefore take precedence (Wilmot, 1997). Employees must act within their delegated authority (*R v Kirklees MBC, ex parte Daykin* [1996]). Thus, where an authority's interpretation is defensible in terms of the statutory mandate and definitions of good practice, it should be followed. If it is not, registered practitioners are entitled and required to uphold their accountability to legal and professional mandates. An employer's claim on its employees becomes problematic where the agency requires staff to implement policies and practices which seem to conflict with the requirements of ethical and conduct codes (Wilmot, 1997). Other aspects of the legal framework provide further protection against the erosion of standards: the Public Interest Disclosure Act 1998 (PIDA 1998), for example, provides protection for employees who disclose in the public interest information that would ordinarily remain confidential, provided they do so in good faith, believing it to be true, and for no personal gain. Of particular relevance to social care workers is the permitted disclosure of failures to comply with legal obligation, and of situations where the health or safety of individuals is being endangered (Braye and Preston-Shoot, 1999).

However, the PIDA 1998 does not provide for mandatory reporting and is seen as an unattractive proposition because it offers too little protection to staff making disclosures. Institutional support is lacking and organizational policies are poorly developed in connecting professional conduct with registration. Additionally, the routine and hierarchical nature of much practice and the very general wording of codified standards render it difficult to demonstrate a breach (De Maria, 1997). However, judges have criticized local authority practice not just in respect of its lawfulness but also with regard to ethics, attitudes and values, for instance in cases involving information disclosure in care proceedings (*Re J (A Child) (Care Proceedings: Disclosure)* [2003], placement for adoption (*Re F (A Child)* [2008]), payments to kinship carers (*R (L) and Others v Manchester CC* [2002]) and manual handling (*R (A&B and X&Y) v East Sussex CC and the Disability Rights Commission (interested party)* [2003]).

Professional control v user or carer control of decision-making

A further dilemma is located in the relationship between professionals and service users and carers themselves. To what extent can and should professionals have control over decision-making? Are service users and carers seen as 'experts by experience', and what role should their expertise play in determining whether and how intervention takes place?

The law has given considerable endorsement to the notion of a partnership in decision-making between professionals and service users and carers. Guidance to the CA 1989 (DH, 1991d, 2000b; DfES, 2006a) is replete with references to partnership with families. More recently, children's participation has taken centre stage. The CA 2004 requirement to consider the wishes and feelings of children prior to determining interventions strengthens earlier provisions in the 1989 Act, and child advocacy is increasingly seen as an important vehicle for ensuring that children's voices are heard in important decisions affecting their lives (Boylan and Braye, 2006). Petrie and colleagues (2006) demonstrate how the legal framework for children's participation in decisions that affect their lives can act as a benchmark for participation in other, less regulated activities, such as research.

In community care services, government policy rhetoric promotes the notion of control by service users over decisions. 'The individual service user and ... any carers, should be involved throughout the assessment and care management process. They should feel that the process is aimed at meeting their wishes' (DH, 1990, p. 25). The Community Care Assessment Directions 2004 further strengthen the legal framework in this respect, recognizing the centrality of participation by users and carers. The subsequent adult services White Paper (DH, 2006a) and personalization agenda (DH, 2008a) place users centre stage in the management and implementation of decisions about care, promising a sea change in the power balance for decision-making about needs and services.

Parallel to child advocacy has developed a stronger legislative emphasis on advocacy for adults, in relation both to mental health needs (Independent Mental Health Advocates introduced by the MHA 2007) and to those lacking capacity (Independent Mental Capacity Advocates introduced by the MCA 2005), with the aim of making representation to decision-makers about the identifiable wishes and feelings of the individual concerned. The mental capacity legislation in fact signals significant shifts in the power balance of decision-making relating to people without capacity to make their own decisions. Keywood (2003) notes that those holding power of attorney have wide-ranging powers of decision-making over both financial and welfare matters and expresses concern that the Act's requirement for decision-makers to act reasonably does not go far enough to ensure that 'best' interests are preserved. This concern is strengthened by evidence that decision-making powers granted under earlier (now repealed) mandates under the Enduring Powers of Attorney Act 1985 may have been assumed without any assessment of an individual's capacity or at best an assessment that was status- or diagnosis-driven (Suto et al., 2002).

In broad terms, participation as envisaged within the legal and policy process is underpinned by notions of consumerism, constructing service users and carers as consumers in a welfare market place rather than as citizens with participatory rights. What is envisaged in law and policy is arguably participation in processes defined and controlled by others rather than user control or, in any meaningful sense, shared responsibility for constructing the process of intervention, negotiating the agenda or determining how needs are to be addressed. Even mechanisms designed to increase levels of user control, such as the provision of direct payments and individualized budgets, are dependent upon professional decision-making and the potentially competing imperative of securing economy and efficiency in the use of public funds. Equally the pursuit of individualized, consumer rights sits uneasily with the decision-making processes in which social workers must be involved. Here people must be considered in the context of their families and communities, within which the pursuit of individual interests is inextricably bound up, and must be balanced with considerations of collective benefit. Practitioners commonly encounter situations in which the expression of individual autonomy conflicts with the interests of others within family and community networks, and where the twin imperatives to work in partnership with both service users and carers requires engagement with complex dynamics of choice and control within relationships.

Social work in the interprofessional arena

The final tricky relationship is that between different professions in the welfare arena. Practice increasingly takes place in a context where different agencies and professions contribute to the promotion of well-being. Social work joins notably with Education and Health in providing services that promote good outcomes for children, and with Health and Housing in responding to the needs of adults relating to older age, disability or mental health. Yet these services draw on very different traditions, funding streams, legal frameworks and policy directives; the professionals who work within them draw on differing knowledge bases, models and orientations to intervention in the lives of people who use services. Whilst the law increasingly provides for interagency collaboration and interprofessional working, it makes no provision for the power dynamics of decision-making. Social workers must negotiate their position within a complex web of power, position, status, knowledge and resources.

Social workers making decisions about the potential removal of children from their parents must inevitably take into account medical opinion on the non-accidental nature of significant harm. That this is problematic and challenging territory is uncontested, evidenced by a long catalogue of enquiry reports that point to failures in interagency and interprofessional systems (Reder et al., 1993; Reder and Duncan, 1999; Sinclair and Corden, 2005) and ongoing policy preoccupations with structures that can facilitate communication and constructive collaboration (CA 2004).

Equally, what weight should be given to medical diagnosis in the decision whether to admit someone compulsorily to psychiatric hospital? Doctors providing recommendations in this context are not required to balance their assessment of the need for medical treatment against the individual's right to liberty – that has been the approved social worker's judgement call. They brought a particular perspective to decisions on the needs of people with mental health problems, particularly pertinent at the crucial point of determining the need to effect compulsory admission to hospital. Their emphasis on social responses to social problems leads them to seek legal mandates that deal with barriers to sustained recovery rather than merely reduce psychiatric symptoms, and increased legal clarity about the pursuit of social objectives (Walton, 2000). It remains to be seen how the role of AMHP, introduced under the MHA 2007 and replacing the ASW with a role that can be held by practitioners from any one of a range of professional disciplines, will affect the balance of decision-making here.

Reconfiguring the relationship

This discussion highlights the need for a decision-making framework that can address these dilemmas of practice. Following the analysis thus far, this framework must draw on values, a knowledge base informed by research and theory, and skills in conceptualizing and negotiating the connections between social work tasks and social work law. It must be accompanied by a critical appraisal of local authority powers and duties, and by skills in gaining information, reflecting on events, identifying and taking action, and developing clarity about the reasons for the action which is proposed (Braye, 1993).

The proposed conceptual frame combines three core elements:

- Good technical knowledge of the law and the ability to apply it to situations encountered in practice;
- Sound awareness of the ethical and moral dimensions of applying the law in practice;
- A critical understanding of the role of law in promoting human rights and social justice.

These elements are in effect different ways of organizing the necessary knowledge, skills and values associated with effective practice of social work law, each prioritizing different aspects of the relationship. They may be viewed as a form of triangulation as shown in Figure 3.1.

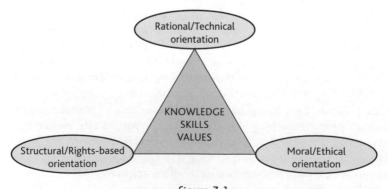

Figure 3.1

	Rational/ Technical orientation	Moral/Ethical orientation	Rights-based/ Structural orientation
Views law as ...	A set of rules to be applied	Part of the professional toolkit	A resource for service users
The driver for practice is ...	Legal mandates	Ethical goals	The search for social justice and human rights
Practitioners need ...	Technical legal knowledge	To locate law within their professional morality	Critical understanding of law
The key practice question is ...	Are the criteria for legal intervention met?	How does law contribute to ethical goals?	How can law confront exclusion and oppression?
The emphasis is on ...	Procedurally correct practice – 'doing things right'	Negotiating dilemmas – 'doing right things'	'Rights thinking'

Table 3.1
Source: Braye and Preston-Shoot, 2006a.

In the centre are located the knowledge, skills and values that inform and drive practice. The points on the triangle are orientations which inform what practitioners view as the driver for practice (law, ethics or rights), what kind of knowledge they need (technical or critical), and what legal rules are used (those for responding to individual need or those promoting collective rights and justice). These perspectives are summarized in Table 3.1.

Integrating all three orientations is important, enabling practitioners to engage with the complexity of practice dilemmas in each unique case by reference to knowledge bases skilfully applied to a situation, capable of informing when limits to a values principle should be imposed, how competing rights might be weighed, and what outcomes are sought. Promoting rights requires technical legal knowledge as well as values commitments. Technical knowledge can counter-balance the potential bias of personal values and organizational cultures. Professional decision-making must meet the requirements of administrative law, but technical application must be approached critically, and located within an awareness of the shortcomings of individualized solutions that ignore a need for social change. Ethical frameworks can interrogate both the legal rules and the purpose of interventions, and justify one course of lawful action in preference to another. Critical appraisal will also identify how law erodes or supports rights, whilst rights themselves must be viewed through the lens of how moral codes build the fundamental social frames of reference within which rights are promoted or restricted. Thus all three elements are required when responding to individual and collective needs, avoiding the limitations inherent in each:

- Codes of practice and values have had limited success in guaranteeing that professionals will meet their ethical responsibilities, especially when codes are ill-defined, leave dilemmas unacknowledged and unresolved or lack sanctions (France, 1996; Clark, 2006; Preston-Shoot, 2008).
- Research has found that practitioners sometimes collude with organizational misuse of power and authority, and that organizational processes can compromise employees and the legal rules (Machin, 1998; Horwath, 2000; Preston-Shoot, 2000b).
- Research finds little evidence of clear and transparent application of legislation, rules and guidance (Bradley, 2003), and variable attitudes towards the use of discretion.
- Rights can fail to address the nature of social power in society and how certain groups are excluded by its exercise (France, 1996).
- Enforcing social rights that have no clear underlying basis in civil rights is difficult (Rummery and Glendinning, 1999). The ECHR is limited to civil and political rights. UN Conventions are more expansive in their scope, including social and economic rights, but are not integrated into UK law.
- Legal rules can focus less on social issues, such as human rights and discrimination than on individuals, their needs and risks they present to themselves and to others. Many of the legal rules are residual in their scope and contain discretion as to when they are triggered.
- Legal entitlements can be seriously compromised by managerial and professional processes (Rummery and Glendinning, 1999).
- The track record of law is not commendable on rights (Swain, 2002).

The National Occupational Standards (TOPSS, 2002) and the social work benchmark (QAA, 2008) endorse the tripartite linkage of law, rights and values and the view, strongly articulated by experts by experience (Braye and Preston-Shoot et al., 2005), that social workers should be competent technicians *and* well-rounded critical professionals. Experts by experience want to be involved in determining the issues that require fixing, as well as how and why, but they expect social workers also to have a view on both. They should have practical legal knowledge, a willingness to debate ethical dilemmas with service users, and an ability to defend their judgements. They should demonstrate a keen awareness of how the law impacts on people and they should scrutinize and speak about how the legal rules are constructed and used. Thus, the subject benchmark (QAA, 2008, at 4.2 and 4.7) urges social workers to think critically, whilst the national occupational standards (TOPSS, 2002, passim) require social workers to understand, critically analyze, evaluate and apply the law. These endorsements, which support the conceptual model in Figure 3.1, are expanded in Table 3.2.

Moral or ethical orientation: law linked with values	Social work is a moral activity (QAA, 2008, at 4.6).
	Social work engages with service users with openness, reciprocity, mutual accountability and explicit recognition of the powers of the social worker and the legal context of intervention (QAA, 2008, at 3.9).
	Social workers exercise authority within complex frameworks of accountability and ethical and legal boundaries (QAA, 2008, at 4.7).
Rational or technical orientation: knowing the legal rules.	Social work education should enable students to acquire, critically evaluate, apply and integrate knowledge and understanding of the significance of legislation and legal frameworks (QAA, 2008, at 5.1.2).
	Social work education includes the relationship between agency policies, legal requirements and legal frameworks (QAA, 2008, at 5.1.1).
	Social workers must be able to identify the need for legal and procedural intervention, including the ability to explain to people their rights and the social worker's powers, and to justify the need for intervention (TOPSS, 2002, at 4.2).
	Social workers must be able to implement legal and policy frameworks for access to records and reports (TOPSS, 2002, at 16.3).
Emancipatory or rights orientation	Social workers must be able to challenge discrimination and to help people regain control, if compatible with their own and other people's rights (QAA, 2008, at 4.6).
	Social work must uphold the law on discrimination (QAA, 2008, at 5.1.3).

Table 3.2

Conclusion

That law, values and rights should be connected in practice is highlighted once more by a description of social work roles and tasks (GSCC, 2008). Social work features equality and human rights, privacy and dignity, and challenges to discrimination. Social workers use legal powers to intervene in complex situations. However, this description does not recognize that social workers may sometimes challenge the legal rules themselves, because they diminish and curtail human rights or depart from the values standards of beneficence and non-maleficence. Nor does it appear to recognize the collision with legal rules when noting that social workers help to ensure the well-being and human rights of refugees and asylum-seeking children and families.

Regrettably, research has found that some practitioners and teams neither debate ethical issues nor explicitly articulate legal rules (Marsh and Triseliotis, 1996; Braye et al., 2007), despite recognizing the complexities of applying values and their anxieties about being held accountable for omissions in performance of statutory requirements. The following chapters aim to provide practitioners and managers with the confidence to bring law, values and rights into greater prominence in their work, articulating the connections in order to engage and work through complexity.

---

putting it into practice

Reflect on these questions and discuss your ideas with others if you have the opportunity:

- Should social workers intervene in parents' decisions about what is best for their children? Would your answer be the same for a parent with learning disability?

- Should an adult who has the capacity to make their own decisions have the right to refuse care or treatment, even if this means they will die? Would your answer be the same for a child or young person? Would your answer be the same for someone who has a serious mental health problem?

- Should social workers intervene to safeguard and protect the welfare of an older person with capacity who is being abused but who does not wish any intervention to take place? How far should social workers be able to go to impose protection? Would your answer be the same for someone without capacity?

Further reading

Herring, J. (2005) 'Farewell welfare?', *Journal of Social Welfare and Family Law*, 27, 2, 159–71. This paper considers how a relationship-based approach to welfare can resolve debates on the welfare principle in decision-making.

Reichert, E. (ed.) (2007) *Challenges in Human Rights: A Social Work Perspective*. New York: Columbia University Press. This text, written in the US context but with international relevance, explores how social work can adopt a more focused and analytical approach to human rights

Ward, H. and Munro, E.M. (2008) 'Balancing parents' and very young children's rights in care proceedings: decision-making in the context of the Human Rights Act 1998', *Child and Family Social Work*, 13, 2, 227–34. This paper explores how the Human Rights Act 1998 has influenced the balancing act between children's and parents' rights.

4 | Adult services, mental well-being and criminal justice

The purpose of this chapter, and the following one, is to outline the breadth of legal knowledge required to guide social work interventions and to illustrate how the legal rules are drawn upon in practice. Our approach is to start with a situation that may be encountered in practice and to identify how law provides a framework for considering what must and may be done.

The cases in this chapter start with a focus initially on an adult service user, whilst in the following chapter the initial focus will be upon children. Both, however, will reflect the complexity of family situations and illustrate how practitioners must draw on a wide legal framework.

William

William, a white British man aged 78, has lived alone since becoming a widower in his late 50s. His home is close to his daughter and son-in-law, Gwen and Don, and their two children, Paul, 15 and Tracey, 13. William is fiercely independent, but has become increasingly frail. He has had a long-standing heart problem, but more recently has also had a series of small strokes that left him with some physical impairment and limited movement. Following a fall, his physical condition deteriorated more rapidly. He can no longer manage stairs without help and is reliant on his family's visits several times a day for help with personal care. Gwen supports him in the mornings, and also does shopping and prepares meals, but she works evenings, so Tracey and Paul take turns to help their grandfather to bed. Don works away from home during the week.

Paul is struggling at school as his GCSEs draw close. There is evidence that he is under some stress – he is sleeping badly and is often reluctant to go to school. He is taking the main responsibility for his grandfather's care, as Tracey has recently refused to help.

William has become very worried about the future, fearing further deterioration in his health. He clings fiercely to his independence and is adamant that he wants to stay in his own home, but doesn't know how he would manage if he has any further loss of health. He becomes tearful when he considers what he sees as the impossibility of his position, and talks about life being not worth living. The additional support made necessary by his gradual deterioration has placed significant demands on Gwen. She is worried about Paul and anxious about Tracey's rebellion. If she gives up her job to care for her father, she knows they cannot manage financially, but equally she doesn't think they can go on like this much longer. She has talked to her GP, who has requested that the family get some help.

This is a finely balanced situation, with stability achieved at a high cost to all involved and in which any one of a number of events could trigger crisis. There are interesting moral questions to be considered – does William have a right to independence and if so, should this be prioritized over his family's well-being? What is it legitimate to expect from the children in the family in respect of their grandfather's care? Government policy seeks to achieve a balance for all concerned, proposing (DH, 2006a) responses in this situation which are intended both to promote William's independence and to recognize and support the contribution of family members involved in his care.

Assessment

The first legal rules to consider are the mandates for assessing need, starting with William and subsequently turning to consider Gwen and her children.

William

The first task is to determine whether William appears to be someone who might be in need of community care services. These are services designed to support people who have needs arising from disability, older age, health problems or mental ill-health, and can include residential or day care, and a wide range of domiciliary provisions. They are provided under duties and powers contained in a range of statutes, notably s.29 and Part 3 of the National Assistance Act 1948 (NAA 1948), s.45 of the Health Services and Public Health Act 1968 (HSPHA 1968), sch.20, NHS Act 2006 (NHSA 2006), s.117, Mental Health Act 1983 (MHA 1983) and s.2, Chronically Sick and Disabled Persons Act 1970 (CSDPA 1970).

The threshold for the level of need required to trigger an assessment is low (*R v Bristol CC ex parte Penfold* [1998], and William's circumstances would certainly meet it, even though his needs are currently being met by his family. Under s.47(1), NHS and Community Care Act 1990 (NHSCCA 1990), the local authority has a duty to carry out an assessment of his needs and then to decide whether services should be provided. During this assessment the local authority must, under s.47(3), inform the Health or Housing Authorities if it appears William may require services they could provide.

A related question is whether William is disabled, as defined by s.29, NAA 1948, by virtue of being 'blind, deaf or dumb, or suffering from a mental disorder, or substantially and permanently handicapped by illness, injury or congenital deformity'. Whilst this definition is framed in the language of its time, it still acts as the gateway to eligibility for certain services. If he meets this definition – and there is guidance that it should be interpreted widely (LAC(93)10) – then under s.47(2) NHSCCA 1990 the local authority must, whilst assessing his community care needs, also make a parallel decision under s.4 of the Disabled Persons (Services, Consultation and Representation) Act 1986 (DPA 1986) on whether he requires services under s.2 of the CSDPA 1970 – essentially domiciliary services for disabled people. Equally, William, as a disabled person, or anyone caring for him could request a s.4 assessment. This amounts to the right to assessment on request for a disabled person, without any threshold test related to the appearance of need.

Assessment is the cornerstone of high quality care (DH, 1990). Need is defined in guidance as requirements to enable people to achieve, maintain or restore an acceptable level of social independence or quality of life (DH, 1991b), where possible in their own home (DH, 1990). Assessment of William's situation should consider a wide constellation of factors, including current and future social and emotional needs as well as physical care, without reference to the availability of, or his eligibility for, services to meet them (*R v Bristol CC ex parte Penfold* [1998]). Need has been much debated in community care case law, viewed variously as an absolute fact, beyond discretion (*R v Gloucestershire County Council, ex parte Barry* [1997]), or as a relative concept requiring careful professional scrutiny (*R v Tower Hamlets ex parte Wahid* [2002]).

Whilst guidance is clear that need is defined by the local authority (DH, 1991b), there is strong emphasis on the involvement of the person being assessed. Need is to be defined on an individual basis, as precisely as possible, recognizing the individual and unique circumstances of each person's situation, and permitting individualized rather than stereotyped responses. Assessment should be aimed at meeting an individual's wishes, actively taking their views into account; when reconciling different perspectives, the assessing practitioner should depart from the user's view only with good reason (DH, 1991c). The emphasis on participation is further strengthened by the Community Care Assessment Directions 2004, requiring consultation and where possible agreement with the individual being assessed (and, if appropriate, any carers).

Early generic guidance on the conduct of assessment (DH 1990, 1991c) has been strengthened and supplemented in relation to specific user groups. Thus, in William's case, practitioners would work under their local authority's interpretation of the Single Assessment Process (SAP), introduced through the National Service Framework for Older People (DH, 2001b) and designed to reduce duplication and gaps between multidisciplinary assessment régimes and to further emphasize the user's expertise.

In its search for consistency, the SAP guidance (LAC(2002)1) outlines the domains of need that should be subject to review:

- *The user's perspective*: William's own view of the issues facing him, his expectations, strength, abilities and motivation;
- *Clinical background*: the history of William's medical conditions, diagnoses and medication;
- *Disease prevention*: William's nutrition and exercise patterns, any history of drug and alcohol use;
- *Personal care and physical well-being*: William's ability to look after himself, his mobility, pain, oral health, continence, sleep patterns;
- *Senses*: William's sight, hearing and communication;
- *Mental health*: William's cognition, orientation and memory, his mood and emotional well-being;
- *Relationships*: William's social contacts, relationships and involvement in leisure, hobbies, the strength of his caring arrangements, including the perspectives of Gwen, Tracey and Paul;
- *Safety*: consideration of any issues of abuse or neglect, other aspects of William's safety, and any risks that he poses to others;
- *Immediate environment and resources*: how William manages daily tasks at home – cooking, cleaning, shopping – his housing situation, amenities and heating, his management of finances, and access to local amenities.

Assessment may be conducted at one of four levels: contact assessment (to identify the presenting problem, and resolve straightforward needs); overview assessment (where the domains are explored in more depth); specialist assessment (where very specific needs are explored in more depth); comprehensive assessment (where the domains are explored in circumstances where support is likely to be intensive or prolonged). For William, initial contact would identify at least the need for an overview assessment, and possibly further specialist assessments, building to a comprehensive picture over time. This is in line with the expectations within the legal framework, which recognizes that in practice the distinction between categories of assessment is likely to be blurred (DH, 2002b).

At the heart of the current legal framework on assessment lies the Fair Access to Care Services (FACS) policy, designed to end the 'postcode lottery' of access to community care provision (DH, 1998). The guidance (DH, 2002b, 2003a) reflects the growing emphasis on independence as the goal for adults with care and support needs, identifying the purpose of assessment as:

> to identify and evaluate an individual's presenting needs and how they constrain or support his/her capacity to live a full and independent life.

> (DH, 2002b, p. 7)

People should not be screened out of the assessment process before sufficient information is known about them; assessment should be rounded and person-centred, taking account of a range of issues such as health and housing, as well as social care needs, whilst being as simple and timely as possible. Individuals are seen as experts on their own situation and partners in the assessment process, which should explore individual and environmental factors, and strengths as well as needs, taking into account the impact of age, gender, ethnicity, religion, disability, caring arrangements, relationships and location. It should be co-ordinated and integrated across agencies to minimize duplication. The goal is to identify the degree of risk to independence through factors that impair autonomy and freedom of choice, health and safety, personal care, and involvement in family and community life.

The assessment duty under s.47(1) NHSCCA 1990 falls into two stages. The local authority must first assess William's needs, then decide whether his needs require service provision. The rules governing the second stage are also contained within the FACS guidance (DH, 2002b, 2003a); decisions on service provision must be made by reference to the risk to independence posed by an individual's presenting needs. The four risk bands – critical, substantial, moderate and low – relate to the identified level of abuse/neglect, choice and control over the immediate environment, ability to carry out essential daily living tasks, maintain essential relationships/support systems, participate in work and learning, and fulfil essential roles and responsibilities. The local authority must prioritize meeting needs that pose the greatest risks to independence, i.e. meet needs that create 'critical' risk before those creating 'substantial' risk, and so on. It is entitled to set a threshold of risk which must be met in order to achieve eligibility; needs falling above that threshold are called 'eligible needs'. In setting its threshold, the authority is entitled to take into account its financial resources, thus the threshold for eligibility can change with the authority's budgetary position and needs previously eligible to be met can subsequently fall below the threshold. In this case, however, there must be full reassessment before services to any individual are changed (*R v Gloucestershire CC ex parte Barry* [1997]). Equally, resources must not be the sole criterion used, either in setting the eligibility threshold or in deciding how an individual's needs will be met.

Gwen, Tracey and Paul

The legal rules make clear that in undertaking William's assessment the local authority should consult and reach agreement with Gwen as his carer (Community Care Assessment Directions 2004). The needs of carers themselves, and their entitlement to assessment, are explicitly recognized in statute. Under s.1 of the Carers (Recognition and Services) Act 1995 (C(RS)A 1995), where a local authority conducts a s.47 NHSCCA 1990 assessment of need for community care services, any carer of any age who provides or intends to provide a substantial amount of care on a regular basis may request an assessment of their own needs. The results of this assessment must be used in subsequent decision-making about whether the needs of the cared-for person call for service provision. Whilst the Act does not define 'substantial' or 'regular', Gwen's position would clearly entitle her to request a carer's assessment.

The 1995 legislation precluded carers' assessments in circumstances where the cared-for person refused a community care assessment. This loophole was closed by the Carers and Disabled Children Act 2000 (CDCA 2000), entitling Gwen to a carer's assessment even if William refuses to be assessed himself. However, the 2000 Act does not apply to carers under 16. Following evidence of low take-up of carers' assessments (Audit Commission, 2004), the Carers (Equal Opportunities) Act 2004 (C(EO)A 2004) created a duty for local authorities to inform carers of their assessment rights. It also added the duty, important for Gwen, Tracey and Paul, to consider carers' work, education, training and leisure needs. The Act marked a major cultural shift in viewing carers no longer as merely unpaid providers of services but as individuals with rights to work and social inclusion. Equally the focus shifts from the carer's 'ability and willingness' (s.8, DP(SCR)A 1986) to whether they are being denied life chances that are available to others.

To be assessed, a carer need not live with the person cared for, nor be the sole carer or a relative, but the legislation does not cover volunteers or paid carers. There is extensive guidance on the conduct of assessments (DH, 2005b), emphasizing a 'carer-centred approach', and outcomes which, whilst assisting a carer to care, also address their life outside caring. It recognizes the complex dynamics of caring relationships, and the importance of addressing 'willingness and ability to care' on the emotional and mental level as well as the physical (Clements, 2005).

There is growing recognition of demands on young carers (Becker and Dearden, 2004) and of how early apparent maturity can mask their needs as children (Cass, 2005). Guidance (DH, 2005b) requires young carers to be assessed under the Children Act 1989 (CA 1989), s.17(10) of which defines a child as a 'child in need' if their health or development is not achieving a reasonable standard, or is being impaired, or they are disabled. Identifying young carers as 'children in need', to whom duties are owed, potentially provides for greater breadth of intervention than is available under the mere powers embedded within carers' legislation. Section 17(1) requires local authorities to safeguard and promote the welfare of children in need, and promote their upbringing by their families by providing a range and level of services appropriate to their needs. Policy guidance (DH, 2000c) identifies a range of environmental conditions that render children vulnerable and regards support for parental coping as the key factor in protecting their health and development. Further detail on assessments relating to children may be found in Chapter 5.

Service provision

Decisions about service provision must be made in relation to both William and his carers, and inevitably these decisions are co-dependent.

William's assessment will have identified risks to his independence within his current situation. Once it has been determined which of his needs are eligible needs (including needs that are currently met by his carers for which that help cannot be sustained), then these needs must be met (DH, 2002b, referring to LASSL(97)13). Lack of resources cannot prevent service provision to an individual once that service has been deemed necessary (*R v Wigan MBC ex parte Tammadge* [1998]). A care plan detailing the services William will receive should be written and agreed with him, along with clear arrangements for review after 3 months and thereafter at least annually.

Guidance on the construction of the care plan is drawn from at least three sources. FACS guidance (DH, 2002b) identifies minimum content requirements – the eligible needs and associated risks, the preferred outcomes of service provision, contingency plans for emergencies, details of services provided (including charges or direct payments), carers' contributions and the review date. Both the original guidance (DH, 1991c) and the SAP guidance (LAC(2002)1) provide more detailed lists, emphasizing the service user's consent, their strengths and abilities, alternative options considered and 'unmet need' (presenting needs falling outside the eligible needs threshold). Any care plan, to be lawful, must have a reasonable chance of meeting the needs identified (*R v Staffordshire CC, ex parte Farley* [1997]).

Domiciliary care

The legal mandates for service provision form a complex jigsaw, reflecting piecemeal developments for different service user groups which have not yet been consolidated into one coherent set of rules.

In relation to disabled people, local authorities must identify the number of disabled people in their area (within the s.29 NAA 1948 definition) and must provide a range of services to promote their welfare. The s.29 definition explicitly includes people with 'a mental disorder of any kind'. LAC(93)10 clarifies the duties authorities have towards disabled people. They include the provision of social work advice and support, facilities for social rehabilitation and adjustment to disability, information, day centres for occupational, social, cultural and recreational activities, employment workshops and hostels. In addition, there are powers to provide holidays, travel, assistance in finding accommodation and warden services.

The mandate is further strengthened by the CSDPA 1970, s.2 of which requires arrangements to be made for any disabled person whose needs warrant practical help at home, support to reduce the social and personal consequences of illness and disability, telephones, adaptations to accommodation, meals at home or elsewhere, recreational facilities, including radio, television and libraries, provision of, or assistance in taking advantage of, holidays and educational facilities. It is likely that William, given his long-standing heart problems and his more recent but nonetheless progressive physical incapacity would be considered disabled within the legal definition, and thus eligible for services.

Local authorities have a power to promote the welfare of older people, whether disabled or not, and to use voluntary organizations to assist (s. 45, HSPHA 1968). Services specified include wardens, home delivery of meals, day care and domiciliary provision. However, a more tangible duty exists to provide home help, meals and laundry services if required because of age, illness or disability, and prevention, care and aftercare services to people who have been ill (s.254 and sch.20, NHSA 2006) and aftercare to people discharged from psychiatric hospital following long-term detentions (s.117, MHA 1983). Again this more specific duty would apply in William's case, given both his age and his health problems.

Social services authorities may request assistance from a housing authority when assessing a person's needs for services (s.47(3)(b), NHSCCA 1990). Housing need can easily be overlooked, but housing authorities should play a full part in community care (LAC(92)12). This circular reinforces the importance of communication with housing authorities to invite assistance with adaptations, safety equipment, daily living, improvements and repairs when a person appears to have a housing need. It encourages joint assessment arrangements with the objective of restoring or maintaining where possible non-institutional living. Such considerations are clearly relevant in William's case. Grants for improvements and facilities for disabled people, whether tenants or owner occupiers, are available (Housing Grants, Construction and Regeneration Act 1996) (H(GCR)A 1996). Disabled Facilities Grants (DFGs) are mandatory to facilitate access to a dwelling, heating, cooking, family rooms, toilet or washing facilities, or to help a disabled person care for others, or to reduce levels of risk (*R (B) v Calderdale MBC* [2004]). For other purposes grants are discretionary. The work must be necessary and appropriate to meet the disabled person's needs, and practicable to carry out. Social services may be asked to contribute to this assessment. The applicant, their spouse and others in the house will be means-tested and grant levels are capped. Equally, the local authority has a responsibility under s.2 CSDPA 1970 to provide assistance to a disabled person in arranging to carry out adaptations. Whilst this in theory could include financial assistance, it is usual for more major structural adaptations to be undertaken through a DFG application, with social services providing more minor equipment, aids and adaptations.

Residential care

The options above relate to a care plan that facilitates William remaining in his own home. He might as an alternative, or indeed to supplement home care, be offered residential care. Residential accommodation must be provided to those who, because of age, illness, disability or other circumstances, require care and attention not otherwise available to them (s.21, NAA 1948). This duty may be delegated to private or voluntary organizations (s26; *R v Wandsworth LBC, ex parte Beckwith* [1996]). Users' ability to pay must be assessed (s.22) and their property (including animals) safeguarded (s.48).

William's financial circumstances could influence the local authority's duty to provide residential accommodation. If his capital exceeds a certain level (specified and regularly reviewed under the charging rules for residential care), it could be argued that care and attention is otherwise available to him – i.e. he can enter into a contract with a care home and meet the full cost himself. The Community Care (Residential Accommodation) Act 1998 (CC(RA)A 1998) clarified that any capital below that specified limit must be disregarded by the local authority (i.e. the duty to accommodate is triggered, even if William contributes to its cost). Even if William does have capital in excess of the limit, the local authority may still be required to make the residential arrangements (e.g. if he does not have capacity to arrange for his own care, and no one else, such as a relative or representative, holds responsibility or authority to do so).

If the local authority decides residential accommodation should be provided for William, it must make arrangements for him to enter the home of his choice, provided it is available, suitable for him and costs no more than the authority would usually pay (NAA 1948 (Choice of Accommodation) Directions 1992, as amended by LAC (2004)20) (*R v Avon CC, ex parte Hazell* [1995]). If William's preferred accommodation is more expensive, then a third party (such as Gwen) could pay the difference (or indeed William himself if he owns his own house and enters into an agreement with the local authority to defer payment of his contribution (see below)). Despite the rhetoric of user choice, it has little statutory backing (Clements and Thompson, 2007) and the courts generally treat user preference as only one consideration in determining a care plan, leaving it open for the authority to act against William's preference if it wishes. Equally the courts have distinguished between preferences and needs. In *R v Avon CC ex parte Hazell* [1995] the court concluded that psychological attachment to a particular residential home by a young man with learning disability constituted a need (rather than a mere preference) and that his placement should be funded despite its greater expense to the local authority. Similar arguments about psychological need were also successfully deployed in *R (T) v Richmond LBC* [2001] involving choice of area for accommodation by a Black mental health service user. Equally the courts have supported local authorities' claims to have discharged their duty to provide accommodation if the service user unreasonably refuses suitable offers (*R v Kensington and Chelsea RLBC ex parte Kujtim* [1999]).

One issue of concern is whether residents of independent care homes are protected by the Human Rights Act 1998 (HRA 1998). Following a House of Lords ruling that they were not (*YL v Birmingham City Council* [2007]), this anomalous position has been partially rectified by s.145

Health and Social Care Act 2008 (HSCA 2008); care provided to a person placed by a local authority under s.21 NAA 1948 is considered a public function, and must therefore be compatible with the HRA 1998. Residents placed privately, however, remain outside the protection of the Act.

The local authority may propose a residential placement for William against his wishes, perhaps because a domiciliary care package exceeds a notional limit on permissible weekly costs. There is clear and long-established guidance (DH, 1990) that remaining at home is to be preferred over residential options. The Disability Discrimination Act 1995 (DDA 1995) (as amended 2005) and Article 8 of the ECHR have strengthened further the push for independent living (Clements and Thompson, 2007). Whilst the courts have been clear that ultimately it is for the local authority to determine how to meet identified need, the principle of independent living should be departed from only for professional, not financial, reasons (*R v Southwark ex parte Khana and Karim* [2001]). FACS guidance (DH, 2003a) clarifies that cost ceilings applied to care packages may be employed as a guide, but not used rigidly, leaving it open to an authority to spend above a cost ceiling if this would make a 'significant difference' to the individual involved.

The local authority may thus draw on a wide range of mandates in constructing William's care plan, and, whilst his choice and preferences must be taken into account, it is essentially for the local authority to determine the form his care package should take, weighing up all the circumstances including costs and resources (*R v Lancashire County Council, ex parte RADAR and Another* [1996]). A key consideration however is the dignity of the service user. The concept of dignity draws heavily on Articles 3 and 8 of the ECHR (right to protection from inhuman and degrading treatment; right to respect for private and family life) and has become a cornerstone principle to underpin decisions on service provision (Cass et al., 2006; SCIE, 2008).

Direct payments

Instead of providing services to meet assessed needs, local authorities must in certain circumstances make direct payments to enable a person to purchase the services they are assessed as needing. The mandate is now contained in the HSCA 2001, repealing the Community Care (Direct Payments) Act 1996 (CC(DP)A 1996) (which gave the local authority a power to make direct payments to more restricted groups of people) and the relevant sections of the CDCA 2000 (which extended them to carers for services to meet their own assessed needs, to parents of disabled children and to disabled children aged 16–17). The Community Care, Services for Carers and Children's Services (Direct Payments) (England) Regulations 2003 extend the scope even further, making it a duty to consider direct payments if the individual agrees. Excluded are people 'whose liberty to arrange their care is restricted by certain mental health or criminal justice legislation' (DH, 2003b, p. 7). Most recently individualized budgets have become a central plank of the government's personalization agenda, and are seen as the way to promote choice and autonomy for those requiring help and support (DH, 2006a). The legal rules are somewhat behind the policy drive here, and the government has signalled its intention to legislate to broaden and strengthen the availability and take-up of individualized budgets.

Charging

Local authorities must charge William for residential care provision (s.22 and s.26, NAA 1948), and must act in line with the national regulations (the National Assistance (Assessment of Resources) Regulations 1992) and regularly updated guidance (*R v Sefton MBC, ex parte Help the Aged and Charlotte Blanchard* [1997]). For non-residential services, charging is optional but encouraged (s.17, Health and Social Services and Social Security Adjudications Act 1983). Where charges are levied they must be reasonable, and in line with guidance (DH/DWP, 2002; DH, 2003c). Inability to pay should not mean withdrawal of services. Exceptions on charging are mental health aftercare services provided under s.117, MHA 1983, which are exempt from charge (*R v Manchester City Council ex parte Stennett* [2002]), and time-limited intermediate care services to assist a return to independence following hospital admission (see below).

Continuing care for health-related reasons

Should William's health deteriorate to the point where he is admitted to hospital and he is subsequently unable to return home to live independently, responsibility for providing and funding his services will depend on where the line is drawn between health care and social care. This boundary has been contested, with fierce debates about the split of responsibility between the NHS and the local authority. The outcome of disputes is of key importance to service users, who are asked to make a financial contribution for care provided by local authorities, whilst care provided by the NHS remains free at the point of delivery.

Concerns about hospital bed-blocking by people ready for discharge but awaiting assessment for social care services led to the Community

Care (Delayed Discharges) Act 2003 (CC(DD)A 2003), under which any delay caused by the local authority to arrangements for someone fit to be discharged from acute medical care leads to a financial penalty on the local authority. Intermediate care (LAC(2001)1) was introduced to bridge the gap for people who were medically fit for discharge but unable to return to independent living. It constitutes 'a structured programme of care provided for a limited period of time to assist a person to maintain or regain the ability to live in his own home' (Community Care (Delayed Discharges etc) Act Regulations 2003). Typically it lasts for no more than six weeks, is provided without charge to the service user in a community or domiciliary setting and involves significant interprofessional collaboration to deliver an integrated package of intensive, restorative interventions, working to a holistic, social model of reablement rather than the more medically-oriented and functionally-focused rehabilitation. Research evidence confirms that reablement schemes are well placed both to meet the preferred outcomes of service users and to achieve cost effectiveness in service delivery, when compared with alternatives such as longer-term care (Braye and Wigley, 2002; Braye et al., 2004).

Where continuing health-care needs remain, however, longer-term responsibility must now be allocated in line with national guidance. The NHS Continuing Healthcare (Responsibilities) Directions 2007 implement the National Framework for NHS Continuing Healthcare and NHS Funded Nursing Care in England (DH, 2007a). The framework reflects important case law (*R v North & East Devon Health Authority ex parte Coughlan* [1999]) which established that local authorities could only be held responsible for nursing care that is incidental or ancillary to the accommodation and social care that a social services authority can be expected to give. The HSCA 2001 subsequently expressly prohibited the provision of health care by a registered nurse as part of a package of community care services provided by the local authority. Equally important was case law (*R (Grogan v Bexley NHS Trust & South East London SHA & Secretary of State for Health* [2006]) which criticized the lack of a clearly articulated test for eligibility for NHS continuing care within local procedures, and indeed the lack of clarity in government guidance on this issue.

The test for eligibility for NHS-funded continuing health care is whether there is a primary health need; if so, the individual remains eligible for continuing NHS health care regardless of the setting in which this is delivered. Continuing care should only be refused if nursing and health needs are 'no more than incidental and ancillary' and are of a nature a local authority can be expected to provide. Financial issues should not be part of the decision. Additional factors to be taken into account, particularly in the context of domiciliary care, include the nature of the condition and/or treatment, the intensity of the needs (the extent to which their severity warrants regular interventions), their complexity (for example symptoms that are difficult to manage or control) and their unpredictability, particularly where changes are difficult to manage and present a risk. A decision-support tool defines categories of need across 11 health-care domains and sets out levels of need that *will* establish a primary health need and those that *might*. The domains to be considered, as part of a holistic assessment, are behaviour, cognition, communication, psychological/emotional needs, mobility, nutrition, continence, skin (including tissue viability), breathing, drug therapies and medication and symptom control, and altered states of consciousness. The guidance is clear that care in the context of terminal illness is covered by the continuing care guidelines. It is possible for ongoing services to comprise elements of both social care and continuing NHS health care.

Services for carers

William's care package will be influenced by the assessed needs of his carers, Gwen, Tracey and Paul, and by both their willingness and ability to continue to care for him and the range of services provided under carers' legislation to support them. The C(RS)A 1995, despite its title, was silent on the question of providing services to carers following assessment, but the CDCA 2000 in part remedied this by conferring the power to make services available to carers over 16. At the same time, a Carers National Strategy (DH, 1999a) promoted a strategic, multi-agency approach to meeting carers' needs. The C(EO)A 2004 emphasizes the importance of interagency collaboration by requiring any public authority (such as health, housing or education) to give due consideration to requests from social services for assistance in planning carers' services.

Guidance on services for carers (DH, 2005b) encourages flexibility in meeting carers' needs. The FACS guidance (DH, 2002b) is used to grade risk to the carer's role and thereby determine eligibility. Provision can range from short-term breaks to direct provision of a service in the home, emotional as well as physical support and, importantly, a duty under the Community Care, Services for Carers and Children's Services (Direct Payments) (England) Regulations 2003 to make direct payments, replacing the earlier mere power to do so. Direct payments can be used to meet the carer's needs but not the cared-for person's needs. Examples given in the guidance (DH, 2003b) include driving lessons, moving and handling classes, a mobile phone, taxis to work, or short holidays.

Services to meet carers' needs can include a service to the cared-for person (for example where that person has refused a community care assessment), although their agreement is required, and the services may not include intimate care. The trend observable in the 2004 Act to promote carers' access to work is further reinforced by the right, under the Work and Families Act 2006, for employees who are carers for an adult to request flexible working.

There is particular concern to protect young carers from inappropriate involvement in caring, or playing a substantial or regular role (Cass, 2005). In addition to proper levels of support to William, family support services as outlined in sch.2 of the CA1989 (and considered in more detail in Chapter 5) might also be considered necessary, although eligibility thresholds (in terms of the degree of impairment to Tracey's and Paul's health and development) would need to be reached.

Local authorities have the option to run short-term break schemes where vouchers enable cared-for people to secure the additional support they need when their carer needs a break, but with flexibility – for example to engage the services of a provider of domiciliary support as an alternative to entering short-term residential care. Under the Carers and Disabled Children (Vouchers) (England) Regulations 2003 the value of a voucher may be expressed in either financial or time value terms (DH, 2003d).

Carers can be charged for services, with local authority decisions on charging regulated by guidance (DH/DWP, 2002; DH, 2003c). They cannot, though, be charged for community care services provided to the people they care for, unless those services arise from a carer's assessment. Cared-for people cannot be charged for the services provided to their carers, including any services provided to them as the cared-for person as a result of the carer's assessment.

These developments in how carers are recognized and valued are reflected within more recent government initiatives. The White Paper (DH, 2006a) heralds a new deal for carers, now contained within a new carers' strategy (HM Government, 2008), which emphasizes the centrality of carers' roles, the importance of integrated, personalized support and the need for a balance between caring and life outside that role. A range of strategic and practical measures is envisaged – a national information service, a training programme, emergency care cover, enhanced short-term breaks, developments in technology, personal budgets, health promotion, measures to prevent financial hardship – with implementation overseen by a Standing Commission on Carers. The main strategic direction for young carers is confirmed as enhanced support for families through integrated children's services and the Every Child Matters outcomes (DfES, 2004a) for all children. Young carers' need for recognition and support from universal services such as schools and health care agencies, as well as from targeted and specialized projects, is emphasized, along with a dedicated national helpline. In the longer term, better understanding of the needs of families affected by disability, illness and substance misuse is intended to inform measures to reduce excessive or inappropriate caring by children.

Safeguarding

The law does not yet provide a unified set of legal rules to assist in safeguarding older people's welfare in situations where consensual measures are not sufficient to manage perceived risks. So, if William's condition further deteriorates, notwithstanding the provision of domiciliary services, and he is thought to be in a situation that poses too many risks, there is little that can be done to impose solutions against his will, provided he retains his mental capacity. He can neither be required to accept services at home, nor removed to a safer living situation against his will.

If William's mental health deteriorates and gives cause for concern, and he refuses assessment or treatment, he could be compulsorily admitted to psychiatric hospital (see Amy's case in this chapter). Equally, he could be subject to guardianship (see the case of Janet, also in this chapter). However, these would be drastic measures in the context of the information in the case study and, although it might be supposed that William has some mental health needs due to his anxiety and possible depression, it is more likely and appropriate that assessment of these needs, and services to meet them, would be provided in the context of the SAP and subsequent care package.

The only other power of removal from home for someone such as William, who retains their mental capacity, is under s.47, NAA 1948, which permits removal of someone who (a) is suffering from grave disease or, being aged, infirm or physically incapacitated, is living in insanitary conditions *and* (b) is unable to devote to him or herself, or is not receiving from others, proper care and attention, when it is in their interests or to prevent nuisance or injury to the health of others. The local authority applies to a court with a recommendation from the Community Physician, giving the individual one week's notice. Removal is to a hospital or other suitable location, and detention may last three months, being thereafter renewable. In cases of urgent necessity, immediate removal is allowed, for three weeks, on application to a magistrate supported by two medical recommendations, including the Community Physician. Such action again is drastic, and is likely only to be justified on the ground of public health hazard posed by William's behaviour, rather than as an intervention that prioritized his interests.

There is no information in the case study relating to William that indicates he is being abused or exploited, or that he lacks capacity to make decisions for himself. Were this the case, then it would be essential to consider the protective measures contained within government guidance on the protection of vulnerable people (DH, 2000a). This would cover physical, emotional or financial abuse or neglect, but whilst William retains capacity there is little intervention that could be made to protect his interests against his wishes, without major infringement of his civil liberties. Safeguarding is explored in more detail in the case of Janet later in this chapter.

If William wishes to have help managing his affairs, then provided he has mental capacity he can appoint someone else to make decisions on his behalf. The Mental Capacity Act 2005 (MCA 2005) makes it possible to create a lasting power of attorney (LPA) to endure beyond any future loss of capacity by William. The LPA can cover either property and financial affairs, or personal welfare (including health care and treatment), or both. It must be registered with the Office of the Public Guardian before it can be used. A property and affairs LPA can be used at any time, but a personal welfare LPA can only be used once the donor has lost capacity to make the welfare decision.

Attorneys must observe the principles of the MCA 2005 and guidance in the Code of Practice (DCA, 2007), and act in the best interests of the donor. These issues are explored in more detail in the Janet case study. They can make any decisions in respect of which power has been conferred, but must observe any conditions or restrictions set by the donor. There are some restrictions, for example the attorney could not consent to or refuse treatment for William if he were detained under the MHA 1983, take decisions that would result in him being deprived of his liberty, make decisions that conflicted with those of a guardian under the MHA 1983, override any advance decisions that William has made about medical treatment, or refuse consent to life-sustaining treatment unless the advance decision contains express provision to that effect.

The attorney is also bound by the legal rules of agency (DCA, 2007) which include exercising a duty of care, avoiding any conflict of interests and personal advantage, acting in good faith, with honesty and integrity and observing confidentiality. The Office of the Public Guardian and the Court of Protection have powers to investigate and if necessary terminate LPAs if the powers are exercised inappropriately.

Also under the MCA 2005, William could make an advance decision on refusal of medical treatment, drawing on the common law principle that an adult with capacity has the right to consent to or refuse medical treatment. An advance decision must be respected in the event of future incapacity when the need for the treatment arises provided there is proof it exists, is valid and applies to the treatment in question. If the decision is to refuse life-sustaining treatment it must be in writing, signed and witnessed, and state that it applies even when life is at risk. An advance decision to refuse treatment for mental disorder, however, will not apply if William is detained under the MHA 1983. Although only advance refusals can be made, requests or preferences on treatment to be given can also be recorded.

Concluding comments

The legal framework for services to adults has remained relatively unchanged, despite the major policy shifts of marketization (mid-1980s–1990s) and modernization (1997 onwards). The newly elected government in 1997 embarked upon a process of modernization of public sector provision intended to address the problems of inconsistency of provision, lack of collaboration between services and failure of protection for vulnerable people (DH, 1998). Whilst a range of studies (DH, 2007b) identify progress towards the goals of independence, well-being and choice, they also identify tensions between some of the core principles of modernization, for example between consistency and flexibility, or between independence and protection. They identify that the relationship between interventions and outcomes is complex, and that institutional barriers remain. Added to this, the early years of the 21st century have been growing government concern that a combination of demographic changes and changing expectations makes the social care system unsustainable (HM Government, 2007a). There are sharp divides between the improving standards in publicly-funded social care and those in self-funded provision; resources remain embedded in institutional care; and high expenditure on those with critical care needs leave those with less complex needs excluded by tightened eligibility criteria (CSCI, 2008a).

A more radical reform agenda is under way, with a cross-government commitment to the transformation of adult social care (HM Government, 2007a) around the organizing principle of personalization, tailoring services to the needs and preferences of citizens empowered to shape their own lives and services (HM Government, 2007b). Whole system change to promote choice and control in social care is seen as the means of securing independence, well-being and dignity (DH, 2008a). Key components include improved information and advocacy, early intervention, self-assessment, brokerage and advocacy by social workers (rather than assessment and gate-keeping), holistic approaches crossing organizational boundaries, and personal or individual budgets.

Personal budgets are to be made available to all social care users and their carers – a transparent allocation of resource either managed on behalf of an individual or paid to them as a cash sum, or both, depending on personal choice. In addition, individual budgets are being piloted, bringing together a number of income streams from different agencies to provide greater flexibility for holistic provision (HM Government, 2008).

The transformation and personalization agendas will bring further major changes in the legal framework for care and support to people with social care needs. The HSCA 2008, for example, has already extended direct payments to people without capacity through provision for the appointment of a third party to manage them.

The legal rules on assessment will not remain static. The Commission for Social Care Inspection (CSCI, 2008a) found little consistency, both within and between councils, on eligibility for services under FACS, and poor outcomes for people deemed ineligible. A subsequent review (CSCI, 2008b) found major concerns relating to transparency, clarity and fairness in application of the criteria. A service-led rather than a needs-led approach persisted, with unduly standardized assessments and neglect of some groups. Assessments were not integrated with a wider range of health, housing and leisure needs, or with other assessment frameworks and processes (continuing care, learning disability services or care programme approach), nor were preventive approaches common. FACS – concerned with standardization, consistency and professional decision-making – was seen as inherently inconsistent in relation to personalization (concerned with self-assessment, individual choice and control). For the future, there are strong calls for 'progressive universalism' (CSCI, 2008b, p. 7) through which some help is offered to all, with additional provision for those with greater needs through application of clear criteria and a resource allocation formula.

Local assessment frameworks will be replaced by a Common Assessment Framework, signalled as an intention in the White Paper (DH, 2006a) and subject to government consultation during 2009. Self-assessment is also high on the agenda and could bring significant shifts in the respective responsibilities and powers of professionals, service users and carers. The adult social care legal framework more broadly is also under review, with the intention of creating a unified statute, following a scoping report (Law Commission, 2008); and extensive consultation is taking place on new systems of funding and delivery (DH, 2008b) with a Green Paper on more radical changes anticipated at the time of writing (Summer 2009).

Amy

Amy's case will be explored in a series of stages as the crisis unfolds, with discussion of the relevant legal rules and possible interventions at each stage.

Amy is aged 29 and of mixed parentage. She has little contact with her parents, who are divorced, although her mother lives locally. Diagnosed with schizophrenia in her late teens, she has had in-patient psychiatric treatment for several prolonged periods of time, and has a history of both self-harm and violent outbursts towards others. For the last couple of years she had been more stable, living in supported housing, but last year she moved in with a new partner, Jim, and since then her mental stability has declined. Both make heavy use of recreational drugs and alcohol and the police have been called to the flat on several occasions following complaints by neighbours, though no further action has been taken. Amy sees a nurse from the community mental health team, who of late has been concerned that Amy is not taking prescribed medication, and that she is experiencing more acute episodes of mental distress related to her schizophrenia. Her consultant has considered whether she should be in hospital, but this is a step that Amy has adamantly refused. An urgent call is now received by the community mental health team from Jim, indicating that Amy has been self-harming with a knife and that he thinks she should be in hospital.

As someone with mental health problems living in the community it is likely that Amy has been receiving services under the Care Programme Approach (CPA). Introduced first following the NHS and Community Care Act 1990, CPA is the interdisciplinary mechanism for managing care and treatment to people receiving psychiatric services, regardless of whether they have been in hospital. It is a core element of the standards set for mental health services by the National Service Framework (NSF) (DH, 1999b). Since October 2008, when distinctions between Standard and Enhanced CPA were removed, it is reserved for those with the most complex needs requiring multi-agency intervention, or for those most risk. The guidance (DH, 2008c) calls for refocusing of interprofessional teamwork to adopt a strengths-based, holistic and relationship-based approach to recovery, which promotes user self-determination and control. Eligibility for the approach arises through severe mental disorder with high clinical complexity, current or potential risks (suicide, harm to others, relapse, self-neglect, vulnerability), severe distress or disengagement, dual diagnosis, multiple agency provision, current or recent detention in hospital, significant reliance on carers or caring responsibilities for others, experience of social disadvantage/exclusion. The comprehensive assessment includes psychiatric, psychological and social functioning, risk to the individual and others, needs arising from co-morbidity, personal circumstances including family and carers, housing needs, financial circumstances and capability, employment, education and training needs, physical health needs, equality and diversity issues, and social inclusion and social contact and independence. CPA provides access to a care co-ordinator, a written care plan, ongoing review, advocacy support and information on carers' assessment. If Amy's multidisciplinary care package to date has included social care services, these will have been provided under the same legislation that provided the framework for services in William's case study.

CPA implementation has not been robust and Amy may have fallen through the net. A review (CHAI, 2007) found that implementation has failed to put people first, or involve them in decisions about care and medication; too few people receive a copy of their care plan or know who their care co-ordinator is; reviews are not carried out. Equally, mental health services are not meeting the needs of black and minority ethnic groups who are disadvantaged both in terms of service experience and the outcome of interventions (Sashidharan, 2003). Although since the introduction of the NSF (DH, 1999b) mental health services have become increasingly responsive, improvements are still required in service user and carer involvement, services for minority ethnic groups, long-term care and the availability of psychological therapies and the identification and support of individuals who are at risk (DH, 2004).

Services to Amy may not have been consistent, but her mental disorder and the levels of risk in this current situation indicate that the initial response is likely to involve consideration of legal rules allowing for her detention and treatment, possibly against her will. Two statutes, the Mental Health Act 1983 (MHA) and the Mental Capacity Act 2005 (MCA) (both as amended by the Mental Health Act 2007 (MHA 2007)), provide different forms of authority and procedural safeguards.

The MCA provides rules applicable to decision-making for people who do not have capacity to make decisions themselves. The MHA provides a lawful procedure for the detention and treatment in hospital (and in certain circumstances elsewhere) of someone with mental disorder without their consent where detention is necessary for their own health and safety or for the protection of others. Fennell (2007) indicates that both acts provide safeguards against arbitrary deprivation of liberty which would contravene articles 5 and 8 of the ECHR, but identifies important distinctions between them: MCA 2005 operates on the basis of incapacity due to mental disability (defined as impairment or disturbance of the functioning of the mind or brain) with best interests as the guiding principle. MHA 1983 operates on the basis of mental disorder (defined as any disorder or disability of mind) with health/safety/protection of others as the guiding principle. Fennell identifies the different and competing drivers they enshrine: reducing stigma and social exclusion; managing risk to the public and to mentally disordered people; and protecting human rights.

As a consequence, the use of compulsory powers, particularly to overrule the wishes of someone who has capacity to decide for themselves, is one area of practice that raises ethical dilemmas for professionals committed to supporting people in the exercise of personal autonomy and seeking the least restrictive care setting. Section 118(2B) of the amended MHA 1983 identifies a number of matters which inform decision-making in this context, including patients' past and present wishes and feelings, their religion, culture and sexual orientation, minimizing restrictions on liberty, involving patients in planning, developing and delivering care, avoidance of unlawful discrimination, seeking effective treatment, the views of carers and other interested parties, patient well-being and safety, and public safety.

These are further shaped into five core principles in the accompanying Code of Practice (DH, 2008d) – respecting diversity of need, circumstances, wishes and feelings; involving patients and their carers in decision-making; seeking the least possible restriction of liberty; minimizing harm and maximizing safety and protection; making effective, efficient and equitable use of resources. However, principles inform decisions, they do not determine them, and the weight given to each will depend on the context, though all must be considered when achieving a balance in any individual case. The Code is intended for professionals exercising powers and duties under the Act, who, whilst under no absolute duty to comply with the code, must not depart from its guidance without a convincing justification. The Act is also accompanied by a Reference Guide (DH, 2008e), intended to provide accessible clarification and explanation of its provisions.

Amy's circumstances are likely to trigger an assessment of the need for admission to hospital, undertaken by an Approved Mental Health Professional (AMHP). The AMHP can be a registered social worker, a registered first level nurse with a qualification in either mental health nursing or learning disabilities nursing, a registered occupational therapist or a chartered psychologist, who has undergone an approved training programme and is approved by the local authority (LA).

If Jim is Amy's nearest relative (NR), then under s.13(4) the social services authority *must* direct an AMHP as soon as practicable to consider making application for her admission to hospital. NR status is a potentially powerful position, with the right to apply for admission, seek discharge and challenge detention, alongside rights to information and consultation about decisions made by AMHPs and in some cases the power to withhold consent. It is not the same as 'next of kin'. Section 26(1) lists, in order of priority, those who qualify, placing civil partners and unmarried same and opposite sex couples alongside married partners at the top.

Powers under the legal rules to impose solutions on Amy rely on her status as a person with a mental disorder. Following the MHA 2007 amendment, there is now a single definition of mental disorder, applicable to all types of detention under the MHA 1983 – 'any disorder or disability of mind'. The Code of Practice (DH, 2008d) indicates this is a broad umbrella, and lists a wide range of conditions covered, including some previously excluded from longer-term detentions under the original MHA 1983. Fennell (2007) points out that this opens the way for sex offenders who have served determinate prison sentences to be subsequently further detained under the non-offender provisions.

There are, however, some restrictions on inclusion. People with learning disability (defined (s.1(4)) as 'a state of arrested or incomplete development of mind which includes significant impairment of intelligence and social functioning') cannot be detained for treatment (s.3), guardianship (s.7), community treatment (s.17A), remands or orders from court to hospital or guardianship (ss.35–38), transfers to hospital from prison (ss.47–48) unless their disability is associated with abnormally aggressive or seriously irresponsible conduct. Autistic spectrum disorders, however, are not classed as learning disabilities (DH, 2008d), and therefore remain eligible for all forms of detention. Dependence on alcohol or drugs cannot be of itself deemed a mental disorder, although disorders may arise from or be associated with dependence. Appropriate medical treatment must be available for detention for treatment (s.3) to take place.

An AMHP from the Community Mental Health Team arranges to meet Amy's doctor at her home, and visits the flat, finding Jim locked out in the stairwell. He says that whilst he was attempting to stop Amy from harming herself, she attacked him with the knife and locked herself in with her pills, saying she is going to take them all. He has phoned the police.

What can be done in this situation to gain access to Amy? Although under s.115 an AMHP has the power to enter premises in which a mentally disordered person is living, if he or she believes that person not to be receiving proper care, this does not extend to entry by force. An occupier can permit entry. Thus, unless Amy has exclusive rights of occupation, Jim could break down his own door or authorize someone else to do so. Where an occupier is unavailable, or unwilling, the police have powers of forcible entry under the Police & Criminal Evidence Act 1984 (PACE 1984) to save life and limb and/or prevent crime. Without either of these justifications, the AMHP must apply to a magistrate for a warrant (s.135, MHA 1983) empowering a police constable to enter, by force if necessary, accompanied by an AMHP and a doctor, and remove Amy to a place of safety with a view to making an application for admission to hospital, or other suitable arrangements. This can be granted if the AMHP has reasonable cause to suspect that a person believed to be suffering from mental disorder (a) has been or is being ill-treated, neglected, or kept otherwise than under proper control, in any place, or (b) is living alone and is unable to care for himself.

Were Amy not at home but in a place to which the public has access, the police hold further emergency powers (s.136) to remove to a place of safety someone who appears to be mentally disordered and in immediate need of care and control, if this is necessary in their interests or for the protection of others. Someone taken to a place of safety on s.136 must be interviewed as soon as possible by an AMHP (along with a doctor) with a view to making arrangements for their care or treatment.

In both these circumstances, the place of safety can be a residential care home, a hospital, a police station, or any other suitable place with the permission of the occupier. Detention may not exceed 72 hours.

In the event, after a conversation through the door, Amy allows the AMHP to enter the flat, accompanied by the police. She has not caused herself any harm, though her pills are scattered about the room and the knife is in evidence. The doctor, her GP, arrives and a discussion reveals that Amy is indeed very distressed and is experiencing the return of some of her more acute symptoms. She talks of being pursued by people who want to hurt her, and appears fearful, anxiously pacing the room and finding it impossible to explain her distress or be calmed or reassured. Physically she looks undernourished and unwell. The doctor is certain that she should be admitted to hospital, but Amy refuses to consider this.

The professionals have powers and duties under the MHA 1983 (as amended by the MHA 2007) to admit Amy to hospital without her consent. Most patients admitted to psychiatric hospital have voluntary status (s.131, MHA 1983), meaning they are not subject to compulsory detention and may leave at any time. They either (a) have capacity and have consented to admission or (b) do not have capacity but are not resistant and the degree of control exercised whilst they are in hospital does not amount to deprivation of liberty. In the light of Amy's refusal the AMHP must find a way forward that sits within the legal rules.

The first issue is whether Amy has the capacity to understand and make a decision to consent to or refuse hospital admission. Capacity is defined simply as 'the ability to make a decision' (DCA, 2007, p. 41), and an individual lacks capacity in relation to any particular decision if they are unable to make the decision because of an impairment of, or a disturbance in the functioning of, the mind or brain (MCA 2005, s.2(1)). Although Amy is distressed and possibly disturbed in her thinking, this does not *per se* equate to lack of capacity to decide whether she wants to be in hospital, and the MCA 2005 is quite clear that incapacity should not be assumed merely because of a condition or behaviour, or because a decision appears unwise to others.

Possible ways forward are:

● If Amy does not have capacity and is not actively resisting admission, and if once in hospital she will not be deprived of her liberty (e.g. by being prevented from leaving), then she could be admitted informally, without the need for recourse to the MHA 1983 powers for compulsory admission. Such action would be lawful under the protection given in s.5, MCA 2005, provided steps have been taken to ascertain that she does not have capacity, and the intervention does not contravene any advance decision she has made, and is believed to be in her best interests. Determining best interests is a two-stage, balance-sheet decision. First, is the proposed intervention in line with what a responsible body of medical opinion would consider to be in the patient's best interests? Second, does the intervention provide the best balance of advantages over disadvantages? In determining best interests, the professionals must (s.4, MCA 2005):

  O Not make assumptions relating to Amy's age, appearance, condition, behaviour;
  O Take all relevant circumstances into account;
  O Consider whether she is likely to have capacity and when;
  O Encourage her participation;

O Take account of her past and present wishes and feelings and beliefs and values or other factors that she would take into account if able to do so;

O Take account of anyone named by her to be consulted, any carer, anyone with Lasting Power of Attorney (LPA) or a court appointed deputy.

The Code of Practice (DCA 2007) gives detailed guidance on interpretation of these requirements, indicating they are merely a starting point, and that in many cases extra factors will need to be considered.

Certain more serious interventions require the approval of the Court of Protection or someone with LPA, and s.37 MCA 2005 requires an Independent Mental Capacity Advocate to be involved where there is no-one to consult

- If Amy does not have capacity and is not actively resisting admission, but once in hospital she will be prevented from leaving, then her admission could take place under the procedure set out in the MCA 2005 Deprivation of Liberty Safeguards (MCADL) (MoJ, 2008a). Under ss.4A, 4b and 16A of the MCA 2005 (as amended by s.50, MHA 2007), as a person over 18 with mental disorder and lacking capacity to decide on admission to a hospital or care home in order to receive treatment, Amy may be deprived of her liberty in her own best interests if this is a necessary and proportionate response to the risk of her suffering harm. This could not be used if she resists or objects to hospital admission (or would object, if able to do so), or has made an advance directive refusing hospital admission for treatment for mental disorder, or if an attorney or court-appointed deputy refuses on her behalf. Such refusals can however be overridden by MHA detention (see below). Equally MCADL could not be used if capacity is fluctuating and when capable Amy is expected not to consent, or the degree of restraint thought necessary to protect others exceeds that which could be said to be proportionate to risk to the patient personally, or detention using this route would not be sufficient to ensure that necessary treatment would be received and harm would ensue (DH, 2008d; MoJ, 2008a). However, admission to residential care homes can be carried out under MCADL even where the individual resists admission.

- If Amy does not have capacity and her admission cannot be made using either of the above MCA 2005 procedures (for example where one of the exclusions above applies, or where detention is for the protection of others rather than in her own best interests), then the professionals involved must consider whether there are grounds under the MHA 1983 (as amended by the MHA 2007).

● If Amy does have capacity and withholds consent to admission, then again she cannot be detained without some formal procedure, and the AMHP must consider whether there are grounds for compulsory admission under the MHA 1983.

> The AMHP and doctor conclude that although Amy has a mental illness and is acutely distressed, she does indeed have capacity to understand what is being advised and therefore her refusal is valid.

In effect this assessment rules out detention using the MCA 2005, and requires consideration of the powers and duties provided by the MHA 1983. Article 5 of the ECHR provides that any deprivation of liberty must be carried out under a procedure prescribed by law and be necessary on grounds of 'unsoundness of mind'. The MHA 1983 provides the necessary procedural safeguards for lawful deprivation of liberty and sets out the grounds for compulsory admission to hospital. Amy could be admitted for assessment (s.2) or for treatment (s.3).

Under s.2, an application for admission can be made in respect of someone who is suffering from a mental disorder of a nature or degree which warrants their detention in a hospital for assessment (or for assessment followed by medical treatment) for at least a limited period, and where they ought to be so detained in the interests of their own health or safety or with a view to protection of others.

The application (which may come from an AMHP or the NR) must be supported by two medical recommendations, one of which should be from a doctor approved under s.12 as having special experience in the diagnosis or treatment of mental disorder, and one where possible from a doctor who knows the patient. The AMHP must take such steps as are practicable to inform the NR of the application and of the NR's power to discharge the patient. Detention is for 28 days. The patient may appeal to the Mental Health Review Tribunal (MHRT) within 14 days.

Where the grounds for admission under s.2 exist but securing the second medical recommendation would involve undesirable delay, then under s.4 MHA 1983 an emergency application may be made, supported by one medical recommendation, preferably from a doctor who knows the patient. Detention is for 72 hours, during which time a second medical recommendation can be given to secure detention under s.2. The Code (DH, 2008d) states that, in order to be satisfied that an emergency has arisen, the applicant and the doctor should have evidence of an immediate and significant risk of mental or physical harm to the patient or to others, danger of serious harm to property or a need for physical restraint of the patient.

Alternatively, under s.3 MHA 1983, application may be made for admission for treatment. Such an application can be made in respect of Amy if:

● she is suffering from a mental disorder of a nature or degree which makes medical treatment in a hospital appropriate, and
● it is necessary for her health or safety, or for the protection of other persons that she should receive such treatment, and
● it cannot be provided unless she is detained under this section, and
● appropriate medical treatment is available for her.

Not relevant in Amy's case, but important to note, is that people with learning disability are not subject to s.3 admission unless their disability is associated with abnormally aggressive or seriously irresponsible conduct.

The s.3 application (which may come from an AMHP or the NR) must be supported by two medical recommendations, one of which should be from a doctor approved under s.12. Detention is for 6 months, renewable for a further 6 months and thereafter for 1 year at a time. The patient may appeal to the MHRT once within the first 6 months, and once in every period of subsequently renewed detention.

The appropriate treatment must merely 'be available', not necessarily consented to by the patient, or likely to be effective. The Code (DH, 2008d) clarifies that it must, however, be an appropriate response to the patient's condition, taking account of the nature and degree of their mental disorder and all other circumstances of their case.

The Code further clarifies the grounds for admission under s.2 and s.3. Where mental disorder of a nature or degree is a condition that must be satisfied,:

[N]ature refers to the particular mental disorder from which the patient is suffering, its chronicity, its prognosis, and the patient's previous response to receiving treatment for the disorder. Degree refers to the current manifestation of the patient's disorder. (p. 25)

The Code outlines factors for consideration in relation to the patient's health and safety. These include risk of suicide, self-harm or self-neglect, jeopardy to health or safety, likelihood of deterioration if treatment is not provided, views of the patient and of any carers, relatives or close friends about the likely course of the disorder, the patient's own skills and experience in managing their condition, potential benefits of treatment weighed against adverse effects of detention, and other methods of managing the risks.

Medical treatment is defined (s.145) as including nursing, psychological intervention and specialist mental health habilitation, rehabilitation and care, provided the purpose is to alleviate or prevent worsening of the disorder or one or more of its symptoms.

On the protection of others, the Code draws attention to the need to consider the nature of the risk, and the likelihood and severity of harm. Past history will be relevant, as well as the ability and willingness of those around the patient to manage the risks.

The Code also discusses the choice between s.2 and s.3 detention, indicating that s.3 is to be preferred where the patient's disorder and treatment plan is already well established.

An important consideration is the extent to which alternatives to s.3 admission might be available. The rule in s.3(2)(c) – that treatment cannot be provided unless the patient is detained under s.3 – must lead the AMHP to consider first whether, in the case of someone lacking capacity, the alternative of using the Deprivation of Liberty procedure (MCADL) would safely and effectively secure their care (Fennell, 2007). The MCA 2005 Code of Practice (DCA 2007) states that if MCADL is not considered appropriate, MHA 1983 detention should be considered where:

- The care and treatment necessary cannot be given without deprivation of liberty;
- The treatment is subject to a valid advance decision under the MCA 2005;
- Restraint beyond that permissible under MCA 2005 may be needed;
- The person cannot be assessed or treated safely or effectively without treatment being compulsory;
- The person has capacity to refuse some aspect of the treatment, and has done so;
- The person, or someone else, may be harmed if the treatment is not given.

Either an AMHP or the NR may make the application for hospital admission. The Code (DH, 2008d) indicates that AMHP application is to be preferred to NR application, given the AMHP's knowledge and training, and the potentially adverse effect on the NR's relationship with the patient if they make the application. If the NR does make the application, an AMHP must after the event make a social circumstances report to the hospital (s.14, MHA 1983).

If the AMHP makes the application they must, before doing so, interview the patient 'in a suitable manner' and determine that detention in hospital is in all the circumstances of the case the most appropriate way of providing the care and medical treatment needed (s.13(2)). The Code (DH, 2008a) emphasizes that alternatives should be considered, and that consideration must be given to the patient's wishes and views (past and present) of their own needs, their age, physical health, cultural background, social and family circumstances, the impact that any future deterioration or lack of improvement in their condition would have on their children, other relatives or carers, and the effect on the patient, and those close to them, of a decision to admit or not to admit under the Act.

For s.3 admissions, the AMHP must consult the NR before making the application, unless it is not reasonably practicable or would involve unreasonable delay. If, once consulted, the NR objects, the admission cannot proceed. For s.2 there is no duty to consult, but the NR must be advised of the admission, and of their power to discharge the patient, within a reasonable time (s.11(3)). The reasons for any departure from the principle of consultation must be recorded. The Code (DH, 2008d) indicates that impracticality can include the prospect of detrimental impact on the patient resulting in unjustifiable breach of their rights to private and family life under article 8, ECHR. Duties to inform NRs are thus not absolute, and in almost all cases information should not be shared if the patient objects. Where information is shared with a NR without a patient's consent, the professional involved 'must consider whether the disclosure would be likely to put the patient at risk of physical harm or financial or other exploitation, cause them emotional distress or lead to a deterioration in their mental health, or have any other detrimental effect on their health or wellbeing, and if so whether the advantages to the patient and the public interest of disclosure to the NR outweigh the disadvantages to the patient (p. 14).

The NR can discharge a patient from s.3 and appeal to a MHRT if blocked from doing so.

The NR may authorize someone else to act on their behalf (Mental Health (Hospital, Guardianship and Treatment) (England) Regulations 2008). A NR can also be displaced, on application to the county court by the patient, any relative, anyone with whom the patient lives or an AMHP, on grounds of unsuitability. Unsuitability can arise because the NR is incapable of acting because of illness or mental disorder, or has objected unreasonably to an application for admission, has exercised the power to discharge a patient without due regard to the patient's health or wellbeing or the safety of the public, or is unsuitable for some other reason (e.g. having abused the patient, being feared by the patient, or their relationship having broken down irretrievably). The county court can also be asked to appoint a NR for a patient who does not have one.

In performing duties under the MHA 1983, although AMHPs act on behalf of a social services authority, they act autonomously as independent professionals and must exercise their own judgement and a social care perspective (DH, 2008d) in deciding whether there are alternatives to detention.

A completed application with medical recommendation(s) provides the applicant with authority to convey the patient to hospital (which may be delegated to someone else). The patient is in legal custody, and the person authorized to convey them has all the powers of a constable (s.137), including the use of reasonable force. The Code indicates that if the patient's behaviour is likely to be violent or dangerous, the police should be asked to assist but that where practicable an ambulance service vehicle should be used. If a police vehicle is used, ambulance personnel should accompany the patient.

If in the event of an admission taking place informally (i.e. without any of the above formal processes) because Amy consents, but once an in-patient she attempts to discharge herself, there is also provision in the MHA 1983 for her to be detained using 'holding powers'. Under s.5(2) a doctor or Approved Clinician (AC) can detain any in-patient for 72 hours (for the purposes of assessment) if of the view that an application for compulsory admission ought to be considered. Under s.5(4) a registered nurse can hold any in-patient who is already receiving treatment for mental disorder for 6 hours if a doctor or approved clinician is not immediately available to take action under s.5(2).

> Amy is admitted to hospital under s.4 of the MHA 1983, the AMHP judging that the situation was acute enough to warrant the use of emergency powers. Subsequently a second medical recommendation was provided by her consultant psychiatrist, and Amy remained in hospital under s.2, MHA 1983. This was then followed by detention for treatment under s.3.

An important provision for detained patients was introduced by the MHA 2007. From October 2009, an Independent Mental Health Advocate (IMHA) must be appointed for all detained patients (except those held on 72-hour detentions), for patients subject to guardianship and community treatment orders, and for any patients for whom treatments regulated under s.57 (and for patients under 18 treatments under ss.58/58A also) are being considered. Thus Amy will benefit from the services of an IMHA whose role is to promote understanding of her detention and treatment, and provide information about, and support in exercising, her rights (MHA 1983, ss.130A–D). The IMHA can visit Amy in private, interview any professionals involved with her care, and (if Amy consents) consult hospital and LA records about her. The MHA 1983 (Independent Mental Health Advocates) (England) Regulations 2008 specify that the IMHA must be someone of integrity and good character, with appropriate experience and/or training, and able to act independently.

Amy has now become much more stable, and is very keen to be discharged from hospital. She has had several short-term leave of absence visits to a community hostel, in which there is a place for her to live should she be discharged. The psychiatric team however consider that there are risks attached to her discharge. They are concerned that in continuing her relationship with Jim, there are risks that she will stop her medication, or that use of non-prescribed drugs and alcohol will once again threaten her stability, with the possibility that she will leave the hostel and lose contact with support services.

Under s.117, MHA 1983, LAs and Primary Care Trusts share a joint duty to provide aftercare to patients discharged following detention on s.3 (and other longer-term detentions under 37, 45A, 47 and 48). The duty to provide services continues until the person is no longer in need of them and should aim to support them in developing skills needed to cope with life outside hospital (DH, 2008d). The Code identifies a wide range of needs that should be considered in the formulation of the aftercare plan. Provision consists of community care services provided following assessment under s.47 NHSCCA 1990 (see William's case study), but a significant difference is that charges cannot be levied if the individual is entitled to s.117 aftercare (*R v Manchester City Council ex parte Stennett* [2002]).

Whilst s.117 places a duty to provide services, it places no obligation on the person receiving them to accept. In Amy's case the team consider that further measures should be applied to ensure her continuing compliance with treatment, and a social care package that meets her needs for assertive support.

Amy's leave of absence so far has been granted by the Responsible Clinician (RC) who, under s.17, MHA 1983, may grant leave indefinitely or for a specified period, and may impose conditions thought necessary in the patient's own interest or to protect others. Patients on s.17 leave can be recalled to hospital. The RC is the approved clinician who has overall responsibility for treatment, one of a range of ACs who may be involved. ACs may be doctors, psychologists, nurses, OTs or social workers, but they must have appropriate competence and, if acting as the RC, must have had relevant RC training. Whilst the broadening of professional qualifications may signal a welcome departure from the dominance of medical models of care and treatment, Fennell (2007) considers that from a legal perspective it departs from a Council of Europe consensus that medical expertise is necessary when making decisions on the involuntary placement and treatment of people with mental disorder.

The MHA 2007 amendments make it possible for Amy to be subject to compulsory treatment whilst living in the community. If leave of absence is to last over 7 days, the RC must consider the need for supervised community treatment (SCT). This is applicable where the criteria for ongoing detention under s.3 are met, and treatment is available, but the treatment can be provided without Amy continuing to stay in hospital. Under s.17A, MHA 1983, the RC may, with the agreement of an AMHP, discharge her from hospital, but retain the power to recall her if necessary. This process creates a community treatment order (CTO), of 6 months in the first instance, renewable for 6 months and thereafter a year at a time. Under s.17B, conditions may be attached, with the agreement of the AMHP, provided they are 'necessary or appropriate' for ensuring Amy receives medical treatment, preventing risk of harm to her health or safety, or protecting others. These could include a requirement to live in a particular place and comply with treatment. She would remain eligible for s.117 services, with a care plan and care co-ordinator, for at least as long as her CTO continues (DH, 2008d). If the RC considers she needs treatment in hospital and there would be risk of harm to her health or safety, or to others, if she failed to comply with a condition of the order, she could be readmitted to hospital initially for 72 hours, whilst the process of revoking the CTO under s.17F is completed. This requires a written order setting out the grounds for revocation and the agreement of an AMHP.

An alternative legal framework for Amy's care outside hospital is guardianship under s.7 of the MHA 1983. An application for guardianship can be made by an AMHP or NR where the patient is suffering from a mental disorder of a nature or degree warranting admission into guardianship, and guardianship is necessary in the interests of their welfare or for the protection of others. It is important to note that people with learning disability are not subject to guardianship unless their disability is associated with abnormally aggressive or seriously irresponsible conduct.

Guardianship essentially creates a relationship of authority to facilitate appropriate care outside hospital. The powers of the guardian are:

(a) to require the patient to reside at a specified place (including the power to convey);
(b) to require the patient to attend at specified places for medical treatment, occupation, education or training (but not for treatment to be provided without consent, unless provided under ss.5/6 MCA 2005);
(c) to require access to the patient to be given to any doctor, AMHP or other specified person.

The requirement to live in a specified place must not amount to deprivation of liberty – in such circumstances the MCADL procedure can be used for someone lacking capacity, and guardianship is not necessary. The Code (DH, 2008d) identifies that guardianship is appropriate where the patient responds well to the authority and attention of a guardian and would therefore comply with their guidance, or there is a particular need for someone to have the authority to make decisions on residence and care plans.

The application (from an AMHP or the NR) must be supported by two medical recommendations, one from a doctor approved under s.12. The NR must be consulted, and the admission cannot proceed if they object. The guardian may be the LSSA, or someone approved by them. Guardianship is for 6 months, renewable for a further 6 months and thereafter for 1 year at a time. The patient may appeal to the MHRT once within the first 6 months, and once in every period of renewal subsequently.

Patients on guardianship should have a comprehensive care plan established through multidisciplinary discussions. Key elements are likely to include suitable accommodation, access to day care, education and training facilities, effective co-operation and communication between all those concerned and (if the guardian is a private individual) support from the LSSA.

The Code (DH, 2008d) indicates that, for patients lacking capacity, one alternative to guardianship is to rely on s.5 of the MCA 2005, which provides permission for care or treatment provided in the person's best interests. Even where a proposed move (e.g. into residential care) amounts to deprivation of liberty, guardianship is unlikely to be necessary when the MCADL safeguards can be used, although guardianship may still be appropriate in order to create a beneficial relationship with a guardian, where statutory authority for their return is likely to be needed, or where the authority of a guardian is necessary in situations of dispute about where someone should live.

The Code (DH, 2008d) also differentiates between guardianship, leave of absence and SCT. Guardianship is essentially social care-led, and is applicable mainly to patients whose welfare needs require community care. Leave of absence is suitable for short-term absences from hospital for patients who are believed still to need in-patient treatment. SCT is suitable when the patient is thought not to need in-patient treatment, but where the hospital recall power remains important.

Should the professional team not formulate a plan that enables Amy to leave hospital, she could have recourse to the MHRT. The Tribunal's role is to review the lawfulness of detention by considering whether the grounds still apply (at the time of the review). It enables the legal framework to meet the requirement of Article 5(4) ECHR that anyone deprived of their liberty must be able to initiate proceedings whereby the lawfulness of their detention will be reviewed. It does not consider the lawfulness of the original detention, which would instead be challenged through habeas corpus, judicial review or civil action for false imprisonment (Fennell, 2007). The Tribunal is essentially a panel consisting of a legal, medical and lay member. Following a ruling of human rights incompatibility (*R (on the application of H) v London North & East Region Mental Health Review Tribunal* [2001]), the burden of proof is on the hospital to justify the continuing detention rather than upon the patient to prove suitability for discharge. As a patient detained on s.3, Amy could apply once during her first 6 months detention, then once within each subsequent period of detention. Previously when detained under s.2, she could have applied once within the first 14 days. Jim as her NR would have similar rights to apply for her release. The MHRT must discharge Amy if the grounds for detention are not met.

The MHA 1983 provides for a wide-ranging set of interventions focused on Amy's mental health, and support for her both to receive treatment deemed necessary, even if she objects, and to have access to a range of health and social care resources. Whilst the powers are wide-ranging, an additional safeguard for detained patients is the Mental Health Act Commission, a body appointed by the Secretary of State to oversee the use of compulsory powers, now merged into the integrated Care Quality Commission.

Achieving the right balance for Amy relies on careful and comprehensive assessment of the complex web of social interactions which affect and are affected by mental health problems, and active consideration of alternative courses of action. All the general welfare legislation regulating community care services (see William's case) applies to Amy, and in this context, as a result of her mental health needs, she would be a disabled person within the meaning of s.29 (NAA 1948).

Janet

Janet is 45 and has severe learning disability. She has lived all her life with her mother and her older brother, Jeff, who is unemployed. Whilst support services for Janet have been offered, they have never been extensively used, Janet's mother having preferred to cope independently. She and Jeff have always met Janet's personal care needs and provided the structure and direction that Janet needs, essentially providing 24-hour care and supervision. Whilst Janet can make minor day-to-day decisions, she does not have the capacity to engage in decisions of any complexity, and is unable to live with any degree of independence. Recently, Janet's mother has died after being admitted to hospital following a heart attack. Jeff has been continuing to care for Janet whilst a multidisciplinary assessment of her needs takes place and a plan for her care is put in place. As far as can be ascertained, Janet wishes to remain living in her home, but Jeff is planning to leave the area. In any event, neighbours have expressed concern about the current arrangements. When they see Janet she seems distressed and unhappy and her appearance is unkempt. Jeff appears to treat her abruptly, ordering her about and at times physically pushing her about. They also notice that Jeff spends periods of time away from the house, and it is unclear what arrangements have been made for Janet's care during these times.

Janet's situation will have triggered the legal rules outlined in William's case – i.e. s.47, NHS and Community Care Act 1990 assessment of her needs for services, with multidisciplinary involvement to identify appropriate ways of meeting her needs, taking account of the impact of her recent bereavement. Care planning could involve a range of options, from remaining in her own family home with domiciliary support, through to a more supported environment, whether residential or not. Any assessment should also have engaged with Jeff's role as a carer (again drawing on the legal rules on carers' assessments and services outlined in William's case), in terms of both his own entitlement to assessment and services and the viability of his future role in relation to Janet. The concerns expressed by neighbours, however, bring additional considerations about risk and safety, and the situation raises a number of complex questions about safety and well-being, autonomy and decision-making by adults, in contexts where there may be some doubt about the capacity of an individual to understand and give consent to what is proposed.

Irrespective of her longer-term needs, the level of risk involved in Janet's current circumstances is likely to trigger safeguarding procedures.

One of the major gaps in the legal rules remains the lack of any statutory framework for safeguarding adults. There is recognition that the current framework for intervention – policy guidance entitled *No Secrets* (DH, 2000a) – has, despite the development of national standards (ADSS, 2005), had patchy and inconsistent implementation (CSCI, 2008c). These considerations have resulted in a review and consultation (DH, 2008f) on the need for statutory powers and duties, which many have advocated (Action on Elder Abuse, 2008), to clarify and strengthen the grounds for potential intervention.

The *No Secrets* guidance (DH, 2000a) frames the need for protection as 'vulnerability', defining this as a person's inability to take care of, or protect, him or herself against significant harm or exploitation. Harm can involve physical, sexual, psychological and financial abuse as well as neglect and discrimination. More recently the focus has shifted from 'protecting vulnerable adults' to 'safeguarding adults', with a focus on enabling people to access their human right to live a life that is free from abuse and neglect (ADSS, 2005). The Mental Capacity Act 2005 (MCA 2005) Code of Practice (DCA, 2007) develops this theme, defining abuse as anything that goes against a person's human and civil rights.

No Secrets (DH, 2000a) places lead responsibility on the local authority (LA) for co-ordinating inter-agency arrangements for safeguarding adults within its local area. It expects local codes of practice to clarify the roles of agencies involved (such as health and police) and set out policies, procedures and protocols for information-sharing and decision-making on individual cases. There are requirements on publicity, service development, implementation and training, but the guidance does not prescribe a process to be followed in cases where abuse is alleged, and there is limited scope for protective intervention where a person with capacity does not wish it. Conversely, where capacity is lacking, an Independent Mental Capacity Advocate (IMCA) may well be called upon to contribute to decision-making (ADASS, 2007).

The information about Janet's situation is likely to give rise to concern that she may be being abused within her relationship with her brother, leading to an interagency strategy meeting seeking agreements on whether and how an investigation is to take place, and identifying the lead roles of those involved. This process will need to be integrated with the broader assessment process taking place to identify Janet's long-term needs, and the development of a care plan to meet these needs.

In relation to the abuse, if such it is, there may be a case for prosecution. The Domestic Violence Crime and Victims Act 2004 makes it a criminal offence to physically or sexually abuse, harm or cause deliberate cruelty by neglect of a child or an adult. Equally, the MCA 2005 makes it an offence to ill-treat or wilfully neglect a person who lacks capacity. The Fraud Act 2006 creates an offence of fraud by abuse of position, which could apply to court appointed deputies, and those exercising financial powers of attorney in respect of a person who lacks capacity. The Office of the Public Guardian, established by the MCA 2005 to supervise the activities of deputies and attorneys and to make reports to the Court of Protection, can also appoint Court of Protection Visitors to enquire into how anyone with powers and responsibilities under the MCA 2005 is exercising their responsibilities. Such a visitor could have a key role in investigating financial abuse. In relation to securing Janet's safety if she is being abused, non-molestation injunctions or occupation orders under the Family Law Act 1996 (FLA 1996) may have a role to play, but clearly any reduction of contact between Janet and her brother has implications for her day-to-day care and personal needs. The overall purpose is likely to be seen as securing a more viable and appropriate living situation for her in the long term.

Plans for Janet's future will be framed within the general goals set out in the White Paper (DH, 2006a), and pursue the policy vision of person-alization – choice and control in the context of personalized support for Janet to maximize her capacity for independence and self-directed support. Additionally relevant in setting the policy framework for respond-ing to her needs is the *Valuing People* agenda. Originally published as a White Paper in 2001 (DH, 2001c), *Valuing People* set a strongly articu-lated vision for improving the life chances of people with learning dis-abilities, and key targets for change driven by the principles of rights, independence, choice and inclusion. Following a progress report in 2005 (DH, 2005c), which found evidence of some very positive but other more patchy implementation, renewed targets were set (DH, 2007c). These tar-gets prioritize person-centred planning, direct payments and individual budgets, socially inclusive education and employment strategies, primary and acute health services as well the development of specialist services, inclusion in mainstream housing provision, home ownership and assured tenancies and organizational structures, commissioning strategies and workforce developments to maintain the pace of change. Renewed tar-gets for advocacy and user-led organizations, partnership with families and measures to promote social inclusion of learning disabled people within their communities have also been set. Changes to the legal rules are being made to support this agenda; for example, the Health and Social Care Act 2008 extended the reach of direct payments to encompass those who do not have capacity to manage their own financial arrangements, making it possible for payments to be made to a 'suitable person' who can manage finances on their behalf.

On capacity and decision-making more generally, the MCA 2005 now provides an integrated framework which favours a presumption of capacity and autonomy wherever possible, whilst also providing for decision-making on behalf of people who lack capacity. The Act is accompanied by a statutory Code of Practice (DCA, 2007) and a supplementary statutory code regulating decisions that will result in deprivation of liberty (MoJ, 2008a). Also created by the Act is a specialist court, the Court of Protection, to make decisions about the property and affairs, health care and personal welfare of people who lack capacity. It can make declarations relating to specific issues in specific cases and/or appoint deputies (such as a family member) to make decisions of an ongoing nature.

The legal rules set out in the Act and its Codes must be followed, whether decisions relate to small everyday matters or to life-changing events. Capacity is defined simply as 'the ability to make a decision' (DCA, 2007, p. 41), and is a fluctuating quality, determined by reference to the decision that is to be made. Assumptions about capacity must never be made on the basis of age, appearance, condition or any aspect of behaviour. Someone who lacks capacity is simply 'a person who lacks capacity to make a particular decision or take a particular action for themselves at the time the decision or action needs to be taken' (DCA, 2007, p. 3). Janet, therefore, may well have capacity to make decisions such as choosing what to eat, doing daily shopping, seeing the doctor, or taking a tablet for a headache; she may not have capacity to make more complex decisions such as deciding where to live or consenting to an operation.

The five statutory principles in the Act are amplified in the Code of Practice (DCA, 2007).

1 A person is assumed to have capacity unless it is established that they lack capacity. The Code recognizes the importance of balancing people's right to decision-making with their right to safety and protection but the starting assumption is of capacity.
2 A person is not to be deemed unable to make a decision unless all practicable steps to help them to do so (e.g. improving accessibility of information and communication; treating a medical condition; developing new skills) have been unsuccessful.
3 A person is not to be deemed unable to make a decision merely because they make an unwise decision or one with which others disagree. A repeated pattern of unwise decisions that are out of character, however, may give cause for concern.

4 Any decision made for a person who lacks capacity must be in their best interests.

5 Before a decision is made, the 'less restrictive alternative' must always be sought, provided that is consistent with the 'best interests' principle.

Assessing Janet's capacity to make decisions will involve a two-stage test, in line with guidance in the Code (DCA, 2007). Does she have a permanent or temporary impairment or disturbance affecting the way her mind or brain works? If so, does that impairment or disturbance mean that she is unable to make the decision in question at the time it needs to be made? Being able to make a decision requires Janet to be able to:

● understand information about the decision to be made (the Act calls this 'relevant information'),
● retain that information in her mind,
● use or weigh that information as part of the decision-making process, and
● communicate her decision.

The assessment of capacity is made by the person intending to make whatever decision is in question should Janet be unable to make it for herself, and before acting they must believe that on the balance of probabilities Janet lacks capacity to make the decision herself.

The requirement to act in the best interests of someone lacking capacity is fundamental to the legal rules; both the Act and the Code amplify the requirement. To establish what is in Janet's best interests in any matter that falls beyond her own capacity requires decision-makers to observe a 'best interests checklist' (s.4). They must encourage her participation and find out her wishes and feelings, beliefs and values, identifying what factors she might take into account were she able to make the decision herself. Indeed they must defer any non-urgent decision if there is a possibility that she might regain capacity, for example as she moves through her bereavement and resolves the loss of her mother. They must not discriminate against her, must avoid restricting her rights, and must consult relevant other people. All these factors must be weighed before determining what is in her best interests. (Additionally in the context of decisions about withdrawal of life-sustaining treatment, no assumptions should be made about quality of life, and any advance decision made in line with the Act's requirements must be respected.) Where doubt exists, the Court of Protection has power to determine best interests in any given circumstances.

Where a health or care intervention is made for someone lacking capacity, s.5 of the MCA 2005 provides protection from any possibility of prosecution for intervening without consent, provided the intervention was in the person's best interests. Thus if Janet needs help with her personal care, or services at home, or medical treatment, and is not thought able to understand sufficiently to give her own consent, then provision can still be made under the s.5 protection. However, decisions involving a change of residence, perhaps admission to residential or supported accommodation, must comply with additional protections involving consultations with family members, carers and others who have an interest in her welfare and, if there is no-one close enough to her to express a view of what is best for her, with an IMCA (see below). Under s.5, interventions can be carried out even if Janet objects, but if the intervention involves restraint (either the use of force, or the restriction of freedom), then under s.6 the restraint must be the least that is necessary to achieve the best interests outcome, must not amount to deprivation of liberty, must be necessary to prevent harm and must be a proportionate response to the likelihood and seriousness of that harm. Section 6 does not provide protection where restraint is such as to deprive someone of their liberty; in this event the Deprivation of Liberty safeguards (MCADL) (MoJ, 2008a) must be applied (see below). Some decisions, such as withdrawal of food and water to a patient in PVS, organ or bone marrow donation, sterilization and cases where best interests is disputed, must be referred to the Court of Protection.

The IMCA is a new provision under the MCA 2005 to support and consult on particularly important decisions by or on behalf of people lacking capacity, where they have no family or friendship networks. An IMCA *must* be appointed and consulted where, in relation to someone who has no-one else to support them, it is proposed either to provide serious medical treatment or to arrange accommodation in a hospital (for more than 28 days) or care home (for more than 8 weeks). An IMCA *may* be appointed and consulted where a care plan is being reviewed, or in adult safeguarding cases (and, in the latter, may be appointed even where family members or others are involved). IMCAs must be approved by the LA and must have specific experience, show integrity and good character, be able to act independently, and have undergone IMCA training. They have important status, including the right to private interviews with the person who lacks capacity and access to records. They can seek a second medical opinion and may also refer cases to the Court of Protection. They may meet with professionals and paid carers in the process of formulating a report, which must then be taken into account by the decision-maker who retains overall responsibility for making the decision.

Where it is thought necessary to restrict the liberty of someone lacking capacity in order to provide 'best interests' care or treatment, or to protect them from harm, the MCADL (MoJ, 2008a) must be observed in order for the restriction on liberty to be lawful. The safeguards ensure that the deprivation of liberty does not breach article 5 of the ECHR, which requires a 'procedure prescribed by law' to be followed in such cases. The lack of procedural safeguards had been noted in the case of *HL v UK* [2004] – the 'Bournewood' judgment – in which detention in hospital had taken place under common law in the best interests of a learning disabled man who did not have capacity to consent, but where the formal safeguards of detention under the Mental Health Act 1983 (MHA 1983) had not been applied.

The Mental Health Act 2007 (MHA 2007) inserts ss.4A and 4B, and schedules A1 and 1A of the MCA 2005, applying in circumstances where it is proposed to detain an adult lacking capacity in a hospital or care home for the purpose of giving care or treatment in circumstances that amount to a deprivation of liberty, where necessary to protect them from harm and in their best interests. The care or treatment may be for physical or mental disorder. The safeguards do not apply if the deprivation of liberty is for the protection of others – in such cases the MHA 1983 must be used.

The MCADL Code (MoJ, 2008a) gives guidance on determining what constitutes deprivation of liberty, identifying the fine distinction between *deprivation of* and *restriction upon* liberty. Deprivation of liberty is seen as a question of degree and intensity of the restriction, not of its nature or substance, and the Code gives examples to guide practitioners' thinking on this issue. Significant factors will include whether:

- Restraint is used, including sedation, to admit to an institution a person who is resisting;
- Complete and effective control is exercised over the care and movement of a person for a significant period;
- Control is exercised over assessments, treatment, contacts and residence;
- The person will not be released into the care of others, or permitted to live elsewhere, unless the staff consider it appropriate;
- A request by carers for a person to be discharged to their care is refused;

- The person is unable to maintain social contacts because of restrictions placed on their access to other people;
- The person loses autonomy because they are under continuous supervision and control.

Deprivation of liberty is lawful if:

(a) Authorized by the Court of Protection under s.16(2)(a) MCA 2005, or
(b) Authorized under the deprivation of liberty procedures in schedule 1A, or
(c) Carried out through necessity to give life-sustaining treatment or prevent serious deterioration of the person's condition pending a decision from the court.

Under schedule 1A (from April 2009) the authorization is sought by the managing authority of the hospital or care home where it is intended the person will be detained. Authority is sought from the supervisory body – for a person in hospital, the primary care trust; for a person in a care home, the LA where the person is ordinarily resident. A standard authorization is sought where, at some point in the next 28 days, deprivation of liberty is likely. An urgent authorization can be made by a managing authority itself in cases of urgent need, with a reasonable expectation that the qualifying requirements will be met, pending a request to the supervisory body which must be made within the subsequent 7 days. The Code lists the information that must be included in the application. The person's family, friends and carers, and any IMCA already involved in their case, must be advised by the managing authority that it has applied for an authorization, unless it is impractical or impossible to do so, or undesirable in terms of the interests of the relevant person's health or safety. If there is no-one involved who could be consulted as to their best interests, then the supervisory body must appoint an IMCA.

An assessment must take place before authorization can be given, and involves two key people: (a) a best interests assessor (an Approved Mental Health Professional (AMHP), social worker, nurse, occupational therapist or chartered psychologist with 2 years' post-registration experience who has completed relevant training and is not involved in the person's care or treatment, nor in line management to the person proposing the deprivation of liberty); and (b) a mental health assessor, who may not also act as the best interest assessor, nor be in line management to them. Neither assessor can be a relative, or have any financial interest in the outcome of the decision. The six requirements to be assessed are:

- *Age*: The person must be over 18. This can be determined by anyone qualified to be a best interest assessor.

- *Mental health*: The person must have a mental disorder and undergo an assessment by a suitably qualified doctor, who must consider the impact of detention on the person's mental health, and notify the best interests assessor.

- *Mental capacity*: The person must lack capacity to determine whether or not they should be accommodated in the proposed location and given the care or treatment in question. This assessment can be undertaken by a doctor or someone qualified to be a best interests assessor.

- *Best interests*: The proposed deprivation of liberty must be (a) in the person's best interests, (b) necessary in order to prevent harm to them, and (c) a proportionate response to the likelihood of them suffering harm (and with no less-restrictive alternative). The best interests assessor must consult with interested parties, including any carers and/or IMCA, lasting power of attorney (LPA) donee or deputy, and make recommendations on the length of detention (for the minimum necessary and not exceeding 1 year) and any conditions to be attached to the authorization.

- *Eligibility*: The person is ineligible if detained as an in-patient under the MHA 1983 or if authorization would conflict with an obligation under the MHA 1983 to live somewhere else (e.g. leave of absence, guardianship, supervised community treatment or conditional discharge). In relation to deprivation of liberty in a hospital for treatment for mental disorder, a person is ineligible if they object and also meet the criteria for admission under s.2 or s.3, or if they are subject to recall under the MHA 1983. This assessment can be conducted by a mental health assessor who is also a s.12 doctor, or a best interests assessor who is also an AMHP.

- *No refusals*: The person must not have made an advance decision refusing some or all the treatment envisaged under the authorization. Equally, the authorization must not conflict with a decision by a LPA donee or court appointed deputy. This can be determined by anyone qualified to be a best interest assessor.

If all requirements are met, the supervisory body issues the authorization and appoints a representative for the person deprived of their liberty, to maintain contact with them, represent and support them in review of the deprivation of liberty, complaints or application to the Court of Protection. Representatives must be independent of any financial interest in the person's residence and from any professional role in the person's care or treatment.

The supervisory body must conduct a review if requested by the managing authority, the person detained or their representative. A review must take place if any one of the requirements is no longer met, or if the reasons for meeting them have changed, or if the situation has otherwise changed. The deprivation of liberty can be terminated by the managing authority at any time, prior to requesting formal termination by the supervising authority. Equally, the person subject to deprivation of liberty, or someone acting on their behalf, can apply to the Court of Protection for review of the lawfulness of their detention (or proposed detention). The Court may also be asked to rule on deprivation of liberty in circumstances that fall outside the remit of the deprivation of liberty safeguards (e.g. at a private address).

Bringing resolution to Janet's situation will involve very careful balancing of needs, rights and risks. The overall goal will be to secure her in a living situation which maximizes her autonomy within the limits set by her capacity for decision-making, and to act in her best interests, both in short-term protective measures (even if these appear unwelcome to her) and in implementing longer-term plans.

Toby

Toby, an African-Caribbean man of 35, is unemployed and lives with his mother. He has a diagnosis of bi-polar disorder. He frequently enters hospital on an informal basis but never stays longer than a few days before discharging himself. He has been compulsorily admitted on four occasions. While on medication his symptoms do not trouble him, but he becomes physically and verbally aggressive without it. He has previous convictions for criminal damage, theft and assault. His relationship with his mother has become very strained following several incidents when he physically assaulted her, and she is reaching the point of saying that he cannot live with her any longer. Following the most recent assault, Toby became very drunk; he damaged furniture and threatened people in the local public house, which resulted in his arrest.

Debates about appropriate interventions in the lives of people with mental health problems who also engage the criminal justice system are fuelled by strong ideologies which prioritize either 'welfare' or 'justice' imperatives, and concerns about risk and dangerousness, in which the effectiveness of both treatment and punishment approaches to offending behaviour is questioned. Overlaying these debates potentially for Toby are strong, stereotypical images relating to race and gender, which can operate powerfully to mediate the experiences of young black men in both the criminal justice and the mental health systems.

Toby is unemployed and has severe mental health problems. He may soon be homeless. His situation and professional responses to it are likely to require recognition of a range of factors – personal turmoil and distress, relationship breakdown, structural inequality and material disadvantage. The range of legal rules potentially applicable in his case is wide. The law relating to homelessness is covered in Chapter 5. Toby could be seen to be in priority need and thus eligible for support. William's case earlier in this chapter covered the law relating to community care services for which, as a person fitting the definition of disability in s.29, National Assistance Act 1948, Toby would be eligible. Amy's case identified how the Care Programme Approach (CPA) attempts to co-ordinate interdisciplinary services for people with high level mental health needs, and how the Mental Health Act 1983 (MHA 1983) provides a framework for the care and treatment of people with mental disorder, where intervention is necessary in the interests of their own health or safety, or for the protection of others. All such frameworks may be drawn upon to create an appropriate set of interventions for Toby. The analysis that follows here will focus particularly upon appropriate responses in the context of Toby's engagement with the criminal justice system.

There has been long recognition of core principles for the provision of care for mentally disordered offenders (DH/Home Office, 1992):

- Proper regard to the quality of care and proper attention to the needs of the individual;
- As far as possible, care in the community rather than in institutional settings;
- Care under conditions of no greater security than is justified by the degree of danger they present to themselves or to others;
- Care in such as way as to maximize rehabilitation and their chances of sustaining an independent life;
- Care as near as possible to their own homes or families.

Fennell (2007) identifies three principles underpinning contemporary criminal justice policy towards mentally disordered people: (a) that special safeguards should guard against false confessions; (b) that diversion from the penal system to health and social care is appropriate (because mental disorder may reduce culpability, and they may be vulnerable to self harm); (c) that the public should be protected from the risks posed.

At their first point of intervention, on being called to the public house disturbance, the police could choose to prioritize Toby's mental health status by using their powers under s.136, MHA 1983 to remove to a place of safety someone who is in a place to which the public have access, and who appears to be mentally disordered and in immediate need of care and control. Toby could have been taken directly from the public house to the police station, or directly to hospital, and detained for up to 72 hours for the purpose of an assessment of the need for psychiatric hospital admission.

Toby has been arrested, however, and under the Police and Criminal Evidence Act 1984 (PACE) he must, as a mentally disordered person, be questioned in the presence of an 'appropriate adult' (AA), unless arranging this would cause detrimental delay or harm to others or property. The AA could be a member of Toby's family, or someone else responsible for his care, someone independent of the police who has appropriate experience in work with mentally disordered people or, in the absence of all those, another adult who is not a police employee. The AA's responsibility, described in detail in Wayne's case in Chapter 5, is to ensure Toby's welfare during his detention and the appropriateness of questioning to his level of understanding.

Whilst diversion from the criminal justice system may be desirable, to undergo a caution Toby must admit the offence, understand the implications of a caution and be able to agree to it. A conditional caution is also possible (s.22, Criminal Justice Act 2003 (CJA 2003)) providing there is sufficient evidence that Toby has committed an offence, he admits the offence and the nature of the caution is explained to him (s.23). Toby must comply with the conditions, designed to facilitate his rehabilitation. In relation to a decision to prosecute, two tests must be applied:

- the evidential test – is there a reasonable prospect of conviction? If the defendant is mentally disordered, it may not be possible to establish *mens rea* (criminal intent);
- the public interest test – is the prosecution in the public interest? This may be served equally or better by diversion from the criminal justice system.

If a decision is made to prosecute, then Toby will be placed on remand. He should be allowed bail (Bail Act 1976 (BA 1976)) unless it is likely that he would fail to surrender to custody or appear in court, commit further offences, interfere with witnesses or otherwise obstruct the course of justice, or that detention is necessary to prevent harm to himself or others, or that bail would render it impracticable for enquiries to be made and reports completed. Bail will not be allowed if he is charged with, or has been convicted previously of, homicide or rape (s.25, Criminal

Justice and Public Order Act 1994), or if offending is connected with Class A drugs (s.19, CJA 2003), or if accused or convicted of committing any offence whilst on bail (s.14, CJA 2003). Conditions may be attached to bail by the police or courts, such as residence in a bail hostel (courts only) or making oneself available for enquiries to be made, where necessary to prevent absconding, interfering with witnesses or obstructing justice. Conditions may also be attached for Toby's own protection (s.13, CJA 2003), such as attendance at mental health services. If magistrates refuse bail they must give reasons (s.5, BA 1976). Application may then be made to a Crown Court.

Toby's mental health needs place a range of other remand options at the disposal of the court.

- Section 30 of the Magistrates Court Act 1980 provides for Toby's remand by magistrates' court for medical examination (on bail or in custody) if he is charged with an imprisonable offence and the court is satisfied that he committed the act giving rise to the charge and considers enquiry into his physical or mental condition is necessary before the court deals with the case.
- Under s.35, MHA 1983 (as amended by the Mental Health Act 2007 (MHA 2007)), if Toby is charged with an imprisonable offence a Crown or Magistrates' Court may remand him to hospital for reports if, on the evidence of one doctor, the court has reason to suspect that he is suffering from mental disorder and a psychiatric report could not be secured if he were given bail. Remand is for 28 days, renewable twice, to facilitate an assessment and recommendations on care and treatment. Treatment may not be given without consent.
- Under s.36, MHA 1983 (as amended by the MHA 2007), if Toby is charged with an imprisonable offence a Crown Court may remand him to hospital for treatment if, on the evidence of two doctors, one of whom is a mental health specialist, he is suffering from mental disorder of a nature or degree that makes it appropriate for him to be detained in hospital for medical treatment, and appropriate treatment is available. Remand is for 28 days, renewable twice, and treatment may be given without consent.
- If Toby is remanded in custody, he may, under s.48, MHA 1983, on the order of the Secretary of State be transferred from prison to hospital for medical treatment if, on the evidence of two doctors, he is suffering from mental disorder of a nature or degree making it appropriate for him to be detained in hospital for treatment, appropriate treatment is available and the need for it is urgent.

Even once in the criminal justice system, prosecution could be dropped, or Toby could be found 'unfit to plead' – unable to understand the charge and trial, enter a plea, instruct a defence, or follow evidence. The consequence of such a finding, under the Criminal Procedure (Insanity and Unfitness to Plead) Act 1991, is that a trial of the facts will determine whether the jury is satisfied that Toby did in fact commit the act(s) he is accused of. The Court then has wide options including absolute discharge, supervision and treatment, or detention in hospital or guardianship.

If Toby is found fit to be tried and the case is heard, again his mental health status raises a range of different options.

● It is possible for the court, on the evidence of two medical reports, to find him incapable of criminal intent and return a verdict of 'not guilty by reason of insanity' on the basis that he has a 'disease of mind' which led to a 'defect of reason' such that he did not know the nature of what he did, or did not know it was wrong. The Court's powers here are as in a finding of 'unfit to plead'. Whilst not applicable to Toby, in a case of murder the concept of 'diminished responsibility' may, under the Homicide Act 1957, reduce the conviction to one of manslaughter, thus allowing any of the disposals for that offence (including a hospital order) rather than the mandatory life sentence for murder.

● If Toby is convicted of an offence punishable by imprisonment (or, in the case of Magistrates, if the court is satisfied Toby committed the offence) then under s.37, MHA 1983 the court may order detention in psychiatric hospital or admission into guardianship. He must, on the evidence of two doctors, be deemed to have a mental disorder of a nature or degree which makes it appropriate for him to be detained in hospital for medical treatment, where appropriate treatment is available, or which warrants admission to guardianship, and where having regard to all the circumstances this is the most suitable disposal. If so hospitalized, Toby may receive compulsory treatment as if he were detained under s.3; the detention is for 6 months, renewable for a further 6 months and thereafter for a year at a time; he may not be discharged by the nearest relative but may apply to the Mental Health Review Tribunal (MHRT). Discharge is determined by the responsible medical officer or MHRT. Section 41 allows a Crown Court to impose restrictions without limit of time on discharge of a hospital order if it is necessary to protect the public from serious harm. Discharge is then regulated by the Secretary of State or, in certain circumstances, by the MHRT.

● If the court is considering the suitability of a hospital order, it may make an interim order for twelve weeks renewable for periods of

28 days up to six months maximum (s.38, MHA 1983). The order includes authority to treat.

- Before making a hospital order (or interim hospital order), under s.39A the court may ask the local authority to consider whether guardianship is a feasible alternative and to report on how the powers of guardianship would be exercised.

- Equally, the courts can at this stage, once Toby is convicted but before passing sentence, exercise their powers under ss.35 and 36 (outlined above) to remand him to hospital for reports or for treatment.

- Under the Domestic Violence, Crime and Victims Act 2004, as amended by the MHA 2007, if Toby has committed a violent or sexual offence and is subject to a hospital order, the victim has rights to information about which hospital he is placed in, and rights to make representation about conditions that should be imposed on any future conditional discharge.

- Under s.207 of the CJA 2003 a community sentence may be made with a mental health treatment requirement. This would require evidence from a doctor approved under s.12 that his mental disorder could be treated without the need for a hospital or guardianship order. The mental health treatment requirement obliges Toby to accept either out-patient or in-patient treatment under the care of a doctor.

Other sentences available to the court are:

- Deferred sentence – a postponement, to which Toby must consent, where there are specific reasons, such as a potential change in circumstances. Conditions may be attached, including a residential requirement (Powers of Criminal Courts (Sentencing) Act 2000 (PCC(S)A 2000; s.278, CJA 2003);

- Absolute discharge;

- Conditional discharge for a specified period to a three-year maximum, with no further sentence if Toby does not commit further offences within this time;

- Fine, with the amount related to the circumstances and seriousness of the offence and the offender's ability to pay;

- Fixed penalties, on the spot fines with 21 days to pay for specified offences such as disorderly behaviour whilst drunk (CJPA 2001);

- Compensation order (s.130, PCCSA 2000);

- Community sentence for a maximum of three years, to which may be added one or more requirements (ss.199–214, CJA 2003). These include unpaid work; activities or programmes; prohibitions; curfew or exclusion; residence; mental health, alcohol or drug treatment;

supervision or attendance centre. Breach of the requirements can result in an order for unpaid work (s.38, Criminal Justice and Immigration Act 2008 (CJIA 2008)). The order and requirements can only be made if Toby's offence and associated offending history is sufficiently serious (s.148, CJIA 2008).

Toby may also, of course, be subject to a custodial sentence, should the court decide that this is necessary. Custody may be suspended and requirements from the community sentence range specified. Where ordinarily custody for less than 12 months would be ordered, Toby could be sentenced to a short custody period (maximum three months) and supervision with the addition of requirements from the range available under the community sentence for a minimum of six months (s.181/182, CJA 2003). For custody beyond 12 months, and if Toby is not considered dangerous, he would spend half the sentence in prison and half on licence. Intermittent custody is also possible (s.183, CJA 2003) as is an indeterminate sentence if Toby is convicted of a serious offence (s.124, CJA 2003) and the court believes him to represent a serious risk of harm to the public. This is a sentence for public protection (s.125), for which the judge sets a tariff on the expiry of which release should be considered by the Parole Board (s.19, CJIA 2008). There are mandatory penalties for certain serious offences (Crime (Sentences) Act 1997). Under s.157 CJA 2003, courts must take a medical report from a s.12 approved doctor prior to passing a custodial sentence on Toby if he appears to be mentally disordered, and must consider how a custodial sentence would impact upon his mental health.

Under s.45A, MHA 1983, the Crown Court can pass a prison sentence along with immediate direction to hospital for a specified period of time if, on the evidence of two doctors, Toby is suffering from a mental disorder of a nature or degree which makes it appropriate for him to be detained in hospital for treatment and appropriate treatment is available. Once treatment is no longer necessary, Toby would return to prison to carry out the remaining period of his sentence.

Under s.47 MHA 1983, the Secretary of State could order Toby's transfer from prison to hospital if he is suffering from mental disorder of a nature or degree making it appropriate for him to be detained in hospital for treatment, and appropriate treatment is available. This has the effect of changing the basis of Toby's detention to that which would apply under a s.37 hospital order (i.e. discharge at the discretion of the doctor in charge of his treatment), unless restrictions on discharge are attached, in which case the restriction would cease to have effect on the earliest possible date on which he would have been released from prison.

If Toby is made the subject of a hospital order under s.37, MHA 1983, then on discharge he would be eligible for aftercare services under s.117. Equally, any of the conditions outlined in Amy's case could be applied to his discharge, including supervised community treatment. He should subsequently benefit from a co-ordinated care package provided under the CPA, as outlined in Amy's case, and from any of the community care services outlined in William's case that would support his independence and stability.

Before the court passes sentence it should consider a pre-sentence report that contains an assessment of the offence and offender, and risk of harm. The report may be given orally (s.12, CJIA 2008). Where the court envisages a specific sentence, it may request a specific sentence report to advise on its appropriateness and proportionality. Sentences should serve the aims of punishment, crime reduction, rehabilitation, public protection and reparation (CJA 2003), the exact outcome depending on an evalua-tion of culpability, seriousness, dangerousness, offender circumstances and proportionality. A Council has been established to issue sentencing guidelines (CJA 2003).

As with youth justice, Toby could find his behaviour regulated by the civil as well as the criminal law, through anti-social behaviour orders (ASBOs) (Crime and Disorder Act 1998, Anti-Social Behaviour Act 2003) and violent offender orders (s.98/99, CJIA 2008). An ASBO could, for example, be imposed to prohibit him visiting his mother (*Leeds City Council v Fawcett* [2008]).

Sardip

Sardip has arrived with his daughter and his niece from Sri Lanka and has claimed asylum. He appears very frail and is diagnosed with can-cer soon after his arrival. His daughter, Yasmine, also has a physical disability. He is looking after his niece at the request of her parents who have remained in Sri Lanka.

The Immigration and Asylum Act 1999 established the National Asylum Support Service (NASS). NASS is responsible for all asylum seekers unless they have additional needs. Provision for unaccompanied asylum seeking children is covered in Istvan's case (Chapter 5). Sardip requires support to meet his needs for care and attention that do not arise solely because of destitution or the effects from it. Yasmine also requires such support by virtue of being a disabled child. Were she not disabled, they could find that the local authority accepts a duty towards Sardip but would not be responsible for the rest of the family (*R (O) v Haringey LBC* [2004]).

By virtue of his condition the local authority is responsible for meeting Sardip's needs (*R (Westminster City Council) v National Asylum Support Service* [2002]; *R (Mani) v Lambeth LBC* [2003]). Services could include accommodation (s.21, National Assistance Act 1948), owing to his need for care and attention, but also community care services outlined in William's case. However, Sardip's eligibility depends on him having a need that he cannot meet for himself, such as domiciliary or personal care (*R (M) v Slough BC* [2008]). He is also a disabled parent, the legal rules for which are discussed in Wayne's case (Chapter 5). Despite these legal rules related to disabled asylum seekers, research has found evidence of unmet care needs, with practitioners and managers uncertain about entitlements to support (Roberts and Harris, 2002).

Were he without dependent children, Sardip's disability would also be relevant to determinations on whether he claimed asylum as soon as reasonably practical, as required by s.55, Nationality, Immigration and Asylum Act 2002 (*R (Q and Others) v Secretary of State for the Home Department* [2003]). The 2002 Act also allows withdrawal or refusal of support to those whose applications have been refused and their dependants. Controversially, s.9, Asylum and Immigration (Treatment of Claimants etc) Act 2004, allows children to be taken into care where families have become destitute following this withdrawal of support. Central government may be backtracking from this provision, especially in light of the House of Lords ruling that the denial of support to destitute asylum seekers breaches Article 3 (ECHR) since it involves intense physical or mental suffering and/or humiliation of a degree that breaks moral and physical resistance (*R (Limbuela and others) v Secretary of State for the Home Department* [2006]). Those who co-operate with arrangements for their return, having failed in their asylum claims, may obtain services, accommodation and travel warrants. However, local authorities should exercise care when proposing that a child should leave the UK with one or both parents. They should complete a detailed assessment to explore the child–parent relationship and to ascertain whether a return would be in the child's best interests (*R (M) v Islington LBC* [2003]).

Yasmine is covered by s.17, Children Act 1989 (CA 1989), discussed in Chapter 5, because of her disability. Thus, in the case of a disabled child being looked after by her mother, the local authority was responsible because NASS meets the essential living needs of an ordinary person with no special circumstances or disabilities (*R (Ouji) v Secretary of State for the Home Department* [2002]).

Sardip is also responsible for his niece. This introduces the issue of private fostering, highlighted in the case of Victoria Climbié (Laming, 2003). Section 66 (CA 1989) defines private foster care and the local authority's responsibilities. Sections 68 and 69 deal with disqualifications from private fostering. New requirements have been added (Children Act 2004), including promoting awareness of private fostering, assessing the suitability of carers and their home environment, monitoring and recording arrangements, and periodic visits where a person notifies the local authority of a private fostering arrangement. The local authority's responsibilities regarding notification, safeguarding and support are elaborated in national standards (DfES, 2005b), which include secondary legislation (Children (Private Arrangements for Fostering) Regulations 2005 SI 1533).

Sardip's situation may be further complicated if he has UK citizenship but his daughter does not. For example, the Housing Act 1996 prohibits people subject to immigration control from accessing its homelessness provisions. Thus, if Sardip became homeless, he might find he could not qualify under homelessness provisions because his daughter and niece were excluded. However, following a declaration of incompatibility with the ECHR (Article 8) (*Westminster City Council v Morris* [2005]), Sardip can now include in his application as a homeless person someone who would otherwise be ineligible because of immigration controls. This would enable him to present as a homeless family, unintentionally homeless and in a priority group.

Such cases challenge social workers because they may find that acting lawfully breaches their ethical obligations to promote children's well-being within their families when safe to do so. The legal rules are particularly coercive and perpetuate poverty and disadvantage.

Concluding comments

The above cases cover a wide range of legal rules, set within the context of contemporary government policy to promote the well-being of people with needs arising from older age, disability and mental or physical ill-health, along with provision for the needs of their carers. They illustrate the tensions and dilemmas that attend practice, along with ways in which the legal rules steer a path between risk, needs and rights. The following chapter will consider cases in which children's legislation is engaged.

> ### putting it into practice
>
> Take the procedures your agency employs for the task of:
>
> - determining eligibility for adult social care, or
> - allocating personal budgets, or
> - conducting carers' assessments, or
> - implementing the care programme approach.
>
> Audit these against the relevant primary legislation, regulations, policy and practice guidance, and case law. Summarize the degree to which the procedures accurately interpret the relevant legal rules and discuss your findings with your supervisor or manager.
>
> If you do not work in an agency providing services of this nature but wish to explore these issues, use the website of your local council to access the information that it makes publicly available about eligibility, personal budgets, carers' assessments or services to people with mental health problems. Consider how the legal rules are being reflected and interpreted.

Further reading

Clements, L. and Thompson, P. (2007) *Community Care and the Law*. London: Legal Action Group. This text provides a detailed exploration of the law relating to adult social care.

Fennell, P. (2007) *Mental Health: The New Law*. Bristol: Jordans. This text provides a detailed review of the Mental Health Act 2007 and its impact for the Mental Health Act 1983 and the Mental Capacity Act 2005.

Glasby, J. and Littlechild, R. (2009) *Direct Payments and Personal Budgets: Putting Personalisation into Practice*. Bristol: Policy Press. This text draws on law, policy and practice to offer guidance on how councils with social services responsibilities and other welfare organizations might work with service users to ensure that service provision meets their needs and aspirations.

5 | Children, young people and their families

As in Chapter 4, the purpose here is to outline the breadth of legal knowledge required to guide social work interventions and to illustrate how the legal rules are drawn upon in practice. Again, the approach is to begin with a situation that may be encountered in practice and show how law provides a framework for considering what must and may be done. Relevant practice dilemmas are explored to locate interventions within the context of the critical issues identified in Chapter 3.

The cases in this chapter focus on children but illustrate the complexity of family situations by demonstrating how practitioners need to draw on a wide legal framework to consider the needs of all involved. This legal literacy involves being mindful that the needs presented by individuals and families, and the relevant legal rules, may span otherwise neat organizational divisions. Social workers must explore a range of options using their knowledge of the law (SWIA, 2005), recalling their positive duty to promote ECHR rights and to act proportionately when intervening. They must act within the law, having no power to remove children from parents without consent or judicial approval (*R (G) v Nottingham City Council* [2008]).

Throughout, social workers must consult with children and young people, providing information about and helping them to engage fully in assessment and decision-making processes. Children's services must co-operate with other agencies to improve young people's life chances: their physical and mental health and emotional well-being; protection from harm and neglect; education, training and recreation; contribution to society; and their social and economic well-being (s. 10, Children Act 2004) (CA 2004). This includes young offenders, to whom local authorities and prison services owe s.17 and s.47 duties (Children Act 1989) (CA 1989), since their welfare depends on protection from ill-treatment (*R (Howard League for Penal Reform) v Secretary of State for the Home Department and the Department of Health (interested party)* [2003]). Relevant partners, who must co-operate with local authorities, are listed in s.10(4), whilst s.10(3) reiterates the importance of parents and other carers to children's well-being.

Martin

Martin (15) is physically disabled, uses a wheelchair and requires 24-hour care. He requires assistance with all daily living tasks and personal care. He uses a specially constructed letter and symbol board to communicate. He lives with his parents. Both Martin and his parents wish to explore the possibility of him living (semi-) independently.

The Education Act 1996 and Special Educational Needs and Disability Act 2001

Children with special educational needs must be educated in mainstream schools unless parents request otherwise or it would be incompatible with the provision of education for other children (Harris, 1997; DfES, 2001; *R v East Sussex CC, ex parte Tandy* [1998]). There are duties on local education authorities (LEAs) to:

- identify and assess all children with (or if aged between two and five, likely to have) special educational needs, make a statement of needs and arrange provision (ss.321, 323, 324, 331, EA 1996);
- comply with a parental request for an assessment or review (s.328) if one has not been undertaken within six months;
- involve parents in the assessment, including the provision of advice, information and reports, and a means of resolving disagreements (DfES, 2001);
- meet all of the needs identified (*R v Secretary of State for Education and Science, ex parte E* [1992]; DfES, 2001). Parents may appeal to a Special Educational Needs and Disability Tribunal if a statement does not match the assessment of the child's needs (s. 326) or if the authority refuses a statement (s.325);
- detail every special educational need identified in an assessment and the provision necessary to meet them. Authorities are not bound to make the best provision but provision that will work (*R v Surrey County Council, ex parte H* [1984]). Provision should be cost-effective but consistent with a child's assessed needs. Statements should clearly specify what the education authority considers should be provided (*R v Cumbria County Council, ex parte P* [1995]);
- accept parental preference for a school unless unsuitable for the child's age, ability, aptitude or special educational needs, or incompatible with the education of other children or with the use of resources (*H v Special Educational Needs and Disability Tribunal and Another* [2004]);

- inform relevant nursing and social services officials, when assessing a child, to ensure relevant information is available;
- disclose to social services the statement of a child's special educational needs to enable obligations under the Disabled Persons Act 1986 (ss.5 and 6) and under the CA 1989 (ss.22(3), 85(4), 86(3) and 87(3)) to be met;
- review statements of need annually and when there are significant changes in a child's circumstances.

LEAs are empowered to assess children aged under two on parental request (s.331), but without duty to make provision. They must also seek to meet the needs of children who do not have statements but have special needs. Health authorities must inform parents and LEAs when they consider a child under five to have special educational needs (s.332). Special educational needs include any kind of learning difficulty significantly greater than that experienced by most similarly aged children, or disability preventing a child from using ordinary educational facilities effectively, and requiring special provision to be made (s.312). This will include dyslexia, emotional and behavioural disorders, physical disabilities and sensory impairment.

LEAs may request assistance from district health authorities and social services, who must comply unless this would be inconsistent with their duties and functions, or they consider that help is unnecessary (s.322). They must observe the code of practice (DfES, 2001), to which a tribunal may refer on questions arising on appeal. The code recommends assessment to take place in a setting where child and family feel comfortable, and that all services should have information about procedures for identifying special educational needs. Regulations (DfES, 2001) lay down time limits for deciding whether to assess a child, completing the assessment, providing copies of the proposed statement to parents following assessment, and finalizing the statement. Ordinarily the process should be completed within 26 weeks. Regulations also specify who should be present at reviews.

Where a school is named in a statement, the LEA must arrange and pay for it (*White and Another v Ealing LBC and Another; Richardson v Solihull MBC and Another; Solihull MBC and Another v Finn* [1997]). Budgetary constraints should not form part of an assessment of a child's special educational needs (*R v Hillingdon LBC, ex parte Governing Body of Queensmead School* [1997]) as only educational matters can be taken into account when identifying suitable education (s.298(7), EA 1996; *R v East Sussex CC, ex parte Tandy* [1998]). Parents may appeal to a tribunal when a statement is made or amended, including where an authority ceases to maintain it, or if an education authority decides not to (re-)assess, or to issue or amend a statement. The decision of the tribunal is binding. It must give reasons for its decisions and may order an education authority to act. If tribunal decisions are not implemented, appeal is to the Secretary of State. Only parents may appeal to the tribunal, not children (*S v Special Educational Needs Tribunal and the City of Westminster* [1996]). This stands in marked contrast to the requirement in the code of practice (DfES, 2001) to take account of children's views.

The Special Educational Needs and Disability Act 2001 extends the Disability Discrimination Act 1995 to education. Education providers unlawfully discriminate if, for reasons related to a young person's disability, they treat them less favourably without justification. Providers must scrutinize policies and procedures relating to admissions, education and services. Further and higher education institutions must make reasonable adjustments to their premises.

The Special Educational Needs (Information) Act 2008 requires the Secretary of State to publish information about children with special educational needs to improve their well-being.

Disabled Persons Act 1986 (DPA 1986)

The DPA 1986, ss.4 and 8, covered in William's case (Chapter 4), apply here. Three other duties exist. Firstly (s.5), LEAs must ascertain from local authority social services (LSSA) whether children with statements are disabled at the first review of the statement after the fourteenth birthday. The LEA must notify them between twelve and eight months before a disabled child is due to leave full-time education. Unless the person, or if under 16 their parent, objects, the LSSA must then assess the need for services. Where possible this assessment should be completed prior to the leaving date. Children's services are responsible for co-ordinating a multi-agency approach to transition, with assessment focusing on current and future needs, and support targeted on social and emotional needs, education and employment, and developing capacity for independent living (CSCI, 2007). Where the LSSA is satisfied that a disabled child needs a service that can be provided under the Chronically Sick and Disabled Persons Act 1970 (CSDPA 1970) (s.2), it must provide that service, whether or not a formal request for an assessment of need has been made. It cannot escape this specific duty to a disabled child by purporting to act under the more general provisions of s.17, CA 1989 (*R v Bexley LBC, ex parte B* [2000]). When a child decides not to leave full-time education the LEA must inform the LSSA, whereupon their assessment may be suspended until subsequent notification.

Secondly (s.6), LEAs must review dates when disabled children are expected to leave full-time education. Thirdly (s.9), local authorities should provide information about their services. There are comparable duties in sch.2(1), CA 1989 and s. 46, NHS and Community Care Act 1990.

The code of practice (DfES, 2001) details how Connexions, health authorities and LSSAs should be involved in transition planning. For example, Connexions has responsibility under the Learning and Skills Act 2000 (s.140) to ensure that Martin's needs are assessed on leaving school and appropriate provision identified. It should also seek the agreement of Martin and his parents for the transfer of information, such as his statement and transition plan, from his school to the continuing education sector, if appropriate.

LSSAs can assist disabled people to take advantage of education facilities (CSDPA 1970). Students in further and higher education may be eligible for grants for non-medical helpers, and major and minor items of equipment, in order to facilitate their attendance at, and completion of, programmes of study. The code of practice (DfES, 2001) requires each local authority to appoint a lead officer for working with and advising schools and LEAs concerning children with special educational needs.

Children Act 1989

The CA 1989 definition of children in need includes disabled children (s.17). Assessments of children in need should follow the policy guidance framework (DH, 2000c). The intended sequence is that local authorities first assess the disabled child's needs and, where appropriate, those of carers and other family members, followed by the production of a care plan and provision of the intended services (*R v Lambeth LBC, ex parte K* [2000]). Practice guidance (DH, 2000b) provides further advice on assessments, which should cover the child's developmental needs (including health, education, emotional development and family relationships), parenting capacity (addressing the needs of parent carers to promote a child's welfare), and family and environmental factors (including housing). Assessment should be multidisciplinary and link mainstream with specialist services. It should involve and take account of children's experience and understanding, consider the direct impact of their disabilities and address disabling barriers.

Local authorities must provide a range and level of services appropriate to disabled children's needs, to safeguard and promote their welfare and, where possible, upbringing by their families (s.17). Services should aim to 'minimise the effect on children of their disabilities and give them opportunities to lead lives as near normal as possible' (Sch.2(6)). Services include advice and counselling, occupational, social, cultural and recreational activities, home help, travelling assistance to take advantage of services, holidays (Sch.2(8)), day care for children under five (s.18); registers (Sch.2(2)) and family centres (Sch.2(9)). Authorities must have regard to different racial groups to which children in need belong (Sch.2 (11)) and, where such children are accommodated by local authorities, place them where practicable and consistent with their welfare near home (s.23 (7)). LSSAs may request help from education, housing and health authorities (s.27) who must comply if the request is compatible with their obligations. When considering whether to provide services under s.17 local authorities must ascertain, and give due consideration to the child's wishes and feelings (s.53, CA 2004).

Section 25, Children and Young Persons Act 2008, amends sch.2, CA 1989, to require that local authorities provide breaks for carers of disabled children to enable them to continue to care more effectively. Nonetheless, care plans can still prove vulnerable to resource-led decision-making as when a judge quashed proposed new arrangements for respite care for a disabled child because due consideration had not been given to the child's wishes (s.20(6), CA 1989) and the plan would not meet her needs (s.23(8)) or minimize the effects of her disability (s.17(2) and sch.2(6)). The proposals also placed insurmountable responsibilities on the child's mother and failed to recognize the importance of the child's foster carers in her life (*R (CD) (a child by her litigation friend VD) v Isle of Anglesey CC* [2004]). A series of short-term breaks of up to 120 days in any one year in the same place count as a single event for the purposes of ensuring placement suitability (DH, 1991a; Children Short-Term Placement Regulations 1995; *R (L) v Merton LBC* [2008]).

Once Martin is 16, he may request accommodation by the local authority (s.20(11)). As a young person his views are increasingly important but not necessarily determinative. For instance, a refusal to place a young person aged 17 in a residential placement of her choice was held not to breach s.20(6)(b) (CA 1989). The requirement to give due consideration to expressed wishes did not impose an obligation to comply with them (*R (Twomey acting by her litigation friend) v Calderdale MBC* [2005]).

The duty on agencies to co-operate with the local authority in improving young people's well-being (CA 2004) is extended to those aged 18 and 19, to those over 19 receiving leaving care services (Children (Leaving Care) Act 2000 (C(LC)A 2000)), and to those over 19 but under 25 with learning difficulties who are receiving services, such as further or higher education, under the Learning and Skills Act 2000. Under s.140, Learning and Skills Act 2000, local authorities must assess the education provision required for a young person. Recommendations should be made in writing. The Learning and Skills Council must then decide which educational services to fund (*R (Alloway) v Bromley LBC* [2008]). Local authorities have not always completed a proper assessment of needs and pathway plans for disabled young people approaching leaving care, despite the legal requirement to do so (C(LC)A 2000; *R (P) v Newham LBC* [2004]).

The NHS and Community Care Act 1990 (NHSCCA 1990) and Carers (Recognition and Services) Act 1995(C(RS)A 1995)

The duties and principles outlined in William's case also apply here but with some specific nuances. The ability of carers to continue to provide for Martin (Carers and Disabled Children Act 2000 (CDCA 2000)) should be taken into account when deciding what services should be provided through s.17, CA 1989. When constructing eligibility criteria for adult social care, local authorities should have systems for identifying individuals whose needs should be reassessed because of their approaching adulthood (DH, 2002b). Disabled Facilities Grants (Housing Grants, Construction and Regeneration Act 1996) are available where the proposed works are necessary and appropriate to meet a disabled child's needs (*R (B) v Calderdale MBC* [2004]) and means testing of families of disabled children under 19 has been abolished (Housing Renewal Grants (Amendment) (England) Regulations 2005). The prohibition on local authorities providing registered nursing care (s. 49, Health and Social Care Act 2001) appears not to apply to services for disabled children provided under the Children Act 1989 (*R (T, B and D) v Haringey LBC*; *R (D) v Haringey PCT* [2005]).

Direct payments are available to parents of disabled children and to disabled young people aged 16 and 17 (CDCA 2000) to promote independent living, choice and control. Parents and disabled young people must be informed of their availability and that the facility may not continue once the young person is 18. Direct payments may comprise part or all of the support package for disabled children, may include limited periods of residential accommodation, should be negotiated in partnership with parents and young people, and may prove helpful in support transition planning (DH, 2001d, 2005b). Where parents and disabled young people express divergent views, precedence should be given to those expressed by the young person providing that they are competent in making informed decisions. A young person may manage a direct payment alone or with assistance.

The 2000 Act also enables local authorities to offer voucher schemes for short-term breaks for carers. Policy guidance (DH, 2002f) envisages vouchers as an alternative to direct payments, with responsibility carried by the local authority and service provider but with similar advantages of flexibility and choice in how and when support is provided. Vouchers may be expressed in time or financial terms. Third party top-up to the amount funded by the voucher is possible but residential breaks are limited to 28 days on each occasion and a maximum of 120 days annually. Nonetheless, to reduce stress and provide more effective support, government has suggested that a step-change is necessary in the provision of short breaks for parents of disabled children (DfES, 2007) and has legislated (s.25, CAYP 2008) to require local authorities to provide breaks not just for parents who are struggling.

Commentary

The law provides a framework for what must happen and when. However the picture painted by Ombudsman investigations (LGO, 2002, 2007) and research (Harris, 1997; Abbott et al., 2001; Beresford and Oldman, 2002; Hendey and Pascall, 2002; Sims, 2004) has been dismal:

- resource shortfalls creating serious problems in implementing legislation;
- difficulties in co-ordinating interagency approaches;
- failures in transition planning, including delayed and inadequate assessments of home care needs or residential placements, poor recording, neglect of carers' contributions and assessments;
- variable support for disabled young people in pursuit of independent living and meaningful citizenship, such as finding employment or maintaining peer relationships;
- limited assistance from statutory agencies regarding housing difficulties, including lack of space and inaccessible rooms, with consequences for confidence, independence, stress, well-being and development;
- variations in numbers of children being statemented and types of needs considered eligible, including difficulties reported by parents in getting statements and contesting decisions that appear driven by budgetary considerations;
- parental views given insufficient weight; inadequate information about procedures and provisions; parental concerns about delays in statementing and hearing appeals;
- teachers reluctant to give evidence to tribunals in support of disabled children against their employing authority.

Transition services for disabled young people need higher priority, and guidance (DfES, 2001) encourages social services departments to work with education and health authorities in developing joint policies, pooling resources and commissioning strategies for moves from residential care or the parental home into suitable accommodation with support services negotiated on an individual basis. Inspectors (CSCI, 2007) report that co-ordination between social care, education, health and housing remains variable, and that transition planning is not consistently meeting national standards for high quality, family-centred services based on assessed needs and promotion of social inclusion (DH, 2004). The result can be confusion, delay and anxiety for disabled young people and their families.

Agencies should provide an equal opportunity, anti-oppressive continuum of care. However, practitioners will sit uncomfortably astride the needs versus resources practice dilemma. Authorities must decide criteria of need reasonably and might be acting *ultra vires* if not providing services to meet assessed needs because of insufficient funds (see Chapter 7). Nonetheless social workers must act vigilantly against restrictive criteria of need and definitions of statutory duties, and any erosion of social work's values. The practitioner's contribution consists of producing, with Martin and his carers, an assessment of needs (physical, emotional, practical, housing, financial, educational, employment and mobility) and maximizing Martin's control over his life decisions. Maintaining inter-agency links and 'feeding' shortfalls of provision into agency planning processes are key tasks too, recognizing that resource-led decisions are frequently uneconomic and ineffective.

Mary

Mary met her husband while he was working in Nigeria, her country of origin. Joshua, their son, is three. Since arriving in England 18 months ago Mary has been aggressive towards her husband and son, painting herself and Joshua white, periodically refusing to eat, afraid of poisoned food, and locking herself away. Her husband wants a divorce but remains at home because of concerns about Mary's behaviour and Joshua's development and safety. He has requested social work assistance but Mary is difficult to engage.

Mental health legislation (see Amy's case in Chapter 4) may be relevant. Domestic violence and housing may be further considerations (see Sharon's case in this chapter). Here the focus will be on the parents' relationship and their son's welfare.

Divorce

Reforms to divorce law (Family Law Act 1996) will not be implemented. Currently, the sole ground for divorce is irretrievable breakdown of the marriage, evidenced by one or more of five facts (Matrimonial Causes Act 1973):

- the respondent has committed adultery and the petitioner finds it intolerable to live with them;
- the respondent has behaved in such a way that the petitioner cannot be expected to live with them;
- the respondent has deserted the petitioner for a continuous period of two years;
- the parties have lived apart continuously for two years and the respondent consents to the divorce;
- the parties have lived apart continuously for five years.

Divorce proceedings cannot commence within the first year of marriage. Legal aid is not available for undefended divorces but may be paid for mediation services and may enable people to obtain advice. A solicitor is not necessary but advisable. The petitioner in cases involving violence may ask the court to withhold their address from the respondent. If the court is satisfied that the evidence, presented in affidavits, supports the petition, a decree nisi is granted. The petitioner may apply for the absolute decree six weeks later, the intervening period being used to settle matters involving children and property.

In determining property and finance questions legal advice is essential. Courts may make financial orders in favour of a party or a child, and may order periodical or lump sum payments, including interim orders (DfES, 2008). In determining maintenance for children, the Children Act 1989 (CA 1989) (sch.1(4)) allowed courts to consider a parent's income, earning capacity, property and other resources; each person's financial needs, obligations and responsibilities; the child's financial needs, income and resources; any physical or mental disability of the child; and the manner in which the child was being, or was expected to be, educated or trained. However, because of concern about defaulters, the Child Support Act 1991 limits the court's jurisdiction, creating a child support agency to assess, review, collect and enforce payments. Subsequent legislation has amended the legal rules, attempting to provide incentives for parents with care responsibilities to work (Child Support Act 1995) and clear routes of appeal against decisions (Social Security Act 1998), simplify how liability is assessed and strengthen measures to ensure compliance and penalize default (Child Support, Pensions and Social Security Act 2000; Child Maintenance and Other Payments Act 2008). The 2008 Act replaces the Child Support Agency with the Child Maintenance and Enforcement Commission and further reforms both the calculation of financial liability of the non-resident parent and options for payment enforcement.

Concerning Joshua within the divorce process, as in all family proceedings the court only makes an order if so doing would be better than making no order at all (s.1(5), CA 1989). There is no presumption either way (*Re G (Children) (Residence: Making of Order)* [2005]). The welfare of the child is paramount, and the court must have regard to risk, the wishes and feelings of a child in light of their age, understanding and circumstances in which they have been expressed, the conduct of the parties in relation to a child's upbringing, and the principle that usually a child's welfare is best served by maintenance of a relationship with family members. If unhappy with any proposed arrangements, the court *could*:

1 Order a welfare report (s.7, CA 1989); there is no obligation to follow a report's recommendation but courts should give reasons when departing from them.
2 Direct the local authority to investigate whether a care or supervision order may be appropriate (s.37). Where the authority decides not to apply for an order, it must inform the court of its reasons, any services or actions proposed, and any decision to review the case subsequently.
3 Regulate parental responsibility by making one or more s.8 orders:

   (a) a residence order, resolving where Joshua will live, where necessary with conditions (s.11(7)) (*B v B (residence: imposition of conditions)* [2004]) and with the possibility of extension beyond the age of 16 to 18 (s.114, Adoption and Children Act 2002 (ACA 2002));
   (b) a contact order, allowing Joshua to visit, stay with and have contact with his other parent;
   (c) a prohibited steps order, limiting the exercise of parental responsibility in specified areas, such as changing the child's surname (*Re C (a minor) (change of surname)* [1998]);
   (d) a specific issue order, namely directions on specific actual or potential questions, such as whether it is in the child's best interests to have medical treatment (*The NHS Trust v A Child* [2007]), or how to resolve disputes about upbringing (*Re J (specific issue order: muslim upbringing and circumcision* [1999]; *Re C (a child) (immunisation: parental rights)* [2003]).

4 A Family Assistance Order (s.16), requiring the local authority to advise, assist and, if appropriate, befriend those named in the order, whose consent (other than the child's) is required. There has been wide variation in use, in the involvement of children, and an absence of consensus about their purpose, which could be to facilitate agreement over contact and other arrangements after divorce (James and Sturgeon-Adams, 1999). The maximum duration is now twelve months (Children and Adoption Act 2006 (CAA 2006)).

Shared residence orders are possible where of positive benefit to a child (*A v A (Minors) (Shared Residence Order)* [1994]; *Re H (Shared Residence)* [1994]; *Re D (Children) (Shared Residence Orders)* [2001]). If someone holding a shared residence order is subsequently made homeless, they will be in priority need (*R v Lambeth LBC, ex parte Vagliviello* [1990]). Parents, with or without parental responsibility, guardians, and those with a residence order, may apply for any s.8 order. Additionally, foster parents who have cared for a child for more than one year (s.113, ACA 2002) may apply for a residence or contact order. Relatives, such as grandparents, who have cared for a child for more than one year, may also apply for a residence order or special guardianship order (s.36, CYPA 2008). Others require leave to apply for s.8 orders (s.10, CA 1989). Leave will depend on the nature of the application, the person's connection with the child, risk to the child, and (if the child is looked after) the local authority's plans. If the child is in care, the court can only make a residence order; when questions about medical treatment arise, wardship must be used. A child must seek leave to apply for a s.8 order, leave being granted if the child has sufficient understanding and the case has merit (reasonably be expected to succeed). There is growing recognition of young people's rights and of how welfare's paternalism, to protect young people from the implications or consequences of their wishes and actions, must sometimes cede ground to their participation and freedom of expression (*Re C (residence: child's application for leave* [1996]; *Mabon v Mabon* [2005]). A child's understanding is assessed in relation to the issues raised by the case (*Re S (A Minor) (Representation)* [1993]; *Re SC (A Minor) (Leave to seek a Residence Order* [1994]).

Grandparents must seek leave for a s.8 order for contact, and leave does not create a right to contact (*Re A (S. 8 Order: Grandparent Application)* [1995]). Applications for s.8 orders may be restricted in exceptional circumstances (s.91(14)), such as risk to the child of emotional and psychological distress (*Re G and M (Child Orders: Restricting Applications)* [1995]). Agreements between parents should only be set aside by a court in exceptional circumstances (*S v E (a minor) (Contact)* [1993]). The court *must*:

1 Give paramount consideration to the child's welfare (s.1(1)), determined by consideration of (s.1(3)): Joshua's wishes and feelings; his physical, emotional and educational needs; the likely effect on him of any change in circumstances; his age, sex, background and relevant characteristics; any harm he has suffered or may suffer; the capabilities of his parents and relevant others in meeting his needs; the powers available to the court. Although the child's wishes and feelings head the welfare checklist, they do not have priority over other matters (*Re W (A Minor) (Medical Treatment: Court's Jurisdiction)* [1992]).
2 Avoid delay (s.1(2)).
3 Appoint a Children's Guardian, and specify the issues for investigation, unless this is not necessary to safeguard Joshua's interests (s.41). The Children's Guardian has a statutory right of access to information and local authority records (s.41(2); *Re J (a child) (care proceedings: disclosure)* [2003]), and must have regard to the welfare checklist and the need to reduce delay. They must assess the child's needs and provide the court with a reasoned and coherent view of the child's situation, the options available, and a clear recommendation of what appears to be in the child's best interests, including assessment of the local authority's application and care plan. It is an active role as representative of the child and adviser to the court on all relevant matters, such as the timetable for proceedings.

Whatever order the court makes, Joshua's parents can still exercise independently their parental responsibility providing this is not incompatible with the order (s.2(8)). This can obviously create difficulties, often coalescing around contact. Unless the child's interests indicate otherwise, there is a strong presumption in favour of contact, to enable a child to retain a sense of identity and to promote their psycho-social development (DH, 1994). Judgements have upheld a separated parent's right to private life and the importance of not adversely destabilizing a child's welfare (*Glaser v UK* [2001]; *Z County Council v R* [2001]). Others have upheld a child's wishes (*Re M (contact: welfare test)* [1995]). Yet others have not tolerated frustration of contact for the non-resident parent (*V v V (children) (contact: implacable hostility)* [2004]), including custodial sentences on mothers (*Re S (a child) (contact dispute: committal)* [2004]). Contact may be indirect to maintain the confidentiality of a parent's address (*A v L (contact)* [1998]). Courts will take a longer-term view of the child's development (*Re O (contact: imposition of conditions)* [1995]) and may require participation in programmes, counselling or unpaid work (CAA 2006) to facilitate or enforce contact. It is questionable, however, whether such legal interventions facilitate contact and reverse relationship difficulties between parents (Trinder et al., 2002). A court may also ask CAFCASS to monitor compliance with a contact order (s.2, CAA 2006). CAFCASS officers must complete a risk assessment for the court when, in connection with any private family law proceedings, a child is suspected of being at risk of harm (s.7).

Joshua's parents may apply for s.8 orders without divorce proceedings. If cohabiting rather than married, Joshua's father would only acquire parental responsibility if ordered by a court or given by Mary (s.4(1)), or if Joshua's birth is jointly registered and his name appears on the birth certificate (s.111, ACA 2002). A court should not withhold parental responsibility in order to exact financial dues (*Re H (Parental Responsibility: Maintenance)* [1996]). The court should consider the degree of commitment shown to the child, the attachment between child and father, and the reason for the application (*Re G (a minor) (parental responsibility order)* [1994]). Section 8 orders can be used subsequently to control exercise of parental responsibility adverse to the child's welfare. A committed father should have the status of parenthood (*Re S (A Minor) (Parental Responsibility)* [1995]; *Re C and V (contact and parental responsibility)* [1998]). Anyone with parental responsibility, or Joshua with leave, could apply for this to be rescinded. Parental responsibility granted by a mother should not be terminated by a court except in serious circumstances, guided by whether the court would be likely to make a parental responsibility order if an application were to be made by *this* person (*Re P (terminating parental responsibility)* [1995]). If without parental responsibility, Joshua's father could still apply for a s.8 order. The court, if making a residence order in his favour, would also make a parental responsibility order (s.12). If a step-parent, he could apply for a residence or contact order (s.10(5)) and, if married to Joshua's mother, obtain parental responsibility by agreement with her and with the birth father if he too has parental responsibility (s.112, ACA 2002). Under this section the court may also give parental responsibility to the step-parent.

Child care/protection

Each children's services authority must promote co-operation with relevant agency partners to improve young people's physical, mental health and emotional well-being, to protect them from harm and neglect, to promote their education and recreation, and to enhance their social and economic well-being and contribution to society (s.10, CA 2004). The agencies named in s.11 must ensure that their work safeguards and promotes children's welfare, pursuing roles and responsibilities outlined in guidance (DfES, 2005a). If a local authority believes that Joshua is suffering, or is likely to suffer, significant harm, enquiries must be made to determine whether action should be taken to safeguard or promote his welfare (s.47, CA 1989). Policy guidance (DH, 2000c) itemizes the dimensions of assessment – child development, parenting capacity, and family and environmental factors. Safeguarding guidance (DfES, 2006a) delineates the steps to be taken where assessment concludes that children are in need but significant harm is (or is not) suspected or likely, or where s.47 (CA 1989) enquiries determine that protection concerns are (or are not) substantiated. Reasonable steps must be taken to gain access to Joshua and to ascertain and give due consideration to his wishes and feelings (s.53, CA 2004). If access is denied an emergency protection or other order must be sought unless his welfare can be safeguarded satisfactorily without doing so.

Joshua may be judged a child in need – unlikely to achieve or maintain a reasonable standard of health or development, or with that standard likely to be significantly or further impaired without service provision. Social workers must, therefore, safeguard and promote his welfare, involving where possible upbringing by his family, by providing appropriate services (s.17, CA 1989, see Martin's case), including cash (no longer just in exceptional circumstances (s.24, CYPA 2008)). Authorities must not define this duty restrictively (DH, 1991d) but take reasonable steps to prevent ill-treatment and neglect, and reduce the need for care proceedings.

The authority must provide Joshua with suitable accommodation if his parents are prevented, temporarily or permanently, from providing it, having ascertained and considered Joshua's wishes as far as practicable (s.20, CA 1989). Policy guidance (DH, 1991a, 1991e) lists the factors to be evaluated to determine placement suitability. Contact must be promoted if practicable and consistent with Joshua's welfare (Sch.2(15)), including assistance with travel expenses. If either parent objected and was willing and able to provide or arrange accommodation, the authority could only provide accommodation if someone with a residence order agreed. Either parent, unless one has a residence order when the right is limited to them, could remove Joshua subsequently. If agreement on a placement cannot be reached, and concerns about significant harm exist, an emergency protection or interim care order should be sought (*R v Tameside MBC, ex parte J* [2000]).

If services are offered and refused, or fail to safeguard and promote Joshua's welfare, or the degree of risk appears serious, or assessment is frustrated, protective measures may be sought. Local authorities must demonstrate the necessity for such orders, providing evidence that service provision has failed or would be likely to (DfES, 2008). Unless there are immediate safeguarding concerns, investigation should precede application (ss.17 and 47) and the local authority should send written notification to those with parental responsibility, using language they will understand to outline their concerns, what needs to be addressed, what support can be provided and plans to apply for a care or supervision order if issues remain unresolved (DfES, 2008; MoJ, 2008b). Investigation must be thorough; lack of parental co-operation should not result in case closure; and managerial decisions should made on the basis of knowledge of the file and consultation with professionals who know the family (*Re E and Others (Minors) (Care Proceedings: Social Work Practice)* [2000]). Equally, intervention must be proportionate to the nature and gravity of (likely) harm, with work focused on supporting and reunifying the family unless the risks are too high (*Re C and B (care order: future harm)* [2001]).

In all child care/safeguarding activities, practitioners must obtain legal advice about which orders to seek, whether the grounds are satisfied, and the evidence to present. Multidisciplinary co-operation (ss.27 and 47, CA 1989; DfES, 2005a, 2006a) in sharing information and decision-making is required, although divergent thresholds across different agencies and variable definitions of what constitutes significant harm may complicate investigations and interventions (Sinclair and Bullock, 2002). Case management begins, unless waiting would jeopardize the court's ability to promote the child's safety and welfare (MoJ, 2008b), with the local authority compiling the case, including the assessment timetable, materials and records, social work statement and care plan, and case chronology (DfES, 2008; MoJ, 2008b). The chronology is especially important in order to note serious and/or deep-seated problems (*Re E and Others (Minors) (Care Proceedings: Social Work Practice)* [2000]).

Courts must regard Joshua's welfare as paramount and be satisfied that making an order is better than not. Where safe and practicable to do so, they should involve families in all proceedings (MoJ, 2008b). Courts should avoid delay, for instance when it appears unlikely that parents can resume responsibility for a child's care, since this might prejudice the child's welfare (s.1(2), CA 1989) (*Re R (Care Proceedings: Adjournment)* [1998]). Some contested questions may need to be determined at an early stage of care proceedings to facilitate a clearer focus on the child's welfare (*Re S (Care Proceedings: Split Hearing)* [1996]). However, cases have established the principle of positive, planned and purposeful delay where the complexity of the case or further assessments require additional time before determining whether an order is necessary (*R v South East Hampshire Family Proceedings Court, ex parte D* [1994]; *Re A and W* [1992]; *C v Solihull MBC* [1993]).

Protective measures available under the CA 1989 are:

1 Prohibited Steps or Specific Issue Order (s.8) if Joshua is not subject to a care order.
2 Child Assessment Order (s.43) where significant harm is suspected but Joshua is not at immediate risk, or no firm evidence exists of actual or likely significant harm (DfES, 2008), and where efforts have failed to secure parental co-operation and assessment of health and development would clarify his needs. Children of sufficient understanding may decline examination or assessment, which should be sensitive to gender, race and culture (DH, 2000c). The purpose is assessment (*X Council v B (Emergency Protection Orders)* [2004]), for instance of persistent concerns about abuse or neglect (DfES, 2008). The order lasts seven days and may specify assessment away from home. A parent's refusal to allow a child about whom there is serious concern to be seen may indicate immediate risk of significant harm, justifying application for an emergency protection order (DfES, 2008).
3 Emergency Protection Order (s.44): The court must be satisfied that Joshua is likely to suffer significant harm or that social workers have had access refused unreasonably and it is required urgently given reason to suspect significant harm. The child must be in imminent danger (DfES, 2008). Given the importance of due process (regarding the parents as significant in the child's life) and proportionality (Human Rights Act 1998), *ex parte* hearings must be exceptional, held only where there are immediate concerns for a child's safety (*P, C and S v UK* [2002]; *Haringey LBC v C (A Child), E and Another Intervening* [2004]; *X Council v B (Emergency Protection Orders)* [2004]). If heard *ex parte* a social worker with direct knowledge of the case must give evidence, minutes of meetings and conferences must be available, and the reasons for the local authority's decisions presented (*Re X (Emergency Protection Orders)* [2006]). Moreover, the child, a parent, or anyone with parental responsibility or with whom Joshua was living beforehand may seek discharge immediately (s.30, CYPA 2008). Joshua must be produced or his whereabouts disclosed. The applicant is given parental responsibility but its exercise is limited to measures necessary to safeguard Joshua's welfare. He may be removed to accommodation but must be returned if it is safe to do

so. He may be removed again if necessary. Contact with parents and others should be reasonable unless the court makes a specific order. If of sufficient understanding, Joshua may refuse any examination or assessment ordered by the court. The order may be extended once, seven days further (maximum), at an *inter partes* hearing if significant harm would be likely otherwise. A power to enter and search specified premises may be given, also a warrant authorizing the police to assist (s.48). The court must be notified of the outcome here.

The police also have powers of protection (s.46) where a child is suffering significant harm. They may remove a child to, or prevent their removal from, a place of safety. The power extends for 72 hours during which they must inform the local authority, which will assume responsibility for the child's welfare, and notify the parents.

4 Care or Supervision Order (s.31):

(a) If the court is satisfied that Joshua is suffering or likely to suffer significant harm, attributable to the care given, or likely to be given if an order is not made, not being what is reasonable to expect a parent to give. The date determining this is that on which the local authority put arrangements in place to protect the child (*Re M (A Minor) (Care Order: Threshold Conditions* [1994]). If the need for such arrangements subsequently ceases, the court cannot look back to a time when they were necessary. Where evidence-gathering continues, new information can be used to demonstrate what the situation was when child protection arrangements, including care proceedings, were put in place (*Re G (care proceedings: threshold conditions)* [2001]). To establish likelihood of significant harm, the proof is the balance of probability where 'likely' means 'real or substantial possibility' (*Re H and R (Child Sexual Abuse: Standard of Proof)* [1996]). The more improbable an event, the stronger the evidence must be (*Re U (a child) (serious injury: standard of proof)* [2004]).

(b) Only if no better way exists to safeguard or promote Joshua's welfare, for example if services had failed to remedy his circumstances (DfES, 2008). In determining whether to make a care order or supervision order, the court will assess future risks by scrutinizing past events and the need for the local authority to hold parental responsibility from which a duty arises to safeguard the child's welfare (s.72, CA 1989). It will consider whether parental compliance is required as opposed to relying solely on their agreement, and the possible need to remove a child that is no longer safe (*Re S(J) (a minor) (care or supervision order)*

[1993]). Courts may make care orders when local authorities are recommending supervision orders if they give reasonable reasons for doing so (*Re C (Care or Supervision Order)* [1999]). Proportionality, then, is the key when responding to risk, evaluating the level of protection available to a child, and judging whether control of parents' parental responsibility is necessary to safeguard a child's welfare (*Re O (A child) (Supervision Order)* [2001]; *Re C and B (care order: future harm)* [2001]).

If parents retain parental responsibility, the local authority acquires it when a care order is made, with the power to restrict the way in which parents exercise their responsibility when necessary to safeguard or promote Joshua's welfare (s.33).

Courts must consider arrangements proposed by social workers (s.34(11)); reasonable contact must be allowed, driven by the needs of the child and family rather than lack of resources (*Re M (care proceedings: judicial review)* [2003]; *X Council v B (Emergency Protection Orders)* [2004]). In urgent situations an authority may refuse contact for up to seven days; courts must determine contact (s.34(5)), including termination on application by local authority or child. The local authority must justify their plan where contact is excluded or restricted, such as practicalities and the burden placed on foster parents (*Re S (a child) (care proceedings: contact)* [2005]), but plans to terminate contact should not be overturned on the remote possibility of rehabilitation in the future (*Re B (Minors) (Care: Contact: Local Authority's Plans)* [1993]). Local authorities should be clear about the purpose of contact, ensure that staff are skilled in managing it, facilitate parents to attend and review contact regularly (DH, 1994b).

An authority may not change Joshua's surname or religion, consent to adoption, appoint a guardian, or remove him from the country without permission for longer than one month.

Interim orders are allowable when reasonable grounds exist for believing that requirements for care orders are met (s.38). Here courts will balance the various risks (of harm and of disruption to attachments), will consider written advice from the Children's Guardian, and must be satisfied that the child's welfare requires the making of *this* order (*Re M (A Child) (Interim Care Order)* [2003]). Changing the child's residence at this point should only rarely be done but the court may add safeguards (*Hampshire County Council v. S* [1993]). Courts should give reasons for decisions on interim care orders. Courts may also issue directions about examinations and assessment (s.38(6)), including residential evaluations, in order to inform decision-making

(*Re C (a minor) (interim care order: residential assessment)* [1996])
but they may not issue directions for treatment or therapy, even if this
might facilitate rehabilitation (*Re M (Residential Assessment Directions*) [1998]; *Re G (a child) (interim care order: residential accommodation)* [2005]). Children of sufficient understanding may refuse
assessments.

Supervision orders require practitioners to advise, assist and
befriend children, to take reasonable steps to enforce the order, and
to consider whether variation or discharge should be sought. Orders
are for one year, renewable to a maximum of three; they may include
specified activities or directions, not exceeding 90 days, or requirements for medical and psychiatric examination, possible only if the
child consents (Sch.3); a child may be required to live in a particular
place and to present themselves to a specified person. Renewal should
normally only be sought after at least nine months and be necessary
for promoting the child's welfare (*T v Wakefield DC* [2008]). An order
cannot be enforced by the court but breakdown could be used as evidence in further proceedings.

A child, local authority, or person with parental responsibility may
apply for variation or discharge (s.39); others must seek a residence
order which would automatically discharge care and supervision
orders (s.91(1)); applications for discharge, variation or contact, without leave of the court, may not be made within six months of previous
applications (s.91(15)(17)).

Active case management in care proceedings (DfES, 2008; MoJ,
2008b) requires the court to be mindful of important steps in a child's
life, such as change of school, to promote co-operation and facilitate
agreement between the parties to narrow the facts at issue, to control
the use of experts and to agree the documents to be disclosed. The first
appointment will confirm the timetable, make arrangements for contested interim hearings, scrutinize the care plan, agree on any need for
experts and give directions. *Practice Direction: Experts in Family Proceedings relating to Children* (MoJ, 2008b) specifies when and how
courts might instruct experts, the duties of experts, the expected contents
of their reports, their involvement in discussions or meetings to clarify
areas of agreement or disagreement, and arrangements for giving evidence. Experts must give objective evidence (*Re C (a child) (immunisation: parental rights)* [2003]) including consideration of facts that may
not support their opinion (*Re X (non-accidental injury: expert evidence*
[2001]). Other directions may include focusing on Joshua and Mary's
ethnicity, language, religion and culture, and/or on Mary's mental health

or capacity and likely need for a litigation friend to assist her (MoJ, 2008b). Further case management conferences will focus on identifying key issues, giving further directions and delineating the evidence to be heard in issues resolution and final hearings.

After a care order is made, the court has no continuing role or power to impose conditions (*Re B (Minors) (Care: Contact: Local Authority's Plans)* [1993]; *Re S (Children: Care Plan) and Re W and B (Children: Care Plan)* [2002]). Consequently, courts have carefully scrutinized local authority care plans and refused orders when dissatisfied with them (*Re T (a minor) (Care Order: Condition)* [1994]). No care order can be made until a care plan has been considered sufficiently firm to indicate the likely way ahead (s.121, ACA 2002).

If Joshua is accommodated by the local authority or subject to a care order, the authority must:

1 Safeguard and promote his welfare; consider his religion, racial origin, cultural and linguistic background; ascertain and consider his wishes, those of his parents and relevant others with or without parental responsibility, prior to decision-making; and use where reasonable services available for children cared for by their own parents (s.22, CA 1989).
2 So far as possible place Joshua near home and with family, relations or friends unless inconsistent with his welfare or impractical (s.23, CA 1989).
3 Establish representations and complaints procedures (enhanced by s.119, ACA 2002) and reviews within regulated timescales (DH, 1991e), which allow full participation and comparison of plans with duties under the act (s.26) and referral to CAFCASS where local authority performance raises concerns (s.118, ACA 2002).
4 Promote his educational achievement (s.52, CA 2004).

Immigration

Marital breakdown may have far-reaching consequences for Mary, in particular her right to remain in the UK (*Harrow LBC v Ibrahim* [2008]; *Teixeira v Lambeth LBC* [2008]). Specialist advice is essential. However, previous restrictions on eligibility for housing as homeless, whereby in claiming eligibility an applicant was unable to include a non-eligible person due to immigration controls (s.185, Housing Act 1996), have been relaxed somewhat. They may now be included in an application which, if successful, entitles the applicant to a twelve month tenancy (s.314 and sch.15, Housing and Regeneration Act 2008).

Observations

Concerns exist about delays in care proceedings due to excessive use of experts, poor court control of cases and constrained resources (McKeigue and Beckett, 2004). It is questionable whether the new case management system and its timetables (MoJ, 2008b) will reduce delay and iron out some of the significant differences between courts regarding use of experts and interim hearings (Masson et al., 2008). Equally, since local authorities carry the financial costs of care proceedings (*R (Hillingdon LBC, Leeds CC, Liverpool CC and Norfolk County Council) v the Lord Chancellor and the Secretary of State for Communities and Local Government, the Law Society and NSPCC intervening* [2008]), they may be discouraged from applying. Certainly they may remain incident-driven, despite recognizing the impact of environmental factors, such as housing and community resources, and the importance of prevention and early intervention to promote child development and enhance parenting capacity (Cleaver and Walker, 2004).

Practitioners' working conditions (high caseloads, variable supervision arrangements and limited access to legal advice), the need to manage resources by limiting demands for core assessments until crises are reached (Sinclair and Corden, 2005), and the chaotic lifestyles and multiple difficulties of many families involved with social workers (Masson et al., 2008) will continue to test safeguarding arrangements and the point at which an appropriate response is conceived along the continuum of need and significant harm. Resources will be further stretched following the Public Law Outline's emphasis on exploring alternatives such as kinship care by means of family group conferences (DfES, 2008), and the shift of legislation from need, harm and risk (CA 1989) to promoting the well-being of *all* children (CA 2004).

Sharon

For several years Sharon has lived in fear of her life. Her husband, a body-building enthusiast, has regularly assaulted and threatened her. He has also been intimidating and aggressive towards neighbours and agency representatives, for example his probation officers. Sharon has two children, aged 8 and 6, who were on the child protection register following suspected assaults by their father, never substantiated. Their names were removed from the register when their father was sent to prison for grievous bodily harm and burglary. His discharge date is approaching and Sharon has sought advice. She believes there is no point in trying to separate, although she wants a divorce, believing that her husband would threaten her extended family if she moved away.

Divorce law was covered in the previous case. So, too, were the legal rules relating to contact and to children in need. However, contact in the context of domestic violence raises particular issues, and children will be 'in need' if they witness or are victims of domestic violence (s.120, Adoption and Children Act 2002). What additional legislation might apply in this case?

Domestic violence

Both criminal and civil remedies are available. The police have powers of arrest (s.5(3), Police and Criminal Evidence Act 1984 (PACE 1984)) where there is a need to prevent injury or protect a child or other vulnerable person. Offences under the Offences Against the Person Act 1861 include common law assault, assault occasioning actual bodily harm, unlawful wounding and assault occasioning grievous bodily harm. Common assault is now an arrestable offence (s.10, Domestic Violence, Crime and Victims Act 2004 (DVCVA 2004)). Arrest and prosecution in domestic violence is increasing but is by no means yet the remedy of automatic recourse. Under s.12 (DVCVA 2004) restraining orders may be made on both conviction and acquittal. If a prosecution is pursued, Sharon can be compelled to give evidence (s.80, PACE 1984). However, witnesses fearful of doing so are afforded some protection by provision in the Youth Justice and Criminal Evidence Act 1999 for giving evidence from behind screens, by live link or in private, separate waiting rooms, and video recording of evidence in chief and cross-examination. Victims must also be provided with information about decision-making relating to prosecution and the impact on them must be considered when decisions about charges are taken (DVCVA 2004). After conviction for sexual and/or violent offences, victims may also make representations regarding licence and supervision conditions, and have the right to information before the offender's discharge.

Civil remedies are threefold. The Family Law Act 1996 (FLA 1996) provides for *ex parte* hearings in an emergency when there is risk of significant harm to the applicant or a child, or where the applicant would otherwise be deterred from making application. Young people may apply under the FLA 1996, requiring leave of the court if they are under 16. Court decisions on making non-molestation, occupation and exclusion orders will be determined by reference to the parties' conduct, their financial and housing resources, the welfare and needs of any children, and the likely effect on the health, safety or well-being of the parties or children. Courts must make an occupation order if the applicant or child is likely to suffer significant harm, unless the respondent or child would suffer significant harm as a result of the order being made which would be greater than the harm to be suffered as a result of the respondent's behaviour if an order was not made. Breaking an injunction constitutes contempt of court. Sharon would have to advise the court and request a warrant for arrest to be issued. The respondent can be ordered to court and cautioned, fined or imprisoned. When issuing occupation orders, courts must also consider making non-molestation orders.

Powers of arrest can be attached to the original injunction if actual injury has occurred and is likely to occur again (Domestic Proceedings and Magistrates Courts Act 1978 (DPMCA 1978)) or if the respondent has used or threatened to use violence to the applicant or a child and, in *ex parte* orders, where there is also a risk of significant harm (FLA 1996), allowing arrest without warrant if the injunction is broken. Under the FLA 1996 no power of arrest can be attached if the court accepts an undertaking, which stands akin to a court order. Time limits may be attached to exclusion orders (DPMCA 1978) and to powers of arrest, which can limit their effectiveness as longer-term solutions, but orders can also be made until further notice.

The FLA 1996 plugs the loophole that Prohibited Steps Orders (s.8, CA 1989) cannot be used to oust a parent (*Nottinghamshire County Council v P* [1993]; *Re D (Prohibited Steps Order)* [1996]). Where emergency action is necessary to protect children, social workers should assess whether providing services and/or accommodation for the alleged abuser (sch.2(5), CA 1989) may be an alternative to removal of the child (DfES, 2008). Courts may now add to an Emergency Protection Order or an Interim Care Order an exclusion requirement if it is likely that a child will cease to (be likely to) suffer significant harm or, in the case of an EPO, it is likely that enquiries will cease to be frustrated. Sharon must be able to care for the child and consent to the order being made. A court may attach a power of arrest or accept an undertaking. A prison sentence may be imposed for persistent breaches (*Re L (Children)* [2001]). The exclusion requirement ceases to have effect if the authority subsequently removes the child from home for a continuous period of more than 24 hours. Exclusion can mean from the house and/or a defined geographical area.

LAC(97)15 emphasizes the effect of the FLA 1996 on the CA 1989, and details what should be good local authority and interagency practice in relation to domestic violence. Subsequent Home Office initiatives (Hester and Westmarland, 2005; Parmar et al., 2005) have introduced Multi-Agency Risk Assessment Conferences concerning high-risk victims such as Sharon, with support, information and advice provided by independent advocates. This partnership approach can be effective in stopping violence, helping women pursue criminal and civil law remedies, understanding the complex issues facing victims and meeting their support needs.

The DVCVA 2004 extends protection from married and unmarried partners to those who are not living together where there has been an intimate relationship of significant duration, and to same-sex couples. The Act makes a criminal offence the breach of a non-molestation order made under the FLA 1996, with a maximum sentence of five years imprisonment.

Housing

Housing departments must assess cases where applicants are homeless or threatened within 28 days with homelessness, to establish if they are eligible for assistance and, if so, what duty is owed (s.184, Housing Act 1996 (HA 1996)). Housing departments must give reasons for their decisions, and have a duty to provide advice (s.179). If a person appears to be homeless, eligible for assistance and in priority need, the housing department has a duty to provide accommodation pending any final decision concerning their duties and irrespective of any possibility of referral to another authority (s.188). Applicants must have the mental capacity to understand and respond to the offer of accommodation and to undertake the responsibilities involved (*R v. Tower Hamlets LBC, ex parte Begum* [1993]).

Sharon would be homeless if:

1 unmarried and not entitled to occupy accommodation (neither (joint) owner nor tenant);
2 married and entitled to live in the matrimonial home (FLA 1996) but locked out or likely to be subjected to actual or threatened violence (s.177, HA 1996);
3 it is not reasonable for her to occupy the accommodation, together with any other person who normally resides or might be reasonably expected to reside with her (s.175(3) and s.176, HA 1996).

The authority might seek to insist that other legal provisions are used to gain entry or prevent violence, but previous history or degree of violence and the inadequacy of legal remedies should be emphasized.

Authorities must provide suitable accommodation for homeless people, and those reasonably expected to live with them, if in priority need, homeless unintentionally and with a local connection. In the original legislation this duty was initially for two years (s.193), after which authorities could continue to provide such accommodation (though not obliged to do so) if the person was in priority need, there was no other suitable accommodation, and the individual requested it, with a review every two years (s.194(2)). Originally, also, where other suitable accommodation was available, the duty of the housing authority towards those for whom it would otherwise have a housing duty was to provide advice and assistance to enable the applicant to acquire accommodation (s.197). The Homelessness Act 2002 (HA 2002) (s.6) repealed both these restrictions so that the duty now is to provide settled accommodation for people who are unintentionally homeless and in priority need.

If people have a priority need but are homeless intentionally, temporary accommodation is provided for a period considered reasonable to enable the applicant to make other arrangements, together with advice and assistance in securing accommodation (s.190(2)). If they are homeless but not a priority need the authority must provide advice and assistance as they consider appropriate to assist the applicant to secure accommodation, whether or not homeless unintentionally (ss.190(3) and 192), but also has the power to secure accommodation (s.5, HA 2002). Under the HA 2002, local authorities must assess need before providing advice and assistance to those not in priority need. Advice includes details of the availability, location and sources of accommodation suitable for the applicant's needs.

Priority need (HA 1996) covers pregnancy, disaster, dependent children, even if living elsewhere because of violence or homelessness (*R v Lewisham LBC, ex parte C* [1992]) and vulnerability of self or another reasonably expected to live with the applicant, owing to age, disability (including mental illness) or special reasons. The HA 2002, by virtue of the Homelessness (Priority Need for Accommodation) (England) Order 2002, automatically extends priority need to young people aged 16 and 17 who are homeless and to care leavers aged between 18 and 20 if they were looked after when 16 or 17. It also extends priority need to people escaping domestic violence, currently in custody or over 21 and previously looked after by a local authority, if they are vulnerable.

Vulnerability means being less able to fend for oneself so that injury or detriment will result, where the less vulnerable person would cope without harmful effect (*R v Camden LBC, ex parte Pereira* [1999]). This definition is very wide and courts will only interfere in local authority decision-making when it is irrational or perverse (*Simms v Islington LBC* [2008]). Intentional homelessness means deliberate actions or omissions, in consequence of which the applicant has ceased to occupy accommodation which it was reasonable to occupy, or is threatened with homelessness. Domestic violence (and any act or omission in good faith because of unawareness of a relevant fact) falls outside definitions of intentional homelessness. The HA 2002 extends domestic violence to include any form of violence or serious threat of it. Unintentional homelessness may result from harassment, the effect on health of local crime and violence, and from inadequate resources/poverty where an applicant maintains children at the expense of rent and arrears (*R v Wandsworth LBC, ex parte Hawthorne* [1995]). Authorities can refer applicants on to others if claimants have a local connection there (s.198) and would not be exposed to domestic violence. Applicants must not be referred back if that would place them at risk of further violence (s.10, HA 2002). A local connection is defined (s.199, HA 1996) as a place where the applicant is/ was normally resident or employed, or a place with family associations. Once an applicant is notified of an authority's intention to refer on, that authority is no longer under a duty to provide accommodation (s.200). If they are entitled to accommodation the authority must help applicants protect property if a danger of loss or damage exists and applicants are unable to make suitable arrangements. This duty includes a power to retrieve property (ss.211 and 212). Where the housing authority requests it (s.213), another housing authority or a social services department must co-operate as far as is reasonable.

An unreasonable refusal of an offer of accommodation may discharge the authority from its duties (s.193(5)). It may not be unreasonable to house Sharon outside the authority to which she has applied, given a shortage of accommodation (*R (Calgin) v Enfield LBC* [2005]). She should be given the benefit of doubt regarding the degree of violence or threat posed, with the authority having to be satisfied that the accommodation is suitable *and* that it is reasonable for her to accept it (*Slater v Lewisham LBC* [2006]). To be suitable, it must protect her from domestic violence and be located close to support networks. Social factors in an area, such as harassment, racism and drug misuse, may also be relevant considerations when determining whether accommodation is suitable and reasonable for Sharon and her children to occupy (*R v Sefton MBC, ex parte Healiss* [1994]; *R v Haringey LBC, ex parte Karaman* [1996]). Living in a refuge does not count as accommodation for the purpose of deciding if someone is homeless. However, a woman evicted for unreasonable behaviour from a refuge may find herself regarded as intentionally homeless (*Manchester CC v Moran* [2008]).

More generally, suitability includes not just the condition of accommodation when the offer is made but also any adaptations and alterations that could be made to it (*Boreh v Ealing LBC* [2008]). Where a council has concluded that current accommodation is not suitable, it has around six weeks to find reasonable alternatives (*R (Aweys) v Birmingham CC* [2008]).

Applicants have the right to request a review of an authority's decisions in a case (s.202) within 21 days. The HA 2002 allows an appeal lodged after three weeks to be heard where there is good reason. If the review finds against them, they may appeal on a point of law, again within 21 days, to the county court. Whilst an application is subject to review or appeal, the authority may provide accommodation. The review must consider afresh the facts at the time of the original decision (*Omar v City of Westminster* [2008]) unless the decision-making process has continued up to the date of the internal review (*Mohammed v Hammersmith and Fulham LBC* [2002]).

Children are not eligible to apply for housing using homelessness provisions when their parents have been found intentionally homeless (*R v Bexley LBC, ex parte B (a minor)* [1993]; *R v Oldham MBC, ex parte G (a minor)* [1993]). However, social services and housing departments should not buck-pass. Indeed, the former may provide financial assistance (s.17(6), CA 1989) to secure accommodation for children in need *and* their families where a housing authority has found a family to be intentionally homeless (*R v Northavon DC, ex parte Smith* [1994]). Sharon may be eligible for this support and the circumstances when this is considered no longer have to be exceptional (s.24, CYPA 2008). If Sharon consents, housing officers may inform children's services of their involvement and subsequent decisions, and assist the latter with their CA 1989 duties.

Violent offenders

Under the Criminal Justice and Court Services Act 2000, probation and police officers should collaborate to assess and manage the risks posed by violent and sex offenders. The Criminal Justice Act 2003 extends this requirement to the prison service. All other agencies must also co-operate regarding services for such offenders. Decision-making is co-ordinated by the Multi-Agency Public Protection Arrangements panels. Additionally, on application from the police or local authority, courts may impose anti-social behaviour orders (Crime and Disorder Act 1998) for people's protection when someone's behaviour is likely to cause harassment, alarm or distress. The terms of the order, where necessary to protect someone from further anti-social behaviour, can prohibit visits to a partner's home (*Leeds CC v Fawcett* [2008]). The standard of proof is the balance of probability, but breach is a criminal offence.

Children in need

Safeguarding policy guidance (DfES, 2006a) refers to the serious impact of domestic violence on children's well-being and on the victim parent's ability to look after them. Such children are children in need and an interagency approach is required to safeguard and promote their welfare (ss.10 and 11, CA 2004). The guidance advises that both family and criminal law remedies should be used – Sharon should be supported to make safe choices, partly through the provision of information about the law – and that the extent of domestic violence should be assessed, especially in cases of child abuse.

Section 17 duties (CA 1989) include assessment of housing needs (*R (G) v Barnet LBC; R (W) v Lambeth LBC; R (A) v Lambeth LBC* [2003]; s.116 ACA 2002), with a subsequent power to provide accommodation for families and children. This does not mean that children are looked after (LAC(2003)13). Accommodation must be suitable, using the definitions derived from housing law. Assessment must be conducted using the framework (DH, 2000c), including the wishes and feelings of the child (s.20(6), CA 1989). The duty under s.17, especially in cases of domestic violence, falls on the local authority in whose area the child is present. Arguments between local authorities concerning responsibility should not delay service provision (*R (Stewart) v Wandsworth LBC, Hammersmith and Fulham LBC and Lambeth LBC* [2001]; *R (M) v Barking and Dagenham LBC and Westminster CC (interested party)* [2003]).

Contact

The judicial presumption that contact between children and non-resident parents (usually fathers) is beneficial has been tested in respect of domestic violence. Welfare reports and judicial decision-making have not always given sufficient focus to allegations of domestic violence (Radford and Hester, 2006). Courts should consider the conduct of both parties towards each other and the children, the effect on the child and the residential parent, and the motivation of the parent seeking contact. The safety of the child and the resident parent is paramount (*Re L (a child) (contact: domestic violence)* [2000]). Indirect or supervised contact may be options given that the need to protect the mental and physical health of the child's primary carer will outweigh the child's need to have direct contact with the father (*Re H (contact order) (no.2)* [2002]).

The Children and Adoption Act 2006 creates new powers to promote contact, such as requiring perpetrators to attend counselling programmes or parenting classes, and to enforce contact. Breach of a contact order (s.8 CA 1989) may result in imposition of an unpaid work requirement or order to pay compensation. Family Assistance Orders (s.16, CA 1989) may now last for twelve as opposed to six months and do not have to be made only in exceptional circumstances. They may be used to facilitate the provision of advice and assistance for improving and maintaining contact.

Observations

Social workers need to use advocacy skills to ensure that Sharon and her children are safeguarded and their well-being promoted through use of the legal rules. Multi-agency working has proved variable. Neither effective communication lines (*R (Bempoa) v Southwark LBC* [2002]) between housing and social services authorities, nor appreciation of their respective legal duties to assess a child's housing needs (*R v Tower Hamlets LBC, ex parte Bradford* [1998]), can be guaranteed. Social workers should assess the adequacy of local arrangements since service provision remains uneven (Humphreys et al., 2000) and support of partner agencies critical to outcomes (Parmar et al., 2005).

Sam

Following serious non-accidental injury Sam, now aged two, was made the subject of a care order. Sam's father does not have parental responsibility. In line with case law, he was notified of the care proceedings as exceptional circumstances to withhold this information did not exist (*Re X (Care: Notice of Proceedings)* [1996]). He did not contest the authority's application for a care order, nor the subsequent termination of contact. Sam has lived with foster parents since he was nine months old. The local authority's care plan ruled out rehabilitation and contact has been terminated between Sam and his parents.

Management of care proceedings was covered in Mary's case. The local authority's task will have been to protect Sam, to assess the issues, and to rely on legal practitioners to advise on the strength and credibility of the medical evidence (*Re U (a child) (serious injury: standard of proof)* [2004]). A residential assessment (s.38(6) Children Act 1989 (CA 1989)) may have been in Sam's best interests to investigate his mother's parental ability, enabling all relevant evidence to be tested, in line with Article 6 (ECHR) rights to a fair hearing, before he was permanently removed and placed for adoption (*Re L and H (Residential Assessment)* [2007]). The threshold criteria (s.31, CA 1989) do not require proof that the harm suffered by Sam was due to a failure by a specifically identified individual. Where care is shared and harm results, Sam will not have been left at risk because the court was unsure which part of the care network failed (*Lancashire CC and Another v Barlow and Another* [2000]; *Re O and N (children) (non-accidental injury)* [2003]).

Care proceedings must be managed so as to reduce delay by the parties minimizing areas of evidential disagreement (MoJ, 2008b). Parents conceding that the threshold criteria have been met, before or during issues resolution hearings, will normally obviate the need to hear and challenge evidence at a (final) hearing. However, where the allegations are so serious, where findings of fact could affect the approach taken in a case (on contact or adoption for instance) and/or where the child might need to feel listened to, a full hearing might be beneficial (*Re M (threshold criteria)* [1999]). Similarly, if Sam's parents declined to answer questions or give evidence in care proceedings, the court can draw an inference that any allegations against them are true (*Re O and Another (children) (care proceedings: evidence)* [2003]). Section 98(2), CA 1989 provides that statements or admissions in proceedings which may incriminate will not be admissible in criminal proceedings. Equally, where legal representatives possess material relevant to the determination of a case but contrary to the interests of their client, such as a psychiatric report, they must disclose it to the court and other parties (*Re DH (minor) (care proceedings: evidence and orders)* [1994]).

In the event of Sam's mother also being a child, his welfare will be paramount (*Birmingham CC v H (a minor) and others* [1993]; *S v Leeds CC* [1994]). Sam's mother may enter into a parental responsibility agreement under s.4, CA 1989, with his father. The local authority cannot interfere with Sam's mother signing an agreement, even when holding a care order (*Re X (parental responsibility agreement: children in care)* [2000]).

Care planning

Prior to placement, or as soon as possible afterwards, a written plan must be compiled in consultation with Sam, his parents and other relevant people and agencies. It should be reviewed four weeks and three months after placement, and at subsequent six-monthly reviews. Amendments should be notified to relevant people in writing. For children on court orders, partnership and agreement with parents should be sought if possible. Planning, to avoid drift, must assess and consider Sam's needs, contact arrangements with parents and significant other people, his parents' capacity to meet his needs, his race, culture, religion and language, placement arrangements (including health care, pre-school and education, support for the carers, and any plans for reunification), contingency plans should placement difficulties occur, and overall responsibility for the plan. It must determine, after full consideration of Sam and his parents' wishes and feelings, objectives to secure Sam's welfare within achievable timeframes (s.22(4), CA 1989; DH, 1991e; LAC(99)29; DfES, 2004b). The court, prior to making a care order, must invite and consider comment upon arrangements proposed or made by the authority (s.34(11), CA 1989; s.121, Adoption and Children Act 2002 (ACA 2002)). If not satisfied that the care plan meets the child's interests, or that it has been prepared in accordance with guidance (DH, 1991e; LAC(99)29), it could refuse to make a care order (*Re J (minors) (Care: Care Plan)* [1994]; *Re C (a child) (care proceedings: care plan)* [2002]). If there are likely to be difficulties in implementing the plan, the court will proceed providing the authority is aware of how to respond to potential problems.

Care plans are often revised as options are tested and ruled out, or plans for reunification discounted and for adoption foregrounded (Masson et al., 2008). Where adoption is, or may become, the preferred option, the care plan should follow a twin track rather than sequential approach in order to avoid delay. The parents should know that both are being considered (*Re D and K (care plan: twin track planning)* [1999]). Where a care plan for rehabilitation is subsequently abandoned, parents should be given opportunities to participate in decision-making, where this does not jeopardize a child's welfare, in order to protect their Article 8 (ECHR) rights (*Re C (a child) (breach of human rights: damages)* [2007]). Where adoption is the preferred option, courts should be advised of likely steps and timeframes, and sufficient assessment will be necessary to discount rehabilitation or placement with relatives using s.8 orders (CA 1989) and/or special guardianship (LAC(99)29). Care orders and placement orders may be made at the same hearing (*Re P-B* [2006]) but they are separate applications dealt with sequentially, each requiring assessment (*Re M (a minor) (care order: freeing application)* [2004]). Normally, where a court makes a care order with adoption being the plan, it will also make a placement order, unless there are very substantial doubts regarding whether adoption is in the child's best interests, in which event further assessment may follow the care order prior to decision-making on whether to pursue a placement order and adoption (*Re T (children: placement order)* [2008]).

Reviews of care plans are governed by the Review of Children's Cases Regulations 1991 and the Review of Children's Cases (Amendment) (England) Regulations 2004. The latter implements the independent reviewing officer's (IRO) role (s.118, ACA 2002) to monitor the local authority's performance regarding implementation of Sam's care plan and to refer the case to a CAFCASS officer when appropriate. The IRO must be a registered social worker, have relevant experience, be outside management of the case, and chair meetings. They must ensure the child's wishes are understood and taken into account, that all involved are assisted to contribute meaningfully, that any failure in the plan is notified to senior managers and that, where the child wishes to apply to the court for contact or discharge of the care order, or to make representations, they are assisted to obtain legal advice and access to advocacy and complaints procedures. Section 10, Children and Young Persons Act 2008 (CYPA 2008) extends IRO responsibilities to require that, for continuity and relationship-building with children, they are appointed by local authorities once young people become looked after, with their role encompassing not just reviews but all local authority functions. Practitioners and managers must co-operate with IROs to enable them to perform their monitoring functions.

Policy guidance (DfES, 2004b) reiterates that care planning must focus on intended outcomes regarding health, education, emotional and behavioural development, identity, family and social relationships, social presentation and self-care skills. Reviews should consider outcomes since the last review, whether further assessments and revision of the plan are needed, and how records are being kept and planning shared where possible and appropriate.

Placement

Where consistent with Sam's welfare and practicable, placement should be considered with a parent, someone with parental responsibility or an individual who had a residence order prior to the care order being made (s.8(3), CYPA 2008). Otherwise, placement with relatives, friends or foster parents should be considered (s.8(6) CYPA 2008). CYPA 2008 also provides for regulations to allow prospective or existing foster parents to request an independent review of a decision of unsuitability to foster. Parents should be involved in decision-making about Sam's future, giving due consideration to their wishes and those of Sam, where this does not jeopardize safeguarding and promoting his welfare. The Act reinforces earlier provision (s.23, CA 1989) that, where appropriate, placements should be near home, promote siblings living together, be suitable for a disabled child's needs and not disrupt education or training.

The practice of paying lower rates to foster carers who are relatives or friends is unlawful because it is discriminatory, irrational, arbitrary and contrary to the welfare requirements of children (*R (L and Others) v Manchester CC*; *R (R and Others) v Manchester CC* [2002]). Schedule 1(15), CA 1989, also permits accommodation and maintenance payments to a person with whom a child is living under a residence order if not the child's parent, if this would promote their welfare and provide an alternative to care proceedings. Local authorities, however, are noted for inconsistent and inadequate financial and other support provision (*R (M) v Birmingham CC* [2008]; Hunt et al., 2008), which may undermine the positive features of kinship care.

Where rehabilitation is excluded:

1 parents may apply for a residence order (s.8, CA 1989) which, if granted, would discharge the care order;
2 relatives may apply for a residence order or special guardianship order, without leave if they have looked after Sam for a continuous period of one year (ss.36 and 38, CYPA 2008); courts will decide questions of leave by considering the applicants' connection with Sam, the order sought, the risk of disruption and harm to Sam's life and, since he is in care, the authority's plans and the feelings and wishes of Sam's parents (s.10(9), CA 1989);
3 after a one-year placement the foster carers may apply for a residence order or a special guardianship order without local authority consent (ss.113 and 115, ACA 2002);
4 the foster parents may apply to adopt Sam.

Courts will use the welfare checklist (s.1(3), CA 1989) to determine what order to make. In adoption proceedings, courts may make any s.8 order as an alternative or in addition to an adoption order if better for the child (DfES, 2008).

Contact

Contact arrangements raise dilemmas and often challenges from parents or courts. Article 8 rights to private and family life apply to children and parents, but may be qualified when there are proportionate reasons for so doing. Contact may have value for Sam even where there is no chance of reunification, for instance having a beneficial impact on placement stability and subsequent emotional development (Cleaver, 2000). Much will depend on Sam's parents' attitude to the care plan and they should be encouraged to remain involved in planning unless this would prejudice his welfare (DH, 1991e).

Contact is the child's right not the parent's and, where there is a conflict, the child's welfare takes priority (*Birmingham CC v H (a minor) and others* [1993]). Reasonable contact must be allowed (s.34, CA 1989) unless defined or terminated by a court. Reviews should focus on contact arrangements, agreement should be reached with parents wherever possible and, if the authority applies for variation or termination of contact, it must notify in writing those affected, giving reasons (DH, 1991e). It may not be sufficient for the local authority to apply for termination of contact because there is no likelihood of finding adopters who would entertain open adoption (*Re E (A Minor) (Care Order: Contact)* [1994]). Contact may support the child's identity and facilitate commitment to a new family knowing that this has the approval of the birth parent(s) (*Re B (minors) (Care: Contact: Local Authority Plans)* [1993]). It may be in the child's best interests to see his mother on a regular basis, even if eventually contact is terminated through adoption (*Berkshire County Council v B* [1997]). Alternatively, indirect contact may be appropriate where a child cannot be reunited with a parent. However, a care order should not be refused when the court believes that direct post-adoption contact may be preferable. Rather, the parent may make an application or the question can be determined separately (*Re K (care proceedings: care plan)* [2008]).

Special guardianship

Sometimes adoption may be inappropriate. Special guardianship (s.115, ACA 2002) provides an alternative form of permanence, allowing a legally secure placement. Anyone over 18 may be a special guardian. Some people may apply without leave – guardians, those with a residence order, and relatives or foster parents who have looked after the child for one year. Others require leave of the court to apply. Applicants then must give three months notice to the local authority (*Birmingham CC v R and Others* [2006]). If an order is made, any care order is discharged; parental responsibility held by others is retained, but the special guardian may limit how it is exercised. Should a care order be made subsequently, the special guardianship order is not necessarily discharged.

The Special Guardianship Regulations 2005 require assessment of the need for support services when requested by the child or special guardian. Assessment should consider the child's developmental needs, the special guardian's parenting capacity, and the family and environmental factors shaping the child's life. When financial support is being considered, assessment should also cover the child's financial needs and the special guardian's financial resources. Services to initiate or support special guardianship, or to meet a child's therapeutic needs, may include counselling, advice, information provision, financial payments, mediation (for instance regarding parental contact), and groupwork. If support involves more than advice and information, and is ongoing, a plan should be produced and periodically reviewed.

The Regulations also itemize the content for a local authority's report to the court when a special guardianship order is being considered. These include the merits of special guardianship as against other possible orders, and proposals for contact. Case law has distinguished between special guardianship and adoption (*Re AJ* [2007]; *Re M-J* [2007]), the former representing less legal interference with birth family ties but providing permanence. There is no presumption that one or other order is preferable; on each occasion the key question is which order will better serve the child's welfare (*Re S (a child) (special guardianship order)* [2007]).

Adoption

Adoption transfers parental responsibility from birth to adoptive parents. The ACA 2002 has aligned adoption law more closely to the CA 1989. Local authorities must maintain an adoption service (s.2), or delegate responsibility to a registered adoption society (s.3), including the provision of services and financial support. National standards (DH, 2001a) specify clear timetables for assessing adoption applicants and matching children with prospective adopters. The child's welfare, safety, needs and views are central. Their wishes and feelings must be sought and considered. Delay must be avoided, the family sought being the best available, and the child's ethnicity and cultural background valued and promoted. Children must not drift within the care system through exclusion of placements with families who do not share a child's heritage but who could offer a suitable home and help a child understand their racial and cultural identity. Courts will balance ethnic origin as a placement factor against attachment to current carers and whether a move would cause psychological damage (*Re P (a minor) (Adoption)* [1990]; *Re JK (Adoption: transracial placement)* [1991]).

Ongoing links with the birth family should be supported, practically and financially, where this is in the child's best interests (DH, 2001a; *Re G (adoption: contact)* [2002]). Prior agreement of the parties is usual (*Re C (a minor) (adoption: conditions)* [1988]), although contact may be allowed against the wishes of the adopters, for example to ensure that a child has knowledge of their cultural heritage (*Re O (Transracial Adoption: Contact)* [1995]). No order should be made where contact has already been agreed between adoptive and birth parents (*Re T (Adoption: Contact)* [1995]). Proposed arrangements must serve the best interests of the child and not threaten successful adoption (*Re R (a child) (adoption: contact)* [2005]). Before adoption placement, the agency should discuss contact with the child, family and prospective adopters (s. 46(6), ACA 2002). The court must also consider contact. Once a child has been placed, any contact orders (s.8 or s.34, CA 1989) cease to have effect. Following review of arrangements, a new order may be made under s.8, CA 1989.

The ACA 2002 provides:

- that the child's welfare is the paramount consideration (s.1);
- a welfare checklist for agencies and courts to assess a child's interests (s.1(4)), including the child's ascertainable wishes and feelings, the long-term implications of an adoption order, the child's needs, their relationship with relatives and their wishes and ability to offer care, the harm suffered or likely to be suffered by the child, and any relevant characteristics such as age or gender;
- that due consideration be given to the child's religion and ethnic origin (s.1(5));
- for adoption by married and unmarried couples, and by single people (s.49), with unmarried couples defined as those of the same or different sex in an enduring family relationship (s.144);
- for prospective adopters to apply for an order after a placement of ten weeks (s.42) and for foster parents after one year;
- an alternative to step parent adoptions – a parental responsibility agreement whereby the birth parent and new spouse are jointly able to exercise parental responsibility without severing links with the child's other birth parent, the courts involved only if the non-resident birth parent dissents;
- for married and unmarried step parents who prefer adoption, a simplified procedure, where they have lived with the child for at least six months, so that the birth parent is not obliged to adopt his/her own child (s.51).

In Sam's case, an adoption process would require that full information is provided to prospective adopters about his needs (DH, 2001a; *A and Another v Essex CC* [2003]). The adoption panel must consider whether adoption is in his best interests and whether prospective adopters are suitable to be adoptive parents, generally and for Sam. Section 12, ACA 2002, allows unsuccessful prospective adopters to seek independent review. The Independent Review of Determinations (Adoption) Regulations 2004 specifies the size and composition of review panels, which make reasoned recommendations to the prospective adopters and the adoption agency. The ACA 2002 register (s.125) aims to facilitate adoption by suggesting matches with approved prospective adopters.

Unless a care order is in place, Sam's parents could consent freely, unconditionally, and with full understanding to his adoption (ss.19 and 52) either generally or for specific prospective adopters. The adoption agency and the prospective adopters obtain parental responsibility. Birth parents with parental responsibility retain it, although its exercise may be restricted by the agency and prospective adopters. They may ask for Sam's return until an adoption application is made by the prospective adopters, after which only the court can order a move (s.37). If consent has been given, Sam's parents can only oppose the adoption application with leave of the court. Section 20 permits advance consent and a declaration that the parent does not wish to know when an adoption order application is made. Such consents may be withdrawn, whereupon the local authority would have to apply for a placement order (s.31).

If Sam's parents do not consent or he is subject to a care order, or the court believes that the threshold conditions (s.31, CA 1989) are met, the local authority should apply for a placement order (ss.1 and 22). The adoption agency and the prospective adopters obtain parental responsibility. Birth parents with parental responsibility retain it, although its exercise may be restricted by the agency and prospective adopters. The care order is suspended and any s.8 (CA 1989) or supervision orders revoked. A parent may seek revocation of a placement order, to the point where a placement is made. Should a parent notify the local authority of an intention to seek revocation, it should reassess the situation to consider whether a different care plan is required (*Re F (a child)* [2008]).

If Sam's parents are unmarried, and his father does not have parental responsibility, the adoption agency must attempt to find him and seek his views, even though his consent is unnecessary. Generally, birth fathers in this position should be informed of proposed placement orders and applications for adoption (*Re B (a child) (adoption by one natural parent)* [2001]) except where their relationship with the birth mother and their demonstrated level of commitment to the child suggest otherwise (*Re J (adoption: contacting father)* [2003]). Confidentiality for the birth mother might carry weight, the nature of the previous relationship being important in establishing whether Article 8 (ECHR) rights are relevant (*Re H and Re G (adoption: consultation of unmarried fathers* [2001]).

An application to dispense with consent (s.52) must demonstrate either that Sam's parents cannot be found or are incapable of giving consent, or that his welfare requires consent to be dispensed with. At the adoption hearing a reporting officer will confirm that consent has been given freely where this is relevant. Where consent has been withheld a Children's Guardian will report to the court. As these are family proceedings the court may make any order under the CA 1989. The local authority, through a social worker with at least three years' relevant experience (Local Authority Adoption Service (England) Regulations 2003) will also report on the suitability and desirability of adoption and of the applicants (ss.44 and 45), including the apparent stability and permanence of their relationship. At this hearing Sam's birth parents may apply for a residence order with the court's permission (s.28). Section 47 specifies the grounds under which an adoption order may be made, namely either that parents have consented and do not oppose adoption, or that their consent has been dispensed with; or that Sam was placed with these prospective adopters by an agency for adoption with parental consent or a placement order. Section 42 identifies the time periods after which different applicants, including foster parents and step parents, may apply for an adoption order.

If the adoption is granted, Sam at 18 may apply to access his birth records, his name having been entered on the Adopted Children's Register (s.77). He may apply for information from the adoption agency (s.60) to facilitate access to his original birth certificate and to what his adopters were originally told. He may enter his name on the Adoption Contact Register (s.80), and his relatives' details, if also registered, will be passed to him (Sch.10(21), CA 1989). The right to such information is not absolute and may be withheld where there is a significant risk to safety or of a serious crime being committed (*R v Registrar General, ex parte Smith* [1990]). The Adoption Information and Intermediary Services Regulations 2005 detail how adopted people and birth parents may be assisted to make contact and how adopted people may veto approaches for contact.

Local authorities must provide adoption support services for children, their parents, prospective adopters, and adopted people and their parents, birth parents and former guardians (s.3, ACA 2002). If requested, local authorities must assess their needs for support services, which may include counselling, advice and information, groups, contact mediation, therapy and financial provision to support a placement or facilitate its continuation, for instance by responding to a child's disability or needs following earlier abuse or neglect (s.4). Where assessment identifies needs, the local authority must decide whether to provide support services. Assessments and services may also be provided under community care law (NHS and Community Care Act 1990) and children in need mandates (CA 1989). Where services are provided, a plan must be compiled and reviewed. The Adoption Support Services Regulations 2005 provide further detail of what services may be provided and to whom, including foster parents wishing to adopt, and outline the key elements of assessment and subsequent decision-making. They require the appointment of an adoption support services adviser to give advice and information, and to enable those surrounding an adoption to obtain support.

Observations

Social workers should explore each option systematically, using research findings to evaluate which placements might achieve best outcomes. Careful assessment will be key (Hunt et al., 2008) and a working environment where supervisors appropriately challenge received wisdom regarding each case, and where evidence about a child's health, education, identity, placement history and relationships is not just collected for reviews but actively evaluated to refine care plans. Despite the closer alignment between adoption and child care legislation, there remain anomalies. For instance, a step parent must be married in order to acquire parental responsibility from a child's birth parents (s.112, ACA 2002). However, an unmarried step parent may adopt a child and acquire parental responsibility.

Wayne

Wayne, aged 16, is at the police station again, suspected of having committed motoring offences. The police have requested that a social worker attends as an 'appropriate adult'. Wayne has periodically been accommodated by the local authority because of his mother's, health needs (Evelyn has multiple sclerosis) and her difficulty managing his behaviour. At other times, he has acted as her main carer. Concerns about his mental well-being have been expressed by various professionals because of the violence he sometimes displays towards his mother. What legislation applies here?

Youth justice

'Appropriate adult' provisions apply to juveniles, people with learning difficulties or mental illness, and anyone who appears unable to understand the significance of questioning. Parents (unless the child objects or has admitted the offence to them, or they are a victim, co-accused or witness), guardians, social workers or other responsible adults independent of the police, may act as appropriate adults. If parents refuse, cannot be contacted or are unavailable or mentally disordered, a social worker may act, unless the child has admitted the offence to them. Training is important if Wayne's interests are to be safeguarded effectively (s.38(4), Crime and Disorder Act 1998) at the police station. Case law illustrates dangers when parents misunderstand the role (*R v Jefferson* [1994]) or have a poor relationship with the young person (*DPP v Blake* [1989]).

Wayne may be detained without charge for 24 hours, extendable by a superintendent or above to 36 hours if the investigation concerns an arrestable offence (s.7, CJA 2003), and by magistrates to a maximum of 96 hours (s.41, Police and Criminal Evidence Act 1984 (PACE 1984)). Wayne must not be interviewed or make a statement without an appropriate adult present unless any delay would involve immediate risk of harm to people or property, and then only until that risk has been averted. The custody officer has discretion regarding making a record of Wayne's property (s.8, CJA 2003), so the appropriate adult should clarify both with Wayne and the custody officer what has been brought with him to the police station.

Before interviewing, the police must attempt to inform the person responsible for Wayne's welfare of the detention (s.57, PACE 1984), including any agency with statutory responsibility for him. Wayne's right to inform someone, and to legal advice before questioning, may be withheld for up to 36 hours if this would alert others, interfere with evidence collection, or risk physical injury to others and the investigation concerns a serious arrestable offence. Wayne has a right to read the codes of practice governing detention and the custody record. The appropriate adult should discuss these rights with Wayne privately and call a solicitor if appropriate, even if he has refused legal advice. The appropriate adult's role is to:

1 Ascertain whether Wayne is detained and the reasons.
2 Note the time of arrest and the request to attend.
3 Inspect the custody record.
4 Actively participate to ensure interviews are fair and facilitate communication between Wayne and the police.
5 Ensure no informal statements are made.
6 Identify the custody officer who makes decisions about detention and charge, is independent of the investigation, and reviews detention after six hours and every nine hours subsequently, deciding whether or not to charge Wayne. The appropriate adult should be present when these decisions are taken.
7 Be present when Wayne is cautioned or charged and ensure his understanding.
8 Read the written statement of the interview and discuss errors.

9   (If a social worker) not consent to treatment, the taking of samples or fingerprinting unless Wayne is in care by court order, but be present during intimate or strip searches, unless he objects and the appropriate adult agrees, or when Wayne is asked to consent to any identification procedure (ss.54–59, CJPOA 1994).

10 Be present when Wayne considers whether to give a sample to test for Class A drugs (s.5, CJA 2003). This provision applies to those over 14 charged with particular offences, including theft, robbery and taking vehicles without consent, where the police believe Class A drugs might have caused or contributed to the offence; the results may inform bail and sentencing decisions, or advice about treatment. The appropriate adult should consider whether the young person has made a fully informed decision in the event of deciding not to co-operate, which may result in prosecution.

11 Ensure Wayne's proper treatment, including meals, breaks, and attendance by the police surgeon if he shows physical or mental health needs.

12 Check the reason for any extensions to detention, make representations, and note the rank of police officers involved.

In court, evidence obtained unfairly may be excluded (s.78, PACE 1984). The prosecution must prove that evidence or confessions were not obtained unreasonably when an appropriate adult has not been present (s.76; *R v Delaney* [1989]).

Once charged, Wayne must be released on bail, possibly with conditions, unless charged with a serious offence (murder, manslaughter, rape, sexual assault) (NACRO, 2008a) or of no certain address, or evidence exists that he might not attend court, or release would interfere with investigations, or detention is necessary for his protection or to prevent injury to others or property loss/damage (s.38, PACE 1984). Equally, bail may be refused to prevent him committing an offence or because it would be in his own interests. If bail is refused, the custody officer must record reasons for Wayne's detention. Wayne must not be placed in a cell unless it is impracticable to supervise him elsewhere. He must be transferred to local authority accommodation (s.20, CA 1989; sch.13(52), CA 1989) unless weather, industrial action, or time of day prevents this, or for young people over 12 because secure accommodation is unavailable and available accommodation would not protect the public from serious harm (NACRO, 2008a). Serious harm refers to violent or sexual offences causing physical and/or psychological injury. A local authority receiving a request to accommodate Wayne from police detention must do so irrespective of the area he comes from (s.38(6), PACE 1984) and must have reasonable systems to respond to requests for secure accommodation (*R (M) v Gateshead MBC* [2006]). The local authority has discretion whether to accede to a police request that Wayne be placed in secure accommodation. On being accommodated, Wayne becomes looked after (CA 1989) and potentially eligible for leaving care support.

After charge, the police may give a reprimand for a first offence that is not too serious. A warning may be given where a reprimand has been issued previously or for a more serious first offence (ss.65 and 66, CDA 1998). Only in exceptional circumstances for minor offences can a warning be repeated, providing two years have elapsed (s.65(3), CDA 1998). The young person must admit the offence and have no previous convictions, an appropriate adult should be present, and parents should provide informed consent. If convicted within the next two years, a higher sentence is likely. The police must explain this and also outline the evidence they regard as sufficient to charge (sch.9(2), CJIA 2008), so that the young person can seek advice about whether to accept the reprimand/warning. When a warning has been given, the police should refer the young person to the youth offending team for assessment and subsequent participation in a rehabilitation programme (s.66, CDA 1998). Reprimands and final warnings may be given at places other than police stations, thereby allowing them to be issued as part of a restorative conference with parents and victims present (Criminal Justice and Court Services Act 2000). This system has been criticized for inflexibility, reducing the potential of diversion, and locating decision-making with the police rather than a multi-agency framework (NACRO, 2006).

The CJIA 2008 (s.48 and sch.9) introduced the youth conditional caution for young offenders where they have not been convicted previously of an offence, have admitted guilt and consented to the caution. The conditions, which must punish the offender as well as facilitate rehabilitation and reparation, may include financial penalty and/or requirement to attend a specified place at directed times for a maximum of 20 hours. The young person can be prosecuted for the original offence if terms are not completed satisfactorily. In this event, and in any court appearance for further offences, a conditional discharge may only be given in exceptional circumstances.

Local authorities must provide support for young people awaiting trial or sentence (s.38, CDA 1998). Normally, young people appear before the Youth Court except for very serious offences or when charged alongside an adult (s.90, PCCSA 2000). If a young person appears in Crown Court, the formality of this setting must be reduced (*V v UK* [1999]). At court, a parent or guardian, or social worker if Wayne is in care or in local authority accommodation, must attend (CJA 1991, s.56).

The local authority has a duty, unless it believes it unnecessary, to investigate and provide a report to court (s.9, CYPA 1969). Wayne should receive a copy of the pre-sentence report unless this would expose him to significant harm (s.159, CJA 2003). His parents should also receive a copy but with the same proviso. Section 156, CJA 2003, requires the court to obtain a pre-sentence report (unless a previous report exists and can be considered) and consider its evaluation of sentencing options where custodial or community sentences are being considered. The report must evaluate offence seriousness, drawing on aggravating and mitigating factors.

Wayne may decline to answer questions out of court and is a non-compellable witness in his own defence (s.35(4), CJPOA 1994). However, inferences may be drawn if Wayne, under caution or charged, fails to mention facts which he then relies on at trial, or refuses to answer questions or give evidence at trial (ss.34–37, CJPOA 1994). Police officers should outline the allegations to be answered (Article 6, ECHR). Section 58 (YJCEA 1999) amends the silence provisions so that inferences cannot be drawn where Wayne has not been able to seek legal advice at the police station. Wayne cannot be convicted if the only evidence is inferences drawn from his silence (*R v Condron* [1997]) and adverse inferences should only be reached if the sole explanation is that Wayne is unable to answer the allegations (*R v Betts and Hall* [2001]).

The *doli incapax* principle, whereby a court had to be satisfied that children had committed an offence and knew this to be wrong, was abolished by the Crime and Disorder Act 1998. The UK age of criminal responsibility is 10, amongst the lowest in Europe, continuing to draw criticism on the UK government's implementation of the Convention on the Rights of the Child (NACRO, 2008c).

Section 9 (CJIA 2008) clarifies that when sentencing the principal aim is to prevent offending or reoffending (s.37, CDA 1998). The child's welfare (s.44, CYPA 1933) remains a consideration but not the principal aim. Furthermore, the purposes of sentencing are to punish, reform and rehabilitate offenders, to protect the public and to enable offenders to make reparations to their victims. Where a young person pleads guilty and is convicted for the first time, the court will make a referral order where either custody or absolute discharge are unnecessary (s.16, PCCSA 2000) unless for more minor offences a restorative justice intervention, such as a fine or reparation order, are more appropriate (Referral Order (Amendment of Referral Conditions) Regulations 2003). Responsibility then passes to a panel constituted by the youth offending team to negotiate a behaviour contract for a period between 3 and 12 months, specified by the court. Failure to agree a contract will result in a return to court for sentencing. Section 35 (CJIA 2008) extends the discretion of courts to make referral orders when young people have one previous conviction for which a referral order was not made, and in exceptional circumstances to make a second order on recommendation from a youth offending team. Section 36 allows a court to revoke a referral order because of good progress but also to extend an order of less than 12 months by up to three months.

Section 172 (CJA 2003) provides for a sentencing guidelines council, with the purpose of improving fairness, consistency and effectiveness of court disposals. Various sentences are available:

1 Absolute discharge, a conviction for the purposes of determining offence seriousness (s.12, PCCSA 2000).

2 Conditional discharge, for a maximum of three years (s.12, PCCSA 2000). If Wayne re-offends, he will also be sentenced for present offences.

3 Deferred sentence (for a maximum of six months) (s.1, PCCSA 2000), if Wayne consents and a change in circumstances is imminent. The court may add conditions, if Wayne consents, such as residence, reparation or activity (s.287, CJA 2003).

4 Fines, to maximum of £250 (10–13 years) or £1000 (over 14) in the Youth Court (s.135, PCCSA 2000). Parents may be held responsible for payment (s.137, PCCSA 2000). Courts must consider ability to pay and offence seriousness (s.138, PCCSA 2000). Local authorities can be ordered to pay the fines of young people who are the subject of care orders.

5 Where the young person is under 16, binding over of parent/guardian for a maximum of three years. This maximum period is shortened if the young person would reach 18 in a period shorter than three years (s.150, PCCSA 2000). Parental/guardian consent (with fines for unreasonable refusal) is required. As they will be required to exercise proper control, the court must assess whether they can exert any influence over the young person before making such an order.

6 Compensation orders, with the court giving reasons where it has decided against making such an order (s.130, PCCSA 2000). The views of parents must be sought before an order is made (s.137, PCCSA 2000) and their responses towards their child's behaviour will also be influential (*R v J-B* [2004]). Where a local authority holds parental responsibility, they can be ordered to pay compensation if their actions, being unreasonable and short of the standard expected, have contributed to the offences taking place (*D (A Minor) v. DPP* [1995]; *Bedfordshire County Council v DPP* [1996]).

7 Reparation orders (s.73, PCCSA 2000) following a written report specifying the type of work for which the offender is suitable, the attitudes of any victim, and proposals. Reparation may be made directly to the victim, or to someone affected by the offence, or to the community. The consent of victims and those affected is required. Reparation cannot exceed work of more than 24 hours, the requirements being proportionate to offence seriousness. Failure to comply may result in resentencing.

8 Youth rehabilitation order (YRO) (s.1, CJIA 2008). This replaces the range of community orders that developed after 1998 for offenders below 16 (CDA 1998, PCCSA 2000, CJA 2003), including action plans, supervision, attendance centre and curfew orders, and additional community orders for young offenders aged 16 and 17 (CJA 2003). To the new order may be attached requirements – activity, supervision, unpaid work (16/17 year olds), programmes, attendance centre, prohibited activity, curfew, exclusion, residence (16/17 year olds), local authority residence, mental health treatment, drug treatment, drug testing (if 14 or over), intoxicating substance treatment, education, electronic monitoring, intensive supervision, fostering. Schedule 1 (CJIA 2008) outlines which requirements may be combined and the specific elements of each. It also requires courts to avoid conflict with religious belief and education, and to specify by when requirements must have been met (to a maximum of three years). There are no restrictions on the number of occasions that Wayne could be sentenced to a YRO with the menu of requirements adapted as required. A YRO with intensive supervision or a YRO with a fostering requirement may only be made where the offence is punishable by imprisonment, and where it and associated offences are so serious that a custodial sentence would otherwise be appropriate. Where the offender is under 15 on conviction, the court must regard them as a persistent offender (s.100, PCCSA 2000).

9 Detention and training order (s.100, PCCSA 2000), for young people over 12 (if under 15, they must be persistent offenders) who are convicted of an imprisonable offence so serious that only a custodial sentence can be justified or where, in the case of a violent or sexual offence, custody is justified to protect the public from harm. Additionally, custody may follow refusal to agree to requirements within a community sentence, where consent is required, or to comply with supplying a sample for a pre-sentence drug test (s.152, CJA 2003). The maximum length is two years, with the court designating a period of between 4 and 24 months. Custodial sentences should be for the shortest term commensurate with offence seriousness (s.153,

CJA 2003). Normally, half the period will be spent in detention and half under supervision.

10 Longer-term detention for murder, where the court will set the minimum tariff to be served (s.90, PCCSA 2000), or for other grave crimes that for adults carry a penalty of at least 14 years (including manslaughter, rape, grievous bodily harm with intent, residential burglary, aggravated vehicle-taking resulting in death, death by dangerous driving (ss.283–7, CJA 2003)), or are sexual offences where the penalty for adults is less than 14 years (Sexual Offences Act 2003), or are firearm offences committed by those aged 16 or 17 (s.289, CJA 2003; s.91, PCCSA 2000).

Wayne could also be sentenced in Crown Court to longer detention for offences of a violent or sexual nature, specified in sch.15, CJA 2003, if the court assesses him as dangerous. The court must be satisfied of a significant risk both that Wayne will commit further such offences and that he will cause serious harm to others (*R v Lang* [2005]), but also that he should spend at least two years in detention when making an indeterminate detention for public protection (s.226, CJA 2003) or four years when making an extended sentence (s.228) of custody followed by supervision in the community (ss.14 and 16, CJIA 2008). Which sentence depends on whether Wayne has committed a serious specified offence carrying a maximum penalty of life imprisonment, other serious offences, or non-serious specified offences.

MAPPA arrangements were discussed earlier (Sharon's case). Designed to ensure effective multi-agency working regarding the supervision and surveillance of those who present a high risk of serious harm to others, they extend to young people (CJCSA 2000; CJA 2003).

A court may depart from a presumption of bail, especially where offences have been committed whilst on bail, a bail condition is broken, or there is a risk of absconding, offending or interference with justice (s.38(6), PACE 1984). A court may impose conditions to bail if risks exist but these are not so substantial as to deny bail. Conditions should be exact, effective and enforceable to prevent offending and ensure attendance at court, and may include curfew and, if aged at least 12, electronic monitoring through tagging (CJPA 2001; CJIA 2008). Prior to sentencing Wayne could be remanded to local authority accommodation (s.21(2) and sch.12(26), CA 1989) which, depending on assessment of the circumstances and the need to prevent offending and ensure court attendance, could mean placement with foster carers, family members or in residential care, and arrested if he breaches the conditions of his remand (NACRO, 2008b). The court may specify with whom Wayne should not be placed. Wayne's parents would retain parental responsibility but he becomes a looked after child.

The court may additionally add a security requirement to the remand to local authority accommodation, giving reasons, where Wayne is over 12, charged with or convicted of violent, sexual or other offences imprisonable for at least 14 years, *or* has a history of absconding and offending when remanded, *and* to protect the public from serious harm (s.97, CDA 1998). The court must consult the local authority. This gives youth offending teams the opportunity to address court concerns through offering intensive supervision and support programmes. In respect of boys aged 15 and 16, it also enables practitioners to assess vulnerability (physical and emotional immaturity, and risk of self-harm) to inform court decisions about remand to custody or to local authority accommodation with a security requirement (s.98, CDA 1998). When considering options, the court may request a local authority report specifying where Wayne would be placed if remanded to accommodation (s.90, Anti-Social Behaviour Act 2003).

Equally, a child bailed on condition that they reside where directed can be subject to a secure accommodation order (*Re C (a minor) (Secure Accommodation Order: Bail)* [1994]) where charged with or convicted of violent, sexual or other offences imprisonable for adults for at least 14 years, or with previous convictions for violent offences, and where secure accommodation is necessary to prevent him absconding or injuring himself or others (NACRO, 2008b). The welfare checklist (s.1(3), CA 1989) does not apply, but the matters contained therein are not irrelevant (*Hereford and Worcester County Council v S* [1993]). When remanded to local authority accommodation, whether or not secure, Wayne becomes looked after. His case should be reviewed, overseen by an IRO (DfES, 2004b), with a view to minimizing his risk of re-offending, providing suitable accommodation and planning for the future.

Assessment

Sentences will be determined by reference to offence seriousness. A guilty plea will reduce seriousness (s.152, PCCSA 2000) whilst racial aggravation will increase it (s.153). Recent offending (s.143, CJA 2003), crime where harm caused was intended and foreseeable, and committing offences on bail (s.151, PCCSA 2000) will increase seriousness, as will behaviour involving incitement to hatred on grounds of sexuality (CJIA 2008).

Courts will consider aggravating and mitigating factors, drawing on sentencing guidelines and pre-sentence reports. Reports should fully analyze the offence, using the ASSET framework (YJB, 2004). This identifies twelve risks and a scale that links their association to offending in a particular case. Thus, reports should consider Wayne's living arrangements, family and personal relationships, education/training/ employment, neighbourhood, lifestyle, substance use, physical health, emotional and mental health, perception of self and others, thinking and behaviour, attitude towards the offence and motivation to change. The current offence, previous offending and the age of entry into the youth justice system are also relevant.

As CJIA 2008 permits sentences other than those for public protection in cases involving specified offences, even where young people have been assessed as presenting significant risks to the public, this further illustrates that pre-sentence reports should evaluate options (NACRO, 2008d).

Secure accommodation

A looked after child may be placed in secure accommodation if there is a history of absconding, the child is likely to abscond and suffer significant harm or, if not in secure accommodation, is likely to injure themselves or others (s.25, CA 1989). This power may be exercised for up to 72 hours without court authority. Otherwise, a court order is necessary, for up to three months on first application and six months thereafter (Children (Secure Accommodation) Regulations 1991). Wayne's welfare is relevant but not the paramount consideration for the court. The welfare checklist (s.1(3), CA 1989) does not apply here (*Re M (a minor) (secure accommodation order)* [1994]). The court must appoint a Children's Guardian unless satisfied that this is unnecessary, and must specify the detention time limit.

The use of secure accommodation does not contravene the right to liberty (Article 5, ECHR) if its purpose is educational supervision (*Re K (secure accommodation order: right to liberty)* [2001]). However, procedural fairness (Article 6, ECHR) requires that Wayne is informed promptly of any application, has adequate time and facilities to prepare a defence, has legal assistance and can cross-examine witnesses (*Re M (a child) (secure accommodation)* [2001]). A review panel of three people, one of whom must be independent of the local authority, evaluates whether the criteria for detention still apply, the placement is necessary, and any other accommodation is appropriate (DfES, 2004b). (The guidance (DfES, 2004b) recommends that the person who is independent of the local authority is not the Independent Reviewing Officer, if they are employed by the local authority.) Policy guidance also emphasizes that secure accommodation should be a placement of choice rather than last resort, where a safe and secure placement meets the child's needs (DfES, 2008). Placement must follow a needs assessment rather than be triggered by resource shortage.

Local authorities must take reasonable steps to encourage children not to commit criminal offences and to avoid the need for secure accommodation placement (s.17 and sch.2(7), CA 1989).

Regulating behaviour

Additional measures are available to regulate Wayne's behaviour and hold his parents responsible. Courts may make parenting orders (s.8, CDA 1998) alongside other sentences, including anti-social behaviour orders, to help parents deal with their child's behaviour through attending counselling (maximum three months), preventing their child from associating with particular people or being in certain areas (maximum twelve months), and attending a youth offender panel meeting when a referral order has been made (sch.34, CJA 2003). A parenting order will normally be made following sentencing, other than for a referral order, and the making of an anti-social behaviour order (s.85, ASBA 2003) for young people under 16, and the court must give reasons if it does not do so. Section 26, ASBA 2003, also allows free-standing parenting orders where it appears on application from a Youth Offending Team or local education authority that a child has engaged in criminal or anti-social behaviour, or been excluded from school, and a parenting order would assist in preventing further such behaviour.

Parenting orders may be made where the court also makes, in respect of children below the age of criminal responsibility who have committed acts that would otherwise constitute an offence, a child safety order on application from a local authority (s.11, CDA 1998). Section 60 (CA 2004) extends the maximum duration of this order from three to twelve months whilst also removing the sanction of a care order as a possible outcome of breach. The court may attach requirements, such as specified activities or prohibition on locations or associations with others, which will be overseen by a local authority supervisor. A similar extension of youth justice below the age of 10 applies to parental compensation orders (s.144 and sch.10, SOCPA 2005). Compensation may be sought, on application from the local authority, where voluntary reparation or compensation measures have been unsuccessful, where children below the age of criminal responsibility have behaved in a manner that would otherwise be deemed theft or criminal damage, or where they have behaved anti-socially. The court will make an order if it believes that this will prevent re-occurrence.

ASBA 2003 (s.25) also creates parenting contracts where children are experiencing difficulties at school or engaging in criminal or anti-social behaviour. Youth Offending Teams and other agencies provide support to assist parents in dealing with the behaviour of their children.

Wayne's behaviour may additionally be regulated by anti-social behaviour orders (ASBOs) (s1, CDA 1998). Applications are normally made by the police or local authority, in consultation with each other, where behaviour has caused serious and persistent alarm, distress or harassment, and an order is necessary to prevent repetition (*R (McCann) v Crown Court at Manchester* [2002]). The burden of proof is the civil standard, a balance of probabilities, but breach is a criminal offence. Interim orders are possible for ASBOs made on application (s.65, PRA 2002) and on conviction (s.139, SOCPA 2005). The court may impose prohibitions designed to prevent further behaviour; these must be proportionate, enforceable, precise and clear (*R (W) v DPP* [2005]; *M v DPP* [2007]). Orders must last longer than two years and may be indefinite. Normally an individual support order will also be made (s.322, CJA 2003), for a maximum of six months, designed to assist Wayne as a counterbalance to the prohibitions in the ASBO.

Wayne may also, on application by the Crown Prosecution Service, be made subject to an ASBO following conviction for an offence that contains an anti-social component (ASBA 2003).

Dispersal orders allow police officers to designate areas where anti-social behaviour has proved problematic and disperse groups if their behaviour is causing people to feel, or likely to result in them feeling, intimidated, harassed, alarmed or distressed (s.30, ASBA 2003). Force may not be used to effect removal (*R (W) v Commissioner of Police of the Metropolis and Another* [2005]). Finally, penalty notices for disorderly behaviour may be issued by police officers (s.87, ASBA 2003) if they believe a child or young person has committed a penalty offence, such as wasting police time, misbehaviour with fireworks, or offences relating to alcohol. If the penalty is paid within 21 days, the matter is closed. The young person may elect to appear in court instead.

Leaving care

All young people qualify for advice and assistance from the local authority (s.24, CA 1989) to promote their welfare when they cease to be looked after. The CLCA 2000 strengthens this with respect to three categories of care leavers (Children (Leaving Care) (England) Regulations 2001):

- eligible children: those in care aged 16 and 17 who have been looked after for more than 13 weeks since the age of 14 (including periods since 16 *(R (Berhe) v Hillingdon LBC* [2003]);
- relevant children: those aged 16 and 17 who meet the criteria of eligible children but have left care, including those detained in young offender institutions or secure training centres;
- former relevant children: those who before reaching 18 were either eligible or relevant.

The responsible local authority is the last one to look after Wayne as an eligible or relevant young person, regardless of where he might live with a pathway plan. The Act creates a duty to assess and meet the care and support needs of eligible, relevant and former relevant young people. Regulations (CLCER 2001) and policy guidance (DH, 2001e) itemize the principles that should underpin provision and the roles of key agencies and specify a timetable for assessment of needs, normally within three months, and its content – Wayne's need for care and accommodation, his health and development, the support available from his family, his financial needs and skills for independent living, and education, training and employment. Wayne's views should be sought and he should receive a copy of the assessment and any subsequent plan. The level of financial support should be above that provided by social security benefits.

All eligible, relevant and former relevant young people must have a pathway plan, until they are at least 21, covering education, training, career plans and support. Regulations (CLCER 2001) require review at least every six months. The contents of the pathway plan are specified (DH, 2001e) and include the contact and support to be provided, accommodation, education, training and/or employment, support for family and personal relationships, skill development, financial support, health considerations, and contingency plans. Planning should consider Wayne's wishes and feelings. The pathway plan should be reviewed if a young person enters the youth justice system. When in custody, the IRO should chair planning and review meetings.

All eligible, relevant and former relevant young people must have a young person's adviser to help compile, implement and review the pathway plan, to provide advice and support, and to keep in touch until at least the age of 21. Policy guidance further amplifies this role (DH, 2001e), which has been extended (s.22, CYPA 2008) to include former relevant children who inform the local authority that they intend to pursue education and training when previously they were ineligible because of being over 21 and having completed or left a programme. The Act requires that this young person's needs are assessed, a plan prepared and assistance provided as necessary to support education and training, even after the age of 25. Local authorities must provide vacation support, including accommodation, during breaks from further or higher education, and assist with the costs of employment, education and training.

Local authorities must arrange advocacy services for children in care or leaving care who wish to make a complaint (s.119, ACA 2002). The functions of the Children's Commissioner extend to young people between 18 and 21 who have learning disabilities or have been looked after by local authorities after the age of 16 (CA 2004). The duties on agencies to co-operate to improve young people's well-being, and to safeguard and promote their welfare (ss.10 and 11, CA 2004), apply to young people aged 18 and 19 receiving leaving care services.

Up to half of those in young offender institutions have been in local authority care. Concerns remain that local authorities are failing in their duties to young people leaving care. Local authorities must complete proper assessment of needs and pathway plans for disabled children in care approaching 18 (*P v Newham LBC* [2004]). Personal advisers must act as advocates, and be separate from those who complete statutory assessments and plans for leaving care. The contents of plans must be adequate and timetables laid out in regulations must be met (*R (J by his litigation friend MW) v Caerphilly CBC* [2005]). Young people can feel swept along by the pace of change, with little time to adapt to independent living and insufficient contact with social workers (Barn et al., 2005), even though they should not be discharged from care placements prematurely but be properly prepared, supported and ready to move on (DfES, 2007). Young people are given too little information about their entitlements under the 2000 Act (Barn et al., 2005), the resource position and culture within social services resulting in variable but modest responses to leaving care legislation (Broad, 2003, 2005). Assessment and planning may be improving, coupled with support for education and training. However, financial support is often minimal, health needs poorly addressed, and duties concerning provision of needs assessments, pathways plans and personal advisers not always implemented. Multi-agency working, especially between social services and housing departments, is patchy and the standard of accommodation variable. Despite the legislation, the importance of young people feeling cared for and evidence that practical and emotional support, stability and relationships with carers can make a difference (Stein, 2005), vulnerability and loneliness too often characterize this important transition.

Housing

The HA 2002 requires that all young people aged 16 and 17, and those between 18 and 21 when leaving care, are vulnerable and in priority need for housing (Homeless (Priority Need for Accommodation) (England) Order 2002). The Act also advises that young people aged 16 and 17 should not be placed in bed and breakfast accommodation. However, a young person aged over 16 may also request to be accommodated (s.20, CA 1989). Moreover, s.17 (CA 1989) includes the duty to assess housing need and the power to make provision (s.116, ACA 2002). The interface between the two jurisdictions remains particularly complex.

Local authorities must take account of *future* needs when young people are over 16, accommodated informally by friends and wishing to be accommodated under s.20 (CA 1989) (*Re T (accommodation by local authority)* [1995]). An imprisoned young offender permitted early release should be considered homeless if he had no accommodation (*R (B) v Southwark LBC* [2003]). Detention in a cell does not qualify as accommodation. Local authorities cannot postpone a decision in order to avoid a duty. Mediation between young people and parents, which may enable a parent's decision to exclude a child from home to be evaluated, should be encouraged only if there is no danger to either party (*Robinson v Hammersmith and Fulham LBC* [2006]). An unreasonable refusal to return home might entitle a local authority to provide assistance under s.17 rather than s.20 (CA 1989), resulting in failure to qualify for enhanced leaving care provision (*R (M) v Barnet LBC* [2008]).

Case law suggests that, to resolve the complexity of the interface, housing departments should take the lead, through a protocol with children's services, regarding homeless young people aged 16 and 17, providing interim accommodation (s.188, HA 1996) pending full assessment using the framework (DH, 2000c). The wishes and feelings of young people should be considered, which includes informing them that s.20 provision acts as a gateway to leaving care services. Young people will not automatically be entitled to s.20 (CA 1989) accommodation although a breakdown in relationships with parents will be significant in decision-making. However, s.20 provision should not be denied simply to pass responsibility to housing officers (*R (M) v Hammersmith and Fulham LBC* [2008]) and to protect resources (*R (S) v Sutton LBC* [2007]).

Assessment (DH, 2000c), including the young person's wishes and feelings, should also be completed prior to deciding whether accommodation duties should be met under s.20 or s.17, CA 1989 (LAC(2003)13). The guidance distinguishes between children who require accommodation and those who require help to obtain it, indicating that assessment should be based on need without regard to financial consequences. Section 20 will be appropriate if Wayne has been abandoned, has no-one with parental responsibility or such a person cannot provide care and accommodation. Local authorities may lawfully conclude that resourceful young homeless people require help with finding accommodation and support their negotiations with housing officials, rather than provide accommodation directly, especially if they do not wish social workers to be involved, understand tenancy agreements and can make housing benefit claims (*R (G) v Southwark LBC* [2009]). However, councils must not bypass their duties under s.20, CA 1989, for those young people whose needs extend beyond housing.

Wayne's mother could find that she loses her council tenancy because of his anti-social behaviour (*Manchester City Council v Higgins* [2005]).

Disabled parents and young carers

The need for support with parenting roles should form part of assessment for community care provision to adults (DH, 2002b). Thus, Wayne's mother should have her needs assessed (s.47, NHSCCA1990; s.4, DPA1986). Disabled parents report negative assumptions of their parenting capacities by social workers (Goodinge 2000); it is important that assessment takes a holistic view of family needs, and that services seek to support and empower Evelyn to continue in the parenting role she wishes to play. A care plan for Evelyn could provide services to meet her personal care needs, but also household tasks and resources to promote her parenting of Wayne, drawing on the mandates outlined in William's case (Chapter 4). The plan should anticipate the need for flexible provision to respond to what may be varying levels of need at different times. Equally, application may be made under the HGRA 1996 for adaptations to the home to ease and facilitate physical mobility.

The children of disabled parents should not automatically be treated as children in need under CA 1989, although once community care services are in place it may be appropriate to conduct an assessment of Wayne's needs if they are not fully met by Evelyn with the support of community care services provided to her. However, Wayne has roles in the family that mean he could be viewed as a young carer (see William's case); guidance (DH, 2000d, 2005b) is clear that his needs and wishes should be considered under CA 1989, with children's and adult services working together to assess family circumstances and relationships, to ensure Evelyn is receiving services and Wayne's future is protected by reducing his carer responsibilities. Further services to support them as a family could be provided under s.17 and sch.2 (CA 1989), drawing appropriately from other agencies (s.27, CA 1989; s.10, CA 2004) and should promote the key outcomes for children specified in CA 2004. Further detail on legislation for young carers is given in William's case.

Mental health

Mental health law was covered in Amy's case (Chapter 4). However, the position of children under the MHA 1983, as amended by the MHA 2007, should be noted in several respects.

Children aged 16/17 with capacity may consent to their own admission and treatment, even if someone with parental responsibility refuses (s.131(3)). Similarly, if they refuse, they may not be admitted or treated on the consent of someone with parental responsibility (s.131(4)). However, their refusal may in certain circumstances be overridden by a court. Children aged 16/17 without capacity may be admitted and treated in circumstances not amounting to deprivation of liberty (s.5/6, MCA 2005). If deprivation of liberty is required, then either the MHA 1983 or the CA 1989 will be used, as the MCA deprivation of liberty provisions are not applicable to people under 18.

Children under 16 who are Gillick competent can consent to informal admission and consent to treatment, but if they refuse their refusal can be overruled by the Court, by someone with parental responsibility or by the local authority for a child in care. The MHA Code (DH, 2008d), however, notes that in an era of greater autonomy accorded to young people, professionals should be cautious about relying on the consent of someone with parental responsibility. Fennell (2007) contends that, in such circumstances, detention under the MHA 1983 should be used.

Children under 16 who are not Gillick competent may be admitted on the consent of a person with parental responsibility, provided the decision falls within the 'zone of parental control' (DH, 2008d). Where decisions fall outside such a zone (perhaps because they are particularly invasive or even experimental), the Code indicates that the MHA should be used, or authority sought from a court.

Specific issue orders (s.8, CA 1989) can be sought on issues relating to treatment for mental disorder, or the court can also be asked to exercise its inherent jurisdiction (DH, 2008d).

Section 131A requires that children admitted are accommodated (from April 2010) 'in an environment that is suitable for their age'. Section 116 requires the local authority for a child on a care order admitted to hospital to arrange visits to the child on their behalf, and to take any other steps that could be expected of a parent of a child in such circumstances.

Sections 85/86 (CA 1989) require notification to social services if a child is accommodated (such as in a hospital) for more than 3 months, with the local authority having a duty to ensure that the child's welfare is safeguarded.

Broad (2005) suggests that young people's emotional health needs are poorly addressed. There are high rates of mental disorder amongst young offenders (NACRO, 2004) but the health professionals within youth offending teams may not have mental health expertise and accessing child and adolescent mental health services can prove difficult. Wayne's mental health may also affect his ability to participate in court proceedings, to instruct a lawyer, and to understand wrongdoing – minimum requirements for a fair trial (*SC v UK* [2004]; *R (TP) v West London Youth Court* [2005]). The Mental Capacity Act 2005 principles should also be considered, therefore, if Wayne appears in court (NACRO, 2007a). Equally, children with mental distress are also children in need (s.17, CA 1989). Provisions therein, covered in earlier case studies, may be a useful alternative to court proceedings.

Observations

Those involved in administering criminal justice must avoid discrimination on grounds of race, sex or other grounds (s.95(1)(b), CJA 1991). However, young black people continue to be over-represented in the criminal justice system, for example in remands to local authority secure accommodation, as a result of social exclusion, socio-economic deprivation, and the operation of the system itself (NACRO, 2007b). Young people also report racial discrimination and prejudice in care (Barn et al., 2005). All public authorities should adopt a strategic approach to tackling over-representation, for instance in school exclusions or custodial sentences, as part of their duties under the RRAA 2000.

Wayne is both a child in need and a young offender. However, statutory duties relating to young offenders as children in need have been given less prominence than have attempts to control young people's behaviour (*R (Howard League for Penal Reform) v Secretary of State for the Home Department and the Department of Health (interested party)* [2003]). Moreover, it is questionable whether these legal rules effectively address the causes of crime. Noteworthy then is s.6, EIA 2006, which requires local authorities to ensure sufficient positive leisure-time activities for young people. The duty to promote a young person's educational achievement (s.52, CA 2004) equally applies to all children.

The increasing complexity of legal rules relating to youth justice, and their divergence from legislation addressing children's well-being, makes it difficult for practitioners to remain up-to-date and to balance public protection against individual rights, and the welfare of a child against community safety, in each case. Such issues are highlighted by the naming and shaming of young people made the subject of anti-social behaviour orders (*R (Stanley and Others) v Commissioner of Police of the Metropolis and Another* [2004]) and by the conflict of interest when a local authority applies for an anti-social behaviour order in respect of a child in its care (*R (M) v Sheffield Magistrates Court* [2004]).

The United Nations remains critical of UK compliance with the UNCRC (UN, 2008); children's welfare is not paramount, detention is not merely a last resort and use of ASBOs is growing (NACRO, 2008c). Concerns about lack of care in institutions, the vulnerability of young people who are detained, the increasing use of detention and the failure to embed human rights have been intensified by the decision to quash the government's introduction of new rules on restraint (*R (C) v The Secretary of State for Justice* [2008]), by failure to identify the needs of young people and provide appropriate services (*R (M) v Hammersmith and Fulham LBC* [2008]) and the European Court's decision (*S and Marper v UK* [2008]) that retaining fingerprints and DNA when suspects are acquitted is a violation of Article 8, ECHR.

Istvan

> Istvan presents as an unaccompanied asylum seeking child on arrival at the local airport. There is some doubt as to his age as he has arrived without any documentation and is somewhat vague about his previous circumstances.

By virtue of being a child, Istvan becomes the responsibility of local authority children's services rather than the National Asylum Support Service (NASS). Provisions in the Children Act 1989, for instance ascertaining and giving due consideration to his wishes and feelings, therefore apply, as do the five outcomes relating to healthy development, safety, contribution and achievement, enshrined in CA 2004 (s.10). Central to his well-being are protection from maltreatment, prevention of impairment to development, safe and effective care, and provision of life chances through which to enter adulthood (DfES, 2005a). The ECHR, integrated into UK law by the HRA 1998, will also apply; articles 3, 6 and 8 will be especially relevant.

Istvan is a child in need (s.17, CA 1989) but accessing services may not prove straightforward. The first question may be his age, especially if he has arrived with limited documentation and has difficulty explaining his history. Particular care and sensitivity will be needed; the possibly traumatic nature of his unsupported arrival may mean that he appears to tell rehearsed stories to placate those in authority (Kohli and Mitchell, 2007). Age must not be determined on appearance alone; background, family circumstances, education history and the credibility of his general chronology will be relevant. The local authority must make its own assessment although it may use information provided by the Home Office. A medical report may be helpful but is not essential if sufficient other information is available. Investigations should be fair (Article 6, ECHR) so the local authority should explain the relevance of interviews to establish his age and the reasons for its decision. Istvan must be allowed to address any matters that might be held against him (*R (B) v Merton LBC* [2003]). In the event of dispute, the court has power to determine his age (*Lambeth LBC v TK* [2008]).

The second issue is whether he should be accommodated under s.20, CA 1989, or provided with services under s.17. Guidance (LAC(2003)13) clarifies that as no-one in the UK has parental responsibility, Istvan should be accommodated under s.20 and have the same standard of care as other children in need. Some local authorities have avoided obligations which then follow, particularly those located in the CLCA 2000 (see Wayne's case). Unaccompanied asylum seeking minors who have been looked after by local authorities are entitled to relevant statutory aftercare provisions. Courts have challenged local authority arguments that services, including accommodation, have been provided under s.17 when, in fact, young people have been accommodated under s.20 (*R (Behre and others) v Hillingdon LBC* [2003]). To qualify for enhanced leaving care services, the required period (13 weeks) does not have to begin before Istvan becomes 16.

The third issue will be placement. Careful matching and respect for diversity are required, alongside encouraging healthy development, promoting educational achievement, and preparation for transition to adulthood (DH, 2002d). However, research suggests that these standards are insufficiently embedded in practice with asylum seeking children (Wade et al., 2005; Chase et al., 2008).

The fourth question will be whether indefinite leave to remain in the UK beyond the age of 18 is given. This is by no means guaranteed. Istvan could be given discretionary leave and humanitarian protection until the age of 18. Uncertainty about his future will complicate planning, which may have to envisage removal from the UK, continued legal disputes, and full refugee status. Should Istvan commit offences, youth justice provisions will apply (see Wayne's case) but he may also become liable to deportation if over 17 (IA 1971).

The fifth issue, if Istvan remains in the UK, will be the interface between local authority leaving care responsibilities and the role of NASS, once he becomes 18. Istvan could remain in his current accommodation, provided through the local authority (Children Leaving Care Regulations 2001), but NASS may seek to include him in their dispersal arrangements for adult asylum seekers. Here, as elsewhere, assessment of his needs, using the framework (DH, 2000c), will be crucial. Otherwise, unless he has needs arising other than as a result of his asylum seeker status, such as disability, Istvan will become the responsibility of NASS. If he has additional needs, then he could become eligible for local authority adult services (see Sardip's case in Chapter 4).

Istvan's case illustrates the limitations of the UK's adoption of United Nations Conventions, for example on children's rights, since these have not been integrated into UK law, unlike the ECHR. The UNCRC requires that unaccompanied child asylum seekers are given special protection and assistance, and provided with care and placements that promote continuity in upbringing and respect for their ethnic, cultural and religious background (Article 20). Other articles amplify this provision with rights to healthy development (Article 6), life free of neglect and abuse (Article 19), psychological recovery services (Article 39) and an adequate standard of living (Article 27). Article 22 requires that Istvan receives protection and humanitarian assistance to an adequate standard and the UK has now lifted its reservation on this obligation (UNICEF, 2008). The UNCRC also enshrines principles of the best interest of children, non-discrimination, regular reviews and listening to their views, which find expression also in the Children Act 1989.

However, research does not give a positive picture, although it does provide good practice indicators. For example, unaccompanied asylum seeking children often occupy unsuitable accommodation, experience legal delays in determining their cases, and have limited social contacts. Social supports and family placements can increase levels of achievement and assist children to access services (Broad and Robbins, 2005). Istvan may experience lonelinesss, isolation and anxiety, which impact on his emotional well-being, yet feel reluctant to access support services. However, foster placements can provide essential supports, especially if his relationship with his primary carer is positive. Access to a mentor or support worker is also important, especially if he is not fostered (Chase et al., 2008).

These research findings indicate the need for close multi-agency co-operation, as mandated by s.27, CA 1989, and ss.10 and 11, CA 2004, for instance in securing prompt health care, therapeutic counselling, and access to education and training. However, Istvan may become trapped in disputes about which local authority should assume responsibility. In *R (Liverpool City Council) v Hillingdon LBC* [2008], without any area qualifying as the child's ordinary residence and given his expressed wishes, the local authority where he resided was responsible.

Concluding comments

Once again, a wide range of interlocking legal rules has been covered, in the implementation of which practitioners should be not just technically competent but also critically reflective. The next two chapters address additional legal rules, and their interface with professional values, which will help guide practitioners through the exercise of authority and the complex interplay of issues that each case presents.

putting it into practice

Take the procedures your agency employs for the task of:

- enabling young disabled people to make the transition into adulthood
- protecting children and young people from significant harm
- addressing the needs of unaccompanied asylum seeking minors
- working with young people who are leaving care and also convicted of criminal offences

Audit these against the relevant primary legislation, regulations, policy and practice guidance, and case law. Summarize the degree to which the procedures accurately interpret the relevant legal rules and discuss your findings with your supervisor or manager.

If you do not work in an agency providing services of this nature but wish to explore these issues, use the website of your local council to access the information that it makes publicly available about safeguarding and promoting the welfare of children and young people, services for children with special educational needs, and provision for children in need. Consider how the legal rules are being reflected and interpreted.

Further reading

Bridge, C. and Swindells, H. (2003) *Adoption: The Modern Law*. Bristol: Family Law. This book gives a detailed review of the Adoption and Children Act 2002.

Bridgeman, J., Lind, C. and Keating, H. (eds) (2008) *Responsibility, Law and the Family*. Aldershot, Ashgate Publishing. This book explores, from a socio-legal perspective, the concept of responsibility in family life, law and practice.

Ward, R. and Bettinson, V. (2008) *Criminal Justice and Immigration Act 2008. A Practitioner's Guide*. Bristol: Jordans. This text provides a detailed review of legislation affecting youth justice and adult offenders.

6 | Frameworks for decision-making and accountability

The next two chapters consider the law *on* social work practice. They demonstrate how legal frameworks can offer positive and constructive contributions to practice. This chapter's focus is on the frameworks that should underpin and ensure quality of practice, particularly important because employers must not place employees in positions of acting unlawfully and because social workers must engage authoritatively with other professionals and negotiate confidently within and across organizational boundaries.

The body of the legal rules

Much of what makes social work practice effective is not legislated for. Sometimes social work research, values and practice forge ahead of regulation and guidance. However an increasing amount of official guidance regulates practice standards, cementing a significant interrelationship between the law and social work values.

Legislation expresses duties and powers that determine how local authorities must or may act. Some duties are absolute, not dependent on the exercise of professional judgement. Others are discretionary, arising from the exercise of professional judgement and/or shaped by how an authority determines the duty is to be implemented. Legislation is then interpreted. Regulations, guidance and codes connect these duties and powers to principles for practice, clarifying how legislation should be understood and implemented. Regulations have the full force of legislation and cannot be ignored just because an officer believes that to observe them would be pointless (*Lambeth LBC v Johnston* [2008]). The law can be elaborated and extended through circulars; government circulars and guidance, when issued under s.7, LASSA 1970, have regulatory status, must be followed, and may be quoted in complaints procedures, Ombudsman investigations, and judicial review proceedings. For instance, directions on choice of accommodation (LAC(92)27) were influential in successfully challenging a local authority's decision on placement for a learning disabled man (*R v Avon County Council, ex parte Hazell* [1995]). Community care assessments (DH, 1990) must draw directly on the views of disabled adults, as well as their family carers (*R v North Yorkshire CC, ex parte Hargreaves* [1997]). Local authority decision-making in respect of children in need has been overturned when assessment has not conformed to s.7 guidance (DH, 2000c) either on timescales (*R (AB and SB) v Nottingham CC* [2001]) or the process of assessing the child's and family's needs prior to producing a care plan and providing identified services (*R v Lambeth LBC, ex parte K* [2000]).

Other guidance not issued under s.7 is intended to promote rather than 'legislate for' good practice. However, authorities must pay regard to such guidance when performing statutory functions (*R v Islington LBC, ex parte Rixon* [1996]) and only depart from it with good reason (*R v Sutton LBC, ex parte Tucker* [1998]). There is no legal duty to comply with codes of practice. Rather they represent good practice principles. For example, the Mental Health Act Code of Practice (DH, 2008d) provides guidance not instruction (*R (Munjaz) v Mersey Care NHS Trust* [2005]). If police officers breach the codes of practice to PACE 1984, courts may decide nonetheless to accept the evidence so obtained (contrast *R v Jefferson* [1994], where evidence was allowed despite the Appropriate Adult acting outside their role, with *R v Aspinall* [1999] where it was held that the evidence obtained without an Appropriate Adult present should not have been admissible).

Non-compliance by local authorities with directions and regulations emerges consistently. For example, judicial reviews have found failures to follow policy guidance on charges for residential care (*R v Sefton MBC, ex parte Help the Aged and Charlotte Blanchard* [1997]), on needs-led assessments and the application of eligibility criteria (*R v Haringey LBC, ex parte Norton* [1998]), on the preparation of care plans for care proceedings (*Re J (Minors) (Care: Care Plan)* [1994]), and on the interface between child care and community care (*R v Bexley LBC, ex parte B* [2000]). Local authorities have sought unlawfully to limit their duties towards young people leaving care (*R (H, Barhanu and B v Wandsworth LBC, Hackney LBC and Islington LBC* [2007]) and young offenders in custody (*R (K) v Manchester City Council* [2007]).

Ombudsman investigations (LGO, 2007) have similarly found agencies infringing regulations and policy guidance by denying or delaying services, failing to assess need in a structured way or to monitor and review the care provided, and neglecting to act on complaints.

The degree to which policy and practice guidance can ensure good practice is questionable. Implementation can be variable within and across local authorities. In relation to direct payments, this has often resulted from practitioners' and managers' lack of knowledge about the legislation and their perceptions about the impact on social work (Glasby and Littlechild, 2002; Leece and Leece, 2006), together with inconsistent leadership (Newbiggin and Lowe, 2005). How agency procedures are written appears significant as local authorities have drawn clearer distinctions between substantial and critical levels of need than is evident in the policy guidance (DH, 2002b; Charles and Manthorpe, 2007). In child care, variation has been found in the sharing of information (Richardson and Asthana, 2006). The rapidity and clarity of policy change, coupled with poor management practice, resource constraints, inadequate post-registration training and supervision, and organizational cultures on risk, have negatively impacted upon care planning, reviews, partnership with parents and listening to the child (Morris, 2005; Dickens et al., 2007).

Other characteristics of guidance will affect its implementation. Conflicting imperatives and practice dilemmas may be identified or left unresolved in regulations and guidance, as with legislation, leaving practitioners confused about how to proceed. This may be evident in child and adult safeguarding (Preston-Shoot, 2001a) in the balance to be struck between autonomy and protection, and between rights and risks. Difficulties arise because guidance lacks clarity, as in the distinction to be drawn between health and social care (*R (Grogan) v Bexley NHS Care Trust and South East London Strategic Health Authority and Secretary of State for Health* [2006]) or in the interface between reviews, reassessment and resources (*R v Gloucestershire CC, ex parte RADAR* [1996]). Often guidance does not prioritize policy objectives. Needs-led assessment, user choice, promoting independence and remaining within available resources are juxtaposed without recognition of conflict. Interpreting the guidance therefore becomes a balancing act. It would appear unlawful to give too much weight to just one component at the expense of the overall context (*Sutton LBC v Davis* [1994]). Guidance in one area should be read in the context of overall guidance – in this instance about day care provision. Otherwise, giving disproportionate and inflexible importance to one issue renders impossible a correct balancing exercise and a reasonable decision based on the case's merits. A similar balancing exercise must be undertaken when following community care guidance which requires proper assessment of need and a move away from resource-led decisions, but also demands value for money and setting provision levels against what is affordable (DH, 1990). It is unlawful to ignore one element of the guidance in reaching a decision about service provision (*R v North Yorkshire CC, ex parte Hargreaves* [1997]). When, however, is a proper assessment of need undermined by the importance attached to resources?

The space between law in theory and law in practice – the law in-between (Jenness and Grattet, 2005) – is where the legal rules are translated into agency procedures. Such translation will reflect the degree to which central government and local communities can exert meaningful influence, and the agency is aligned with the proposed policy. Thereafter, distance between managers and practitioners will also affect implementation, and whether practitioners have access to, and understand, the guidance. Implementation is determined by how they strike a balance between a bureaucratic approach (emphasizing procedures and accountability to the authority) and a professional approach (emphasizing what contributes to lawful and ethical practice).

Legal rules on decision-making

Statutory duties, regulations and local authorities' own procedures have not been applied consistently, knowledge of legislation has been inconsistent, and the discretion which can be exercised in respect of powers and duties has meant that similar cases have been treated differently, even within the same local authority (Davis et al., 1998; Bradley, 2003; Cestari et al., 2006). Practising outside the legal rules on decision-making can render people and their needs invisible. Differential levels of support can lead to accusations of discrimination. Increasingly, therefore, social services authorities can expect scrutiny of their decision-making, and their approach to rights and duties, by advocates, judges and experts by experience. Indeed, guidance has stressed the importance of the values underpinning care and standards (LAC(2001)6). Service provision should be underpinned by honesty, dignity and partnership. People should have sufficient information to make choices, be involved in decisions, and feel able to use advocates to express their views and to complain. Increasingly decisions are made in the context of time and work pressures, and insufficient information, where delay may increase the likelihood of poor outcomes, and where confidence and judgement are affected by the probability of criticism for interfering over-zealously or for risk-taking (Ellis et al., 1999; McKeigue and Beckett, 2004; Platt, 2006).

Statute has remained relatively silent on the question of professional and agency decision-making. However, both the Mental Capacity Act 2005 and the Mental Health Act 2007 specify principles that should underpin practice. The former refers to presumption of capacity and the right to support to exercise capacity and make one's own decisions. It asserts people's rights to make eccentric or unwise decisions and, where capacity is lacking, requires the least restrictive intervention to preserve a person's basic rights and freedoms, based on an understanding of that individual's best interests. The latter requires respect for diversity and for patients' past and present feelings and wishes. Patients should be involved in the planning and delivery of their care and treatment, and carers' views should also be sought. Once again, intervention should be proportional, with the minimum restrictions necessary imposed on liberty. Unlawful discrimination should be avoided.

Principles of good practice in child care (DH, 2000c) centre on the manner in which help is offered and interventions conducted. These procedural rights – to information, involvement in decision-making, careful assessment, clear explanations of local authority powers and reasons for concern, integrated multi-agency child-centred practice, reviews and complaints procedures – are embodied in the CA 1989 and regulatory guidance which underpins it. This should strengthen accountability. However phraseology such as 'due consideration' and 'as they [local authorities] consider appropriate' invites discretion, and questions the degree of involvement really being offered. Needs and opinions, as defined or expressed by service users, can still be ignored, even though in other respects the Act and regulatory guidance do specify how social workers and local authorities must act in implementing their duties and powers. Indeed, complaints from young people highlight ineffective communication over decisions, for instance concerning contact between looked after children and their families (Pithouse and Crowley, 2007). Much depends, ultimately, on the attitudes and values of agencies and employees; on their skills in partnership, use of authority, assessment, direct work and supervision; and on whether their resource base facilitates good practice.

Section 13 of the Mental Health Act 1983, which requires an AMHP to consider all the circumstances of the case before deciding the most appropriate way of providing care and treatment to a patient, is unusual in giving statutory expression to the process of decision-making. However, a growing body of case law clarifies the law's position on decision-making by public bodies, and is thus relevant to the exercise of skilled professional judgement by social workers. Equally, the Mental Health (Approved Mental Health Professionals) (Approval) England Regulations 2008 specify the key competences for practice, namely values, knowledge and skills relating to the role, legal rules, mental distress and decision-making.

The primary emphasis is that decision-making should be reasonable and rational, based on a full examination of the facts and all the relevant factors, arrived at in good faith, rooted in correct identification of the law, and reached according to guidance, such as Codes of Practice, where that exists (*R v DHSS and Kent County Council, ex parte Bruce* [1986];

R v LB of Harrow, ex parte Deal [1989]; *R v North Yorkshire County Council, ex parte Hargreaves* [1997]; *R v Islington LBC, ex parte Rixon* [1996]). A balance must be struck between the factors relevant to a decision. For example, in *Re H* [1991] the judge described the process as one of gathering evidence, both factual and expert opinion, then, with the test of the child's welfare paramount, assessing the relative weight of advantages and risks to a child of each possible course of action.

The law requires discretion to be exercised in every case. Operating blanket policies in community care would breach the duty to assess an *individual's* need for services (s.47, NHSCCA 1990), and fetter discretion by neglecting issues relevant to an individual's case and thereby the possibility that this case may require departure from agreed policy or eligibility criteria. Similarly, pursuing a blanket policy of same race placements for children is open to challenge through judicial review, on the basis that other factors in addition to race may also be relevant in deciding an individual child's welfare (*Re P (A Minor: Adoption)* [1990]).

Legal judgements have supported principles of consultation and transparency with service users. Authorities must consult with users whilst proposals or assessments are still at a formative stage, clearly presenting reasons for the former and grounds for the latter. Crucial information should be disclosed to those being consulted (*R (Easai Ltd) v NICE* [2008]). Users must have reasonable time to present their views. Reasons must be given for decisions which must themselves be reasonable (*R v Devon CC, ex parte Baker and Johns* [1995]; *R v LB of Barnet, ex parte B* [1994]). Decisions must be explained rather than merely described (*R (Secretary of State for Justice) v the MHRT* [2008]). This approach applies to local authorities, including decisions regarding housing homeless people (*Hall v Wandsworth LBC* [2005]) and to health authorities (*R v North and East Devon Health Authority and North Devon Healthcare NHS Trust, ex parte Pow and Others; R v Same, ex parte Metcalfe* [1999]). This latter case also established that authorities should not wait until a development or variation of services is urgently required and then seek to limit the consultation process.

Thus, in *R (Madden) v Bury MBC* [2002], a decision to close a residential home was quashed because residents had not been given true reasons for the closure. Nor had there been any consideration of whether interference in their article 8 rights was proportionate. However, in *R (Dudley) v East Sussex CC* [2003] application for judicial review was refused. The consultation process was fair, each resident had been able to make representations, care and risk assessments had been sufficient and article 8 rights had to be balanced against high demand and the residential care budget.

These 'rules' about consultation also apply to voluntary groups supplying community care services. They should be able to put their case before the local authority makes any decision to reduce grant aid. They should also receive written notice and reasons for the final decision (*R v Haringey LBC, ex parte Haringey Consortium of Disabled People and Carers Association* [2001]; *R (Capenhurst, Kirby, King, Mistry and Joachim) v Leicester CC* [2004]).

Decisions on provision must again be rational, based on consideration of need and supported by adequate reasons (*R v North Yorkshire County Council, ex parte Hargreaves* [1997]). Thus, in *R (Ireneschild) v Lambeth LBC* [2006] an assessment was unlawful because it did not take all available reports into account. FACS guidance on risk assessment (DH, 2002b) had not been followed and the service user had not confirmed the accuracy of factual matters before the assessor relied upon them. Similarly, in a case involving a child with autism and learning disabilities (*R (LH and MH) v Lambeth LBC* [2006]), a support package was unlawful because the care plan had not identified the necessary measures and the assessment had not properly identified the needs to be met. When withdrawing or amending provision, adequate reasons must be given, together with an opportunity to comment. Regard must be paid to the effect of change on an individual before a final decision is made. Policy guidance must be followed (*R v Rochdale MBC, ex parte Schemet* [1993]; *R v Lancashire CC, ex parte Ingham and Whalley* [1995]). Decisions must be made without undue delay, or within a reasonable time, which depends on the circumstances of the case, unless specific time limits are laid out in statute or guidance (*R v Sutton LBC, ex parte Tucker* [1998]).

The courts may interfere with decisions only where the local authority has exceeded or misused its powers, has misdirected itself in fact or in law, has exercised its discretion wrongly or for no good reason, or has acted perversely (*Smith and others v ILEA* [1978]; *Puhlhofer and Another v. Hillingdon LBC* [1986]). Courts are generally reluctant to interfere because they have no knowledge of competing claims on an authority's resources, nor access to the specialist knowledge required to weigh the relevant factors in decision-making, and are in no position to express a view as to how an authority should deploy resources (*Re J (a minor) (Wardship: Medical Treatment)* [1992]; *R v RB of Kingston-upon-Thames, ex parte T* [1994]; *R v Cambridge Health Authority, ex parte B* [1995]). Courts can only consider the lawfulness of a decision at issue, and cannot arbitrate between conflicting medical opinions or competing claims on limited budgetary resources.

Local authority decisions may, of course, be challenged through the Local Commissioner for Administration (Ombudsman) on the basis of maladministration. This could cover bias, inattention to facts, delay, incompetence and arbitrariness. Maladministration has been established, for example, when an authority has not given a clear indication of likely delays in making an assessment or providing a service, or for failing to keep a complainant updated.

Decision-making must integrate ECHR principles, incorporated into UK law by the HRA 1998. Public authorities have a positive duty to promote Convention rights. Any interference with someone's Convention rights must be proportional, namely the least intervention appropriate for the objectives sought. Thus, local authorities should balance which order is the appropriate level of intervention into family life when preparing care plans in care proceedings, observing article 8 ECHR (*Re O (A Child) (Supervision Order)* [2001]). Proposed action must be proportionate to the nature and gravity of actual or likely significant harm, with work focused on supporting and reuniting the family unless the risks are too high (*Re C and B (Care Order: Future Harm)* [2001]). Similarly, an Emergency Protection Order must be supported by relevant and sufficient reasons, pay close attention to Convention rights and be necessary for the purpose of safeguarding the child (*P, C and S v UK* [2002]; *X Council v B (Emergency Protection Orders)* [2004]; *Re X (Emergency Protection Orders)* [2006]). The latter two cases stated that evidence should be given by the social worker with direct knowledge of the case. Oral evidence must be recorded and *ex parte* applications made only in genuine emergencies where giving notice to parents is impossible.

Available remedies, such as complaints procedures, must be effective, with experts by experience enjoying 'equality of arms' in respect of representation and information. Thus, procedural fairness (Article 6(3) ECHR – right to a fair hearing) requires a number of minimum rights, for example in secure accommodation proceedings where the child should be informed promptly of the application, have adequate time and facilities to prepare a defence, be able to defend themselves via legal assistance, be able to examine and cross-examine witnesses, and have an interpreter (*Re M (A Child) (Secure Accommodation)* [2001]). In care proceedings, fair decision-making requires that parties are aware of concerns, have been advised of the changes expected of them, and have had access to relevant documentation (*Re C (Care Proceedings: Disclosure of Local Authority's Decision-Making Process* [2002]). In the contested and complex decisions that surround initiation of care proceedings, the duty to protect children means that a decision to bring care proceedings, subsequently shown to be mistaken, is capable of justification under ECHR (*RK and AK v UK* [2008]).

In mental health, Article 6 rights have informed the Mental Health (Conflicts of Interest) (England) Regulations 2008. Assessors should not be members of the same team working together routinely or in a line management relationship. The same rights have effected a reversal of the burden of proof in the MHA 1983 (ss.72 and 73) the onus now residing on the hospital to show that continued detention is appropriate (*R (H) v MHRT, North and East London and Another* [2001]). Delays in referrals to Mental Health Review Tribunals have been found to infringe Article 5 rights (*R (C) v South West MHRT* [2001]; *R (Rayner) v Secretary of State for Justice* [2008]). The obligatory involvement of the Nearest Relative in certain sections under the MHA1983 was found incompatible with a patient's Article 8 rights (*R (M) v Secretary of State for Health* [2003]), as was discrimination against same gender couples in the original rules for the selection of the Nearest Relative (*R (SSG) v Liverpool CC and Others* [2002]).

Returning, therefore, to the proposition of the 'law in-between' (Jenness and Grattet, 2005), practitioners and managers should audit the degree to which Convention rights do underpin assessment, service delivery and redress.

Accountability and responsibility

The modernization agenda for social services (DH, 1998) aimed to create a competent and confident workforce, better supervision and management, and codes of practice and national standards so that service users and carers know what to expect and are protected from poor and abusive practice. The Care Standards Act 2000, creating the General Social Care Council and social work registration, is one legislative expression of the search for consistent quality and enforceable standards. The Act also created an independent commission for social care, which became the Care Quality Commission under the Health and Social Care Act 2008.

Another is the ACA 2002 resolution of the problem highlighted in *Re W and B (Children: Care Plan)* [2002], where the court could not repeatedly postpone a decision on a care order even where concerned about a local authority's planning, as this contravened the no delay principle. The CA 1989 was amended to require local authorities to submit a care plan to court (s.121) and to appoint IROs (s.118) whose role is to monitor implementation of the care plan and refer the case to CAFCASS, who may return it to court where problems arise that cannot be rectified through normal review mechanisms.

A common question social workers ask is whether they can be sued for their decisions. Legal powers and duties are placed on Local Social Services Authorities, who may delegate them to independent organizations. Otherwise, the translation of the legal mandate into service provision is achieved by assigning legal functions to individual local authority employees.

One means of achieving this is *designation*. For example, only AMHPs, approved in accordance with s.18, MHA 2007, amending s.114, MHA1983, are designated with the powers and duties to perform certain functions under mental health legislation. In these instances, they can be held individually accountable for their actions, for example if they do not work to practitioner standards.

More usually, the means employed is *delegation*. The local authority delegates powers and duties to its employees who, in turn, must adhere to statute. Here the local authority is vicariously liable for its employees' actions. Employees must not act outside their delegated authority (*R v Kirklees MBC, ex parte Daykin* [1996]). In *Lister and Others v Hesley Hall Ltd* [2001] the employer was held vicariously liable for an employee's acts of sexual abuse because the behaviour was an unauthorized way of performing an authorized activity (residential care) as opposed to an illegal activity outside the scope of an employment contract. Accountability to an employer takes precedence over professional or service user accountability where an employer's interpretation is defensible in terms of the statutory mandate and definitions of good practice. If it is not, however, employees will be in a stronger position to defend themselves in any disciplinary action (or, if dismissed, in an industrial tribunal) by drawing on their accountability to legal, professional and service user mandates (Braye and Preston-Shoot, 1999). Indeed, if employees are instructed to act in ways that are unlawful or contrary to professional ethics, they should refuse and, if necessary, defend their actions in an industrial tribunal (Preston-Shoot, 2000b). The Public Interest Disclosure Act 1998 affords some protection if employees notify the GSCC that their employer is requiring unlawful and/or unethical action that could jeopardize registration of someone qualified and licensed to practise.

Courts were historically reluctant to allow service users to sue local authorities for breach of statutory duty and for negligence (*X and Others (Minors) v Bedfordshire CC* [1995]), but immunity from suit in negligence was successfully challenged in the European Court as contrary to Article 13 (ECHR), which guarantees right to an effective remedy (*Z and Others v UK* [2001]). Failure to protect children from sexual abuse by inadequate investigation, assessment and communication with other agencies did not constitute effective management of a local authority's responsibilities and violated Articles 3 and 13 of the ECHR (*E and Others v UK* [2002]). The HRA 1998 has also changed how far courts will hold local authorities *and* individual practitioners accountable. Courts have found local authorities negligent and open to claims for damages in respect of young people who have been sexually abused by foster parents (*S v Gloucestershire County Council* [2000]), carelessness concerning important decisions for looked after young people (*Barrett v Enfield LBC* [1999]), and failing in assessment and service provision (*R (Bernard) v Enfield LBC* [2002]). Damages have been awarded for psychological injuries suffered in residential care by young people (*C v Flintshire CC* [2001]) and for the return of a young person to parental care without proper assessment or follow-up monitoring (*Pierce v Doncaster MBC* [2007]). These judgements highlight the importance of responsiveness to young people's complaints about their placements. Courts have extended accountability also to individual practitioners where they have failed to exercise professional standards of care in giving advice, information or guidance (*W and Others v Essex County Council and Another* [2000]).

Similar extension of accountability is emerging in adult social care, where there is a clear relationship between a public body and a complainant, and links between the events complained of and the degree of care exercised. Thus, in *AK v Central and North West London Mental Health NHS Trust and Kensington and Chelsea LBC* [2008], aftercare providers (s.117, MHA 1983) might be liable in damages for the negligent failure to discharge their duties.

Where more than one party is involved in social work intervention, as in child protection investigations, courts have been reluctant to allow a duty of care to parents to obscure the duty of care to the child (*D v East Berkshire Community Health NHS Trust and Others* [2005]; *L and Another v Reading Borough Council and Another (No 2)* [2007]). Safeguarding the child's welfare is paramount and, currently, it is held that investigations of sexual and physical abuse might be jeopardized if practitioners were distracted when conducting inquiries and assessments in good faith. A similar approach was taken on sharing information with prospective adopters (*A and Another v Essex County Council* [2003]); no duty of care was owed to the adopters when deciding what information about the child to share unless practitioners took a decision which no reasonable authority would have taken.

Employees must take responsibility for improving their knowledge and skills, promoting equal opportunities, helping people to make complaints, and notifying employers of resource or other difficulties impacting on safe care. They must be accountable, adhering to standards of practice and working in a lawful way (GSCC, 2002). A standard of care will be unreasonable where a responsible and skilled social worker would not have acted in the same way as the practitioner complained of (*Bolam v Friern Hospital Management Committee* [1957]). Thus, where social workers face difficult decisions, involving dilemmas, disputed facts and the balancing of different interests, the test is to ask what social work would define as competent practice (Preston-Shoot, 2000b). However, even if a body of responsible opinion supports the practitioner, courts are free to determine the standard of care required in particular cases and to disregard expert opinion in circumstances where it is considered unreasonable, imbalanced when considering the risks and benefits of different options, and incapable of withstanding logical analysis (*Bolitho v City and Hackney Health Authority* [1997]).

Thus, practitioners will have met their duty of care when they act in good faith, interfere with people's ECHR rights only with cogent justification, involve them and share information and concerns unless this would place someone at risk of harm, and follow decision-making principles when reaching sound professional judgements (*D v East Berkshire Community Health NHS Trust and Others* [2005]). The MHA 1983, as amended by the MHA 2007, remains unique, however, in requiring practitioners to possess an appropriate level of competence to act as AMHPs. No such requirement exists elsewhere. The Act also defines *how* they should act: in good faith and with reasonable care.

Employers too have responsibilities. They must give staff information about relevant legislation (GSCC, 2002) and should support them in protecting practice standards (Brand, 1999). They should provide appropriate training and support (*Lancaster v Birmingham CC* [1999]; *Fraser v Winchester Health Authority* [1999]), such as manual handling (*R (A & B by their litigation friends X & Y) v East Sussex CC and the Disability Rights Commission (interested party) (no 2)* [2003]). They must provide a safe place of work, incorporating psychiatric as well as physical health (*Walker v Northumberland County Council* [1995]). Indeed, emotional exhaustion is high amongst mental health practitioners, working conditions appear in need of improvement, and stress occasions job dissatisfaction (Evans et al., 2005). An employer is entitled to assume that employees can manage work pressures (*Barber v Somerset CC* [2004]), as no job inherently leads to psychiatric injury, but they should act when there are indications of impending harm to health. The steps taken must be reasonable, based on assessment of the magnitude of risk and the seriousness of harm that may occur (*Hatton v Sutherland* [2002]). Thus, in *LA v General Social Care Council* [2007] a decision to remove a social worker from the register was overturned by the Care Standards Tribunal because she lacked guidance from supportive and competent managers. In *R v Kensington and Chelsea RLBC, ex parte Kujtim* [1999], duty to a service user was held to have been discharged where, by his or her conduct, he or she had persistently and unreasonably refused to comply with reasonable requests from staff.

However, there is evidence of significant failures because of ill-trained, poorly supported and overworked staff (Sheppard, 1996; Balloch et al., 1999; Laming, 2003, 2009), who remain reticent about complaining of bullying and workloads, thereby reducing employer liability. Ombudsman investigations have found a lack of support, training and monitoring of staff dealing with complaints (LGO, 2002), officers not understanding adult protection policies and inadequate supervision leading to case drift and delay in meeting people's needs (LGO, 2007). Managers may be unfamiliar with health and safety law. Inquiry reports involving people with mental distress (Sheppard, 1996) have found staff carrying complex cases without consideration of their knowledge and skills, and erratic approaches to induction, training in risk assessment, and space for liaison and communication. Such evidence has stimulated calls to hold employers more accountable for their lack of observance of the GSCC code of practice (2002). Of note, therefore, here is the CMCHA 2007, which enables prosecution of corporate bodies, rather than just individuals, if failure to comply with health and safety law results in the death of someone owed a duty of care.

The introduction of national service frameworks (DH, 1999b, 2001b) and national minimum standards (NCSC, 2001; DfES, 2007), similarly highlights accountability for practice. The Integrated Children's System (DfES, 2005a) aims to improve practice by tracing the progress of individual children against key outcomes and by highlighting when key responsibilities, such as placement reviews, are due. However, such initiatives will only improve the well-being of children in care, or choice and levels of care for vulnerable adults, when they are expressed not just as targets but as individual social rights that are enforceable. Also key to standards are the leadership demonstrated by managers and an organization's culture of learning (Bell et al., 2007).

Judicial review, the local government ombudsman and complaints procedures may all inquire and provide redress. However, given the questions of liberty, violence, risk and compulsion faced daily by social workers, given the abuses of power known to occur within welfare services and the power imbalance between service providers and users, it is questionable whether such post-event protection is sufficient. Recent statutory interest in advocacy (ACA 2002, MCA 2005, MHA 2007) may prove a useful, if partial, corrective.

Social workers are expected to manage the tensions arising from multiple accountabilities to employers, codes of conduct and ethics, and experts by experience (GSCC, 2008). Whilst legal developments codify and support good practice, accountability remains a complex web of obligations to different stakeholders whose demands are not necessarily compatible (Braye and Preston-Shoot, 1999). Evolving mechanisms for delineating and enforcing standards may still be insufficient for promoting ECHR rights and preventing poor practice. Professional practice and moral responsibility can be compromised by perceived accountability to an employing agency (Wells, 1997), evidence continuing that some practitioners collude with organizational misuse of power. Agency processes can undermine policy guidance by restricting or refusing assessments and services (Davis et al., 1998; Tanner, 1998) and erode service users' legal entitlements and protections (Machin, 1998; Rummery and Glendinning, 1999; Horwath, 2000; Preston-Shoot, 2001a). This leads some to suggest that commitment to values should not be taken for granted (Millar and Corby, 2006).

The availability and quality of supervision and post-qualifying training, especially its legal content, remain variable. Practitioners report limited confidence in their legal literacy; the law is often implicit rather than explicit in agency practice (Braye et al., 2007). Social workers struggle to challenge ingrained organizational cultures. Their employment status has considerable impact on their willingness to assert their knowledge and value base (Preston-Shoot, 2000b). The Public Interest Disclosure Act 1998 has not established mandatory reporting and offers limited protection to whistleblowers. Whilst the code of practice (GSCC, 2002) requires that social workers point out breaches to employers, more needs to be done to embed it in practice (Roche and Rankin, 2004). It remains similarly discomforting for experts by experience to challenge agencies which devalue, frustrate and disbelieve them (Flynn, 2004; Goldsmith, 2005). They argue that agencies should give more priority to those they are meant to serve and that social workers should challenge their employers more and be prepared by social work education to do so (Allain et al., 2006).

Although the accountability mosaic has developed substantially, it remains incomplete. The code of practice (GSCC, 2002) aims to offer people a guarantee of what they can expect (Roche and Rankin, 2004). However, its very general wording makes proving a breach difficult. It is an amalgam of values, standards and practice prescriptions, which does not clearly distinguish between acting well and acting correctly, or resolve situations where different principles compete (Orme and Rennie, 2006). Sanctions against employers are insufficiently robust, leaving practitioners exposed when negotiating ethical issues in practice and when confronting conflicts between individual, organizational, professional and social values, or clashes between the rights and wishes of different individuals, particularly in settings where opportunities for critical reflection are limited and moral sensibility is discouraged.

Advocacy, representation and complaints

New Labour administrations have embraced advocacy for young people and vulnerable adults, prompted in part by abuses and poor practice in residential care. The ACA 2002 places a duty on local authorities to make arrangements for advocacy to looked after children and those leaving care who make or intend to make complaints and representations. Policy guidance on safeguarding children (DfES, 2006a) also requires that young people are supported by advocacy. Community care practice guidance (DH, 1991c) promotes independent advocacy, recommending that service users and carers should receive information about advocacy services which can intervene when assessor and provider roles conflict and when provision may not be based on need and people's wishes. The MCA 2005 and the MHA 2007 both introduce independent advocacy to make representations to decision-makers (considered in more detail in Chapter 4 cases).

Providing or arranging advocacy for people is a key social work role (GSCC, 2008). Research continues to identify the need for advocacy: to challenge incomplete assessments of need, failures of information-sharing and inappropriate patterns of support for young people (Coles et al., 2004); to support looked after children (Boylan and Braye, 2006); to resist reviews of residential care that view care as a commodity rather than a human interaction (Scourfield, 2007). If the imbalance of power between service providers and users is to be challenged effectively, a statutory right to advocacy should be extended to all client groups, as recommended for disabled people (Clark, 2003).

IMCAs appear to have improved decision-making on accommodation issues, care reviews, adult protection and medical treatment but medical treatment referrals are very low, and awareness of, and compliance with, the duty to refer has proved variable (DH, 2008g). Guidance reinforces NHS Trust and local authority duties to instruct independent advocates when considering serious medical treatment and changes of accommodation, and their power to refer cases of adult protection and reviews of accommodation (LAC(2008)4). It notes that the necessary culture shift has not really begun, highlighting again the significance of the law 'in-between'.

Young people value independent services, especially the time, resources and listening offered, but still experience difficulty fully participating in decisions (Cleaver et al., 2004; Boylan and Braye, 2006). Pithouse and Crowley (2007) found limited involvement of advocates in supporting young people with complaints. Children found it difficult to access advocates. They concluded that advocacy services may be insufficiently proactive in case finding and that practitioners, anxious about criticism, may not guide young people to such provision.

A Children's Commissioner now exists in each of the four UK nations, in England with a narrower role, the functions being listed in s.2, CA 2004. Whilst England's Children's Commissioner may advise government on the views and interests of children, and consider or research the operation of complaints procedures and other matters relating to their interests, the role is tied tightly to the five outcomes of *Every Child Matters* (DfES, 2004a). Moreover, an advocacy role in respect of government implementation of the UNCRC is excluded, and the Commissioner cannot provide advice or assistance to individual young people or investigate individual cases unless this would not duplicate the work of other agencies and would explore issues of public policy relevant to other children. This lack of independence has prompted criticism that England's Children's Commissioner is a government listening officer rather than a champion for children (Dobson, 2004; Gilligan, 2007).

By contrast, in divorce proceedings, courts are accepting that children should have separate representation to ensure their participation (*Mabon v Mabon* [2005]; *Re S (A Child: Unmarried Parents: Financial Provision)* [2006]). Policy guidance on standards for children's advocacy (DH, 2002e) notes that young people are able to form and express opinions and participate in decision-making. Advocacy services should be led by their wishes and views. However, ambivalent views of children remain, with services not always listening or responding with positive regard (Pithouse and Crowley, 2007).

The local authority duty to establish complaints procedures now resides in the HSCCHSA 2003 and the CA 1989. Additionally, the CQC may investigate complaints on clinical judgement and non-clinical matters, from or on behalf of detained patients. Voluntary organizations providing services for children must have complaints procedures (CA 1989, s.59(4)). The significance of these procedures has been enhanced by courts criticizing the use of judicial review to challenge local authority decisions when a more appropriate remedy exists – a mandate to consider the matter afresh and to exercise an independent judgement on the merits of the facts, and the power to make recommendations to which an authority must pay due regard (*R v Birmingham City Council, ex parte*

A [1997]). Service users must usually exhaust complaints procedures before seeking leave for a judicial review or an ombudsman investigation (*R (Cowl) v Plymouth CC* [2002]). Courts do warn that legal proceedings may not be appropriate for resolving disputes, being likely to exacerbate differences between clients and agencies (*R (C, M, P and HM) v Brent, Kensington and Chelsea and Westminster Mental Health NHS Trust* [2003]). Judicial review is then reserved for challenging the use made by an authority of a complaint panel's findings, or for an authoritative resolution of a legal issue (*R v Durham CC, ex parte Curtis and Broxson* [1995]; *R v RB of Kingston-upon-Thames, ex parte T* [1994]; *R v LB of Barnet, ex parte B* [1994]; *R v Cambridge Health Authority, ex parte B* [1995]; *R v Gloucestershire CC, ex parte RADAR* [1996]; *R v Sutton LBC, ex parte Tucker* [1998]). Modifications by an authority to a panel's recommendations will not necessarily be unreasonable (*R v North Yorkshire County Council, ex parte Hargreaves* [1997]). Judicial review can only scrutinize the legality of a decision rather than compel an authority to follow a panel recommendation (*Re T (Accommodation by Local Authority)* [1995]).

The procedures local authorities must establish are governed by regulations (Local Authority Social Services Complaints (England) Regulations 2006; Children Act 1989 Representations Procedure (England) Regulations, 2006) and policy guidance (DfES, 2006c; DH, 2006c). There are three stages for both adults' and children's services procedures – an informal problem-solving stage, a formal stage, and a review stage, with a one-year time limit for making complaints and clear time frames for conclusion of each stage. Complainants must be given information about the procedures and about advocacy services. Local authorities must appoint a complaints manager who is independent of line management and of direct service providers. Procedures should be clear and easy to use, complainants treated with dignity and respect. Where possible, local resolution is encouraged and outcomes should be monitored so that organizations can learn and improve. There are two important differences between the procedures. An independent person must be involved at stage 2 in children's complaints but only at this stage in community care complaints if there are concerns about an individual's vulnerability, otherwise at stage 3. All three members of the review panel must be independent of the local authority under children's procedures but only two in community care complaints.

The purpose of the independent person is to ensure that the process is fair and transparent. However, Bridge and Street (2001) found variation in local authority attitudes and behaviour towards the independent person, and in the training, support and co-operation they receive, also difficulty in matching young people with independent persons, defensive staff attitudes in agencies characterized by a blame culture, and role uncertainty in terms of balancing attempts at conciliation with formal investigation. Moreover, there was doubt about their degree of actual independence and on their influence upon local authority practice once the complaints procedure had concluded. Pithouse and Crowley (2007) stress the importance of the independent person as young people regard social workers as employees and, therefore, not independent. However, they also found that, where social workers and complaints managers are child-friendly, an independent person may be less necessary. Indeed, concerns about independence and the tightness of the time frames, given the level of complexity often involved, have prompted a further review of the complaints system (DH, 2008h).

Social workers should assist service users and carers to make complaints (GSCC, 2002). However, the reasons why services users and carers do not complain are complex and varied. Some may be sceptical of the benefits or daunted by the procedures. Others are anxious about the potential adverse consequences of complaining, such as withdrawal of services or being regarded as troublesome. They may feel deterred by a lack of information, both about the procedures and their wider rights, unequal power relations, low expectations, delays and dependence on service providers (Brand, 1999; Braye and Preston-Shoot, 1999; Williams and Robinson, 2000; Bridge and Street, 2001; Preston-Shoot, 2001c; Scourfield, 2007). Both Goldsmith (2005) and Flynn (2004) provide first-hand accounts of using complaints procedures. They describe delays, non-response, neglect of statutory policy guidance, and disrespectful attitudes. Complaints were not seen as information about practice standards or as indicating a need to initiate adult protection procedures to investigate potential abuses. Pithouse and Crowley (2007) found the complaints officer's attitude crucial in terms of respect shown and timekeeping, in systems often characterized by adult domination, delay and daunting procedures. Thus, a culture shift is required if people are to feel empowered to overcome a reluctance to complain. The provision of procedures alone is insufficient.

Ombudsman reports (LGO, 2002, 2007) have censured local authorities' failure to comply with statutory time limits for handling complaints, and to investigate complaints properly, including deficiencies in gathering facts, recording meetings, conveying decisions, giving reasons and using clear criteria for decisions. Reports have also highlighted failures to treat complainants appropriately, to train staff in investigation, to implement recommendations, and to understand the extent of their responsibilities under legislation. Judges have also criticized the management of complaints procedures, for instance the consideration given to panel findings (*R v Avon CC, ex parte Hazell* [1995]). Finally, inquiries have sometimes deemed it necessary to recommend systematic recording of complaints and guidelines for managing them (Sheppard, 1996).

Courts have also reminded local authorities of ECHR rights to a fair hearing (Article 6) and an effective remedy (Article 13). However, the availability of social services complaints review panels, coupled with judicial review, affords Article 6 remedies for alleged failures to lawfully determine civil rights (*R (Beeson) v Secretary of State for Health* [2003]). The new Care Quality Commission will monitor how NHS Trusts and local authorities deal with complaints.

Once complaints procedures have been exhausted, service users must first seek leave for a judicial review, for which they may not have all the available evidence. Moreover judicial review is only concerned with the decision-making process and its legality, with procedural propriety and reasonableness, not with the merits of the case. It is not, therefore, a reappraisal of the case and can prove both slow and expensive. Complainants may find the review upholds their complaint but that the local authority makes the same decision again via correct procedures. Goldsmith (2005) experienced judicial review as a blunt instrument which cannot fully protect individual rights or uphold quality provision.

Alternatively, it is possible to complain to the Commissioner for Local Administration, the Local Government Ombudsman. The Ombudsman may investigate maladministration – unreasonable delay or failure to comply with legal requirements, to investigate an issue, to take appropriate action, or to provide adequate information or explanation. The Ombudsman's inquiries are not restricted to the legality of an authority's actions, but focus more broadly on the administration of the case. Ombudsman investigations have set standards to which reference can be made, namely that shortage of funds and staff is not an answer to complaints about delay or failing to meet duties; that any delay must be reasonable and practice competent; that there should be high standards of decision-making, demonstrating fairness, absence of bias, and due regard for procedures. However, even if the Ombudsman finds in the complainant's favour, s/he has no power to enforce recommendations to rectify injustice arising out of discrimination, incompetence, delay or other maladministration. The process is also lengthy.

As constructed by legislation, complaints procedures fall within a consumerist model of individual service use, representation and redress. There is little focus on collective action or on the public interest dimensions of an organization's practice. Redress is *post hoc* and limited mainly to procedural correction when, for service users and carers, what matters is the effectiveness of provision and the relationships through which it is delivered.

Fitness to practise

The commitment to quality and standards (DH, 1998) includes protection of the public from poor and abusive practice. The PCA 1999, which covers education and social services, creates lists of people dismissed for misconduct or who resigned or retired prior to dismissal, or who were transferred to a position where they do not have regular contact with children, or who are suspended pending decisions about misconduct. The Act allows inclusion of people where new information emerges that would probably have resulted in dismissal or any of the other outcomes just described. The Act creates the Care Standards Tribunal to hear appeals against inclusion. Misconduct includes actions or inactions which place young people at risk or which result in harm. Child care organizations must check the list prior to offering paid or unpaid employment in a child care position. The employment of a person named on the list is prohibited.

The CSA 2000 creates a similar register of people unsuitable to work with vulnerable adults. Care providers and employment agencies must refer people to the list when misconduct is found or suspected, even if transferred to a non-care role, and check the register prior to offering employment. The Act extends the scope of the PCA 1999 provisions to include people disqualified from working in independent schools. Appeals against inclusion are heard by the Care Standards Tribunal. Provisional listing may also be challenged by representation to the Secretary of State and/or judicial review (*R (Wright and Others) v Secretary of State for Health and Another* [2007]). The CQC may refer individuals as a result of evidence gathered during their registration and inspection functions if they have not been referred previously for the alleged misconduct (s.84).

The SVGA 2006 replaces these registers with a new vetting and barring service, operated by the Independent Safeguarding Authority (ISA). For a fee, this agency will assess every individual wishing to take paid employment or voluntary activity with vulnerable people. This includes reconsidering all those who are currently barred because of inclusion on the registers created by the 1999 and 2000 legislation. When new offences are notified by the CRB, decision-making will be updated. Once approved for work by the ISA, individuals will not need to apply again, for instance when changing jobs, but employers will check their status prior to offering employment. The SVGA 2006 implements the recommendations of the Bichard Inquiry (2004), which criticized failures to share information and to keep adequate records. It extends the reach of safeguarding beyond social (care) work. One objective in creating the ISA is to introduce greater consistency in decision-making about an individual's fitness to practise. There has been inconsistency in how serious criminal convictions and their non-disclosure have been viewed by local authorities (Smith, 1999). Another is to remove the problem of poor co-ordination between the different barring lists.

Crucial to effectiveness will be whether employers check on new staff, how providers understand the new system and whether staff are willing to challenge poor and abusive practice. There is concern about how employers take up references, refer unsuitable social workers to the GSCC and check existing registers (*Christopher Onyeka Nwokoro v GSCC* [2007]). In this context, training to support staff making appropriate referrals will be important, alongside routine sharing of information, which the ICS is intended to facilitate by recording information available and to whom it has been passed. Employees disclosing poor practice may have their identity protected when an employer has collected detailed statements, considered the reliability of the evidence and the genuineness of the employee's fear of retribution from the accused, and shared all other parts of the employee's statement with the accused and their representative (*Linford Cash and Carry v Thompson* [1989]).

The CSA 2000 also creates the GSCC, responsible for the publication of codes of practice (s.62) and the registration of social (care) workers (s.56). The Council may refuse an application for registration (s.58) (GSCC (Registration of Social Workers) Rules 2003), if it is not satisfied that the applicant is of good character. It is also responsible for regulating social work education.

Legislation also details offences that constitute an abuse of a position of trust (Sexual Offences (Amendment) Act 2000; Sexual Offences Act 2003), such as sexual activity when working with children or providing care, assistance and services to learning disabled people and people with mental distress.

Case law is accruing regarding disqualification from employment. The Care Standards Tribunal is the appropriate forum to hear appeals by social workers whose names have been placed on the barring registers following accusations of sexual abuse of children (*R (M) v Bromley LBC* [2002]). Referrals should follow a structured risk assessment and decisions should be based on evidence (*Turner v Secretary of State for Health* [2007]). Unsuitability involves consideration of an individual's character, disposition and capacity, including their ability to act appropriately in difficult or frustrating circumstances. Past performance will be relevant alongside the nature and extent of the admitted or proved misconduct resulting in harm or the risk of harm, and any extenuating circumstances. Also relevant will be the number and gravity of incidents, the time that has elapsed, the individual's recognition that their behaviour equated to misconduct, and steps taken by them to prevent recurrence (*Close v Secretary of State for Health* [2007]). Individuals have been barred for lacking insight into the seriousness of deficient care and minimizing its significance when managing a residential home (*AB v Secretary of State for Health* [2007]), for callous acts and falsifying records (*Johnson v Secretary of State for Health* [2007]) and for theft of a service user's direct payments (*Nkala v Secretary of State for Health* [2007]). The agency that recruited and placed the live-in carer was criticized in this last case, underscoring debates about the degree of evidence of abuse relating to direct payments and the need to train, monitor and quality assure those whom service users wish to employ.

The Care Standards Tribunal, considering a case already the subject of statutory inquiries, may exercise its own judgement and reach different, and possibly less serious decisions regarding an individual's suitability (*Secretary of State for Education and Skills v Mairs* [2005]; *LA v General Social Care Council* [2007]), recognizing the part that lack of institutional support may play when good practice breaks down.

Case law on registration is also building. Registration was refused where an applicant had failed to disclose past misconduct and poor performance to the GSCC or a previous employer. Honesty and trustworthiness are key components of good character (GSCC, 2002). Once again, the degree of recognition and the individual's response will be important (*Skervin v GSCC* [2007]). More critically, refusals of registration and deregistration have to date almost exclusively centred on inappropriate relationships with service users and non-disclosure of criminal convictions. Poor performance as highlighted in judicial reviews and ombudsman investigations has yet to trigger evaluation of suitability.

Registration and inspection

One means of ensuring accountability and raising standards is through registration and inspection of service provision. Here too the legislative map has evolved significantly owing to the modernization agenda (DH, 1998). The CSA 2000 replaces provisions in the CA 1989 regarding registration and inspection of children's homes. The regulatory framework is extended to small children's homes and local authority foster care, the relevant regulations being the Children's Homes Regulations 2001. All homes must have a statement of purpose, a guide to the establishment, and detailed arrangements for management, staffing, training, complaints procedures and record keeping. Every child must have a placement plan. Homes can be prosecuted by the CQC once notice has been given for failure to comply with the regulations. National minimum standards (DH, 2002g), published under the CSA 2000 (s.23(1)), have also been issued, again with provisions for management, staffing, complaints procedures, planning and protection of young people.

The CA 2004 (ss.20 and 21) requires the CQC to work with other inspectorates, such as Ofsted, in conducting Joint Area Reviews (JARS) using a common assessment framework (Ofsted, 2005, 2007) which focuses on the five outcome areas for young people (DfES, 2004a). JARS is due to be replaced in 2009 by Common Area Assessment where inspection is particularly triggered by poor performance, declining services and young people's under-achievement. Inspection will cover safeguarding, looked after children and disabled children and take account of the views expressed by young people, parents and carers.

The EIA 2006 formally transfers responsibility for the regulation and inspection of children's social care services, whether provided by local authorities or the private sector, to the Chief Inspector for Education, Children's Services and Skills. The CA 2004 also strengthens regulation of private fostering but registration is not compulsory. The Childcare Act 2006 provides a new framework for regulating and inspecting all early years settings, including childminders, with the intention of integrating early years provision with health and social services, securing sufficient child care for young people up to 14 (16 for disabled children) and improving outcomes.

The CQC (formerly the CSCI) is responsible for adult care and residential services across local authority, voluntary agencies and independent organizations. All domiciliary care agencies must be registered and inspected annually. Its functions include evaluating the quality of information provision and the effectiveness of services, which must incorporate assessment of value for money (s.76, HSCCHSA 2003). It registers, inspects and reports on service providers, including their record-keeping, management, staffing, facilities and training (ss.22 and 31, CSA 2000), using the seven outcomes for adult services, which include health and well-being, quality of life, freedom from discrimination, and dignity. In what has been described as a remarkably complex statutory scheme (*Bamgbala v CSCI* [2008]), registration as a care owner must follow an application if the CQC, or the CST on appeal, believe that the Care Homes Regulations 2001 will be complied with (s.13, CSA 2000). It is a criminal offence to run a care home without registration (s.11). The regulations require managers and providers to be physically and mentally fit, of good character, with integrity, to employ sufficient care, competence and skill and to possess the qualities, skills and experience necessary. The CQC may take enforcement action for a breach of the fitness provisions. National minimum standards have been issued, for instance on care homes for older people (DH, 2002h). These cover staffing, management and administration, including supervision and record-keeping, choice (including contracts), interpersonal care (incorporating dignity, privacy and care plans) and daily life (including cultural needs, complaints and protection). Unlike the regulations, which are mandatory, compliance with the standards is not enforceable.

Case law is evolving on registration. Care home providers are unlikely to be registered without good understanding of the regulatory requirements and sufficient experience, care, competence, and skill to comply with them (*Hunt v CSCI* [2007]). Registration as a provider or manager may be cancelled because of serious breaches of regulations, such as failing to record administered medication or serious incidents. The CQC must cancel registration if a provider or manager is unfit, or where there have been long-standing breaches of requirements and an unwillingness to acknowledge and provide a remedy (*Bamgbala v CSCI* [2008]). Inspectorates and the CST must adhere to decision-making standards, namely due process, when preparing and hearing evidence. Concerns should be discussed openly, interviewees must know what will be discussed so that they have time to prepare; records of meetings should be adequate to enable fair consideration of the evidence, and conclusions should be evidenced (*Hunt v CSCI* [2007]; *Joseph v CSCI* [2007]).

Under the HSCCHSA 2003 inspectorates may access records for purposes of carrying out their inspection functions or dealing with complaints. More critically, all the legislation quoted here refers to safeguarding and promoting people's welfare rather than to giving individuals rights. It is, therefore, out of step with both European and United Nations Conventions. The quality of care homes remains variable, with the suggestion that inspectorates cannot distinguish between poor and excellent care (Valios, 2006). Arguably, minimum standards are set too low and the inspection framework focused on quality control – standards which are measurable (Scourfield, 2007) – rather than on quality of life measures and the less tangible, but no less significant, components within care relationships.

In a potentially significant extension to partnership with experts by experience, the LGPIHA 2007, elaborated in secondary legislation (the

Local Involvement Networks (Duty of Service Providers to Allow Entry) Regulations 2008), gives local involvement networks the role of scrutinizing local authority adult social care provision. Lay involvement in inspections dates back at least to LAC(94)16, with consultation between service providers and users on standards, open reports, and follow-up. Networks have the right of entry to inspect adult social services premises, which can entail observing activities provided this will not harm service users or compromise either their dignity or the provision itself. Local authorities (s.221) must have strategies for promoting the involvement of local people in the commissioning, provision, monitoring and scrutiny of health and social care services. Local authorities will receive reports of the views of networks on the quality of provision and must (s.226) consider how to respond to matters referred to them.

This legislative schema changed with the implementation of the Health and Social Care Act 2008. This merges health and social care regulators, including the CSCI and the MHAC, into the Care Quality Commission. The new commission, charged with improving health and social care services, encouraging provision based on need and the experiences of people who use services, but also with ensuring efficient and effective use of resources (s.3), has new powers of enforcement, including warning and fixed penalty notices. There will be increased fines for criminal breaches of care home regulations. Inspection will be lighter touch for providers with good records, an approach to proportionate monitoring that is also recommended in respect of corporate parenting and the outcomes for children in care (DfES, 2007).

What is the evidence for the effectiveness of inspection and registration systems? Bainbridge and Ricketts (2003) found good systems for safeguarding vulnerable older people from abuse and poor practice. The Audit Commission (2002) found significant progress in departments subject to special measures but some weaknesses in enforcement of performance standards. Lymbery (2007) observes that performance measures can have a beneficial impact on service quality but questions whether current frameworks capture the essence of what social services organizations must accomplish. Laming (2003) recommended that senior managers should inspect case files and supervision notes at least every three months. Braye and Preston-Shoot (1999) note that inspection is a retrospective rather than developmental activity. It may prevent poor practice but will not, of itself, promote staff development or provide support through the difficulties encountered in trying to improve practice. Equally, it does not address the dynamics and forces that lead to abusive practice.

Conclusion

Policy guidance, regulations, national service frameworks and national minimum standards have proliferated, attempting to promote accountability by making clear requirements and frameworks within which professional judgement is to be exercised. The national minimum standards for fostering services (DH, 2002d) requires clear aims and objectives, accessible written policies and procedures for use by decision-making panels, and transparent systems for promoting children's welfare. Complaints should be monitored for evidence of the quality of care provided and staff must possess adequate knowledge and experience. The national service framework for children (DfES, 2004c) requires planning, both generally and in individual cases, oriented around care standards, identifying needs and intervening early, promoting health and well-being, supporting parents and carers, and making information available. Care packages should be co-ordinated and services both integrated and age appropriate. There are standards for urgent mental health assessments and short breaks for disabled children.

Critics argue, however, that such standards have a negative effect by elevating coercion and removing discretion from practitioners (Blaug, 1995; Ward, 1996) – that the approach hinders good workers whilst not assisting (or effectively regulating) weak practitioners. Indeed, practitioners have reported that one impact of assessment frameworks and national standards is that agency managers focus on performance measures to the exclusion of the legislative aims and the needs of service users (Braye et al., 2007). Harlow (2004) argues that if guidance is too prescriptive, it may undermine reflexivity, dialogue and the relational aspects of social work. Lymbery (2007) questions whether accountability is really enhanced when service users are unaware of the regulatory framework, and whether separating out social services performance measures is fair and appropriate in a context of increasing integration across health, housing, education and social care.

Regulation will only be effective if service users and carers have the necessary knowledge and support to challenge harmful decision-making (Flynn, 2004), hence the importance of giving information not just about service provision and complaints procedures but also about the legal standards that should underpin decision-making. Wistow (2005) also reports that experts by experience believe that too much emphasis is placed on the personal and too little on the social aspects of their lives and roles.

Whilst much of the detail within regulatory frameworks is constructive for social work practice, its potential impact is reduced by being too distant from the personal encounters between practitioners, service users and carers. The language used is general and framed in welfare rather than rights-based terms, making enforcement problematic (Braye and Preston-Shoot, 1999). Sinclair and Corden (2005) are critical of the belief, for instance within the Climbié report (Laming, 2003), that safety will be enhanced through regulation, procedures, information collection and a management hierarchy. The quality of the experience of service provision depends on much else besides, which is the focus of the next chapter.

---

putting it into practice

Take one key piece of social work law, such as a local authority circular, a guidance document, a code of practice, or an inquiry report investigating practice. Summarize the document chosen, identifying the key points and their implications for practice. Prepare a short presentation for colleagues, identifying the importance of the material. Finally, take a case with which you are working and consider how the material you have read impacts upon your work.

Further reading

Boylan, J. and Braye, S. (2006) 'Paid, professionalised and proceduralised: can legal and policy frameworks for child advocacy give voice to children and young people?', *Journal of Social Welfare and Family Law*, 28, 3–4, 233–49. This paper explores emerging concerns about the nature and direction of advocacy with young people in public care.

Ellis, K. (2004) 'Promoting rights or avoiding litigation? The introduction of the Human Rights Act 1998 into adult social care in England', *European Journal of Social Work*, 7 (3), 321–40. This article evaluates the impact of human rights legislation on social work practice.

Fairgrieve, D. and Green, S. (eds) (2004) *Child Abuse Tort Claims Against Public Bodies: A Comparative Law View*. Aldershot: Ashgate. This text reviews how different legislative systems approach accountability.

7 | Frameworks for partnership work

The second chapter on social work practice focuses on relationships: between agencies, between service providers and communities, and between social workers, service users and carers. Once again, the emphasis falls on how legal frameworks support practice that is in line with social work values and knowledge.

Anti-discriminatory policies and practice

Social workers must not discriminate unlawfully or unjustifiably (GSCC, 2002). They must promote social justice, challenge individual, institutional and structural discrimination, and combat processes that lead to marginalization and social exclusion (QAA, 2008). They must respect people's human rights, and enable them to maintain independence and develop their potential. This involves practising by equality and diversity principles, dismantling barriers, and resisting stereotyping (GSCC, 2008). These key commitments find increasing support in legal rules, including the ECHR, article 14 of which provides that Convention rights themselves must be enjoyed without discrimination on grounds such as sex, race, language, religion, political opinion or birth status.

Section 71 of the RRA 1976 imposes a duty on local authorities to ensure that their functions are performed with due regard for the need to eliminate unlawful racial discrimination, and to promote equality of opportunity and good relations between people of different racial groups. Section 20 makes it unlawful for anyone providing goods, facilities or services to the public to discriminate by refusing or deliberately omitting to provide them or by the quality, manner or terms in which they are provided. Section 35 allows the special education, training and welfare needs of particular racial groups to be met by preferential allocation or restriction of access to such groups.

The RR(A)A 2000 was one outcome of the Stephen Lawrence inquiry report (Macpherson, 1999), which recognized that systematic disadvantage occurs through institutional procedures, policies and practices, including the unequal distribution of power, opportunity and resources. The Act imposes active requirements on public authorities for tackling behaviour, attitudes and processes, a trend that continues with the Disability Discrimination Act 2005 and the Equality Act 2006. Thus in respect of race, disability and gender, public authorities must consider the equality implications of what they do, prepare impact statements and adopt schemes for equality in employment and services. The duties on public authorities thereby shift from focusing merely on individual acts of discrimination to taking positive action.

The RR(A)A 2000 brings all public services within its scope, making it unlawful for any public authority to discriminate, directly or indirectly, in the performance of their functions. Public authorities, such as central and local government, NHS trusts, prisons, voluntary agencies and the courts, must work towards the elimination of unlawful discrimination and promote equality of opportunity and good race relations. They must have strategies to prevent, investigate and record racist incidents. Exemptions are allowed for certain immigration and nationality functions, and judicial proceedings, including decisions not to prosecute. Noteworthy, then, is judgement against a local authority for having failed to conduct a race equality impact assessment before changing funding criteria for voluntary organizations (*R (Kaur and Shah) v Ealing LBC* [2008]).

The Race Relations Act (Amendment) Regulations 2003 implements the EU Article 13 Race Directive (2000/43/EC) into UK law, outlawing discrimination on grounds of racial or ethnic origin in employment, vocational training, goods and services, social protection, education and housing. The regulations bring more informal practices within the scope of indirect discrimination and revise the rules such that any job may be subject to a genuine occupational requirement for a person of a particular race. There is a statutory prohibition of harassment, being when someone's actions or words are unwelcome and violate another person's dignity or create an environment that is intimidating, hostile, degrading, humiliating or offensive. The burden of proof is revised so that where a claimant has established a *prima facie* case of discrimination or harassment, the complaint will be upheld unless respondents provide evidence to support denial. Business partnerships, charities, landlord/tenant relationships and employment in private homes are now covered.

The track record of local authorities in developing anti-discriminatory policies and services is hardly impressive, despite community care guidance (DH, 1990, 1991f, 2002b) requiring that eligibility criteria, assessment, and care provision respect cultural, ethnic and emotional needs, and that information provided takes account of special needs, different languages and cultural backgrounds. Myths continue that minority communities look after their own people and will not participate in service development (Begum, 2006). Some providers continue to lack cultural knowledge and expect people from minority groups to fit into existing provision (Vernon, 2002). A study of black young people caring for disabled family members found poor understanding of problems faced by the families and examples of discrimination by race and/or disability (Jones et al., 2002). Guidance says little about funding the voluntary sector, where many black projects exist, to ensure its survival. The emphasis on value for money leads to standardization which invariably reflects majority group needs.

The MHA 2007 lists principles later developed in the code of practice (DH, 2008d). One refers to respect for diversity, including religion, culture and sexual orientation. Another refers to avoidance of unlawful discrimination. However, these principles are set alongside others that direct attention to public safety and the effectiveness of treatment. This juxtaposition, alongside the omission of overt reference to human rights in the principles, reinforces long-standing concerns about institutional racism, cultural relevance of assessments and services, and marginalization of the ethnicity agenda within mental health provision. Black people remain over-represented in social control measures and under-represented in supportive, facilitative service provision; their experiences of acute care are frequently poor (Sheppard, 1996; Sashidharan, 2003).

Similarly, s.95, CJA 1991 requires those administering justice to avoid discrimination on grounds of race. National Standards (Home Office, 1995) require that work should be free from discrimination. The CDA 1998 (s.28) creates racially aggravated offences, crimes rendered more serious by racial motivation, attracting tougher sentences (*R v Saunders* [2000]). However, African-Caribbean people are more likely to be stopped or arrested by the police, less likely to receive unconditional bail, and over-represented in the prison population. Young black men continue to lack confidence in the police and services for victims lack accessibility (Yarrow, 2005).

The CA 1989 and the ACA 2002, and the regulatory guidance issued subsequently, affirm anti-discriminatory practice. Building on the principle (DH, 1989a) that services and practices must not reflect or reinforce discrimination, the CA 1989 includes:

1 race, culture and religion as characteristics which courts should consider in determining children's welfare (s.1(3)(d));
2 religious persuasion, racial origin, cultural and linguistic background as features to which local authorities must give due consideration in making decisions about looked after children (s.22(5));

3 a duty to consider racial groups to which children in need belong and, in respect of day and foster care, to have regard to different racial groups (Sch.2(11)).

Similar duties exist for voluntary organizations (s.61(3)(c)), registered children's homes (s.64 (3)(c)), and cancellation of registration of those providing day care and childminding (s.74(6)), where seriously inadequate care includes lack of attention to children's race, culture, language and religion. The ACA 2002 contains similar requirements concerning racial background and religion (s.1 (5)).

Regulatory guidance refers to:

1 Valuing children's religious, cultural, racial and linguistic identity (DH, 1991d).
2 Ensuring availability of experience and expertise to assess needs, including ethnic origins, religion and special needs (DH, 1991e).
3 Ensuring equal opportunities when working together to safeguard children, securing for children their best possible development regardless of gender, ability, race and age (DfES, 2006a).
4 Considering the effects of racism when families respond to assessment and enquiry procedures (DfES, 2006a).
5 Respecting differences of religion, culture and ethnic origins, working knowledgeably with diversity, and neither reflecting nor reinforcing people's experiences of discrimination (DH, 2000c).
6 Promoting equality issues and monitoring discrimination through children's advocacy services (DH, 2002e).
7 Drawing on awareness of social factors discriminating against black and minority ethnic groups, understanding the effects of racial history, racial discrimination and institutional racism, and assessing how religious beliefs and cultural traditions influence attitudes, values and behaviour, without condoning abuse and neglect for religious or cultural reasons (DfES, 2006a).

Practice guidance (DH, 2000b) on assessing children in need acknowledges institutional racism, reflected in the numbers of black and minority ethnic children in care, and applies knowledge about black families to the three domains of assessment. It recognizes the difficulties involved but recommends that assessment should address the impact of racism on children and families, and not reinforce it through stereotyping. Standards for fostering services (DH, 2002d) require that placements take account of, and address needs relating to, ethnic origin, religion, gender, disability and sexuality.

Thus the legal rules endorse anti-discriminatory practice. Lack of resources will not excuse discrimination. Resources must reflect the profile of the communities served, especially if the goal of social inclusion (CA 2004) is to be achieved.

What is due consideration? To what extent are questions of race, culture and religion to be determinative? Here the law balances the importance of race against other matters, such as attachment to present carers, in deciding a child's welfare (*Re P (a minor) (Adoption)* [1990]). Accordingly placement regulations (DH, 1991e) endorse same-race placements as most likely to meet a child's needs and safeguard their welfare, 'other things being equal'. Generally there are no grounds for complacency. Cleaver et al. (2004) find that greater attention still should be paid to assessing children from black and minority ethnic groups to ensure equality of access to services.

The SDA 1975 (amended 1986) parallels the RRA 1976 in making it unlawful to discriminate on grounds of sex and marital status in employment, education and provision of goods, facilities and services. Sex discrimination must be avoided by those administering justice (s.95, CJA 1991). The Employment Equality (Sex Discrimination) Regulations 2005 bring the EU Equal Treatment Directive (2002/73/EC) into UK law, requiring equal treatment for men and women in access to employment, vocational training and promotion, and working conditions. A further EU Directive (2006/54/EC) reinforces the prohibition on sexual harassment as both a form of sex discrimination and a violation of dignity in the workplace.

The Equality Act 2006 requires that public authorities promote equality of opportunity to counter sex discrimination, again paralleling positive actions demanded in respect of racial equality. The Gender Recognition Act 2004 enables people who have decided to live permanently and fully in their chosen gender to apply for legal recognition of that change.

Regulatory (DH, 1991d) and other guidance in relation to children (DH, 1989a) refers to equal opportunities, including the importance of practice avoiding gender stereotyping. However, policy guidance on community care is either silent on promoting equality for women (DH, 1990) or non-specific when requiring that assessments do not unfairly discriminate but take account of gender and other social divisions when responding to presenting needs (DH, 2002b). Gender must be taken into account when providing services to a cared for person as part of support to their carer (DH, 2005b). Equally, the Carers (Equal Opportunities) Act 2004, designed to minimize disadvantage to carers, engages consideration of gender in assessments, which must consider carers' work, education, training and leisure needs. Nonetheless, assumptions about gender and care giving continue to influence policy and practice. Cestari et al. (2006), for example, show that women receive poorer access to, or a lower level of, resources.

In relation to disability, the range of services which may be provided under the CA 1989 and the CSDPA 1970 do little to challenge discrimination because they reflect the non-disabled assumptions and orientation of social arrangements. They emphasize individualized needs and resources, rather than rights and inclusion. Problematic assumptions continue to be held about disabled people and direct payments (Bewley and McCulloch, 2004; Ellis, 2007). Services for people with physical and sensory disabilities are insufficiently culturally sensitive (Clark, 2003), with mixed experiences of how well direct payments and individual budgets offer flexibility to access culturally appropriate services (SCIE, 2007). There remain wide variations in opportunities for learning disabled people to make choices about where to live, what to do and who will support them (Stalker et al., 1999; HM Government, 2009), coupled with disturbing evidence of poor quality care, inadequate performance monitoring, stereotyping, poor communication between NHS Trusts and social services, sidelining of carers and mishandling of complaints (LGO, 2008; Michael, 2008). Pejorative attitudes and judgements regarding disabled parents also continue (Wates, 2002; Law Commission, 2008), notwithstanding policy guidance (DH, 2002b) on supporting their parenting capacity through community care services. There remain in law no guarantees to independent living or to transferring care packages when disabled people move across local authority boundaries.

Local authorities must provide services to disabled children that are designed to minimize the effects of disability and to give children the opportunity to lead lives that are as normal as possible (Sch.2(9), CA 1989). Accommodation for disabled children should be suitable for their needs (s.23(8), CA 1989). A register of disabled children should be kept to assist with future planning of services (Sch.2(2), CA 1989). Guidance (DH, 1991g) lists the principles for such work: the child's welfare is paramount; disabled children are children first and should access the same range of services as others; the importance of partnership with families must be recognized. Responding to research evidence about the variable quality of assessments, practice guidance (DH, 2000b) applies the three domains of the assessment framework – a child's developmental needs, parenting capacity, and family and environmental factors (DH, 2000c) – to provision for disabled children. However, case law indicates that assessments of children in need do not always conform to guidance that local authorities should first assess the needs of the disabled child and, where appropriate, the carers and other family members; second, produce a care plan; and third, provide the identified services (*R v Lambeth LBC, ex parte K* [2000]). In one instance (*R (CD) (a child by her litigation friend VD) v Isle of Anglesey CC* [2004]) a care plan was overruled because it did not minimize the effects of a young person's disability (s.17(2) and sch.2(6), CA 1989), or give due consideration to the child's wishes (s.20(6)) and did not meet her needs (s.23(8)). Case law also shows that obligations to disabled children under the CSDPA 1970, which are duties owed to individual children, are ignored by reliance on s.17, the Children Act 1989, where the legislation is couched in more general terms, effectively conferring target duties, failure to implement which is more difficult to challenge (*R v Bexley LBC, ex parte B* [2000]). Ombudsman investigations also find failures to make appropriate provision for disabled children (LGO, 2002).

The Disability Discrimination Act 1995 makes it unlawful to discriminate in connection with employment, access to buildings, and the provision of goods, facilities and services. Discrimination is defined as the refusal of a service or less favourable treatment that cannot be justified for reasons relating to disability. Disability is defined as a physical or mental impairment which has substantial and long-term adverse effects on an individual's ability to carry out normal daily activities. Employers and service providers must make reasonable adjustments, changing practice, policy and procedures that make it unreasonably difficult for disabled people to access jobs and services, and giving extra help or providing aids and other facilities to promote inclusion (*Roads v Central Trains* [2004]; *Ross v Ryanair and Stansted Airport* [2004]). What is reasonable depends on the resources available and the practicality of the adjustments, and should be based on a proper assessment of what is required to eliminate any substantial disadvantage (*Southampton City Council v Randall* [2006]).

The Act's provisions were vague and not comprehensive in terms of groups of disabled people or areas of daily living covered. It was unlikely to promote integration into economic and social life, to assist disabled people in community participation and presence, or to free disabled people from constraints affecting their lives, especially since service provision legislation is narrowly focused on particular types of care-based services.

Partial strengthening and extension of the legal rules has followed. The Disability Rights Commission Act 1999 provided for a commission with powers of enforcement, the preparation of statutory codes of practice, the availability of advice and formal investigations, and the facility for assistance to disabled people to secure their rights. Exemptions for small employers were removed in 2004. The Special Educational

Needs and Disability Act 2001 extends the DDA 1995 to cover education, training and any services provided wholly or mainly for students. It is unlawful for those providing such services to treat a disabled person less favourably than a non-disabled person for a reason that relates to the person's disability. If a disabled person is at a substantial disadvantage, those providing services must take reasonable steps to prevent it, such as changes to policy and practice, course requirements and timetables, physical features of a building, provision of interpreters, and alternative forms of delivery materials.

The Employment Act 2002 allows flexible working hours for parents (men and women) of disabled children. However, knowledge of the legislation is limited. Evidence indicates a lack of understanding and flexibility by employers, and employees uncertain of their rights (Harrison and Shelley, 2004). Nor does this Act necessarily prevent unfavourable treatment and harassment, which may now constitute discrimination by association (*Coleman v Attridge Law* [2008]).

The Disability Discrimination Act 2005 (s.2) amends the DDA 1995, making it unlawful for a public authority to discriminate against a disabled person in carrying out its functions. A public authority must not discriminate unless:

● Non-compliance is necessary in order not to endanger the health or safety of others.
● The person is not capable of giving informed consent and non-compliance is reasonable.
● Substantial extra costs are involved and having regard to resources these would be too great.
● Non-compliance is necessary for the protection of the rights and freedoms of others.
● The non-compliance is a proportionate means of achieving a legitimate aim.

Public authorities must make reasonable adjustments to practice, policy and procedures which make it unreasonably difficult for a disabled person to access or use a service. Section 3 amends the 1995 Act to require public authorities to perform their functions with due regard to the need to eliminate unlawful discrimination or harassment of disabled people, to promote equality of opportunity, to take account of disabled people's disabilities (even where this involves treating disabled people more favourably than others) and to encourage participation by disabled people in public life. Section 18 amends the definition of disability to include people with some cancers, HIV infection and multiple sclerosis. Protection is extended for people with mental health difficulties by removing the requirement that the condition is clinically recognized. As yet legislation does not provide rights for independent living, nor require disabled housing registers or technology in public transport to assist people with sensory and/or learning disabilities. However, s.3 DDA 2005 requirements have been used successfully to challenge a local authority's amendment to its eligibility criteria for access to community care services (*R (Chavda) v Harrow LBC* [2007]).

Social work's engagement with inequality also embraces sexuality, religion, age and class. Here too change is apparent. Section 28 of the LGA 1988, which viewed homosexual partnerships as 'pretended family relationships' and prohibited local authorities from promoting them, was repealed by s.127 of the LGA 2003. The CPA 2004 has given legal recognition to same-sex partners. Discrimination against gay and lesbian nearest relatives under the MHA 1983 was successfully challenged (*R (SSG) v Liverpool City Council and others* [2002]) resulting in amendment to ensure equal treatment. The HFEA 1990 (s.13(5)), requiring that deliberations on the welfare of the child must include consideration of their need for a father, has been revoked (HFEA 2008). People in same-sex relationships are no longer disqualified from adoption, provided they can demonstrate an 'enduring family relationship'. Civil partners may acquire parental responsibility in a similar way to step parents (s.144(4), ACA 2002). Finally, incitement to hatred on grounds of sexual orientation is now a criminal offence (s.74, CJIA 2008).

Policy guidance (DH, 1991a) covering preparation of young people for leaving care, requires that the needs and concerns of 'gay young men and women' must be recognized and approached sympathetically. However, the guidance on foster care (DH, 1991e) still refers to the chosen way of life of some adults rendering them unable to provide a suitable environment for care of children. Guidance on assessment of children in need (DH, 2000b, 2000c) is silent on sexuality. This falls considerably short of positive social work practice (Macdonald, 1991) which ensures availability of information and literature, challenges heterosexist behaviour and language, promotes clear messages about the validity of being lesbian, gay or heterosexual and provides confidential discussion space.

The Employment Equality (Sexual Orientation) Regulations 2003, Employment Equality (Religion or Belief) Regulations 2003 and Employment Equality (Age) Regulations 2006 outlaw discrimination in employment and vocational training. They were introduced to comply with EU Employment Directive (2000/78/EC), again reflecting the influence of Europe on the development of UK law, which prohibited discrimination on grounds of sexuality, religion or belief, disability and age in employment and vocational training. The regulations outlaw direct and indirect discrimination, harassment and victimization. They apply throughout the employment relationship and to all employers/businesses, qualification bodies and further and higher education institutions.

The sexual orientation regulations cover persons of the same sex (lesbians and gay men), opposite sex (heterosexuals) and same and opposite sex (bisexuals). They cover discrimination on grounds of perceived and actual sexual orientation. The religion or belief regulations cover actual or perceived religion, religious belief or similar philosophical belief, but not other kinds of belief.

Under the age regulations, employers must consider requests to continue working beyond retirement age. However, employers can still, with six months notice, retire people over 65 and refuse applications for employment from people within six months of 65. Thus, the regulations do not tackle institutionalized ageism comprehensively.

In respect of service provision, the Equality Act 2006 prohibits discrimination in the provision of goods, facilities and services on the grounds of religion or belief and sexuality, with further guidance in the Equality Act (Sexual Orientation) Regulations 2007. Whilst the national service framework for older people (DH, 2001b) sets a standard for services that do not discriminate on grounds of age, there is no public sector equality duty covering age, and discriminatory practice is often not even identified, let alone addressed (Postle et al., 2005). Evidence of discrimination through reduced service provision emerges when people make the transition between adults' services and specialist services for older people (Clark et al., 2004). Barriers to involvement and participation remain for older people, characterized by blanket assumptions and stereotypes about lifestyles, as evidenced in poor provision of information and limited encouragement to use direct payments (Bainbridge and Ricketts, 2003; Hasler, 2003; Postle et al., 2005).

The Equality Act 2006 also creates a single Equality and Human Rights Commission, with investigation and enforcement powers, to disseminate awareness of human rights and secure equality and good relations between diverse groups. It may intervene in court cases covering equality and human rights issues. However, its remit is extensive – disability, age, gender, sexuality, race, and religion or belief – and its resources may be stretched to give each aspect, as well as their interlocking features, the same focused attention as previously available for sex, disability and race through separate commissions.

Not all legislation has moved closer to social work's commitment to anti-discriminatory practice. The CAA 2006 continues to enforce contact between children and non-resident parents, even where this might destabilize the care being given by the resident parent. The AI(TC)A 2004 allows the withdrawal of support from failed asylum seeking families. Its provision in s.19 relating to marriages by people subject to immigration rules was declared unlawful (*R (Baiai and Others) v Secretary of State for the Home Department* [2006]). It contravened Articles 12 and 14 of the ECHR by distinguishing between Anglican and other marriages, with permission only being required for the latter. The ABA 2003, with its provision for dispersal orders, may antagonize and alienate young people who feel stigmatized when in public places. Public authorities will need to avoid unwarranted discrimination and assess the impact of these powers on the promotion of race equality (Crawford and Lister, 2007).

These disjunctions leave practitioners with a dilemma: what action should they take when they believe agencies are discriminating? The variable outcome of social work's commitment to anti-discriminatory practice highlights the importance of exploring how public authorities respond to the intentions expressed in legal rules. Otherwise they may remain comfortable rhetoric only (Humphries, 2004). Possible responses are discussed in Chapter 8.

Confidentiality

Confidentiality is where the tension between partnership and protective duties is particularly prominent. Principles of privacy, safety and public interest converge; practitioners must respond to two injunctions simultaneously – defending individual interests, and promoting the public good (Clark, 2006). Either may require information-sharing or confidentiality. These different imperatives must be weighed in each case, presenting moral and practical dilemmas, and requiring judgement and discretion. Too tight an adherence to confidentiality can place users at risk; too loose and there emerge risks of labelling and injustice.

Confidentiality is an established social work value. Social workers must maintain trust and confidence, respecting confidential information and explaining agency policies on information-sharing (GSCC, 2002). Facts must be distinguished from opinion or hearsay, information should be checked for accuracy and fully shared with service users unless there is a clear risk of significant harm, and practitioners should openly discuss their duties and roles. However, safeguarding responsibilities may require disclosure of information without the individual's consent. A failure to weigh up gathered information, to place it in context and to form a decision based on a vulnerable person's best interest (Goldsmith, 2005) can have quite devastating effects on quality of life. Sometimes Article 6 and Article 8 (ECHR) have to be balanced, or one individual's Article 8 rights against another's. In *R (S) v Plymouth City Council* [2002] a mother was given access to data relating to her son, who was the subject of a Guardianship Order (MHA1983) and who lacked capacity to consent to disclosure, so that she could evaluate whether further action was needed to protect her son's interests. However, in another case (*R v Kent CC, ex parte Marston* [1997]) an Approved Social Worker was held to have acted lawfully in refusing to disclose the whereabouts of an individual on guardianship to a NR because of concerns about possible abuse. In *Re B (Disclosure to Other Parties)* [2001], a father who was alleged to be violent and had not had recent contact with his child, requested documents relating to care proceedings, asserting Article 6. The mother claimed her right to private and family life (Article 8). The court held that qualification of the father's right was acceptable if the reasons were compelling.

This complexity, coupled with that of the legal rules themselves, results in practitioners being uncertain about the lawfulness of sharing information (DCA, 2003; Laming, 2003; Bichard, 2004). Additionally, there are differences of approach across professions, rooted in values, role and status (Frost et al., 2005; Clark, 2006; Richardson and Asthana, 2006); child protection and mental health inquiries have identified divergent understandings of confidentiality, consent and referral behind inadequate communication and sharing of knowledge (Munro, 1996; Sheppard, 1996; Reder and Duncan, 2003). Failures to communicate have resulted in flawed risk assessments and undermined effective care planning. Information-sharing behaviours have, as a result, variously been over-open (stressing the public interest and disclosing inappropriately), over-cautious (emphasizing confidentiality and withholding inappropriately), or chaotic (Richardson and Asthana, 2006), The General Teaching Council, GSCC and Nursing and Midwifery Council (GTC et al., 2007) have issued a joint values statement, seeking to resolve the tension between information-sharing and confidentiality by establishing clarity on when professionals are obliged to share information, noting the primary duty to safeguard and promote the welfare of the child.

The law recognizes that strong public interest in disclosure may override a professional's duty to maintain confidentiality (*W v Egdell* [1989], DPA 1998; DCA, 2003; *Re B (Children: Patient Confidentiality)* [2003]). Thus, information disclosure to third parties will normally be with the subject's consent (DH, 2000e) unless there is evidence for, or a serious risk of, significant harm to children or adults, or a case requires some information-sharing in order to decide what further action may be necessary (DH, 2000a, 2000c; DfES, 2006a). Confidentiality is not intended to prevent exchange of information to assess significant harm but records should be kept of the reasons for disclosure or the request for information, and the agencies contacted (DH, 2000c). A child's welfare is paramount.

Where children have the capacity to enter into a confidential relationship, then, as with adults, the obligation of confidentiality is not total if disclosure in the child's best interests is compelling on the grounds of serious risk or harm (*Re C (A Minor) (Evidence: Confidential Information)* [1991]; *Re G (A Minor)* [1996]).

Similarly, in mental health services, disclosure of confidential information should normally be with the individual's consent or responding to a specific legal obligation (such as production of reports for MHRTs) or an overriding public interest, such as protecting others from serious harm (DH, 2008d). When seeking consent, practitioners should convey how information-sharing will benefit the individual or others. Decision-making regarding disclosure should be recorded fully. Practitioners should only exceptionally disclose without consent, where, for example, an individual lacks capacity, and then following MCA 2005 best interests procedures (NICE, 2006).

'Public interest' has also allowed disclosure of information to employers, universities offering professional training and/or regulatory bodies in respect of individuals who have abused children (*A County Council v W (Disclosure)* [1997]; *Re L (Care Proceedings: Disclosure to a Third Party)* [2000]; *Woolgar v Chief Constable of Sussex Police and UKCC* [2000]; *Maddock v Devon County Council* [2004]; *Brent LBC v SK HK (A Minor)* [2007]). Compelling reasons following risk assessment may also justify disclosure to housing and other authorities, and family members, of information relating to a sex offender (*Re C (Sexual Abuse: Disclosure)* [2002]; *R (J and Another) v West Sussex County Council and Another* [2002]).

Workers may disclose information to the police if (a) it can help prevent, detect or prosecute serious crime; (b) the crime is sufficiently serious for the public interest to prevail; or (c) without disclosure, the task of preventing or detecting the crime would be seriously prejudiced or delayed (DPA 1998). Thus, disclosures may be made to the police where this is necessary to allow investigation of possible criminal activity against children (*L v UK (Disclosure of Expert Evidence* [2000]; DfES, 2006a). Similarly, on medical advice, it may be necessary to disclose health information to prevent serious risk to the public (DH, 2000e). In line with the ECHR principle of proportionality, information disclosed should be the minimum necessary to meet the requirements of the situation (DH, 2000e).

Not infrequently social workers must consider whether to respect the confidences of children. Children's rights under the CA 1989, for example to seek leave to apply for a s.8 order or to discharge a parental responsibility order, are not restricted by age limits but rather by concepts of maturity, welfare and sufficient understanding (*Gillick v West Norfolk and Wisbech AHA* [1986]). Children may be given information or advice on request (Hamilton, 2005). Mature children have a right to seek independent advice and representation (*Mabon v Mabon* [2005]), to expect confidentiality from their advocates (DH, 2002e) and to receive medical treatment or counselling (Hamilton, 2005). They are entitled to the same duty of confidentiality (except in the circumstances discussed earlier) and if workers propose to disclose information for welfare reasons, the young person should be consulted (DH, 2000c). Where children are unable to consent to disclosure, any one person with parental responsibility may do so (CA 1989, s.2(7)). Professionals working with children and young people, however, should never promise absolute confidentiality because breach may be needed to safeguard their welfare (Hamilton, 2005). It is good practice to discuss with the child parental involvement, to provide information in a manner they can understand, and to assess how far they understand the advice given, appreciate its implications and significance, and comprehend the implications of the help sought. Also relevant is whether the practitioner believes that it is in the child's best interests to receive the advice or treatment. It is a matter of judgement.

Guidance has been issued to inform decision-making about disclosing information (DCA, 2003), namely:

- Is there a legal power to share the information? The power may be expressly stated. The CDA 1998 (s.115) allows disclosure to the local authority, police, probation service and NHS Trusts where necessary for the purposes of the Act. The DVCVA 2004 (s.54) contains a similar provision. The CA 2004 establishes databases to facilitate agencies working together and sharing information to identify family difficulties and provide appropriate support (s.12). Health and education authorities, and care homes, must notify the local authority when they provide accommodation for a child (s.85, CA 1989). Alternatively, the power may be implied. The CA 1989 implies that data should be shared for the protection of children (*R (A) v Hertfordshire County Council* [2001]).
- Is disclosure proportional? This is where Article 8 (ECHR) rights to private and family life are engaged. Such rights may be limited in accordance with law, for the purposes of a legitimate aim, such as safeguarding, and where necessary in a democratic society.
- Does the public interest lie in protecting confidentiality or sharing the data? Case law and policy guidance here have been discussed above.
- Does the DPA 1998 allow disclosure? Social workers are allowed to disclose information without consent for particular purposes (DH, 2000e).

To assist with data-sharing, local authorities must have information protocols with partner organizations on safeguarding and promoting the welfare of children and vulnerable adults (DH, 2000a, 2000e; DCA, 2003; Richardson and Asthana, 2006). Information-sharing and assessment systems also underpin the five outcomes in *Every Child Matters* (DfES, 2004a). Local authorities must promote co-operation between agencies to improve children's well-being (s.10) and partner agencies must co-operate (s.11), which includes (s.11(1)) a duty on some, such as NHS Trusts, police authorities and Youth Offending Teams to disclose information for inclusion on the databases. Section 12(4), CA 2004, details the information to be kept on children. The Integrated Children's System (LAC(2005)3) intends to facilitate collection and understanding of significant information, such as key events, legal status of the child and services received, to promote early intervention and co-ordinate referrals, assessments and planning across agencies. Establishing such systems has been affected by shortage of resources, lack of management support, difficulties changing mainstream practice and reluctance amidst some voluntary sector and health care professionals (Cleaver et al., 2004). The databases may reduce staff time when tracking down the child's professional network and may indicate who holds additional information and is engaged in direct work. Information is held in one location, facilitating easier access, and the structured format can lead to greater focus in assessments and reviews (Bell et al., 2007). However, it may prove difficult to differentiate between children at risk and those about whom there are concerns. The faith placed in information technology to reduce variability in practice, to overcome partial views of individual children, to minimize duplicated assessments, and to enhance children's safety may be overly optimistic (Bell et al., 2007; Peckover et al., 2009). Further guidance has been issued (DfES, 2006b; CWDC, 2007); information that is provided on the understanding that it would be shared with some people for some purposes may be shared and disclosure is allowable to promote the welfare of children and to prevent crime and disorder. Information-sharing should be proportionate. Young people under 16 with capacity to understand may consent to information being shared. As difficulties remain, perhaps because available guidance lacks subtlety for complex practice situations (Clark, 2006), it must remain doubtful whether regulatory guidance alone is sufficient to overcome professional reluctance to co-operate. Thus, Richardson and Asthana (2006) call for more outward-looking professional values, whilst training, supervision, and leadership in culture change are also necessary (Cleaver et al., 2004; Lord et al., 2008).

Advocates (MCA 2005, s.35(6); MHA 2007, s.30) may examine and take copies of health and local authority records relevant to their investigation. Inspectorates may access personal information in order to fulfil their inspection functions (HSC(CHS)A 2003). Personal information may also be used without consent for clinical audit, record validation, research or public health (DH, 2000e; HSCA 2001). Courts, Tribunals and the Ombudsman can all order disclosure of records to them. Consent of third parties is not required here but they should be informed. Children's Guardians have statutory rights of access to information relating to the children in question (s.42(1), CA 1989; *Manchester City Council v T and another* [1993]).

Social workers can be compelled to give evidence and cannot, therefore, guarantee confidentiality except as to the identity of informants (*D v NSPCC* [1978]). Children's Guardians should not promise complete confidentiality since the courts must determine what is disclosed (*Re D (minors)* [1994]). Decision-making on confidentiality of what people say to a Children's Guardian belongs to the court, whose permission is required, therefore, before information that is part of care proceedings is disclosed to any person or agency not a party to them (*Oxfordshire CC v P* [1995]). Factors taken into account here include the child's interests balanced against confidentiality (*Re EC (Disclosure of Material)* [1996]). In private law proceedings concerns about harm may also be passed on to relevant agencies, as the ultimate aim is to safeguard children. Practitioners must be alert to the danger of enmeshment and should assess the information to be shared for plausibility and evidence of risk and significant harm (*Re M (A Child) (Disclosure: Child and Family Reporter)* [2002]).

Article 6 rights (ECHR) ordinarily require that a person be informed of accusations against them and have opportunity to question witnesses. On whether parties to a dispute should, therefore, disclose documents, whether or not they intend to rely on them in legal proceedings, professional privilege has to yield to the paramount interests of the child (*Oxfordshire CC v M* [1994]) since to determine a child's welfare requires that reports are disclosed, irrespective of whether these contain unfavourable statements relating to a party, since any right to privacy must give way to the protection of the child's interests (*L v UK (Disclosure of Expert Evidence)* [2000]). A local authority must disclose documents to other parties in care proceedings, including notes of conversations and minutes of meetings (*Re G (Care: Challenge to Local Authority's Decision)* [2003]), whether or not the documents support its case. Parties should ensure that all relevant material is available to the court, having validated the information as much as possible (*Re R (Care: Disclosure: Nature of Proceedings)* [2002]).

The presumption is one of disclosure. Those seeking disclosure must show why documents should be produced. Courts may authorize that the evidence of one party, and reports, are not disclosed to another party if there are exceptional and compelling circumstances relating to the welfare of the child that outweigh the normal Article 6 requirements of a fair trial (*Re B (A Minor) (Disclosure of Evidence)* [1993]; *Re M (Disclosure)* [1998]; *Re W (Children) (Care Proceedings: Disclosure)* [2003]). Where a local authority believes that public interest immunity should apply, it should inform the other parties and apply to court for permission to withhold a document (*Re C (Care Proceedings: Disclosure of Local Authority's Decision-Making Process)* [2002]). Local authorities have been criticized for defensive and obstructive attitudes regarding disclosure (*Re J (A Child) (Care Proceedings: Disclosure)* [2003]). The implications for recording are discussed in Chapter 8.

The strong presumption of disclosure to a party of material relating to them applies to adoption (*Re D and Another (Minors) (Adoption Reports: Confidentiality)* [1995]). Again, the child's welfare may justify the court's use of discretion not to disclose but a court must consider the degree of likelihood that harm will occur and the gravity if it does. Both likelihood and seriousness are required for refusal to disclose. Thus, in *Re X (Children) (Adoption: Confidentiality)* [2002] disclosure of prospective adopters' identity to the birth parents was refused because of the likelihood of significant harm to the child and the destabilization of the placement.

Finally, it is worth noting that family proceedings are held in private, although the CA 2004 (s.62) does allow publication of information about cases in exceptional circumstances in the public interest. Youth Courts, however, are open and cases may be reported providing a young person's identity is not disclosed. This may be lifted if it is in the public interest and must be when courts are considering breach of anti-social behaviour orders (SOCPA 2005, s.141). There are no automatic reporting restrictions when courts make anti-social behaviour orders (ABA 2003) although courts must consider the young person's welfare (CYPA 1933).

Access to information

Access to information is a core component of integrated, effective services for people with complex needs (DH, 1998; Wistow, 2005). However, the legislation can be implemented passively or actively. For instance, the Health Services Ombudsman (2003) has been critical of poor information about continuing care funding, especially at the point of discharge from hospital to care homes.

Local authorities have a duty to publicize information about the services they offer (DPA 1986; CA 1989; NHSCCA 1990). This now includes the duty to provide information, advice and assistance on services, facilities and publications that are available, for instance concerning disabled children or employer-supported child care (Childcare Act 2006, s.12), and local authorities must also provide information, advice and training to childcare providers (s.13). The SEN(I)A 2008 requires councils to collect, and the Secretary of State to publish, data on outcomes for young people with special educational needs in order to improve planning for their well-being. Information should be accessible (language and location) to all potential users, especially on services, eligibility criteria, costs and timescales (DH, 1990, 2002c). It should be straightforward, relevant, accurate, and enable people to make informed choices and to understand how personal information will be shared with others (DH, 1991f, 2000c, 2002e).

Policy guidance requires local authorities to detail clearly the community care needs that they will support, including a jointly agreed strategy for providing information on long-term care services across health, housing and social care (DH/DETR, 2001). They must inform disabled adults and their carers about the standards they can expect, and what they can do if expectations are disappointed. The focus is on working in partnership to sustain people's independence, to treat people responsively and fairly on the basis of need, and to involve them in service improvement. For people with dementia and their carers (NICE, 2006) up-to-date information about local arrangements should be given. For detained patients and their NRs, information should be given orally and in writing, covering their rights and the legal rules surrounding detention and treatment (DH, 2008d). For children's services, information-sharing systems should support achievement by young people of beneficial outcomes. Service directories should be designed to help practitioners and the public know what is available locally and to facilitate finding services to meet children's needs. However, the quality of the data is not always reliable or comprehensive (Cleaver et al., 2004). Equally, some young people do not recall having been given information, for instance about how to complain, and struggle to make sense of the details they did receive (Pithouse and Crowley, 2007).

Inspections and research studies have been critical of performance in terms of the accessibility, consistency and clarity of information provision

(Fryer, 1998; Bradley, 2003; Baxter et al., 2008). Information systems had not worked adequately (DH, 2001b). Inspections of older people's services found patchy availability of information and poor provision for minority groups (Bainbridge and Ricketts, 2003). Disabled people, including parents and refugees, need more information, in a wider range of formats and languages (Clark, 2003), about their entitlements and how to access services, such as equipment, child care (Roberts and Harris, 2002; Vernon, 2002; Morris, 2004) and direct payments (Clark et al., 2004). Indeed, awareness within some departments about direct payments and eligibility criteria (Cestari et al., 2006) appears poor and service users are not informed even though offering direct payments is now mandatory (Leece and Leece, 2006). Parents of disabled children require clearer information about decision-making processes regarding placements (Abbott et al., 2001). Awareness of the notification requirements regarding private fostering (CA 2004, s.44) should be promoted (Morris, J., 2005). Young people leaving care receive little information about their entitlements (Harris and Broad, 2005). Publicity also fails to reach carers, including kinship carers, about assessment and provision (Williams and Robinson, 2000; Broad et al., 2001). Accessibility of information is crucial for people to make informed choices (Baxter et al., 2008) and to assert their rights. However, there is limited research evidence on the specific access needs for some service user groups, such as ethnic minority groups, young carers and people with multiple disabilities, and on how best to provide accessible information so as to reduce existing inequalities, expand the range of data available, and target people facing life transitions or particular barriers (Baxter et al., 2008).

In *Gaskin v UK* [1986] the ECtHR held that refusal of access to a social services file containing information about a person's family and life in local authority care violated Article 8. Access to files legislation was a direct result, now governed by the DPA 1998 and the FoIA 2000. Specific regulations for social services have been issued (Data Protection (Subject Access Modification) (Social Work) Order 2000) along with guidance (DH, 2000e). Similar orders have been made with respect to health and education.

The FoIA 2000 provides a general right to information held by public authorities concerning their functions, rather than their involvement with particular individuals. Specific timeframes operate within which organizations receiving requests for information must respond. Some exceptions to the principle of transparency are allowed, such as commercially sensitive information or documentation which, if disclosed, would prejudice the prevention or detection of crime. Organizations should provide training for staff on the procedures involved and have systems for tracking the location and movement of records, and for monitoring compliance with the Act.

The DPA 1998 requires that information is processed lawfully and fairly. Processing of data must be done with the consent of the data subject or be necessary either to protect their or other people's vital interests or to facilitate a function conferred by legislation or government department. Data may be used only for the legitimate purpose for which it was obtained and must be accurate and up-to-date. Data should not be kept for longer than is necessary and must be adequate, relevant and not excessive for its purpose.

Subject to certain safeguards and exceptions, individuals may have access to data held on them. They are entitled to a description of the personal information held, the purposes for which it is processed, the recipients of the information and its source. This includes children where the authority is satisfied they understand the nature of their request or someone with parental responsibility approves. Parents may seek access to a child's records if the child is not competent to make an application *and* access is in the child's best interests, or if the child is competent and consents. If another individual could be identified from data, that part of the information may be withheld unless that other individual has consented, or it is reasonable to comply with the data subject's request anyway without such consent.

Social Services must have an access procedure, although there is no duty to publicize it actively or widely. Having received a written request and, if required, a fee, departments must inform applicants within 40 days what information is held, and provide access and copies when requested. Applicants can request amendment of recorded information which they consider inaccurate. If the authority disagrees, a notice must be attached to the record specifying the disputed part and a copy given to the applicant. Where an authority refuses to grant access or amend information held, appeal is possible either to the Data Protection Commissioner or to the courts. Courts may order disclosure or amendment. The Commissioner can issue enforcement notices.

Exceptions to access (DH, 2000e) are:

1 adoption information;
2 certain court reports;
3 information held for purposes of crime prevention or detection, or the prosecution of offenders, where disclosure could prejudice such matters;
4 information which would reveal the identity of another person to whom the information partly relates or a source of that information,

with that individual refusing to consent to the disclosure on written request from the local authority; this does not normally apply to social services employees or to those providing services to enable the authority to exercise its functions; moreover the information can be supplied in ways in which the identity cannot be discerned;

5 information which would cause serious harm to the physical or mental health of the applicant or another person;

6 where disclosure would possibly prejudice social work functions, including any case for legal proceedings.

Where access involves personal physical or mental health information, the authority must not disclose this information without first consulting an appropriate health professional, normally the person responsible for the individual's clinical care (Data Protection (Subject Access Modification) (Health) Order 2000).

For recording and data access to be effective (DH, 2000e; DfES, 2006a), information must be accessible in terms of structure, language and style. Users and practitioners should be clear what information is recorded or exchanged, how, and why. Each should participate in compiling records, including assessments, reviews and closing summaries. Records should contain the process of decision-making, and observed or verified facts. Opinions, when stated, should be clearly differentiated from facts, with evidence for them. Record-keeping must enable service users to know and understand their development and other fundamental and essential aspects of their private and family life (*MG v UK* [2002]). It must help them come to terms with the emotional and psychological impact of significant events in their lives and understand their impact on subsequent and related behaviour. Practice guidance (DH, 2000e) emphasizes that recording helps to focus work, monitor practice and maintain continuity when new workers become involved. Case records should contain evidence of objectives, assessment and periodic summaries, and of how information has been shared with service users. Judges have reminded practitioners that files must have an adequate chronology of significant events and present a clear picture of serious and/or deep-rooted problems. Clear, accurate, full and balanced notes should be kept of all relevant conversations and meetings (*Re E and Others (Minors) (Care Proceedings: Social Work Practice)* [2000]; *Re C (Care Proceedings: Disclosure of Local Authority's Decision-Making Process)* [2002]) However, recording practice has often been associated with poor or tragic outcomes (Goldsmith and Beaver, 1999; Daniel and Baldwin, 2001; Preston-Shoot, 2003b).

Planning

Children's services plans were made mandatory by the Children Act 1989 (Amendment) (Children's Services Planning) Order 1996, partly to ensure co-ordination, efficiency and coherence within and between services, and to improve outcomes for young people (DH, 2000c). Concern, however, about the proliferation and duplication of planning requirements for children services, involving education and early years (Hamer, 2003), has led to some streamlining. The 1996 Order has been repealed and the CA 2004 (s.17) requires that local authorities prepare and review annually a single children and young people's plan. As in community care the plan should be strategic and collaborative, agreed between all the agencies responsible for safeguarding and promoting the welfare of children. The Integrated Children's System (LAC(2005)3) is also intended to support planning processes at individual case and strategic levels. However, patterns of need are often not understood or analyzed systematically (Huber, 1999; Little, 1999). Need profiles and decision-making on resource allocation have not necessarily been aligned. Joint planning arrangements with voluntary organizations (Stepney, 2006) and other statutory agencies (Preston-Shoot and Wigley, 2005) have proved variable. This highlights ongoing strains within interagency collaboration, for example on meeting the housing and social care needs of care leavers and homeless families, where the potential for buck-passing has drawn judicial criticism (*R v Northavon DC, ex parte Smith* [1994]). Initiatives to involve children are not always supported by the necessary resources, and appear confused on whether young people are consumers or citizens. Service development therefore reflects management strategies with insufficient testing against young people's experience (Gunn, 2005).

Significantly, however, and further reinforcing the policy differentiation between children in need and young offenders, local authorities are still required to produce a separate annual youth justice plan (CDA 1998, s.40), detailing the provision and operation of youth offending teams and strategies with targets to reduce youth offending. Additionally, local authorities, in partnership with the police, probation service, health and other stakeholders, must produce and implement local strategies for reducing crime and disorder (s.6).

Community care plans were originally required by s.46, NHSCCA 1990, again prepared and reviewed in partnership with health, housing and voluntary bodies. This requirement was repealed in England by Care Plans (England) Directions 2003. The C(EO)A 2004 requires housing and health authorities to give due consideration to requests from local authorities for assistance in planning services for carers. Good practice involves carers in planning and service development, and makes available information about local population needs. However, stereotypes continue to influence services for carers (Robinson and Williams, 2002).

Community care planning has been made more difficult by tight budgets and anxieties about the legal implications of recording unmet need for individuals. One reason why the duty to assess arises where the local authority has a legal power to provide community care to an individual (*R v Bristol City Council, ex parte Penfold* [1998]) is that assessment can inform future service plans. Some research (Tanner, 2003), nonetheless, suggests that managers rarely record gaps in services, despite this being a requirement in practice guidance (DH, 1991c), such that this information is not used to inform planning. Joint planning and commissioning with PCTs may also be impeded by interprofessional and organizational differences (Leece, 2007). Elsewhere, however, inspections have found better inclusion of service users in planning and consultation, and more integrated strategic planning between health and social care (Bainbridge and Ricketts, 2003) but population needs analysis and contracting for quality remain weak (Preston-Shoot and Wigley, 2004). Research with disabled people from ethnic minority groups (Vernon, 2002), and with learning disabled people (Flynn et al., 1996; Fyson et al., 2004), continues to find divergent views between service providers and users about what provision is valuable, and to recommend improvements in consultation. Planning for dementia services should include service users in order to highlight and address problems specific to localities (NICE, 2006). Equally, however, involving service users may prove difficult because of participation-fatigue and disillusion with the limited evidence of a return for the time and energy invested (Leece, 2007). Evidence would suggest that planning is still some way from systematically consulting with experts by experience, equating services to needs, and defining user-led outcomes as objectives.

Community care planning now falls within the LGA 2000, which empowers local authorities to promote and improve the economic, social and environmental well-being of their area (s.2). Section 4 requires preparation of community plans, utilizing local strategic partnerships between statutory and voluntary agencies, community groups and individuals. Social care's position within these plans, which cover children and adults, is not yet fully developed (Wistow, 2005). Policy guidance (DH/ DETR, 2001) requires experiences of provision to be sought, in order to inform planning and standards for health, housing and social services.

The LGPIHA 2007 (s.106) requires local authorities, with partner agencies, to prepare and publish local area agreements and community strategies. With targets, these are designed to improve the economic, social and environmental well-being of an area. Additionally, s.116 requires the production of a joint strategic needs assessment concerning health and social care needs.

Resources

There is no absolute right for an individual to receive a service or treatment. Instead, health and local authorities have powers and duties. Duties are sometimes owed to particular groups, such as children in need, and are known as target duties. Sometimes duties refer to individuals who might qualify for a service. They are stronger than target duties and, therefore, possibly easier to enforce; local authority decisions must be related to each individual to whom the duty is owed.

However, additional duties do not attract additional funding, and identifying need has serious consequences for local authority resources. Resource constraints are:

1 Creating a restrictive rather than broad interpretation of family support to children in need (s.17, CA 1989), despite guidance which cautions against employing narrow definitions (DH, 1991d; Colton et al., 1995; Platt, 2006).

2 Restricting the focus to children in greatest need at the expense of preventive services (Morris, K., 2005).

3 Limiting recognition and promotion of the human rights of unaccompanied asylum seeking children, disabled children at residential schools and privately fostered children (Morris, J., 2005).

4 Resulting in inexperienced practitioners handling child protection situations (Laming, 2003) and practitioner concern about assessment timescales, meeting identified needs and staffing resources (Millar and Corby, 2006; Platt, 2006). The failure to provide sufficient experienced staff and other resources, such as supervision, leads to important issues being overlooked, impaired thinking, ineffective monitoring, rationing, and optimistic assumptions that children are safe (Reder and Duncan, 2004; Sinclair and Corden, 2005).

5 Limiting service development and assistance to people who need community care services, and inflating some people's needs to ensure they receive a service (Clark, 2003; Fyson et al., 2004; Cestari et al., 2006; Charles and Manthorpe, 2007).

6 Limiting local authority use of alternatives to MHA 1983 hospital admission (Evans et al., 2005).

7 Constraining support for young people leaving care (Harris and Broad, 2005).

8 Encouraging local authorities to promote special guardianship with foster carers as, under the Special Guardianship Regulations 2005, councils are only obliged to support former foster parents for two years once the order is granted (Gillen, 2008).

9 Leading to residential care placements because finance is not available to support foster care provision for young children (Selwyn et al., 2006).

10 Prompting local authorities to disregard policy guidance (DH, 2002b) that recommends the adoption of low thresholds when considering whether someone may require a community care service (Tanner, 2003).

The net effect is that standards promoted in guidance are eroded. Practitioners become gate-keepers to resources rather than advocates (Richards, 2000; Lymbery, 2006). The ideology of curtailing welfare expenditure is sometimes quite explicit. The principles within the MHA 2007 juxtapose respect for patients' wishes and feelings, and their involvement in planning, with efficient use of resources. The NSF for Older People (DH, 2001b) suggests that resources have been duplicated and the Single Assessment Process (DH, 2002c) is therefore designed to ensure that professional resources are used effectively. Guidance on the Common Assessment Framework (CWDC, 2007) makes similar points regarding children's services.

At other times the question of resources is sidestepped completely. For instance, the CC(DC)A Act 2003 could result in local authorities assessing individuals in hospital, because of financial penalties, ahead of those in the community with similar or greater needs. Rebalancing adult social care between high- and low-intensity needs will require explicit choices and good financial management (Wistow, 2005). Laming (2003) recommends that no case should be closed until the child and their carer has been spoken to and a plan for safeguarding agreed. The CA 2004 moves the policy and practice focus beyond children in need and child protection to the well-being of all children in the community. Sinclair and Corden (2005) question the feasibility in the current financial context of local authorities and their partners delivering an adequate response to all children in local communities, whilst also ensuring children in need are protected from harm and high quality care for children removed from home. They are critical of the Laming Report (2003) for identifying shortage of resources but failing to recommend increased investment and to question whether all the recommendations could in fact be implemented within current financial constraints. Similarly, Stepney (2006) argues that any switch to prevention will prove unrealistic if it takes resources away from safeguarding children, whilst Platt (2006) suggests that refocusing needs to be financially front-loaded. Only rarely is service user anxiety about the likely availability or continuity of provision acknowledged; only rarely has lack of resources been acknowledged in policy pronouncements (DH, 1998).

What is the legal position on services and resources? Unless ring-fenced for particular purposes, the annual financial allocation is to each local authority. Indeed, this corporate identity and responsibility underpins guidance on assessing children in need and their families (DH, 2000c). Social workers commonly find their practice influenced and their recommendations delayed through lack of funds in particular budgets, but authorities should only plead lack of resources for statutory duties once all budgets, in whatever departments they were originally allocated, are spent.

Local authorities must have sufficient staff to perform their social services functions (s.6, LASSA 1970), but discretion in local authority standards here may prove difficult to contest. Ombudsman investigations have, however, referred to this duty in cases involving delay. In relation to absolute duties, provision cannot be fettered by resource considerations (DH, 1990; *R v Brent LBC, ex parte Connery* [1990]). The financial situation is not relevant where there is an absolute duty to do something; funds must be found to enable that duty to be fulfilled. Nor can resources be used as a reason for failing to follow s.7 (LASSA 1970) guidance, for example concerning reviews and reassessment of the need for provision (*R v Gloucestershire County Council, ex parte Radar* [1996]), or the provision of residential accommodation chosen by an individual which they are already providing to others (*R v Avon County Council, ex parte Hazell* [1995]).

Eligibility criteria may be shaped by resource considerations. However, criteria must be fair, reasonable and non-discriminatory (DH, 1990, 2002b), and not set so narrowly that the discretion to assess and provide services where it appears necessary excludes those who might need provision. Courts have begun to scrutinize how agencies use the FACS criteria. For example, significant health problems are serious (*R (Hefferman) v Sheffield City Council* [2004]) and must be allocated to the critical band so that care needs are met. When raising the threshold for assessment, local authorities must consider the impact this may have on disabled people (*R (Chavda) v Harrow LBC* [2007]). Equally, discretion must be exercised in every case. Operating blanket policies would breach the duty to assess an individual's need for services and fetter discretion by neglecting all the issues relevant to an individual case, thereby neglecting the possibility that *this case* may require departure from agreed eligibility criteria.

In relation to discretionary duties owed to the general population or specific groups, courts are reluctant to interfere in an authority's exercise of discretion and are likely to accept that financial restrictions are legitimate factors to take into account, for instance in respect of children in need (*R v RB of Kingston-upon-Thames, ex parte T* [1994]; *Re J (a minor) (Specific Issues Order)* [1995]; *Re C* [1996]). This is providing the authority's actions are neither perverse nor unreasonable (*Puhlhofer and Another v LB of Hillingdon* [1986]) and authorities have not exceeded or misused their powers, misdirected themselves in law or fact, or exercised discretion wrongly or for no good reason.

In relation to discretionary duties owed to individuals, it may prove harder for local authorities to take resources into consideration on decisions concerning assessment and service provision. The NHSCCA 1990 provides for assessment where the local authority is satisfied that a person might be in need of community care services. The duty (s.47) is discretionary, with the local authority deciding whether an assessment is appropriate and necessary. However, the duty to assess is not dependent on the physical availability of services but arises where the local authority has a legal power to provide community care to an individual (*R v Berkshire County Council, ex parte P* [1998]; *R v Bristol City Council, ex parte Penfold* [1998]).

The House of Lords ruled that, for community care, resources may be taken into consideration when assessing needs (*R v Gloucestershire County Council, ex parte Barry* [1997]) although subsequent policy guidance (DH, 2002b) appears to allow resource considerations only to influence how eligibility criteria are set and care plans constructed following assessment of need. Resources may be considered when deciding *how* to meet assessed needs, either when need is first established or on review and reassessment, providing all issues relevant to the case are evaluated (*R v Lancashire County Council, ex parte RADAR and Another* [1996]) and resource considerations do not dominate decision-making (DH, 2002b). To be lawful, assessment and review must take all of a person's needs into account (*R v Haringey LBC, ex parte Norton* [1998]). Services provided must have a reasonable chance of meeting the need identified (*R v Staffordshire County Council, ex parte Farley* [1997]). Care plans must follow policy guidance requirements, and reviews must contain an adequate analysis of why care is being reduced when the service user's needs remain unchanged, and reduction in care must not be driven solely or mainly by resource considerations (*R v Birmingham City Council, ex parte Killigrew* [2000]). A decision to move an older person from residential to nursing care was quashed because she could have remained there, as she and her family wished, providing resources were made available (*R (Goldsmith) v Wandsworth LBC* [2004]). The authority in choosing a cheaper option had not considered Article 8 rights and proportionality, and had not given appropriate consideration to a community care assessment stating that the woman could have remained settled in residential care. A similar Article 8 balancing exercise had not been done, and therefore a care plan was unlawful, when moving a person into residential care to save money without giving proper weight to her remaining at home (*R (Gunter) v SW Staffordshire PCT* [2006]).

So, whilst local authorities may decide how to balance needs versus resources in community care, and determine the weight to be given to each, service users' needs must be properly met. A balancing exercise must be carried out and any change in provision must not expose an individual to significant risk or detriment. Decision-making must be sensitive and reasonable.

The *Barry* case has been distinguished from other judgements about resources elsewhere in the social work landscape. Thus, a local housing authority must not take its resources into account when calculating a reasonable time for an applicant to secure accommodation. What was reasonable for an applicant would depend on her circumstances and the range of accommodation potentially available (*R (Conville) v Richmond upon Thames LBC* [2006]). Local housing authorities are also not entitled to take resources into account in deciding whether or not to approve a disabled facilities grant (s.23(1), H(GCR)A 1996; *R v Birmingham City Council, ex parte Taj Mohammed* [1998]). In *R v East Sussex County Council, ex parte Tandy* [1998]) the House of Lords held that an authority cannot plead lack of resources to avoid or limit duties regarding provision of a suitable education, including meeting special education needs (EA 1996, s.298). This illustrates the importance of social workers carefully reading how the legal rules are constructed when entering advocacy for their clients.

In children's services there is evidence of local authorities attempting to limit their responsibilities. For example, they have unsuccessfully sought to frame provision for asylum seeking minors and other children who have been looked after as s.17 provision rather than accommodation under s.20, Children Act 1989, thereby limiting young people's entitlement to statutory aftercare provisions on reaching adulthood (*R (Behre and Others) v Hillingdon LBC* [2003]; *R (S) v Sutton LBC* [2007]). The practice of paying kinship carers at a lower rate than foster carers has been successfully challenged as irrational, discriminatory, arbitrary and failing to meet the welfare requirements of the child (*R (L and Others) v Manchester City Council* [2002]).

In *Re C (A Minor) (Interim Care Order: Residential Assessment)* [1996] the House of Lords held that it may give mandatory directions in care proceedings (s.38(6), CA 1989) for the purposes of medical or psychiatric examination or other assessment of the child and family, and may override the local authority's view. The Court must consider the financial implications of its direction but needs-led assessment is the core principle. Concerning supervised contact (*X Council v B (Emergency Protection Orders* [2004]; *Re S (a child) (care proceedings: contact)* [2005]), some regard must be paid to the practicalities and burdens placed on foster carers and to the local authority's resources, but arrangements must be driven by the needs of the family and not skewed by lack of resources. The resource position has been seen as a computer virus infecting local authority decision-making (*R (CD) (a child by her litigation friend VD) v Isle of Anglesey CC* [2004]). In this case a care plan for a disabled child was ruled unlawful because it was contrary to her wishes, placed unsustainable responsibilities on the child's mother, failed to recognize the importance of the foster carers to the child, and therefore ignored CA 1989 requirements to minimize the effects of disability (s.17(2)), give due consideration to the child's wishes (s.20(6)) and meet her needs (s.23(8)). On occasion, then, courts are not reticent to weigh resources against other factors, and to challenge how authorities resolve the difficult judgements facing them.

The Ombudsman has found maladministration in how authorities have approached assessment of need and have defined appropriateness of provision in relation to need. The Ombudsman has been reluctant to accept shortage of funds as an answer to complaints about delay or failure to meet a duty (LGO, 2002, 2007) and has criticized the strict application of policies when this has inhibited a proper assessment of need. Even when the Ombudsman has been sympathetic to an authority's position, recognizing that priority has to be given to those in greatest need, it has found maladministration when an authority has not given a clear indication of likely delays in making an assessment or providing a service.

Partnership between professionals

The modernization agenda (DH, 1998) was premised on a view of services as inflexible, reflective of institutional rather than individual needs, fragmented and poorly co-ordinated. Statute and guidance continue to encourage or mandate working together. Multidisciplinary practice is a key feature in mental health work, for example when liaising to search for alternatives to hospital. The code of practice (DH, 2008d) pinpoints the need for good working relationships based on knowledge and understanding of roles and responsibilities, and agreement on how these can best be discharged. It outlines specific responsibilities of doctors and AMHPs, and offers advice for resolving disagreements – consulting colleagues, exploring alternatives and positively reframing disputes as opportunities to safeguard patients' interests.

In criminal justice, the CDA 1998 makes local authorities responsible for youth justice provision through youth offending teams (s.39). The police, probation services, health and education authorities must co-operate, including by financial contribution (s.39(4)). The CJA 2003 (s.325) imposes a duty to co-operate on responsible authorities, such as police, probation and prison services, together with agencies such as housing, education, social services and youth offending teams. The aim is to clarify roles and responsibilities, and to encourage joint working. It is designed to reinforce the MAPPA (CJCSA 2000), whereby police and probation services, drawing on the support of other agencies, must have joint arrangements for assessing and managing violent, sexual and other dangerous offenders. Local agencies will need to have protocols or memoranda to define how they will co-operate.

In community care, the NHSA 2006 imposes a duty on health authorities to co-operate with each other and on health organizations and local authorities to co-operate to secure and advance people's health and welfare (s.82, formerly s.22, NHS Act 1977). Section 26, NAA 1948 allows local authorities to delegate to voluntary bodies the provision of residential accommodation (*R v Wandsworth LBC, ex parte Beckwith* [1996]). Section 47(3), NHSCCA 1990 allows the local authority when undertaking an assessment to request assistance and services from health and/or housing authorities. The C(EO)A 2004 provides for co-operation between authorities and other bodies in planning and provision of services relevant to carers. The CC(DC)A 2003 takes a harder line on co-operation. Local authorities can be fined for delays in moving people from hospital into residential care or back home with community care support. Once notified by an NHS body of the likely need for community care services, and given a discharge date, the local authority has two days to put together a discharge plan. This applies to people in receipt of acute medical care but not to those in mental health, maternity, palliative, intermediate, recuperative or rehabilitative care (LAC(2003)21).

The DPA 1986 (ss.5 and 6) and the EA1996 require an interagency approach to services for young people with disabilities, for instance when approaching transition from children's to adults' services. LEAs (s.322(1), EA 1996) may request help from health and social services in relation to young people with special educational needs. Schools must also co-operate with safeguarding investigations and promote and safeguard children's well-being (s.175, EA 2002).

More recently a different legislative direction has emerged. Powers and duties to collaborate have been accompanied by new organizational configurations, indicative of a policy shift from collaboration to integration. The HA 1999 (now consolidated into the NHSA 2006) gives statutory backing to partnerships between health and local authorities. It allows transfer of money between the NHS and local government and permits new funding partnerships to facilitate health and social services working together. Partners may create lead commissioning arrangements, delegating to one agency responsibility for commissioning all services for a service user group, transferring funds and transferring or seconding staff to facilitate this (s.75, NHSA 2006). Partners may create integrated provision, allowing different professions to work together within one management, budgetary and administrative structure. Implementation of the Act is governed by secondary legislation (NHS Bodies and Local Authorities Partnership Arrangements Regulations 2000; Commencement of Sections 29 and 30, Health Act 1999 Regulations 2000) and guidance (LAC(2000)9); LAC(2000)10). These rules place no limit on the size of partnerships or numbers of partners. Arrangements must follow consultation with all stakeholders and must be shown to be likely to improve services. Arrangements can cover all health-related local authority functions, including social services, education and housing. Funds may be transferred from the NHS to any health-related function of local government, and to the voluntary sector, to improve the health of people more effectively; equally funds may be transferred from local authorities to PCTs or health authorities.

The HSCA 2001 attempts to dismantle barriers between health and social care. It permits local and health authorities to merge their powers into Care Trusts, responsible for commissioning services. Where services are failing, the Secretary of State may direct local partners to enter into partnership arrangements. Local authorities may scrutinize the NHS and represent local views on the development of local health services.

The CA 2004 similarly facilitates the creation of Children's Trusts by allowing pooled financial and staffing resources to promote co-operation (s.10(6)). Local authorities must promote co-operation between partner agencies and other bodies, which are listed in s.10(4), to improve the well-being of young people. Partner agencies must co-operate in these arrangements, and other relevant bodies such as voluntary agencies are expected to do so, and ensure that their functions are discharged having regard to the need to safeguard and promote the welfare of children. Local Safeguarding Children Boards are established (s.13). Children's services authorities, together with named partner agencies including the police, NHS and youth offending teams, must ensure the effectiveness of safeguarding and promoting the welfare of children. Their role is elaborated in policy guidance (DfES, 2006a) and includes planning and commissioning, enhancing awareness, constructing policies and investigating serious case failures. Finally, the Act creates an integrated inspection framework (s.20) for children's social care and education.

The theme of integration and new organization and practice configurations is continued by the Childcare Act 2006. This requires early childhood services to be provided in an integrated manner (s.3) that facilitates access, with the NHS and Jobcentre Plus working in partnership with the local authority. Section 4 creates a duty to work together to deliver integrated early childhood services to improve outcomes for children and to reduce inequalities in achievement. There is a power to share resources and pool budgets to deliver fully integrated front-line services. The Act also introduces a new legal framework for integrated regulation and inspection of education and childcare services.

Arguably, both approaches have failed to address obstacles that have traditionally undermined collaboration and interdisciplinarity: fragmentation of responsibility, non-coterminosity of boundaries, differences in planning and financial cycles, differing status and patterns of discretion and accountability, uni-professional training, territoriality and overlap of functions, non-alignment of performance measures for health and social care bodies, nervousness that pooled budgets means a loss of financial control, and value differences (Hudson and Henwood, 2002; Glasby, 2003; Wistow, 2005; Lymbery, 2006).

These obstacles continue to surface in relation to continuing care (*R (Grogan) v Bexley NHS Care Trust and South East London Strategic Health Authority and Secretary of State for Health* [2006]), where the balance between local authority and PCT responsibilities must be determined. Guidance (DH, 2007a) indicates that social services and health professionals should make multidisciplinary assessments and recommendations, which PCT decision-makers should depart from only in exceptional circumstances. It claims joint working renders decision-making more effective and consistent, and notes the possibility that Directions will be issued. Whilst the PCT is not bound by the local authority's view on what services are needed, the outcome of s.47, NHSCCA 1990 assessment is an important contribution to decisions. In *St Helens BC v Manchester PCT* [2008], the local authority took the extreme step of bringing judicial review proceedings against the NHS. The PCT had refused to act on, or accept, a recommendation of a multidisciplinary assessment. PCTs and LAs must have local dispute resolution processes for resolving failures of agreement about their respective responsibilities for meeting continuing care needs.

Obstacles remain in the relationship between Care Management and the Care Programme Approach in mental health, with ongoing differences between health and social care approaches to eligibility determination, assessment and priorities (Cestari et al., 2006). There has been separation rather than integration of mental health and social care perspectives and assessment practices when CPA and FACS have to be grafted together at local level.

Mental health inquiries (Sheppard, 1996; Stanley and Manthorpe, 2004) and research (Onyett et al., 1997) have pointed to poor interagency collaboration in multidisciplinary assessments, discharge-planning, and linkages between departments within local authorities, and between them and other public authorities, concluding that a highly compartmental-ized view is inappropriate. Poor information-sharing and collaboration reduces the effectiveness of other professionals' contributions, generat-ing a need for regular reviews of multi-agency working, and training in risk assessments, mental illness, partnership working with families, legal rules, multi-agency roles, and managing violent behaviour. They recom-mend strategies for joint commissioning and planning future provision, and for liaison and communication on individual cases.

The boundary between health and social care remains problematic. Wistow (2005) reports concern that integration will result in a return to the medical model and concludes that it is difficult to avoid negative assessment of health and social care partnerships. More integrated plan-ning between health and social care in services for older people has been achieved, with some pioneering work involving commissioning of inter-mediate care and housing-based support services. However, seamless working between agencies has proved variable, with uncertain progress in forging partnerships with independent providers, and poor leadership in transforming strategic direction into achievable plans and outcomes (Bainbridge and Ricketts, 2003). Implementation of single assessment processes for older people (DH, 2002c), which should merge disparate approaches to assessment, has foundered on professional boundaries, resources and absence of agreed documentation (Clarkson and Challis, 2004). Perceptions of the purpose and content of assessments differed, with some practitioners reluctant to accept others' assessment. Where a lead person co-ordinated the assessment and information was pooled, older people benefited.

The legal rules on delayed discharges do not tackle the problem of insufficient capacity in social care. They may create a divisive system that weakens the interprofessional nature of discharge processes (Lymbery, 2006). Professional and organizational differences have also impeded partnership work and joint commissioning, for instance surrounding user-controlled support (Leece, 2007) and there remain barriers to the integration of health funding within individual budgets.

A joint health and local government ombudsman report (LGO, 2008) into the transfer of learning disability services found serious maladministration because insufficient scrutiny was given to the quality of the services being transferred (03/A/04618 against Buckinghamshire CC; HS-2608 against Oxfordshire and Buckinghamshire Mental Health Partnership Trust). The investigation found poor integration of human rights considerations at all decision-making levels and poor communication between the two authorities. The vulnerable adult at the centre of the investigation did not have his needs regularly assessed or an individual care plan. Similarly, an investigation into alleged abuse in Cornwall concerning people with learning difficulties found poor working relationships (Healthcare Commission and CSCI, 2006).

The drive towards integration – of health and social care, and of education with children's services – creates boundaries as well as demolishing them. Thus, there appears to be a lack of coherence between children's and adults' services in assessing the needs of young carers in black families (Jones et al., 2002). Disabled parents report difficulties in securing adult services to support their parenting alongside children's services (Goodinge, 2000; Wates, 2002). Multi-agency work is patchy for young people leaving care (Harris and Broad, 2005). The interface between housing and social care appears particularly problematic. In *R v Northavon District Council, ex parte Smith* [1994], where a housing need existed that was not met by other agencies, social services had to provide appropriate services. In *R (M) v Hammersmith and Fulham LBC* [2008], the House of Lords gave detailed guidance on how housing and children's services should work together to meet the needs of homeless 16 and 17 year olds. Both bodies have accommodation obligations (HA 1996, HA 2002, CA 1989) and the borderline is unclear. Housing authorities should lead and, where necessary, provide interim accommodation whilst the longer-term position is resolved. For this purpose a framework for joint assessment should underpin working together in specific cases. In *R (Bernard and Another) v Enfield LBC* [2002] an integrated approach to the needs of disabled adults broke down, leaving them without necessary adaptations for a substantial period.

In both child care (*R (Stewart) v Wandsworth LBC, Hammersmith and Fulham LBC and Lambeth LBC* [2001]; *R (M) v Barking and Dagenham LBC and Westminster City Council (interested party)* [2003] and community care, disagreements arise between local authorities about which is responsible for providing services because an individual or family is ordinarily resident there. Courts have had to remind authorities that the welfare of children should not become subservient to arguments about resources and that local authorities must co-operate in preparing a care plan when, during care proceedings, parents and children move (*Hackney LBC v C* [1996]). In *Hertfordshire CC v FM* [2007], the court criticized the initial failure of mental health and children's services to work together to ensure the safety of the children of a mentally distressed father.

The initial outcomes of integrating support for families appear positive, with evidence of culture and role change, better social work recording, improved multi-agency working around making referrals and co-ordinated follow-through in delivering services. However, familiar challenges resurface (Cleaver and Walker, 2004; Frost et al., 2005; Morris, K. 2005; Brandon et al., 2006; Lord et al., 2008):

● workloads;
● developing an explicit knowledge base and shared language;
● boundary disputes and differences in thresholds for action;
● mistrust and misunderstanding others' expertise;
● refusal to accept others' assessments.

Having a clear and shared high profile vision is crucial, together with strong leadership and clear funding and accountability arrangements. Elsewhere, a lack of effective partnership working, for instance between Children's Guardians and social workers around assessment and evidence, and between lawyers and social workers, has contributed to delays in care proceedings (McKeigue and Beckett, 2004; Selwyn et al., 2006). Platt (2006) stresses the importance of robust, locally negotiated, interagency processes covering both assessment of children in need and children's safeguarding, especially in borderline cases.

The fragile nature of interagency collaboration has been most obvious in children's safeguarding. Teamwork is fundamental to the implementation of duties in the CA 1989 for young people leaving care (s.24), children in need (s.17) and day care (s.18). Sections 27, 28 and 30 provide duties and powers involving co-operation between social services, education, housing, health and independent authorities (DH, 1991d). Whilst a co-ordinated approach to policy-making and service delivery is required, collaborative working arrangements have been undermined by divergent ideologies or priorities, separate training, blurred roles and responsibilities, financial constraints, competitiveness and different case approaches. Reports (Butler-Sloss, 1988; Sinclair and Bullock, 2002; Laming, 2003) regularly highlight limited interagency work on post-protection plans, confusion about information-sharing duties, divergent interpretations of safeguarding responsibilities, and limited integration between services for children and adults. This suggests again that law and guidance are insufficient to achieve role clarity and relationships which foster interprofessional understanding and use of expertise. This message is reinforced in a critical evaluation of inquiry reports (Reder et al., 1993; Reder and Duncan, 2004; Sinclair and Corden, 2005), which document the need to understand and monitor relational and communication processes in interprofessional contacts, including the context in which they occur, if polarization, exaggeration of hierarchy, isolation, and closed systems are to be avoided.

Concern about interagency collaboration has resulted in further revisions to guidance. *Working Together* (DfES, 2006a) is designed to promote multidisciplinary teamwork with a shared understanding of aims and good practice, and with an ability to act decisively when necessary. It requires social workers, when undertaking child protection investigations (ss.37 and 47, CA 1989), to gather information from key professionals, and to liaise and act in collaboration with other agencies. In decision-making about looked after children, social workers must seek the views of relevant people (s.22(4)(d)). The corporate responsibility for children in need and children requiring protection is emphasized. A range of professionals and agencies are identified as having roles in children's well-being, their knowledge seen as essential to decision-making. An interagency collaborative model is promoted to ensure an effective service response for children and families about whom there is concern. The roles and responsibilities of different bodies are described, with staff required to understand the perspectives and language of other agencies. Senior management commitment, interagency training, and protocols are seen as the means by which working collaboratively will be valued, tasks and responsibilities appreciated, communication improved and intervention integrated at strategic and individual case levels.

However the document does not explore the reasons for past difficulties in interagency co-operation. The CA 1989 only provided a power, not a duty on local authority social services to seek assistance, with other authorities under a duty to comply only if it did not unduly prejudice the discharge of their own functions (s.27) or if it was not unreasonable in the circumstances to assist (s.47). The stronger compulsory duties in the CA 2004, to co-operate to ensure children's well-being, may overcome long-standing problems with information-sharing. Arguably, though, partnership between professionals requires more than a reinstatement and reinforcement of previous guidance, including values statements (GSCC, 2002; GTC et al., 2007) on recognition and respect for other professionals' roles, knowledge and expertise. Some prerequisite knowledge, attitudes and skills are considered in Chapter 8.

Partnership with service users

Service user and carer involvement is now a cornerstone of social work practice (Braye, 2000), and includes open records, attendance at case conferences and reviews, participation in decision-making, and access to complaints procedures. Besides serving as a check on the way practitioners exercise authority, this partnership is based on the centrality to effective and ethical practice of:

- honesty and openness;
- providing information and checking understanding;
- developing and retaining clarity of purpose by negotiating expectations, defining and agreeing problem areas and tasks, and reviewing work regularly;
- taking users' comments seriously, openly acknowledging differences;
- identifying and promoting users' strengths and skills;
- mobilizing the active support of significant others; and
- using contracts or working agreements.

Accordingly, social workers must respect and promote individuals' views and wishes, communicate accurately, use power responsibly, and help people to manage potential and actual risks to themselves and others (GSCC, 2002). They should engage with openness and reciprocity, acknowledging explicitly their powers and the legal context of any intervention (QAA, 2008).

In this development the law has been variably responsive. It does not embrace fully the concept of partnership, discriminating between different user groups on the degree of partnership it will underscore. The power imbalance between providers and users remains largely weighted in favour of service providers. In adult services, policy refers to expert patients and expert carers (DH, 2006a), and to people being at the centre of their care, with greater say over where, how and by whom they are supported. The HSCA 2008 requires the Care Quality Commission to state how it will engage with experts by experience and take account of their views. However, care packages are not transferable across local authority boundaries; there is no right to independent living; statutory advocacy provision is limited to certain groups, and eligibility criteria reflect drives to manage demand rather than commitment to address social exclusion and guarantee quality of life.

The MHA 1983 Code (DH, 2008d) promotes the involvement of patients, as far as possible, in the formulation and delivery of care and treatment. AMHPs must provide reasons for their decisions, and take into account, as far as urgency allows, the views of relatives and friends. Guardianship is seen as requiring both parties to be willing to work together. Patients should be given, orally and in writing, as much information as possible about their care and treatment, and about their rights (s.132, MHA 1983). Questions should be answered openly and honestly, checking to ensure understanding of the information given. The information given should be clearly recorded.

However mental health service users' experiences are such as to question the degree of partnership offered. Their perspectives should inform assessments and outcome-setting but research evidence points to geographic inequities in community support, failure to distribute care plans routinely, and inadequate participation in management (Newton et al., 1996; Godfrey and Wistow, 1997; Onyett et al., 1997).

Sections 1–3 and 4b, DPA 1986 would have given all disabled people the right to appoint representatives to assist them in dealing with local authorities, and requesting and receiving an assessment of their needs. These sections have not been implemented and provisions in the MCA 2005 and MHA 2007 do not extend to all adults. Potentially empowering legislation remains dormant.

Local authorities have a duty to consider the needs of disabled people for services under s.2, CSDPA 1970, when requested by a disabled person or their carer (s.4, DPA 1986), and to meet an established need for services. However, in respect of others who may need community care, local authorities control the decision whether to assess (s.47, NHSCCA 1990).

Perhaps more positively, direct payments allow people to purchase their own care. Earlier restrictions on which service user groups could apply (CC(DP)A 1996) have been removed and a duty created to offer direct payments and make them available to any eligible person who requests them (HSCA 2001; DH, 2003a). Disabled people are positive about the flexibility and control that direct payments offer, but schemes are not always well promoted and service users are not involved in their introduction and operation (Wates, 2002; Hasler, 2003; SCIE, 2007).

The NHSCCA 1990 and subsequent government guidance (DH, 1989c, 1990; Community Care Assessment Directions 2004) demonstrate equivocal attitudes towards partnership. People should be active partners in their assessments, since they are experts on their own situation, with

their perspectives uppermost (DH, 2002b). Social workers must consult the individual and, where appropriate, their carers when conducting
assessments, a written statement of the outcome should be provided if
a continuing service is to be offered, and efforts made to reach agreement (DH, 1990; Community Care Assessment Directions 2004). Where
agreement is not possible, points of difference should be recorded. Care
plans should contain statements of objectives, criteria for evaluation of
their achievement, services to be provided and by whom, the cost to the
user, other options considered, differences of opinion, unmet needs with
reasons, location of responsibility for monitoring and review, and the
date of the first review. Reviews should also be recorded. The ultimate
responsibility for defining need, however, rests with the assessing professional (DH, 1991c).

Assessment then is participative. Users and carers must be involved,
and should feel that assessment and care management processes are aimed
at meeting their wishes, with services tailored to meet assessed needs
(DH, 1990). However assessment is not user-led. Rather the objective is
to determine the *best available* way to meet needs. Assessment must take
account of the local authority's criteria for determining when services
should be provided and the types of service *they* have decided to make
available. Consequently choice, a feature of the policy, is compromised
by the local authority's responsibility to meet needs *within available
resources*. Even where choice appears endorsed, for instance in respect
of residential care (LAC(2004)20), this is only where the local authority
deems a person's choice to be suitable in relation to assessed needs, and
where it would not cost the authority more than it would usually expect
to pay. Given that the local authority remains the major source of provision and the gate-keeper to other provision, the power of users is severely
limited. Thus, as Tanner observes (2003), need is what local authorities
will provide for. Policy guidance on eligibility criteria (DH, 2002b) does
not explicitly recognize unmet need, whilst that on single assessment
(DH, 2002c) does not clarify the distinction made between presenting
need, eligible need and identified need.

It is certainly the case that the balance of power between professionals and service users is set to change, with the culture of personalization,
choice and control already bringing fundamental changes to assessment
practice and professional roles within it. Statute law lags some way
behind policy shifts here, but is set to change radically once the review
that follows the Law Commission's (2008) scoping report is complete.
Changes will be timely, as research indicates that older people are concerned about the quality of advice and support available to those using
direct payments or individual budgets (SCIE, 2007) and disillusioned

with tokenistic forms of participation (Postle et al., 2005). Black and minority ethnic groups are rarely engaged by policy-makers and practitioners in efforts to improve social care (Begum, 2006). Care plans may be overlooked for disabled parents, or be service-led and not routinely reviewed (Goodinge, 2000). Assessments may be experienced as fragmentary, confusing, superficial and irrelevant, marginalizing and distorting service user perspectives (Davis et al., 1998; Tanner, 2003). Reviews appear inconsistent, routinized and bureaucratized, with practitioners reporting that policy guidance (DH, 2002b) does not much influence their practice and that interaction is focused on eligibility, need and cost rather than identity and life goals (Charles and Manthorpe, 2007; Scourfield, 2007). Both carers and service users report sometimes being excluded from complaints procedures (Flynn, 2004).

Carers should be involved in the design, monitoring, delivery and management of carer support services (DH, 2005b). However, they too report that significant areas such as housing and health are not covered in assessments (Robinson and Williams, 2002; Bainbridge and Ricketts, 2003) and they experience exclusion from decision-making panels (Goldsmith, 2005).

Furthermore, redress through judicial review is only possible where a local authority has acted irrationally or illegally. Some authorities, however, have had judicial review against them for failing to consult, to assess needs and/or to involve users and carers in assessments and reviews (*R v North Yorkshire County Council, ex parte Hargreaves* [1997]; *R v Gloucestershire County Council, ex parte Mahfood and others* [1995]; *R (Bernard and Another) v Enfield LBC* [2002]). Nonetheless, rather than partnership, what exists at best is participation in a pre-set agenda. Much is dependent, therefore, on attitudes and approaches adopted by service providers. These values and skills in practising social work law are discussed in Chapter 8.

The CA 1989, the ACA 2002, the CA 2004 and accompanying policy guidance, in attempting to reconcile the conflicting imperatives of state intervention and children's and parents' rights, have brought partnership and written agreements to centre stage. Guidance on safeguarding (DfES, 2006a), family support (DH, 2000c) and day care (DH, 1991d) requires practitioners to involve parents as fully as possible. Within a context that the welfare of children is paramount, partnership with parents is seen as likely to improve the quality of information and decision-making, reduce their scapegoating of the agency, lessen feelings of powerlessness and failure, build on family strengths as well as tackle difficulties, promote respect, and maximize the potential for co-operation (DH, 2000b, 2000c; DfES, 2006a). Effective prevention and intervention rest on these elements (Sinclair and Corden, 2005). Partnership in the CA 1989 resides in the provision of information (Sch.2, 1(2)), consultation (ss.22, 61 and 64), reviews of services (ss.19 and 26), access to complaints procedures (s.26) and advocacy by representatives (s.41(2); Sch.2(17)). No notice is required from parents prior to removing children from s.20 accommodation. Rather there is informed participation, encapsulated in written contracts, based on clear understanding of the powers, duties and roles of agencies, the legal rights of parents and children and, where possible, negotiation and agreement.

The ACA 2002 extends advocacy provision for young people (s.119) and requires preparation of care plans whenever application for a care order is made (s.121). The CA 2004 (s.53) requires local authorities to ascertain children's wishes when considering service provision under s.17, Childcare Act 1989 and when completing investigations under s.47. Policy guidance on safeguarding (DfES, 2006a) also requires that social workers listen to the child and be clear about the legislative basis of their work. The CA 2006 (s.3) encourages local authorities to involve parents and providers of early years provision when developing integrated services and to have regard to the views of children. Engaging with the common assessment framework also requires consent from children and parents, with whom concerns should be discussed before deciding to proceed (CWDC, 2007). Children and young people's views should inform Joint Areas Reviews (Ofsted, 2007) and decision-making on the transition from care to independent living (DH, 2002i).

Due consideration must be given to children's wishes and feelings, and to parents and relevant other people who may or may not have parental responsibility. Written agreements with parents are required for children accommodated by the local authority or in care and placed with parents (DH, 1991e). They include the purpose of the placement, contact arrangements, any delegation of parental responsibility to the local authority, and plans for the children. They must specify services to be provided by the local authority, review dates and contingency plans. For children in care, arrangements should be made with parental agreement where possible. For accommodated children the arrangements in the plan must be agreed between the local authority and a person with parental responsibility, or the young person if aged 16 or 17 (Arrangements for the Placement of Children (General) Regulations 1991). Placement agreements with foster parents are also required, covering care and contact arrangements, and circumstances in which the child could be removed (Foster Placement (Children) Regulations 1991; DH, 1991e). Foster carers must also be provided with information necessary to enable them to care for the child.

The partnership approach extends to making reasonable efforts, prior to applying for a Child Assessment Order, to secure parental co-operation and to involving parents fully in decisions about the process the assessment will follow once an order is made. It extends to children in care, with social workers required to consult and notify parents about decisions affecting children, to promote contact where appropriate to a child's welfare, and to work with parents to secure a safe return home or a satisfactory alternative placement (DH, 1991e). It extends to the safeguarding process (DfES, 2006a) where local authority practice should be characterized by openness and honesty regarding concerns, roles and planning, negotiation where possible and allowed by the legal mandate, and parental involvement throughout.

Several critical points arise concerning partnership and how the balance between autonomy and state intervention has been codified. In weighing the duty to safeguard and promote a child's welfare, social workers must determine whether provision of accommodation by agreement with parents is sufficient to safeguard the child's welfare in the context of significant harm (DH, 1991d). Local authorities must consider court applications if parents wish to remove children under 16 from accommodation. Voluntary contingency plans in placement agreements will not be binding, although agreements could be used as evidence in legal proceedings subsequently. Furthermore it remains unclear how far authorities, or foster carers, may use the s.3(5), CA 1989) permission to do what is reasonable to safeguard or promote the child's welfare.

The CA 1989 also assumes that people will act reasonably when children are in care. Local authorities and parents may act independently, the former only able to limit the latter's exercise of parental responsibility when necessary to safeguard and promote a child's welfare. Such co-operation will not always be possible. Social workers must record these cases fully, indicating in particular why collaboration proved impossible and how an order might improve it (Adcock et al., 1991). Nor does regulatory guidance assist greatly when the views of children under 16 and parents conflict. The child's views do not have primacy and are not determinative. If a child requests to be accommodated but a parent objects, only a court order will settle the dispute.

Case law has reinforced the importance of partnership with children and their families. Thus, parents of children in care must be involved in decision-making and enabled to answer allegations and criticism of their parenting and behaviour (*TP and KM v UK* [2001]; *Re C (Care Proceedings: Disclosure of Local Authority's Decision-Making Process)* [2002]). Where parents do not attend case conferences, they should be given minutes (*Re X (Emergency Protection Orders)* [2006]). Lack of parental co-operation is never a reason to close a file or remove children from registration, whilst work should provide a clear time frame in which changes are required (*Re E and Others (Minors) (Care Proceedings: Social Work Practice)* [2000]). Birth parents should have their rights and feelings respected in adoption work, and they should not be prevented from being heard (*Re F (a child* [2008]). A young person's wishes must be ascertained before s.20 CA 1989 accommodation is provided, and the onus should not be on the child to identify and request the services they require (*R (M) v Hammersmith and Fulham LBC* [2008]). Due consideration should be given to the views of disabled children and their parents, as well as to minimizing the effects of disability, when setting or reviewing care packages (*R (CD) (a child by her litigation friend VD) v Isle of Anglesey CC* [2004]).

Research suggests that children are sceptical about, and not routinely offered, involvement in decision-making. They want reliability, practical help, support and staff who listen and respond (Statham and Aldgate, 2003). There are varying patterns of participation by young people in policy-making (Gunn, 2005). Young people expect to be consulted before information about them is shared and to be reassured that data will be accurate and used appropriately (Cleaver et al., 2004). Serious case reviews point to insufficient attention being paid to what children say and how they look and behave (Sinclair and Bullock, 2002). A culture in reviews that adults know best may prove difficult to challenge and decision-making can appear to young people to be exclusive rather than inclusive (Lumley, 1998). Nonetheless, there is some evidence of a culture shift in communicating with, and involving, children in planning and decisions, even if meetings could be more child-friendly (Statham and Aldgate, 2003).

The Common Assessment Framework appears to improve communication with families and to facilitate skilled work through clear processes which promote family involvement (Cleaver and Walker, 2004; Brandon et al., 2006). However, research also concludes that some professionals find working in partnership with parents hard to grasp and not all families had been given copies of their assessments (Brandon et al., 2006; Millar and Corby, 2006). Similarly, some professionals conclude that documentation derived from the Integrated Children's System is too complex to share with parents (Bell et al., 2007). More positively, partnership practice that establishes shared understandings of problems and possibilities, and clarifies legal powers and how they may be used, is welcomed by parents and the assessment framework has been successful in involving parents and children, and in promoting therapeutic as well as diagnostic outcomes (Corby et al., 2002; Millar and Corby, 2006; Platt, 2006).

However, delay and drift can be caused by lack of assessment, planning and action, for instance concerning permanency planning (Selwyn et al., 2006). There is increasing use of compulsion, contrary to the intention of the CA 1989 (McKeigue and Beckett, 2004). Parents of disabled children sometimes receive little help in maintaining contact with their children or in attending reviews (Abbott et al., 2001).

The duty to give 'due consideration' to the wishes of children and parents may be interpreted broadly or restrictively. Authorities need not implement their wishes. Nor are they guided on the relative importance to attach to their respective views, other than that a child's age and understanding will be influential. Indeed, law and practice reflect an ambivalent attitude towards partnership with children. The MHA 1983 Code (DH, 2008d) recommends that young people should be kept informed about their care and treatment and regarded generally as having the right to make their own decisions when they have sufficient understanding. Any intervention should be the least restrictive possible. Children can make application in family proceedings, although they sometimes require leave to do so. They may refuse medical assessments and examinations as part of child assessment orders, emergency protection orders and interim care orders (ss.38(6), 43(8), 44(7), CA 1989) and refuse medical and psychiatric treatment when on supervision (sch.3, CA 1989). However, cases (*Re R (a minor) (Wardship: Consent to Treatment)* [1991]; *Re W (A Minor) (Medical Treatment: Court's Jurisdiction)* [1992]) have eroded many of the gains derived. The CA 1989 requires courts to listen to and consider a child's views, but the court's view of best interests decides (*Re P (minors)* [1992]). However, a young person with special educational needs cannot appeal to a SEN Tribunal against a decision of the local education authority (*S v Special Educational Needs Tribunal and Another* [1996]). Only a parent has standing here.

There remains no right of attendance for children and parents at case conferences, nor any guidance on what chairs of conferences should consider, beyond a clear conflict of interests or continued hostility, persistent denial of abuse, or severe illness, in determining whether parental attendance will preclude proper consideration of the child's interests, and whether children are old enough to participate (DfES, 2006a). Similarly, the focus is on outcomes for children and young people, which means that social workers have to make explicit links to ECHR rights. Indeed, Morris (K., 2005) is concerned that the CA 2004 has diluted the voices of children and families, and that services may not prove participative or needs-led. Sinclair and Corden (2005) are similarly concerned that a risk-averse approach, subsequent to the Laming report (2003), may jeopardize preventive and collaborative work and alienate families.

Once again attitudes and skills are central to practising social work law, respecting and building on the competence of children, ensuring that services are informed by their views, promoting realistic dialogue with parents, and constructing accessible routes for representation. In particular, where anxiety to control outcomes is high, and where defensive practice could subvert partnership, social workers must guard against agreements becoming institutionalized coercion – hurdles for users to jump to obtain services rather than tools of negotiation. Sharing information and critical opinions with parents is not easy, and therefore must be underpinned by supportive leadership, organizational and individual commitment, and the provision of supervision and other spaces for critical reflection.

---

putting it into practice

Reflect on these questions and discuss your ideas with others if you have the opportunity:

- Do your agency guidance and procedures clearly articulate the legal content of the work that is being undertaken?

- Is there written guidance on how the authority interprets its legal duties?

- Are there commonly agreed criteria and thresholds for triggering intevention?

- Where powers rather than duties are involved, is it clear how and when the authority uses those powers?

Further reading

Clark, C. and McGhee, J. (eds) (2008) *Private and Confidential: Handling Personal Information in the Social and Health Services*. Bristol: Policy Press. This book explores philosophical, ethical, legal and professional practice issues in privacy and confidentiality, exploring their implications for policy and practice.

Glasby, J. and Dickinson, H. (2008) *Partnership Working in Health and Social Care*. Bristol: Policy Press. This is a policy and practice guide to interprofessional working.

Kemshall, H. and Littlechild, R. (eds) (2000) *User Involvement and Participation in Social Care*. London: Jessica Kingsley. This text provides both an overview of the drivers for participation and examples of its development in practice.

8 | Making sense of practice

Social workers practise in unpredictable and complex situations where often they must balance competing rights and ethical principles, resolve dilemmas and manage stress. Decisions call for skilled professional judgement (GSCC, 2008) in which knowledge of legal mandates alone is insufficient to promote the exercise of human rights and achieve valued outcomes. Indeed, to be the 'critical fixers' valued by experts by experience (Braye and Preston-Shoot et al., 2005), practitioners must engage in dialogue not only about what may or must be done but also why and how. This demands that social workers act confidently in and with authority.

Social workers practise in environments where the law is too often implicit rather than explicit, where human rights are not embedded in agency procedures (Braye et al., 2007), and where bureaucratic or managerialist orientations downgrade the importance of understanding and negotiating complexity (Reder and Duncan, 2004). Evidence highlighted in this book has demonstrated how managers and practitioners become party to unlawful or unethical practice – complying with inappropriate care plans and compromising assessments because of resource concerns (Preston-Shoot, 2000b), neglecting support for newly qualified or promoted staff (*Forbes v GSCC* [2008]), or overriding professional values, such as respect for people and maintaining trust, for more proceduralized forms of decision-making (*Re F(a child)* [2008]).

This final chapter, therefore, turns attention to the skills required in the practice of social work law within the context of an active commitment to social work values. The law itself is a relatively blunt instrument. It is practice skills that enable it to be applied with any degree of precision and social workers to maintain practice standards lawfully (GSCC, 2002). The objective is not to create legal experts so much as to ensure that social workers can operate confidently when interpreting legal mandates, credibly when taking or recommending decisions, critically when balancing competing perspectives and creatively when problem-solving. Skills and values help to make sense of the complexity and dilemmas inherent in the task when practitioners may feel apprehensive about their use of legal knowledge.

Translating personal and professional values into practice

Earlier chapters have demonstrated how the law embodies beliefs about how society should operate, based on principles which are collectively 'valued' and embedded within society's functioning. Ethical practice uses evidence to challenge such received ideas and explores the legal rules to identify where they support social work's values. In addition to awareness of the law's value base, scrutiny is needed of the way *personal* values and organizational *culture* affect the practice of social work law. Personal values, for instance concerning risk, interdependence and independence, health and well-being, acquired from upbringing and experience, filter what is seen and the sense made of it. Organizational values too influence the range of options open to practitioners and the way the law is applied. Safeguarding inquiries routinely identify the impact upon judgement of pervasive belief systems, such as optimism about family care or pessimism about local authority provision (Reder et al., 1993; Reder and Duncan, 1999, 2003; Laming, 2009). Crawford and Wates (2005) demonstrate how implementation of the legal rules concerning disabled parents is affected by assumptions and values, for instance regarding need or parenting.

The values arena is equally complex. Social work embodies core values of human rights, equality and social justice (GSCC, 2008). Definitions of scope, however, differ. Traditional professional values, such as respect for persons, and their contemporary incarnation in equality of opportunity and partnership, contrast with a more radical agenda which tackles structural inequality and prioritizes empowerment and citizenship. Faced with such complexity there is a danger that the term 'values' tends to be indiscriminate, rich in nuance and evocation but often thin in descriptive and informative content. Equally, social workers will hold particular orientations when responding to need, deciding whether to challenge agency priorities, or determining whether and how to use the legal rules in situations involving risk and autonomy. The orientations are not inherently right or wrong but bring different emphases to the task of practising within the legal framework (Braye and Preston-Shoot, 2007). Thus:

- A technical orientation emphasizes technical legal knowledge. Action is underpinned by reference to accurate legal knowledge, for which access to the latest guidance and influential case law is essential.
- A needs orientation seeks to understand people's experience. Intervention enacts obligations society owes to vulnerable people, for which needs are matched with resources or services.

- A procedural orientation focuses on employers' policies and procedures for implementing the legal rules. Action is based on guidance from managers.
- A rights orientation prioritizes how the law confers or limits rights for people who use services. Action seeks to promote people's rights in relation to agency practice and in other areas of their lives. Rights are the guiding principle of decision-making.

There is, therefore, a responsibility for questioning and critical appraisal, on personal, professional and organizational levels, how values, beliefs and experiences influence perspectives on law, assessments, options being considered and interactions with experts by experience (Braye and Preston-Shoot, 2006a).

Families and relationships

Practitioners are inevitably affected by, and in turn affect, the family and relationship patterns they observe in their work. Underlying an individual's professional functioning is a complex personal history that will influence where they stand in relation to the conflicting imperatives and practice dilemmas of using the law. Early experience and subsequent learning will profoundly affect what practitioners want to use the law to achieve – what are the merits of permanent placement for children as opposed to continuing contact and possible rehabilitation with birth families; how far should community presence and participation be promoted over protection from possible danger and exploitation; what work should be prioritized with young people living in the public care system? Such decisions are often value-led.

Authority and power

Ironically, for a profession deemed to possess limitless and sometimes inappropriate power, social work faces its social control function with considerable unease, and individual practitioners often describe feeling *powerless*, both within their employing bureaucracies and in relation to helping people change their lives.

Analysis of the power that resides in the social work role, balanced with understanding of the factors that influence personal authority in that role, is essential if the law is to be used appropriately. It must be accompanied by an awareness of power in the lives of service users.

The law is one obvious source of power since it confers the capacity to make decisions, to allocate resources, to coerce and ensure compliance. Individuals will again carry personal experiences which affect the way they value the power of the law.

It is tempting to conflate law with power to control and coerce in a negative sense. A more positive view is necessary which recognizes the empowering aspects of legislation also – how it enables protection and resources to be offered. Choosing to empower, however, presupposes the possession and transferability of power in the first place. Empowerment is not just a matter of transferring a finite amount of power, but also of working with people to discover their own sources of power, sometimes through the law, and valuing those in encounters with professionals.

Other sources of power include the helping role, the advantage of professional status, access to information and resources, agency status, knowledge and expertise, and membership of dominant groups. By contrast, service users can be disempowered by material and social disadvantage, by lack of knowledge of agency role and status, by jargon and the mystique of professionalism, by discrimination and oppression on both a corporate and an individual level. A 'power audit' of this kind can be developed into action.

Prejudice, discrimination and oppression

The theme of personal values and power leads to exploration of both personal and professional understandings of power used oppressively. Social work and law can promote social cohesion, human rights and social justice but can also threaten it (Braye and Preston-Shoot et al., 2005). Increasingly, how professional practice and organizational behaviour are implicated in the major structural oppressions is being addressed in the extension of equalities legislation. Personal values and awareness are an important part of this process. It is this that influences when, how and why social workers reach for the law, and underpins skills in combatting differential use of law in relation to certain groups. It can be built from clarification of the patterns of understanding, messages, anxieties and feelings arising from early learning and experience.

The tendency is to notice only what one can see from one's own position and to prefer it as the 'true' version of reality. Developing awareness of what the world looks like from other people's perspectives brings new information that can be incorporated into an anti-oppressive position. Thus, when experts by experience encourage social workers to be 'critical fixers' (Braye and Preston-Shoot et al., 2005), they are advocating practice which identifies commonalities as well as differences and which utilizes the opportunities created by the legal rules, such as advocacy or the extension of equalities legislation to service provision, to challenge disabling barriers and to work for structural change as well as individual outcomes.

Organizational debates

The nature of the interaction between the law, agency policy and individual practice makes it essential that individual practitioners are not left to grapple alone with the intricacies of ethical decision-making on the use of legal powers and duties. To be effective, social work policies and procedures need to be underpinned by a clear philosophy and value base (CWDC, 2007). Clearly articulated organizational values can provide considerable support to workers attempting to make sense of conflicting imperatives and practice dilemmas. Formal policy statements provide the security and anchors necessary to promote effective decision-making.

There are dangers in written guidelines. One is that they remain glowingly principled but, in offering no guidance about how to prioritize competing principles, they leave practitioners with the same insoluble dilemmas as the legislation itself. Alternatively, they might not mention practice dilemmas at all. However, it is vital that consideration is given to prioritizing: when must workers be gate-keepers of resources and when may users exercise choice; when may the rights of carers take precedence over the rights of people being cared for; when does inspection become more important than support and guidance; at what point may the need to safeguard welfare overtake the right to autonomy?

Another danger is that, in attempting to give clear guidance, procedures tend to encourage linear thinking and solutions, as if by working logically through the procedures will produce a good enough solution, almost without the use of professional judgement. A third danger is that procedures inaccurately interpret the requirements of the legal rules. Finally, they may essentially be top-down, bureaucratic approaches, which do not encourage thoughtfulness about the influence of such contextual factors as workloads, resources and communication (Reder and Duncan, 2003, 2004), or promote understanding and ownership at all organizational levels of new procedures and practices (Cleaver and Walker, 2004; Cleaver et al., 2004; Lord et al., 2008). Organizational values, then, may remain distant, unachievable goals or resented constraints that seem irrelevant to practice. A balance will not be achieved without organizational debates, active monitoring and wide discussion of when, how and why decisions to use the law are made, identification of where decision-making power and responsibility are located, what influences the way they are exercised, what objectives are to be achieved and how learning from outcomes is incorporated into future practice.

Core skills

The core skills for competent practice of social work law are of course none other than core skills for practice in general. There are, however, some emphases that are particularly significant in the light of a critical understanding of the law. Individual competence will be emphasized alongside the organization's responsibility to provide a competent context for practice.

Challenging discrimination

Social work law offers both opportunities and responsibilities for anti-discriminatory practice: using equalities legislation to challenge discrimination, and vigilance to ensure that the law is not applied in a discriminatory way. The wider context of oppressive law and legal structures makes it necessary to prioritize awareness of legislation such as the RR(A)A 2000, the DDA 2005 and the CA 1989, which lay down specific responsibilities that can be used as standards against which other proposed actions involving the law can be measured. The skills that follow will take the challenge forward.

Skills in thinking systemically

The law has encouraged individual explanations for social problems and their solutions. Even where welfare law has recognized discrimination it has individualized the solution. In requiring a focus upon a presenting problem, such as 'significant harm' or 'mental disorder of a nature or degree that warrants detention in hospital', much welfare legislation has obscured the presence of structural oppression in the lives of individuals and collective unmet need across communities or social divisions.

Thinking systemically helps practitioners balance the individual and the structural elements in explanations of and solutions to problems, drawing on equalities legislation for the mandate to challenge discrimination in service provision, and assessment frameworks (DH, 2000c; CWDC, 2007) that direct focus beyond individuals and families to the wider environment and its impact on opportunities and experiences. Such recognitions enable interventions to be directed at social need arising from poverty, exclusion, and gendered or racist assumptions about care-giving.

Challenging normative or stereotypical assumptions

Practitioners must avoid the twin pitfalls of either failing to recognize difference or doing so in a way that uses stereotypical understandings. Current legislation and the way in which it is applied contain the potential for both. On the one hand, normative explanations and expectations which treat everyone the same are pervasive throughout welfare law and the practice it supports. The ideology of the NHSCCA 1990 reflects firmly-entrenched social values, beliefs and Western market models. In following normalization principles which tackle discrimination of one form, practitioners must avoid the danger of perpetuating other forms of discrimination. White Eurocentric norms have also influenced expectations of child development, family patterns and parenting styles.

On the other hand, attempts to recognize difference and to move away from a colour-blind approach have resulted in cultural stereotyping, demonstrated by assumptions that 'families will care' (Begum, 2006). Recognition of cultural diversity must take place in the context of a broader understanding of racism, so that a balance is achieved between sensitivities to culture and to structural inequalities. This is particularly so in relation to protective legal measures, where stereotypical assumptions can result in both over- and under-use. Assumptions about gender roles, capacity and family structure are also a danger to practitioners if they define both focus and outcome of intervention. Interventions derived from a family welfare model can fail to support disabled parents but instead regard such cases as automatically raising questions about children in need (Goodinge, 2000; Wates, 2002).

Challenging myths and stereotypes takes place on both personal and political levels. Legislation such as the NHSCCA 1990 and the CA 1989, providing for individual need, offer opportunity to move away from assumptions and take full account of race, culture, language, religion, class, gender and ability. In relation to race and disability in particular, the emphasis on resources should not mean providing services that cannot realistically meet the needs identified. Monitoring, for example of the impact of eligibility criteria, must include consideration of whether services are being used by all communities (*R (Chavda) v Harrow LBC* [2008]). Market diversity offers opportunities to purchase services from black voluntary organizations, not to avoid making relevant mainstream provision but to increase accessibility. Additionally the RR(A)A 2000, the DDA 2005 and the EA 2006 require local authorities more proactively to examine the impact of policy decisions and the relevance and accessibility of services.

Developing a language

Skill in communicating *about* discrimination is crucial to the development of a strong challenge. Practice is strengthened by appropriate language, underpinned by shared understandings about definitions and terminologies. Misconceptions are common, for example that equal opportunities means treating everyone the same, partly because individuals hold different systems of meaning (Reder and Duncan, 2003). Organizations and multi-agency networks need to agree a shared vocabulary that gives a strong base from which to challenge discriminatory language and interventions. This involves making explicit implicit values and knowledge (Frost et al., 2005). The language used to frame communications is a powerful indicator and influencer of values; the words that are used to describe actions are challenges in themselves to discriminatory processes. For instance, experts by experience prefer the term 'self-directed support', directing focus to the exercise of rights, over 'personalization', which is associated with consumer choice (Henwood, 2008).

Skills in campaigning and empowering

Challenging discrimination at a wider level than in individual practice involves taking a personal and corporate stance against practices that are oppressive yet condoned by legislation. Immigration, housing and income support are three examples of areas in which practitioners find themselves called upon to advise, assist, advocate and support the lawful attainment of rights and meeting of needs. Where discrimination is covered by legislation it is important to monitor and illustrate the profile and ethos of services, to encourage and support individuals to take action through tribunals and courts, and to involve the investigative powers of the EHRC. This may mean initiating action through the organizational hierarchy, and using legal knowledge, advocacy skills, and equal opportunity policy statements to empower such action, where discrimination against service users is apparent in the workings of one's own employing organization.

It is vital, while working to challenge discrimination at an individual level, to work in partnership with groups of service users and others who, through validating the strengths and upholding the rights of oppressed groups, can begin to make a difference. Social workers have a key role in linking individuals into groups of common interest and experience, thereby enhancing their opportunity for collective action and access to political processes. Taking this one step further, it can be argued that social work's concern with power leads inevitably to engagement with political action as an integral component of practice.

Working in partnership

The word 'partnership' means different things to different people. It remains ill-defined in the legal rules and in statements of social work roles and tasks (GSCC, 2008). It is, therefore, open to infinite interpretation in practice. Essential to the development of skills in partnership is a clearer understanding of what the principle covers and what the aims of working in partnership are.

The concept of partnership has a complex aetiology, reflecting influences from both consumerism and citizenship. The term is used to describe anything from token consultation to a total devolution of power and control (Braye and Preston-Shoot, 1995) or to distinguish between user-centred and management-centred involvement (Begum, 2006). Understandings about power, and recognition that partnership and empowerment are linked in a dynamic developmental process, are crucial; certain aspects of partnership – consultation, participation in social processes that affect people's lives – are in themselves empowering, and transfer in the balance of power alters the nature of subsequent partnership. Thus, evidence suggests that participatory assessment frameworks offer benefits in terms of process and outcome (Cleaver and Walker, 2004; Lloyd, 2006; Platt, 2006).

The implications of a partnership ethos for practising social work law are that recognition must be given to the power at the centre of the relationship. Partners in a relationship do not always have equal power. Social workers have power, and indeed duties, to act in certain circumstances. They cannot deny, delegate or ignore this. However, in their exercise of this authority they can be held accountable by service users and care councils. Service users and the communities to which they belong also have power and strengths. One of the skills of partnership is recognizing how power is initially distributed in a relationship, and promoting the exercise of users' power within it (Braye and Preston-Shoot, 2006a). It is tempting to assume that partnership is easier to achieve when drawing on legislation to exercise helping functions rather than controlling functions. This is not necessarily the case, however, and skills are transferable from one to the other.

Skills for partnership in practising social work law will certainly involve the following:

- conveying accurate information about the powers and duties of the local authority; information that is jargon-free in accessible language, conveyed through effective channels of communication;
- relationship-building that tackles expectations, distrust and fears with clear communication, and demonstrates availability and accessibility,

practically and emotionally, through responsive listening and continuity of contact (Godfrey and Wistow, 1997; Robinson and Williams, 2002; Gunn, 2005; Begum, 2006; Brandon et al., 2006; Lloyd, 2006; Millar and Corby, 2006);

● involving service users in problem definition and analysis of need, at both an individual and general planning level, exploring how they make sense of their situation, recognizing the knowledge they possess as well as professionals' skills of assessment (Richards, 2000);

● exploring options (Robinson and Williams, 2002; NICE, 2006), taking account of what legislation empowers or requires and searching for the proportional intervention that responds to risk and need but also utilizes strengths (Begum, 2006; CWDC, 2007; Henwood, 2008);

● widening consultation: service users' agendas must be included alongside those of professionals – there are many different opinions about what is the right service development to follow, and consultation reveals potentially contradictory options; exploring diversity and commonality across different social divisions is important (Begum, 2006);

● communicating in different ways with different groups of people (Robson et al., 2003) to ascertain wishes and feelings, paying attention to what children, family members and, where appropriate, neighbours and community members say (Sinclair and Bullock, 2002);

● providing material and emotional support to facilitate participation;

● clarifying the aims of consultation or assessment: what is the purpose; what is the power structure; can those being consulted influence the outcome; how will their views be taken forward?

The legal rules will impact upon the extent of partnership and power transfer. Original policy guidance on community care (DH, 1990) made it clear, for instance, that legislation forbade cash payments in lieu of services. Subsequent legislation (CC(DP)A 1996, HSCA 2001, HSCA 2008) has positively promoted them, although to exercise choice and determine how services are personalized, users must still qualify for support and thus navigate through the local authority's control of budgets.

What of the more coercive and controlling aspects of practising social work law, the points at which self-determination may be overruled for purposes of control or protection?

Policy guidance (DH, 2000c; DfES, 2006a) emphasizes that partnership has the objective of safeguarding children and promoting their welfare. Partnership with families should not put children at risk. Nonetheless, professionals must be open and honest, and keep parents informed about their rights and what action is being taken. Research also strongly endorses practice wherein concerns and issues are shared straightfor-wardly but sensitively and disagreement or conflict is openly discussed (Millar and Corby, 2006; Platt, 2006). The same guidance identifies opportunities for good partnership practice at key stages through the safeguarding process, and additionally recognizes the importance of a facilitative organizational framework involving senior managers, elected members, and Local Safeguarding Children Boards.

It is entirely consistent with an ethos of partnership to identify what cannot be changed – that the social worker has a duty to act – but within that context to use the authority positively, applying the same skills of informing, involving and consulting. Underpinning skill in the positive use of authority are:

- role clarity; the clear setting of boundaries and understandings of who has what powers, duties and resources; what principles are used in their application; what can or cannot be done; what is or is not negotiable;
- clear communication about what is happening and why, using clear and unequivocal language, avoiding euphemisms, jargon and the mystique of legalistic language;
- clarity of purpose: how the use of compulsory legal powers supports the overall purpose of intervention;
- clarity about foregoing consent to a course of action if judgement indicates this is required, and then using the minimum coercive action necessary to secure safety or protection;
- openness to other possible means of achieving goals; the over-use of controlling legislation can sometimes be a defensive strategy to reduce the anxiety inherent in the levels of responsibility carried by practitioners;
- preparing and supporting participants to facilitate their involvement and managing group processes to ensure that the goals of working together are achieved.

Finally partnership skills include the ability to connect individuals with networks, tapping the strength that can arise from peer support, especially from organizations controlled by experts by experience (Begum, 2006; Henwood, 2008), putting individuals in touch with resources such as law centres, offering information about rights and complaints procedures, proactively encouraging independent representation and advocacy so professional power may be balanced by active strengthening of users' rights, opinions and perspectives.

Skills in assessment

The importance of assessment in contributing to the skilled and effective use of legislation has been emphasized in child protection (DfES, 2006a), in family support (DH, 1991d, 2000c) and in adult services (DH, 1991c, 2002c). The principle of open, accessible, needs-based assessment has, however, been difficult to activate. Inquiries have found assessment to be poor, with insufficient linkages between planning and outcomes, failure to integrate information or clarify how it has influenced decision-making, and limitations in the recognition and consideration of risk (Statham and Aldgate, 2003; Cleaver and Walker, 2004; Reder and Duncan, 2004). Service users and carers have expressed dissatisfaction with the assessment process, experiencing it as fleeting, superficial, procedural and resource-dominated, and unlikely to capture their perspectives or the complexity of carer/cared-for relationships (Godfrey and Wistow, 1997; Richards, 2000; Tanner, 2003; Lloyd, 2006). More positively, use of assessment frameworks appears to have improved the quality of assessment, planning and decision-making (Cleaver and Walker, 2004; Selwyn et al., 2006) and can have therapeutic benefits (Millar and Corby, 2006). Assessment should be an ongoing process rather than a single event; several component skills can sharpen practice and contribute to a more accurate use of law.

Clarity of purpose

The legal rules define the reasons for undertaking assessment. In adults' services, the purpose is 'to identify and evaluate an individual's presenting needs and how they constrain or support his/her capacity to live a full and independent life' (DH, 2002b, p. 7). Some situations may contain a range of legal mandates. Assessment under the NHSCCA 1990 may run parallel to one under the DPA 1986 (where the goal is to assess need for specific services – those provided under CSDPA 1970) and another under the C(RS)A 1995 (where the goal is to assess the needs of carers). A key objective is to evaluate 'presenting needs' to determine whether they are also 'eligible needs' by reference to the degree of risk they pose to autonomy, health and safety, ability to manage daily routines, and involvement in family and wider community life. Evaluation of risk is also a central purpose of assessment in children's services and mental health, both the CA 1989 and the MHA 1983 permitting coercive action to facilitate this. Since the legislation prioritizes different objectives at different times, it is important in every assessment to understand the primary focus of the legal mandate.

An associated issue is clarity over *who* is being assessed. In certain circumstances the needs of carers may be prioritized even though the person being cared for has refused assistance (CDCA 2000). The need for services arises not from an individual's need alone but from the pattern of relationships available to that individual, thus requiring that the whole situation is assessed, which includes the willingness and ability of the carer to care (DPA 1986, s.8; Robinson and Williams, 2002). Clearly there will be changes over time, so the purpose and focus of assessment will need to be kept under review. When assessing children in need, for example, the young person must be seen and interviewed (DH, 2000c) but the assessment focus also includes parents and other care-givers, and the wider environment.

A systematic process

The process of assessment can be broken down into stages or steps. In adults' services, these are defined both in generic guidance for assessments under the NHSCCA 1990 (DH, 1991c, 2002b) and in specific frameworks relating to different user groups, such as the NSFs (DH, 1999b, 2001b), the Care Programme Approach (DH, 2008c), those in continuing care (DH, 2007a), and carers (DH, 2005b). Thus a systematic approach involves familiarity with the most relevant guidance on each individual assessment. The degree of systematization may vary with the type of assessment being undertaken. FACS (DH, 2002b) indicates the scale and depth of the assessment should be proportionate to the individual's presenting needs and circumstances. The SAP (DH, 2002c) refers to four levels or types of assessment – contact, overview, specialist and comprehensive, the last of which is reserved for cases where needs are particularly problematic or where prolonged and intensive support is likely. Assessment tools and scales are intended to promote standardization and systematicity of the process.

Of a different order of systematization are the *components* of comprehensive assessment, for example those offered to structure children's needs and safeguarding assessments (DH, 2000c; DfES, 2006a), child and family welfare (CWDC, 2007) and mental health admissions (DH, 2008d). These lead practitioners through a range of areas of enquiry deemed relevant to the task.

Research (Rummery and Glendinning, 1999; Richards, 2000; Cleaver and Walker, 2004; Tanner, 2005) highlights how assessment and professional judgement can become distorted by the availability of services and resource pressures. It becomes agency-centred rather than user-centred. It may focus only on immediate rather than longer-term needs and neglect to evaluate the likely outcome if help is not offered. Working through a systematic process and content will help practitioners to maintain a needs-based focus and to challenge the negative impact on people's social rights of resource-led gate-keeping. An important caveat, however, is that the structure should not dominate to the extent that it pre-empts exploration of factors 'not on the list', whereupon assessment practice becomes mechanical (Cleaver and Walker, 2004; Bell et al., 2007). Checklists become dangerous if they encourage practitioners to sidestep the subtlety of situations, the relative importance of different features, and information that is difficult to organize and interpret (Munro, 1998; Richards, 2000). An essential stance is one of curiosity, an openness of mind that makes room for the 'not so obvious' and avoids prescribing the solution before defining the problem. The assessor tailors the standardized format to the situation, demonstrating empathy and respect (Corby et al., 2002).

Matching information to criteria and standards

It is crucial to define the criteria against which assessment is being made, and within those criteria to set standards, expressed in terms of specific behaviour, against which presenting information can be judged. What is the 'nature or degree' of mental disorder (s.2, MHA 1983) that warrants detention in hospital? When is harm significant (s.31, CA 1989)?

Theoretical frameworks and research evidence are crucial in enabling social workers to make sense of data from assessment (Munro, 1998; Reder and Duncan, 2004). Without systematically using such knowledge-bases, planning and decision-making may be naïve, if not dangerous, and difficult to justify when accountability is demanded. Indeed, social workers have an ethical responsibility to present knowledge-informed, needs-led reasoning for particular recommendations and to evaluate knowledge-bases and practice outcomes both to extend evidence-based approaches to intervention and to enhance their own competence (Magill, 2006).

Assessment must also consider the referrer's position. The widespread use of eligibility criteria will influence how referrers describe their concerns (Richards, 2000; Cleaver and Walker, 2004).

The skill, then, is in matching the information to the criteria. It is important to be specific in terms of language used, and to recognize the power of legal definitions as opposed to, for example, medical definitions. 'Mental impairment' is a phrase commonly used about a whole range of learning and behavioural difficulties, yet within the context of the MHA 1983 it has a precise legal meaning. Terminology, particularly that which confers legal status and thus requires legal action, such as the duty to admit to hospital, must be used with precision and understanding of the implications.

A danger when setting criteria and standards is that they can reflect dominant norms and thus discriminate against people from minority groups in the context of assessment. Frameworks for assessment of child development (DH, 2000b), for example, do offer guidance for work with black families and disabled children, but practitioners matching information against standards must critically appraise any framework and ensure that in neither content nor application does it lead to discriminatory assessment.

Skills in opening up assessment to a process of participation

Despite emphasis upon openness, accessibility, participation and person-centred approaches (DH 2002b, 2003c), assessment as construed in guidance remains firmly in the domain of professional activity. In this respect, the legal rules lag behind the policy rhetoric of personalization (DH, 2008a). Clearly there are skills of communication, negotiation, relationship-building, exploration and openness that need to be engaged if involvement is to be more than tokenistic. They include creating a positive atmosphere and reducing tension (Millar and Corby, 2006), believing in people's ability to change (Corby et al., 2002), and seeing them as expert in assessing their needs and problem-solving (Tanner, 2003). Enabling people to use their preferred forms of communication, engaging with their individual meanings, lived experience and desired outcomes (Godfrey and Wistow, 1997; Tanner, 2005), demands time, trust, continuity and sensitivity, and the routine involvement of advocates and interpreters who can offer assistance in self-expression.

One challenge, with enhanced significance following the MCA 2005, is how to involve service users who do not have decision-making capacity. It is important not to assume incapacity for judgement, but to check levels of comprehension at each decision point. Capacity can fluctuate and is function-specific – different levels of capacity can be required for different decisions. Capacity and communication can be affected by time, medication and location, by trust and types of interaction, and by the quality of the relationship that is developed. The MCA 2005 and its guidance (DCA, 2007) articulate the principle of support for people to take decisions they are able to take. Mechanisms include anticipatory decision-making by a competent person making arrangements for future incapacity. Knowledge of an individual's former views and wishes on an issue are of great importance, and ascertaining them may involve consultation with a wide range of people. Where capacity does not exist, the concept of 'best interests' is a key foundation for professional judgement. A related challenge is to ascertain children's capacity to understand and engage in decisions and to develop communication that will facilitate their participation (Lefevre, 2008; Lefevre et al., 2008). Traditional views of capacity must of necessity be challenged in everyday practice. The use of advocates and interpreters in outlining, clarifying and taking forward assessment processes is crucial to effective communication: a skill not merely in working with a representative or 'linguistic technician' but in valuing and drawing upon crucial knowledge and interpretation of fine nuance and detail in what is being communicated.

Decision-making inevitably remains the responsibility of the local authority. Resource allocation has to take place within strict constraints. Individual practitioners are accountable for their decisions and, in assessments which have a high political profile, such as children's safeguarding, the stakes are high. Within that broad framework, however, there is considerable scope for assessment to be enhanced by fuller levels of partnership between the parties involved, and further developments will follow as personalization takes shape.

Reflection and review

Sometimes policy guidance dictates a timetable for reviews, as when community care assessments (DH, 2002b) must be reviewed after three months and at least annually thereafter. Reflection and review is, however, good practice, especially because practitioners can be slow or reluctant to revise their judgements (Munro, 1996; Reder and Duncan, 2004). Sinclair and Corden (2005) advise an open-minded approach to young people's requests to be accommodated under the CA 1989, embracing considerations of need as well as risk. White and Featherstone (2005) advocate interrupting established mindsets so that discomforting or disconfirming facts can be considered, for instance around decision-making at the threshold between s.17 and s.47 (CA 1989). Inquiries (Sheppard, 1996; Laming, 2003) have recommended that cases should only be closed after reassessment and consultation, including checking that recommendations have been followed through and adequate safeguarding arrangements are in place.

Skills in recording

Social workers must maintain accurate records (GSCC, 2002, 2008). Agencies should have policies on record-keeping, covering such issues as purpose, confidentiality, file structure, user involvement, content and retention, with key principles being openness about information-sharing, clarity in distinguishing fact from opinion, and partnership in compilation (DH, 2000e). Files should be clear, up-to-date, balanced, accurate and comprehensive, detailing chronology, nature and quality of care provided, and integrating reasons for decisions or differences of opinion within the professional network that will help people to understand their past lives (*Re C (Care Proceedings: Disclosure of Local Authority's Decision-Making* [2002]; *Re G (Care: Challenge to Local Authority's Decision)* [2003]; CWDC, 2007; DH, 2002d). Details of advance decisions (MCA 2005) should be kept to avoid any later uncertainty.

These standards are necessary to promote service users' Article 8 rights to private and family life. Records should bring focus to practice, for example detailing the intricate processes of decision-making, particularly in situations where professionals must choose between options, none of which are risk-free. It is not uncommon for decisions to be made in supervision, or in *ad hoc* consultation in urgent situations, and legal opinion may have contributed. As such, an accurate record of the decision-making *process* may not be made, with perhaps the final decision logged, but no detailed account of the reasoning behind it. Yet it is precisely this reasoning, or balancing act, that is called to account when professionals must justify their actions. The implications for record-keeping are clear – where decisions to pursue one course of action in preference to another are made, records must clearly demonstrate the attention paid to the advantages and disadvantages of each course of action.

Research and inquiry evidence is critical of poor recording (Sheppard, 1996; Goldsmith and Beaver, 1999; Laming, 2003). It reveals insufficient attention to case history, scattered or inadequately recorded assessments, and missing chronologies (Daniel and Baldwin, 2001; Sinclair and Bullock, 2002; Preston-Shoot, 2003b; Cleaver and Walker, 2004; Selwyn et al., 2006). Children's views on proposed plans or delays in decision-making (Daniel and Baldwin, 2001; Selwyn et al., 2006) can be hard to locate, as are carers' needs and wishes (Robinson and Williams, 2002). Records may not disclose who took particular decisions and why, or contain evidence of management oversight (Preston-Shoot, 2003b). More positively, there is evidence that assessment frameworks (Cleaver and Walker, 2004) and the ICS (Bell et al., 2007) are improving the quality of recording, including analysis of children's needs, the outcome of child protection investigations and strategy discussions, and planning. Indeed, the ICS requires a chronology of key events, detail of a child's legal status, referral, assessment, plan, intervention and review, and analysis of information (LAC(2005)3). Nonetheless Bell et al. (2007) found that greater attention was needed to contingency planning, monitoring progress, and compiling records that are easier for parents to understand.

King and Trowell (1992) suggest that professional worries about scrutiny of files in the legal arena lead to less rather than more recording – omitting impressions, opinions and hypotheses which could be challenged. Clearly, the form of recording is important, and unsubstantiated judgements can and should be open to challenge. Hypotheses and impressions should be clearly identified as such, but do have a place in the formulation of professional judgement and are thus legitimately recorded.

Skills in court craft

Practising social work law will inevitably bring practitioners into the legal arena of the courts. This is often experienced as threatening (Braye and Preston-Shoot, 2007), partly because of the low esteem in which practice may be held (Dickens, 2003; Davis, 2007). Indeed, delays in care proceedings have sometimes resulted from a lack of assessment, planning and managerial oversight (Selwyn et al., 2006) and from a lack of confidence in decisions involving risk (McKeigue and Beckett, 2004).

There are several areas of skill development. One requires the completion of local authority pre-proceedings work before court applications are made, other than in emergency situations (MoJ, 2008b). Another concerns the preparation and presentation of evidence, namely the ability to give meaning to concepts such as significant harm and to make a case for particular outcomes with coherent arguments. Good practice can be undermined by poor presentation in terms of focus and analysis. Techniques of reasoning and logic, fact analysis and categorization and interpretation, need to be matched by preparation for the types of questioning likely to be encountered in cross-examination and recognition of the skills in giving evidence effectively (Braye and Preston-Shoot, 2007; Davis, 2007). Social work of necessity deals in shades of opinion, probability and uncertainty. Legal process emphasizes factual evidence, and social workers operating in the courts need to recognize and use this effectively. Familiarity with court rules and roles can contribute to the ability to assert one's position with credibility and authority. Familiarity with relevant research makes an important contribution, and is needed both in the presentation of evidence and in cross-examination.

Practitioners must maintain high standards of reporting to derive maximum benefit for children of court actions, accurately linking, therefore, the content of statements and reports to the legal context in which they will be read, and to the requirements of the relevant parts of the legislation being used. A systematic and thorough approach is advocated by Plotnikoff and Woolfson (1996) who offer the following overall checklist to ensure that statements are well focused:

- take account of the principles of the CA 1989;
- reflect the requirements of the relevant sections;
- ensure balance and overall fairness;
- include all relevant facts, whether or not supportive of the local authority's conclusion;
- verify significant facts and justify opinions;
- avoid repetition;
- present information with sensitivity;
- make relevant references to race;
- avoid applying cultural/moral values;
- take account of changes during the court proceedings.

Similarly, the Public Law Outline (MoJ, 2008b) reinforces the key importance and necessary content of a chronology, social work statement and case summary. These must include details of previous court proceedings, present living arrangements for the child and contact with family members, information on ethnicity, culture and gender and services provided, key issues in the case and the circumstances triggering the application, proposals for the child, including placement, contact and services, and details of the parties involved.

A third skill is working closely with the local authority's lawyers, for instance when preparing for hearings and anticipating where evidence might be challenged. This also incorporates co-operating with other parties' representatives in order to avoid delay (MoJ, 2008b). A fourth skill is supporting service users through court processes, ensuring that people have information about their rights, about the nature and course of proceedings, and being sensitive to the emotional impact of the occasion (Dickens, 2003). In the adversarial atmosphere of the court, such support may be difficult to give. However, in the wider context of law as a necessary part of the relationship with service users, the court setting is no different from other situations where power and authority are key factors, to be incorporated positively.

Skills for interaction with other professions and agencies

The statutory foundations for interprofessional and interagency collaboration outlined in Chapter 7 cannot alone guarantee effective and efficient interdisciplinary working. Yet such collaboration is crucial to effective use of law. Moreover, research (Statham and Aldgate, 2003; Clarkson and Challis, 2004; Frost et al., 2005; White and Featherstone, 2005; Cestari et al., 2006) shows considerable mistrust between agencies regarding assessment, and demonstrates that a common language does not exist for articulating social care needs. More positively, perhaps, use of assessment frameworks across children's services has helped to promote interagency work (Cleaver and Walker, 2004). Equally, the flexibilities introduced by the HA 1999 have led in some quarters to closer co-ordination and working relationships (Hudson and Henwood, 2002).

Much can be learned from analyses of what goes wrong in both inter-professional and interagency communication and processes: there are implications both for skills development and for procedures. Studies and reports (Sheppard, 1996; Sinclair and Bullock, 2002; Laming, 2003; Reder and Duncan, 2004) have identified a number of problems:

- lack of clarity about the contributions of various agencies and individuals, arising from unclear roles and responsibilities, and boundary disputes;
- differing levels of knowledge;
- individual workers asked to fulfil several roles at once, but those roles not clearly distinguished;
- failure to communicate within and between agencies, and to share information and decision-making;
- responsibilities allocated, to give a semblance of the task being done, but lack of attention to the resources required or the realities of resource constraint;
- overlap of functions common to more than one agency;
- lack of differentiation between degrees of risk;
- stereotyping, competitiveness, hostility and hidden agendas between different professional groups;
- attitudinal differences, for example about the involvement of service users, the culpability of victims, the treatment/punishment of offenders, the credibility of children – leading to goal differences and conflicts about how to proceed;
- tendency to avoid contentious areas of difference and to consider only that which can be agreed upon;
- lack of recourse to specialist advice (legal/medical);
- differences in professional power and status affecting decision-making;
- dysfunctional patterns of relationships within professional networks;
- inappropriately closed or open professional systems in relation to their interaction with others outside the system.

These findings point to the skills that need to be developed, irrespective of whether services are integrating to create new organizational configurations for service delivery or merely working together more closely. A previous history of effective multi-agency working facilitates this agenda but is not essential (Bell et al., 2007).

Establishing a common value system and language

Common aims and vision are fundamental to integration (CWDC, 2007). Accordingly, alongside uni-professional statements (GSCC, 2002; GTC, 2006), joint values statements have been issued for health and social care (QAA, 2004) and for the children's workforce (GTC et al., 2007), all of which emphasize respect for the roles and expertise of colleagues, team-working, and sharing knowledge. However, different professional values continue to impact on collaborative working. They emerge, for instance, in different approaches to confidentiality (Frost et al., 2005) and refusal to accept assessments from other professionals concerning older people (Clarkson and Challis, 2004) or children (Brandon et al., 2006).

Dialogue between professions must take issues further, however, into an understanding of the dynamics of professional/institutional power in people's lives. This is crucial if decisions to use the law are to reflect anti-discriminatory values, and the law is to be used positively to counteract oppression and abuse rather than maintain and institutionalize it.

Skill in converging and differentiating

Co-locating different professions around common assessment processes or in new organizational configurations does not automatically improve communication or collaboration. Practitioners from different professions also use different systems of meaning (Reder and Duncan, 2003). They use different terms to understand prevention (Morris, K., 2005) and the needs of children and families (Cleaver et al., 2004). Understanding roles and responsibilities requires recognizing where and how professional roles differ from one another, in terms of legal mandates and professional culture, ideology, attitudes and expertise, and finding a common language and conceptual framework. This includes making explicit, and discussing the relevance for collaborative or integrated practice of, implicit knowledge, which demands commitment to share and learn, and to articulate similarities and differences (Frost et al., 2005). It involves opening up practice to scrutiny and challenge, and monitoring how inter-professional communication is affected by the degree of mutual understanding (White and Featherstone, 2005).

For instance, most professions in regular contact with service users would maintain that they have a role in assessment; yet within that generic concern there are a number of specialist areas that become the focus of different professional groups. It is essential that knowledge is shared about the legal boundaries which determine the work focus, that legal duties are made explicit and limitations on powers are understood. This can contribute to understanding how each profession thinks and approaches its task, its agendas and priorities.

This skill is certainly tested in relationship-building between lawyers and social workers. Relationships between them can be characterized by resentment at over-intrusion or frustration at under-involvement, and by impressions that their aims and skills are different (Braye and Preston-Shoot et al., 2005; Dickens, 2008). The skill here lies in establishing how the values and skills underpinning the work of both professions, such as information collection, assessment and advocacy, and the goals to which they aspire for people they are working with, are characterized as much by similarity as difference. It moves on to learning from each other's perspective and developing a language that makes practice accessible to the other. It concludes with recognizing those settings where lawyers' roles, knowledge and skills may be foregrounded and feeling able to challenge and moderate the other's practice (Braye and Preston-Shoot, 2006a, 2006b; Dickens, 2008).

Skill in negotiating

A next step from the recognition of difference is the negotiation of position. Who is going to fulfil what role? Who is accountable for what to whom? The aim is to avoid overlap and gaps, to reach for a workable compromise. Of related importance is clarity of responsibility for decision-making and for implementing decisions. This will depend both on individual agency accountability structures and upon the power accorded to any joint forum. Written notes of agreements made can often be helpful, and form the basis of continuing review and evaluation. Here, as elsewhere, social workers should contribute their knowledge and practice models (GSCC, 2008) and may find that their perspective and approach is valued by multidisciplinary teams (Lymbery, 2006).

Skill in networking

The task here is to bring the interagency system together, balancing views and opinions, working for clear definitions of need and articulation of risk, backed by understanding of the need for hard evidence in the legal arena. Networking seeks a collective approach to people's well-being in a context frequently preoccupied with single agencies' eligibility criteria and procedures for assessment and records (Clarkson and Challis, 2004; Bell et al., 2007). Where all parts of the system congregate together, as in case conferences, the skill extends into the arena of group process to ensure it is a positive rather than a negative force. The existence of chairpersons who are independent of line management responsibility or agency allegiance makes an important contribution to establishing constructive processes in such forums, such as clear and shared objectives, realistic plans, the availability of specialist information, and explicit roles and timeframes.

Also important is a forum for interagency networking that is independent of the need to meet for decision-making on individual situations. Local Safeguarding Children Boards, for example, can promote the channels of communication and trust which can then facilitate effective collaboration in day-to-day decisions. Housing and social services authorities should agree protocols concerning the accommodation of young people aged 16 and 17, which provide a framework within which practitioners can communicate confidently and constructively. Similarly, managers should co-ordinate and integrate work surrounding people with dementia through written procedures regarding care and treatment (NICE, 2006). Key NHS and education personnel should be identified to co-ordinate and facilitate effective contributions from other healthcare and teaching staff to the children's safeguarding process (DfES, 2006a).

Networking, however, also includes drawing on knowledge of local communities and organizations (Begum, 2006; Stepney, 2006; SCIE, 2007). This may facilitate take-up of services such as direct payments, and the development of advocacy and direct action by groups of (potential) service users.

Skill in working within power structures

It is important to understand and respond to the ways in which power and status influence interprofessional communication. In addition to the differences of status between professions, there are hierarchies of gender, race and other individual characteristics which make interaction more complex. Attention must be given both to others' participation and to asserting one's own position and ensuring appropriate account is taken of this. Equally, attention must be given to the dangers of groupthink (SWIA, 2005), where patterns of thinking appear entrenched, and of mirroring, where professional networks act out a family's relationships (Reder and Duncan, 2003).

The organizational context for effective and competent practice in social work

This book has made frequent reference to the organizational context – the structures, procedures and forums – in which practice is located. It has explored the evidence of how organizational cultures can corrode professional standards and compromise core tasks, such as assessment and decision-making. Adverse work contexts do impact on professionals' ability to safeguard and promote well-being and to question organizational practice (Richards, 2000; Preston-Shoot, 2000b; Reder and Duncan, 2003; Sinclair and Corden, 2005; SWIA, 2005). Indeed, Care Standards Tribunals have reinstated some social workers to the register precisely because they were inadequately supported by management (*LA v General Social Care Council* [2007]; *Forbes v GSCC* [2008]). Practising social work law requires a competent organization – a culture which supports employees as well as service users, a set of organizational goals disseminated at all levels and giving rise to clear procedural guidance, and measures to facilitate staff in achieving those goals. Three specific organizational mechanisms will resource practitioners to develop their practice of social work law.

Supervision and consultation

Supervision should fulfil an accountability function, to ensure that legal duties and powers are being used appropriately and that policies and procedures are being complied with, and a reflective function, where the dynamics of the work and the elements of new working practices can be explored in detail (Cleaver and Walker, 2004; Reder and Duncan, 2004; Brandon et al., 2006). Supervision has been criticized across adult (Evans et al., 2005) and children's services (Laming, 2003; Sinclair and Corden, 2005) for taking place with inadequate frequency and having an unclear influence on case management. Practitioners have not felt supported in implementing the Common Assessment Framework, for instance, and lack confidence in the (new) skills required (Brandon et al., 2006).

Practising social work law is fraught with uncertainty, concern about rights and liberty, potential for discrimination, anxiety about risk management, ambiguity from conflicting imperatives and practice dilemmas, culminating in fear of getting it wrong and pressure to get it right. Decisions to use the law to protect or control may bring workers into situations where they are more likely than in any other activity to encounter fear and intimidation (Selwyn et al., 2006). Action is often required quickly, yet with partial information. Decisions not to act under the law, not to allocate resources or offer services can leave workers facing hostility, blame, disappointment and distress.

Moreover, practitioners are concerned about the lack of resources to meet identified needs and about management expectations and government targets (Platt, 2006). They perceive a threat to their discretion and an increasing surveillance of their practice through such measures as the ICS (Bell et al., 2007), and express concern about timeframes and staffing resources to meet the increasing demands of assessment frameworks (Cleaver and Walker, 2004; Millar and Corby, 2006). Inquiries, similarly, point to the impact of staffing levels, caseloads and failures of supervision and strategic management (Sheppard 1996; Reder and Duncan, 2004; SWIA, 2005).

This must be the substance of supervision, along with exploration of the processes that affect decision-making, personal values and their interplay with agency priorities, feelings about using authority, the draining emotions in the situations in which the law requires or sanctions intervention, and the effects of anxiety and defence in human interaction. The supervisor's role is to provide a sufficiently supportive environment for challenges to be made constructively, to help practitioners consider alternative interpretations and actions, to reflect on and weigh in the balance the likely effects of differing interventions, to acknowledge fears and feelings, to face the task to be done, to gain courage and to see the law as a positive tool for practice rather than a constraint or imposition; in short, to attend both to task, the job to be done, and to process, how it is done and how it affects the person doing it. Supervision must be a space for reflection and thinking about cases (Munro, 1996; Reder and Duncan, 2004) and how to meet the joint demands of legally and professionally accountable practice.

Consultation with people with specialist knowledge from other disciplines will be important, in particular with lawyers whose interpretations can clarify areas of uncertainty and help construct the detailed working knowledge that contributes to confidence. Doubts, however, have been expressed about the availability to social workers of good-quality legal advice (Sheppard, 1996; Hunt and Macleod, 1998) and concerns about tensions in the relationships between social workers and lawyers (Preston-Shoot et al., 1998c; Dickens, 2005, 2006). There is also concern about social workers' access to employer support, continuing professional development, and supervisors with up-to-date legal knowledge (Preston-Shoot et al., 1997, 1998b; Braye et al., 2007).

Access to information

Qualified social workers will have benefited from the emphasis placed on law within qualifying programmes. The complexity of social work law, however, can lead to a feeling of being swamped, exacerbated by the rapidly changing and diversifying legal context. Continuing professional development is essential, therefore, to update knowledge (Braye and Preston-Shoot, 2006a) but practitioners appear poorly resourced for maintaining their legal literacy (Preston-Shoot et al., 1997; Braye et al., 2007), with knowledge gaps relating to eligibility for housing and other services (Chase et al., 2008) and community care provision (Cestari et al., 2006).

In this context it is worth noting the employer's obligation to ensure that social workers understand their roles and responsibilities, through the provision of training and other developmental opportunities (GSCC, 2002). Inquiry recommendations about training have not been adequately implemented (Reder and Duncan, 2004) and training requirements for new procedures, such as the CAF and the ICS, have been underestimated (Cleaver and Walker, 2004; Brandon et al., 2006; Bell et al., 2007).

Every practitioner should have easy access to certain resources. There is no substitute for referring to the law as written in Acts of Parliament. Basic information must also routinely include associated regulations, policy guidance and codes of practice. The third essential component is information on local policies and procedures: how the law is interpreted and implemented in criteria and standards by the employing authority; what strategies and priorities for policy implementation the organization has devised. Of equal importance are judicial decisions which themselves alter, amend, clarify or innovate in relation to legal duties, powers and processes. Access to journals, news-sheets and case reports can help individual practitioners keep in touch with developments influencing lawyers and courts in their interpretations of the law. One exercise that individual practitioners and teams can undertake routinely is compiling and maintaining materials appropriate to their work (Braye and Preston-Shoot, 2006a).

Practitioners must also expect to be familiar with policy guidance and research that both support and challenge the position they are taking in any given situation, updating their knowledge and practice. This includes being familiar with key research findings and also researching their own practice. Social work skills and research skills are not exclusive specialisms since both require information collection, assessment and analysis, recording and reporting. Integrating research into practice is a key process in the task of reclaiming professionalism from the control of managerialism and bureaucracy.

Action planning

Finally, standing back to monitor one's work and review its effectiveness is a vital process that can help identify impediments to practising social work law and plan the necessary personal and organizational resources. The results of such scrutiny, which may routinely include self-audits of knowledge and skills (Braye and Preston-Shoot, 2006a), may usefully be incorporated into action planning for the future. Action plans can be both personal and organizational, carried out individually or in teams, involving both personal developmental tasks and collective approaches. By promoting open communication they help practitioners and managers take a proactive stance in creating a work environment that facilitates the effective use of law within the wider context of practice. They work on the principle of breaking down apparently big or insoluble problems into smaller, more manageable parts, making commitments to strategy and tackling each step in turn. It is of crucial importance to identify those in an organization who have the power and authority to take issues forward, to establish dialogue and engage key people in processes of development and change.

Figure 8.1 demonstrates the process of creating an action plan.

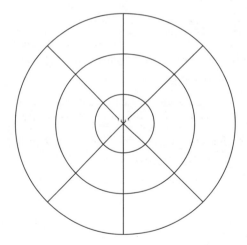

In the centre of the diagram, make a note of what concerns you about using the law in your practice. In the second circle, indicate what effect this concern has on your practice. In the outer circle, specify the tasks, however small, that will enable you to start addressing the issue that is of concern; who else will need to be involved; when you will do these tasks; when you will review progress. Now commit yourself to your action plan by sharing it with a colleague and using your discussion to develop and fine-tune your tasks.

Figure 8.1   Creating an action plan

Action plans – examples

Possible concerns about using the law which might appear in the central circle of the diagram are:

- I fear cross-examination in court;
- I'm uncomfortable involving parents in case conferences;
- I have insufficient factual knowledge about powers and duties;
- I have no guidance on acceptable risk definitions;
- There is no legislation to protect older people from abuse;
- I'm not sure I should be crushing these tablets up into her food;
- Our services discriminate;
- I have to admit people to psychiatric hospital because there are no suitable community alternatives;
- I don't know if the standards we apply discriminate against black families;
- I'm supposed to take into account the needs of both the service user and her carer, but they are diametrically opposed.

The beginnings of an action plan might look like Figure 8.2, taking two concerns from this list and working outwards from the concern at the centre towards the concrete steps that can assist in resolving it.

putting it into practice

Reflect on these questions and discuss your ideas with others if you have the opportunity:

- When have you accepted or not accepted authority from others? What factors influenced your acceptance?
- When (in your work) do you feel powerful? Where does that power come from? Do you feel comfortable with that power?
- When (in your work) do you feel powerless? What is it like to feel powerless?
- What power do service users have? How are service users disempowered?
- How does your power affect people you work with?
- Is it possible to work in partnership when depriving someone of their liberty through compulsory admission to hospital, or when intervening in the exercise of parental responsibility without that person's agreement?

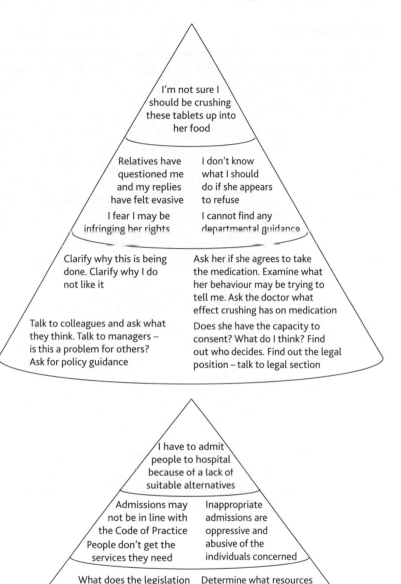

I'm not sure I should be crushing these tablets up into her food

Relatives have questioned me and my replies have felt evasive

I don't know what I should do if she appears to refuse

I fear I may be infringing her rights

I cannot find any departmental guidance

Clarify why this is being done. Clarify why I do not like it

Ask her if she agrees to take the medication. Examine what her behaviour may be trying to tell me. Ask the doctor what effect crushing has on medication

Talk to colleagues and ask what they think. Talk to managers – is this a problem for others? Ask for policy guidance

Does she have the capacity to consent? What do I think? Find out who decides. Find out the legal position – talk to legal section

I have to admit people to hospital because of a lack of suitable alternatives

Admissions may not be in line with the Code of Practice People don't get the services they need

Inappropriate admissions are oppressive and abusive of the individuals concerned

What does the legislation require me to do? Check Mental Health Act 1983. Discuss legal implications of being constrained to deprive someone of their liberty because of lack of resources

Determine what resources would help. Talk to colleagues, users and doctors. Find out from volunteer groups what resources they need to develop viable services

Make representation to health and social care purchasers about budget allocations

figure 8.2   Example action plans

Further reading

Baxter, S. and Carr, H. (2007) *Supported Housing and the Law*. London: Legal Action Group. This provides an introduction to an area spanning young people and adult services where social workers are often asked for advice and advocacy

Clifford, D. and Burke, B. (2009) *Anti-Oppressive Ethics and Values in Social Work*. Basingstoke: Palgrave Macmillan. This book explores the contribution of different ethical perspectives to practice.

Dalrymple, J. and Burke, B. (2007) *Anti-Oppressive Practice: Social Care and the Law*, 2nd edn. Maidenhead: Open University Press/McGraw-Hill. This provides an exploration of how law can support anti-oppressive practice.

Conclusion

The purpose of this book has been to provide social workers and their managers with a reflective, secure and critical legal and ethical literacy. It is our belief that such literacy is essential for navigation through the difficult dilemmas and challenging contexts which practice inevitably presents. It is also our belief that knowledge of the law and its skilled application in practice, coupled with the same in respect of other knowledge frameworks and social work values, can significantly assist the experts by experience with whom practitioners and managers work.

A particular challenge, however, resides in the speed with which legal rules, and their policy context, can change. Social workers bound by the GSCC Code of Practice (2002) will know that they have responsibility to maintain and improve their knowledge and skills. In the legal context, this means taking personal responsibility for ensuring the currency of one's knowledge about statutory developments and judicial interpretations in case law, and about policy and practice guidance and codes of practice, all of which impact upon daily practice. Importantly, it means continuing to subject the legal rules to critical scrutiny by reference to the moral rules embedded within professional ethics and values. This conceptualization of legal and ethical literacy, and its expression in practice, forms a crucial resource for a profession which is confident, credible and critical.

References

Abbott, D., Morris, J. and Ward, L. (2001) *The Best Place to Be? Policy, Practice and the Experiences of Residential School Placements for Disabled Children.* York: Joseph Rowntree Foundation.

Action on Elder Abuse (2008) http://www.elderabuse.org.uk/Mainpages/ Campaigns.htm.

ADASS (2007) *Practice Guidance – Criteria for the Use of IMCAs in Safeguarding Adults Cases.* London: Association of Directors of Adult Social Services.

Adcock, M., White, R. and Hollows, A. (1991) *Significant Harm: Its Management and Outcome.* Croydon: Significant Publications.

ADSS (2005) *Safeguarding Adults: A National Framework of Standards for Good Practice and Outcomes in Adult Protection Work.* London: Association of Directors of Social Services.

Ahmed, S. (2005) 'What is the evidence of early intervention, preventative services for black and minority ethnic group children and their families?', *Practice*, 17, 2, 89–102.

Allain, L. (2007) 'An investigation of how a group of social workers respond to the cultural needs of Black, Minority Ethnic looked after children', *Practice*, 19, 2, 127–41.

Allain, L., Cosis-Brown, H., Danso, C., Dillon, J., Finnegan, P., Gadhoke, S., Shamash, M. and Whittaker, F. (2006) 'User and carer involvement in social work education – a university case study: manipulation or citizen control?', *Social Work Education*, 25, 4, 403–13.

Audit Commission (1994) *Seen but not Heard.* London: HMSO.

Audit Commission (2002) *Recruitment and Retention: A Public Service Workforce for the 21st Century.* London: The Stationery Office.

Audit Commission (2003) *Services for Disabled Children: A Review of Services for Disabled Children and their Families.* London: Audit Commission.

Audit Commission (2004) *Support for Carers of Older People.* London: Audit Commission.

Baglietto, C. (2005) 'Children's rights in the UK: an overview of issues raised by the Council for Europe's Commissioner for Human Rights', *Childright*, 218, 14–16.

Bainbridge, I. and Ricketts, A. (2003) *Improving Older People's Services: An Overview of Performance*. London: Department of Health.

Ball, C., Harris, R., Roberts, G. and Vernon, S. (1988) *The Law Report. Teaching and Assessment of Law in Social Work Education*. London: CCETSW, paper 4:1.

Ball, C., Preston-Shoot, M., Roberts, G. and Vernon, S. (1995) *Law for Social Workers in England and Wales*. London: CCETSW.

Balloch, S., McLean, J. and Fisher, M. (1999) *Social Services: Working under Pressure*. Bristol: Policy Press.

Barn, R. (2006) *Improving Services to Meet the Needs of Minority Ethnic Children and Families*. Department for Education & Skills/Research in Practice. http://www.rip.org.uk/publications/researchbriefings.asp.

Barn, R., Andrew, L. and Mantovani, N. (2005) *Life After Care: The Experiences of Young People from Different Ethnic Groups*. York: Joseph Rowntree Foundation.

Barnes, J. (2002) *Focus on the Future. Key Messages from Focus Groups about the Future of Social Work Training*. London: Department of Health.

Barnes, M., Evans, R., Plumridge, G., and McCabe, A. (2006) *Preventative Services for Disabled Children: A Final Report of the National Evaluation of the Children's Fund*. London: Department for Children Schools and Families.

Bartlett, P. (2003) 'Adults, mental illness and incapacity: convergence and overlap in legal regulation', *Journal of Social Welfare and Family Law*, 25, 4, 341–53.

Baxter, K., Glendinning, C. and Clarke, S. (2008) 'Making informed choices in social care: the importance of accessible information', *Health and Social Care in the Community*, 16, 2, 197–207.

Becker, S. and Dearden, C. (2004) *Young Carers in the UK: The 2004 Report*, London: Carers UK.

Begum, N. (2006) *Doing it for Themselves: Participation and Black and Minority Ethnic Service Users*. London: Race Equality Unit and Social Care Institute for Excellence.

Bell, M., Shaw, I., Sinclair, I., Sloper, P. and Rafferty, J. (2007) *An Evaluation of the Practice, Process and Consequences of the Integrated Children's System in Councils with Social Services Responsibilities*. London: Department for Education and Skills.

Beresford, B. and Oldman, C. (2002) *Housing Matters: National Evidence relating to Disabled Children and their Housing*. Bristol: Policy Press.

Besson, S. (2007) 'Enforcing the child's right to know her origins: contrasting approaches under the Convention on the Rights of the Child and the European Convention on Human Rights', *International Journal of Law, Policy and the Family*, 21, 2, 137–59.

Bewley, C. and McCulloch, L. (2004) *Helping Ourselves. Direct Payments and the Development of Peer Support*. London: Values into Action.

Bichard, M. (2004) *The Bichard Inquiry Report*. London: The Stationery Office.

Blaug, R. (1995) 'Distortion of the face to face: communicative reason and social work practice', *British Journal of Social Work*, 25, 4, 423–39.

Blom-Cooper, L.J. (1985) *A Child in Trust: The Report of the Panel of Inquiry into the Circumstances surrounding the Death of Jasmine Beckford.* London Borough of Brent.

Boneham, M., Williams, K., Copeland, J., McKibbin, P., Wilson, K., Scott, A. and Saunders, P. (1997) 'Elderly people from ethnic minorities in Liverpool: mental illness, unmet need and barriers to service use', *Health and Social Care in the Community*, 5, 3, 173–80.

Boylan, J. and Braye, S. (2006) 'Paid, professionalised and proceduralised: can legal and policy frameworks for child advocacy give voice to children and young people?', *Journal of Social Welfare and Family Law,* 28, 3–4, 233–49.

Bradley, G. (2003) 'Administrative justice and charging for long-term care', *British Journal of Social Work*, 33, 5, 641–57.

Brammer, A. (2007) *Social Work Law*, 2nd edn. Harlow: Pearson Education.

Brand, D. (1999) *Accountable Care. Developing the General Social Care Council.* York: Joseph Rowntree Foundation.

Brandon, M., Howe, A., Dagley, V., Salter, C., Warren, C. and Black, J. (2006) *Evaluating the Common Assessment Framework and Lead Professional Guidance and Implementation in 2005–6.* London: Department for Education and Skills.

Braye, S. (1993) 'Building competence in social work law for the Diploma in Social Work', *Social Work Education*, 12, 28–38.

Braye, S. (2000) 'Participation and involvement in social care: an overview', in H. Kemshall and R. Littlechild (eds) *User Involvement and Participation in Social Care: Research Informing Practice.* London: Jessica Kingsley.

Braye, S. and Preston-Shoot, M. (1990) 'On teaching and applying the law in social work: it is not that simple', *British Journal of Social Work*, 20, 4, 333–53.

Braye, S. and Preston-Shoot, M. (1995) *Empowering Practice in Social Care.* Buckingham: Open University Press.

Braye, S. and Preston-Shoot, M. (1999) 'Accountability, administrative law and social work practice: redressing or reinforcing the power imbalance?', *Journal of Social Welfare and Family Law*, 21, 3, 235–56.

Braye, S. and Preston-Shoot, M. (with Cull, L.-A., Johns, R. and Roche, J.) (2005) *Knowledge Review: Teaching, Learning and Assessment of Law in Social Work Education.* London: Social Care Institute for Excellence.

Braye, S. and Preston-Shoot, M. (2006a) *Teaching, Learning and Assessment of Law in Social Work Education: Resource Guide.* London: Social Care Institute for Excellence.

Braye, S. and Preston-Shoot, M. (2006b) 'The role of law in welfare reform: critical perspectives on the relationship between law and social work practice', *International Journal of Social Welfare*, 15, 1, 19–26.

Braye, S. and Preston-Shoot, M. (2007) *Law and Social Work E-Learning Resources.* London: Social Care Institute for Excellence (www.scie.org.uk/publications/elearning).

Braye, S. and Wigley, V. (2002) *Promoting Independence – Reablement Provision for Older People in Staffordshire.* Stoke-on-Trent: Staffordshire University.

Braye, S. (with Melville, R., Pope, A. and Rangel, M.) (2004) *Promoting Independence: Reablement in St Helens*. Liverpool: University of Liverpool.

Braye, S., Preston-Shoot, M. and Thorpe, A. (2007) 'Beyond the classroom: learning social work law in practice', *Journal of Social Work*, 7, 3, 322–40.

Brayne, H. and Carr, H. (2008) *Law for Social* Workers, 10th edn. Oxford: Oxford University Press.

Bridge, G. and Street, C. (2001) 'When things go wrong: being an independent person under the Children Act 1989 complaints procedure', *Social Policy and Administration*, 35, 6, 716–31.

Broad, B. (2003) 'Young people leaving care: the impact of the Children (Leaving Care) Act 2000', *Childright*, September, 16–18.

Broad, B. (2005) 'Young people leaving care: implementing the Children (Leaving Care) Act 2000?', *Children and Society*, 19, 371–84.

Broad, B. and Robbins, I. (2005) 'The wellbeing of unaccompanied asylum seekers leaving care', *Diversity in Health and Social Care*, 2, 271–7.

Broad, B., Hayes, R. and Rushforth, C. (2001) *Kith and Kin: Kinship Care for Vulnerable Young People*. London: National Children's Bureau.

Brophy, J. (2008) 'Child maltreatment in diverse households: challenges to law, theory, and practice', *Journal of Law and Society*, 35, 1, 75–94.

Buckner, L. and Yeandle, S. (2007) *Valuing Carers: Calculating the Value of Unpaid Care*. London: Carers UK.

Butler-Sloss, E. (1988) *Report of the Inquiry into Child Abuse in Cleveland*. London: HMSO.

Butt, J. and O'Neil, A. (2004) *'Let's Move On': Black and Minority Ethnic Older People's Views on Research Findings*. York: Joseph Rowntree Foundation.

Cass, E. (2005) *Implementing the Carers (Equal Opportunities) Act 2004*. London: Social Care Institute for Excellence.

Cass, E., Robbins, D. and Richardson, A. (2006) *Dignity in Care. Adult Services Practice Guide 9*. London: Social Care Institute for Excellence.

Cestari, L., Munroe, M., Evans, S., Smith, A. and Huxley, P. (2006) 'Fair Access to Care Services (FACS): implementation in the mental health context of the UK', *Health and Social Care in the Community*, 14, 6, 474–81.

CHAI (2006) *Joint Investigation into the Provision of Services for People with Learning Disabilities at Cornwall Partnership NHS Trust*. London: Commission for Healthcare Audit and Inspection.

CHAI (2007) *No Choice, No Voice: A Joint Review of Adult Community Mental Health Services in England*. London: Commission for Healthcare Audit and Inspection.

Charles, N. and Manthorpe, J. (2007) 'FACS or fiction? The impact of the policy Fair Access to Care Services on social care assessments of older visually impaired people', *Practice*, 19, 2, 143–57.

Chase, E., Knight, A. and Statham, J (2008) *The Emotional Well-Being of Young People Seeking Asylum in the UK*. London: British Association of Adoption and Fostering.

Chau, P.-L. and Herring, J. (2002) 'Defining, assigning and designing sex', *International Journal of Law, Policy and the Family*, 16, 3, 327–67.

Choudhry, S. and Herring, J. (2006) 'Righting domestic violence', *International Journal of Law, Policy and the Family*, 20, 95–119.

Clark, C. (2006) 'Against confidentiality? Privacy, safety and the public good in professional communications', *Journal of Social Work*, 6, 2, 117–36.

Clark, H., Dyer, S. and Horwood, J. (1998) *'That Bit of Help': The High Value of Low Level Preventive Services for Older People*. Bristol: Policy Press.

Clark, H., Gough, H. and Macfarlane, A. (2004) *'It Pays Dividends': Direct Payments and Older People*. Bristol: Policy Press.

Clark, J. (2003) *Independence Matters: An Overview of the Performance of Social Care Services for Physically and Sensory Disabled People*. London: Department of Health.

Clarkson, P. and Challis, D. (2004) 'The assessment gap', *Community Care*, 15–21 July, 38–9.

Cleaver, H. (2000) *Fostering Family Contact*. London: The Stationery Office.

Cleaver, H. and Walker, S. (2004) 'From policy to practice: the implementation of a new framework for social work assessments of children and families', *Child and Family Social Work*, 9, 81–90.

Cleaver, H., Barnes, J., Bliss, D. and Cleaver, D. (2004) *Developing Identification, Referral and Tracking Systems: An Evaluation of the Processes Undertaken by Trailblazer Authorities*. London: Department for Education and Skills.

Clements, L. (2005) *Carers and Their Rights: The Law Relating to Carers*. London: Carers UK.

Clements, L. and Thompson, P. (2007) *Community Care and the Law*. London: Legal Action Group.

Coles, B., Britton, L. and Hicks, L. (2004) *Building Better Connections: Interagency Work and the Connexions Service*. Bristol: Policy Press.

Colton, M., Drury, C. and Williams, M. (1995) 'Children in need: definition, identification and support', *British Journal of Social Work*, 25, 6, 711–28.

Corby, B., Millar, M. and Pope, A. (2002) 'Assessing children in need assessments – a parental perspective', *Practice*, 14, 4, 5–15.

CPS (2001) *Provision of Therapy for Child Witnesses prior to a Criminal Trial*. London: Crown Prosecution Service.

Crawford, A. and Lister, S. (2007) *The Use and Impact of Dispersal Orders: Sticking Plasters and Wake-Up Calls*. Bristol: Policy Press.

Crawshaw, M. and Wates, M. (2005) 'Mind the gap: a case study for changing organisational responses to disabled parents and their families using evidence based practice', *Research Policy and Planning*, 23, 2, 111–22.

CSCI (2007) *Growing Up Matters. Better Transition Planning for Young People with Complex Needs*. London: Commission for Social Care Inspection.

CSCI (2008a) *The State of Social Care in England 2006–07*. London: Commission for Social Care Inspection.

CSCI (2008b) *Cutting the Cake Fairly: CSCI Review of Eligibility Criteria for Social Care*. London: Commission for Social Care Inspection.

CSCI (2008c) *Safeguarding Adults: A Study of the Effectiveness of Arrangements to Safeguard Adults from Abuse*. London: Commission for Social Care Inspection.

CWDC (2007) *Common Assessment Framework for Children and Young People: Practitioners' Guide*. Leeds: Children's Workforce Development Council.

Daniel, B. and Baldwin, N. (2001) 'Assessment practice in cases of child neglect: a developmental project', *Practice*, 13, 4, 21–38.

Davis, A., Ellis, K. and Rummery, K. (1998) *Access to Assessment: Perspectives of Practitioners, Disabled People and Carers*. Bristol: Joseph Rowntree Foundation/Policy Press.

Davis, L. (2007) *See You In Court. A Social Worker's Guide to Presenting Evidence in Care Proceedings*. London: Jessica Kingsley Publishers.

Day Sclater, S. and Piper, C. (2000) 'Re-moralising the family?: family policy, family law and youth justice', *Child and Family Law Quarterly*, 12, 135.

DCA (2003) *Public Sector Data Sharing. Guidance on the Law*. London: Department for Constitutional Affairs.

DCA (2007) *Mental Capacity Act 2005: Code of Practice*. London: Department for Constitutional Affairs/The Stationery Office.

De Maria, W. (1997) 'Flapping clipped wings: social work ethics in the age of activism', *Australian Social Work*, 50, 4, 3–19.

DfES (2001) *Special Educational Needs. Code of Practice*. London: Department for Education and Skills.

DfES (2004a) *Every Child Matters: Change for Children*. London: The Stationery Office.

DfES (2004b) *Independent Reviewing Officers Guidance: Adoption and Children Act 2002*. London: The Stationery Office.

DfES (2004c) *National Service Framework for Children, Young People and Maternity Services*. London: Department for Education and Skills.

DfES (2005a) *Statutory Guidance on Making Arrangements to Safeguard and Promote the Welfare of Children under Section 11 of the Children Act 2004*. London: Department for Education and Skills.

DfES (2005b) *National Minimum Standards for Private Fostering*. London: The Stationery Office.

DfES (2006a) *Working Together to Safeguard Children: A Guide to Inter-Agency Working to Safeguard and Promote the Welfare of Children*. London: Department for Education and Skills.

DfES (2006b) *Every Child Matters: Change for Children. Practitioner's Guide to Information Sharing*. London: Department for Education and Skills.

DfES (2006c) *Getting the Best from Complaints. Social Care Complaints and Representations for Children, Young People and Others*. London: Department for Education and Skills.

DfES (2006d) *Care Matters: Time for Change*. London: The Stationery Office.

DfES (2007) *Care Matters: Time for Change. Summary*. London: Department for Education and Skills.

DfES (2008) *The Children Act 1989 Guidance and Regulations. Volume 1: Court Orders*. London: The Stationery Office.

DH (1989a) *The Care of Children. Principles and Practice in Regulations and Guidance*. London: HMSO.

DH (1989b) *An Introduction to the Children Act 1989*. London: HMSO.

DH (1989c) *Caring for People; Community Care in the Next Decade and Beyond.* London: HMSO.

DH (1990) *Community Care in the Next Decade and Beyond; Policy Guidance.* London: HMSO.

DH (1991a) *The Children Act 1989 Guidance and Regulations, Volume 4, Residential Care.* London: HMSO.

DH (1991b) *Care Management and Assessment: Summary of Practice Guidance.* London: HMSO.

DH (1991c) *Care Management and Assessment: Practitioners' Guide,* London: HMSO.

DH (1991d) *The Children Act 1989 Guidance and Regulations, Volume 2, Family Support, Day Care and Educational Provision.* London: HMSO.

DH (1991e) *The Children Act 1989 Guidance and Regulations, Volume 3, Family Placements,* London: HMSO.

DH (1991f) *Getting the Message Across: A Guide to Developing and Communicating Policies, Principles and Procedures on Assessment.* London: HMSO.

DH (1991g) *The Children Act 1989 Guidance and Regulations, Volume 6, Children with Disabilities.* London: HMSO.

DH (1994) *The Children Act 1989: Contact Orders Study.* London: HMSO.

DH (1995) *Child Protection – Messages from Research.* London: HMSO.

DH (1998) *Modernising Social Services.* London: The Stationery Office.

DH (1999a) *Caring About Carers: A National Strategy for Carers.* London: Department of Health.

DH (1999b) *National Service Framework for Mental Health.* London: Department of Health.

DH (2000a) *No Secrets: Guidance on Developing and Implementing Multi-Agency Policies and Procedures to Protect Vulnerable Adults from Abuse.* London: The Stationery Office.

DH (2000b) *Assessing Children in Need and their Families: Practice Guidance.* London: The Stationery Office.

DH (2000c) *Framework for the Assessment of Children in Need and their Families.* London: The Stationery Office.

DH (2000d) *A Practitioner's Guide to Carers' Assessments under the Carers and Disabled Children Act 2000.* London: Department of Health.

DH (2000e) *Data Protection Act 1998: Guidance to Social Services.* London: Department of Health.

DH (2001a) *National Adoption Standards for England.* London: The Stationery Office.

DH (2001b) *National Service Framework for Older People.* London: Department of Health.

DH (2001c) *Valuing People: A New Strategy for Learning Disability for the 21st Century.* London: Department of Health.

DH (2001d) *Direct Payments for Young Disabled People. Policy Guidance and Practice Guidance.* London: Department of Health.

DH (2001e) *Children (Leaving Care) Act 2000: Regulations and Guidance*. London: Department of Health.

DH (2002a) *Requirements for Social Work Training*. London: Department of Health.

DH (2002b) *Fair Access to Care Services. Guidance on Eligibility Criteria for Adult Social Care*. Issued with LAC(2002)13. London: Department of Health.

DH (2002c) *Guidance on the Single Assessment Process for Older People* (LAC(2002)1). London: Department of Health.

DH (2002d) *Fostering Services: National Minimum Standards Fostering Services Regulations*. London: The Stationery Office.

DH (2002e) *National Standards for the Provision of Children's Advocacy Services*. London: The Stationery Office.

DH (2002f) *Carers and Disabled Children Act 2000: Short Break Voucher Schemes*. London: Department of Health.

DH (2002g) *Children's Homes. National Minimum Standards. Children's Homes Regulations*. London: The Stationery Office.

DH (2002h) *Care Homes for Older People: National Minimum Standards and the Care Homes Regulations: Third Edition (Revised)*. London: The Stationery Office.

DH (2002i) *Promoting the Health of Looked-After Children*. London: The Stationery Office.

DH (2003a) *Fair Access to Care Services: Practice Guidance. Implementation Questions and Answers*. London: Department of Health.

DH (2003b) *Community Care, Services for Carers and Children's Services (Direct Payments) Guidance England 2003*. London: Department of Health.

DH (2003c) *Fairer Charging Policies for Home Care and Other Non-residential Social Services: Guidance for Councils with Social Services Responsibilities*. London: Department of Health.

DH (2003d) *Carers and Disabled Children Act 2000: Vouchers for Short Term Breaks. Policy and Practice Guidance*. London: Department of Health.

DH (2004) *The NSF for Mental Health – Five Years On*. London: Department of Health.

DH (2005a) *Independence, Well-Being and Choice*. London: Department of Health.

DH (2005b) *Carers and Disabled Children Act 2000 & Carers (Equal Opportunities) Act 2004 Combined Policy Guidance*. London: Department of Health.

DH (2005c) *Valuing People: The Story So Far*. London: Department of Health.

DH (2006a) *Our Health, Our Care, Our Say*. London: The Stationery Office.

DH (2006b) *Reviewing the Care Programme Approach*. London: Department of Health.

DH (2006c) *Learning From Complaints. Social Services Complaints Procedure for Adults*. London: Department of Health.

DH (2007a) *The National Framework for NHS Continuing Healthcare and NHS-funded Nursing Care*. London: Department of Health.

DH (2007b) *Modernising Adult Social Care: What's Working.* London: Department of Health.

DH (2007c) *Valuing People Now: From Progress to Transformation.* London: Department of Health.

DH (2008a) *Transforming Social Care: LAC(DH)(2008)1.* London: Department of Health.

DH (2008b) *The Case for Change: Why England Needs A New Care and Support System.* London: Department of Health.

DH (2008c) *Refocusing the Care Programme Approach: Policy and Positive Practice Guidance.* London: Department of Health.

DH (2008d) *Code of Practice: Mental Health Act 1983.* London: The Stationery Office.

DH (2008e) *Reference Guide to the Mental Health Act 1983 as amended by the Mental Health Act 2007.* London: The Stationery Office.

DH (2008f) *Safeguarding Adults: A Consultation on the Review of the No Secrets Guidance.* London: Department of Health.

DH (2008g) *The First Annual Report of the Independent Mental Capacity Advocacy Service.* London: Department of Health.

DH (2008h) *Making Experiences Count: Reform of the Health and Social Care Complaints Arrangements.* London: Department of Health.

DH/DfES (2006) *Options for Excellence: Building on the Social Care Workforce of the Future.* London: Department of Health/Department for Education and Skills.

DH/DETR (2001) *Better Care, Higher Standards.* London: Department of Health.

DH/DWP (2002) *Fairer Charging Policies for Home Care and Other Non-residential Social Services: Practice Guidance.* London: Department of Health/Department for Work and Pensions.

DH/Home Office (1992) *Review of Mental Health and Social Services for Mentally Disordered Offenders and Others Requiring Similar Services (The Reed Committee).* London: HMSO.

DHSS (1974) *Report of the Committee of Inquiry into the Care and Supervision provided in relation to Maria Colwell.* London: HMSO.

DHSS (1982) *Child Abuse: A Study of Inquiry Reports, 1973–1981.* London: HMSO.

DHSS (1985) *Social Work Decisions in Child Care.* London: HMSO.

Dickens, J. (2003) 'How to hold court', *Community Care*, 13–19 March, 38–9.

Dickens, J. (2005) 'Being "the epitome of reason": the challenges for lawyers and social workers in child care proceedings', *International Journal of Law Policy and the Family*, 19, 73–101.

Dickens, J. (2006) 'Social work, law, money and trust: paying for lawyers in child protection work', *Journal of Social Welfare and Family Law*, 28, 3 and 4, 283–95.

Dickens, J. (2008) 'Welfare, law and managerialism: inter-discursivity and inter-professional practice in child care social work', *Journal of Social Work*, 8, 1, 45–64.

Dickens, J., Howell, D., Thoburn, J. and Schofield, G. (2007) 'Children starting to be looked after by local authorities in England: an analysis of inter-authority variation and case-centred decision-making', *British Journal of Social Work*, 37, 4, 597–617.

Dobson, A. (2004) 'A pale imitation', *Community Care*, 11–17 May, 18–19.

Dunn, M., Clare, I., Holland, A. and Gunn, M. (2007) 'Constructing and reconstructing "best interests": an interpretative examination of substitute decision-making under the Mental Capacity Act 2005', *Journal of Social Welfare and Family Law*, 29, 2, 117–33.

Ellis, K. (2004) 'Promoting rights or avoiding litigation? The introduction of the Human Rights Act 1998 into adult social care in England', *European Journal of Social Work*, 7, 3, 321–40.

Ellis, K. (2007) 'Direct payments and social work practice: the significance of "street-level bureaucracy" in determining eligibility', *British Journal of Social Work*, 37, 3, 405–22.

Ellis, K., Davis, A. and Rummery, K. (1999) 'Needs assessment, "street-level bureaucracy" and the new community care', *Social Policy and Administration*, 33, 3, 262–80.

Evans, S., Huxley, P., Webber, M., Katona, C., Gately, C., Mears, A., Medina, J., Palak, S. and Kendall, T. (2005) 'The impact of "statutory duties" on mental health social workers in the UK', *Health and Social Care in the Community*, 13, 2, 145–54.

Fennell, P. (2007) *Mental Health: The New Law.* Bristol: Jordans.

Flynn, M. (2004) 'Challenging poor practice, abusive practice and inadequate complaints procedures: a personal narrative', *Journal of Adult Protection*, 6, 3, 34–44.

Flynn, M., Cotterill, L., Hayes, L. and Sloper, T. (1996) *A Break with Tradition: The Findings of a Survey of Respite Services for Adult Citizens with Learning Disabilities in England.* Manchester: National Development Team.

France, A. (1996) 'Exploitation or empowerment? Gaining access to young people's reflections on crime prevention strategies', *Groupwork*, 9, 2, 169–85.

Francis, E., David, J., Johnson, N. and Sashidharan, S. (1989) 'Black people and psychiatry in the UK', *Psychiatric Bulletin*, 13, 482–5.

Frost, N., Robinson, M. and Anning, A. (2005) 'Social workers in multidisciplinary teams: issues and dilemmas for professional practice', *Child and Family Social Work*, 10, 187–96.

Fryer, R. (1998) *Signposts to Services: Inspection of Social Services Information to the Public.* London: Department of Health/Social Services Inspectorate.

Fyson, R., Tarleton, B. and Ward, L. (2004) *Support for Living? The Impact of the Supporting People Programme on Housing and Support for Adults with Learning Disabilities.* Bristol: Policy Press.

Garrett, P. (2003) 'Swimming with dolphins: the assessment framework, New Labour, and new tools for social work with children and families', *British Journal of Social Work*, 33, 4, 441–63.

Gillen, S. (2008) 'Not so special relationship', *Community Care*, 10 July, 16–17.

Gilligan, P. (2007) 'Well motivated reformists or nascent radicals: how do applicants to the degree in social work see social problems, their origins and solutions?', *British Journal of Social Work*, 37, 4, 735–60.

Glasby, J. (2003) 'Critical commentary: bringing down the "Berlin Wall": the health and social care divide', *British Journal of Social Work*, 33, 7, 969–75.

Glasby, J. and Littlechild, R. (2002) 'Independence pays? Barriers to the progress of direct payments', *Practice*, 14, 1, 55–66.

Glendinning, C., Davies, B., Pickard, L. and Comas-Herrera, A. (2004) *Funding Long-Term Care for Older People: Lessons from Other Countries*. York: Joseph Rowntree Foundation.

Glover-Thomas, N. (2007) 'Joint working: reality or rhetoric in housing the mentally vulnerable?' *Journal of Social Welfare & Family Law*, 29, 3–4, 217–31.

Godfrey, M. and Wistow, G. (1997) 'The user perspective on managing for health outcomes: the case of mental health', *Health and Social Care in the Community*, 5, 5, 325–32.

Goldsmith, L. (2005) 'A daughter's battle', *Professional Social Work*, January, 8–9.

Goldsmith, L. and Beaver, R. (1999) *Recording with Care. Inspection of Case Recording in Social Services Departments*. London: Department of Health.

Goldson, B. (2002) 'New Labour, social justice and children: political calculation and the deserving–undeserving schism', *British Journal of Social Work*, 32, 6, 683–95.

Goodinge, S. (2000) *A Jigsaw of Services. Inspection of Services to Support Disabled Adults in their Parenting Role*. London: Department of Health.

Grimwood, C. and Popplestone, R. (1993) *Women, Management and Care*. London: Macmillan.

GSCC (2002) *Codes of Practice for Social Care Workers and Employers*. London: General Social Care Council.

GSCC (2008) *Social Work at its Best. A Statement of Social Work Roles and Tasks for the 21st Century*. London: General Social Care Council.

GTC (2006) *The Statement of Professional Values and Practice for Teachers*. London: General Teaching Council.

GTC, GSCC and NMC (2007) *Values for Integrated Working with Children and Young People*. London: General Teaching Council.

Gunn, R. (2005) 'Young people's participation in social services policy making', *Research Policy and Planning*, 23, 3, 127–37.

Hale, B. (2003) 'Editorial', *Journal of Social Welfare and Family Law*, 25, 4, iii–v.

Hamer, L. (2003) *Planning with a Purpose*. London: Health Development Agency, Local Government Association and the NHS Confederation.

Hamilton, C. (2005) *Working with Young People: Legal Responsibility and Liability*, 6th edn. Colchester: The Children's Legal Centre.

Harlow, E. (2003) 'New managerialism, social services departments, and social work practice today', *Practice*, 15, 2, 29–44.

Harlow, E. (2004) 'Protecting children: why don't core groups work? Lessons from the literature', *Practice*, 16, 1, 31–42.

Harne, L. and Radford, J. (1994) 'Reinstating patriarchy: the politics of the family and the new legislation', in A. Mullender and R. Morley (eds) *Children Living with Domestic Violence. Putting Men's Abuse of Women on the Child Care Agenda.* London: Whiting & Birch.

Harris, J. and Broad, B. (2005) *In My Own Time: Achieving Positive Outcomes for Young People Leaving Care.* Leicester: De Montfort University, Children and Families Research Unit.

Harris, N. (1997) *Special Educational Needs and Access to Justice.* Bristol: Jordans.

Harris-Short, S. (2008) 'Making and breaking family life: adoption, the state, and human rights', *Journal of Law and Society*, 35, 1, 28–51.

Harrison, J. and Shelley, P. (2004) 'Bending the rules', *Community Care*, 14–20 September, 39.

Hasler, F. (2003) 'Making choice a reality', *Community Care*, 23 April–6 May, 22–3.

Healthcare Commission and CSCI (2006) *Joint Investigation into the Provision of Services for People with Learning Disabilities at Cornwall Partnership NHS Trust.* London: Commission for Healthcare Audit and Inspection.

Health Services Ombudsman (2003) *NHS Funding for Long-Term Care.* London: The Stationery Office.

Hendey, N. and Pascall, G. (2002) *Disability and Transition to Adulthood: Achieving Independent Living.* Brighton: Pavilion Publishing.

Henricson, C. (2003) *Government and Parenting: Is there a Case for a Policy Review and a Parent's Code?* York: Joseph Rowntree Foundation.

Henwood, M. (2008) 'Self directed support: grounds for optimism', *Community Care*, 15 May, 34–5.

Herring, J. (2005) 'Farewell welfare?', *Journal of Social Welfare and Family Law*, 27, 2, 159–71.

Hester, M. and Westmarland, N. (2005) *Tackling Domestic Violence: Effective Interventions and Approaches.* London: Home Office.

HM Government (2007a) *Putting People First: A Shared Vision and Commitment to Transformation of Adult Social Care.* London: Department of Health.

HM Government (2007b) *Building on Progress: Public Services. HM Government Policy Review.* London: Prime Minister's Strategy Unit. .

HM Government (2008) *Carers at the Heart of 21st Century Families and Communities.* London: Department of Health.

HM Government (2009) *Valuing People Now: A New 3-Year Strategy for People with Learning Disabilities.* London: Department of Health.

Hoggett, B. (1990) *Mental Health Law*, 3rd edn. London: Sweet & Maxwell.

Hollingsworth, K. (2007) 'Responsibility and rights: children and their parents in the youth justice system', *International Journal of Law, Policy and the Family*, 21, 190–219.

Home Office (1995) *National Standards for the Supervision of Offenders in the Community.* London: Home Office.

Home Office (2001) *Achieving Best Evidence in Criminal Proceedings. Guidance for Vulnerable or Intimidated Witnesses, including Children*. London: The Stationery Office.

Horwath, J. (2000) 'Child care with gloves on: protecting children and young people in residential care', *British Journal of Social Work*, 30, 2, 179–91.

Huber, N. (1999) 'Children's services suffer from variable performance', *Community Care*, 21–27 October, 10–11.

Hudson, B. and Henwood, M. (2002) 'The NHS and social care: the final countdown?', *Policy and Politics*, 30, 2, 153–66.

Humphreys, C., Hester, M., Hague, G., Mullender, A., Abrahams, H. and Lowe, P. (2000) *From Good Intentions to Good Practice: Mapping Services Working with Families where there is Domestic Violence*. Bristol: Policy Press.

Humphries, B. (1997) 'Reading social work competing discourses in the Rules and Requirements for the Diploma in Social Work', *British Journal of Social Work*, 27 (5), 641–58.

Humphries, B. (2004) 'An unacceptable role for social work: implementing immigration policy', *British Journal of Social Work*, 34, 1, 93–107.

Hunt, J. and Macleod, A (1998) *Statutory Intervention in Child Protection*. Bristol: Centre for Socio-Legal Studies.

Hunt, J., Waterhouse, S. and Lutman, E. (2008) *Keeping Them in the Family: Outcomes for Children Placed in Kinship Care through Care Proceedings*. London: British Association of Adoption and Fostering.

Hunter, M. (2004) 'Councils demand coherent guidance on information-sharing systems', *Community Care*, 9–15 September, 18–19.

IASSW (2001) *International Definition of Social Work*. Copenhagen: International Association of Schools of Social Work and the International Federation of Social Workers.

James, A. and Sturgeon-Adams, L. (1999) *Helping Families after Divorce: Assistance by Order?* Bristol: Policy Press.

Jenness, V. and Grattet, R. (2005) 'The law-in-between: the effects of organizational perviousness on the policing of hate crime', *Social Problems*, 52, 3, 337–59.

Jones, A., Dharman, J. and Rajasooriya, S. (2002) *Invisible Families: The Strengths and Needs of Black Families in which Young People have Caring Responsibilities*. Bristol: Policy Press.

Jones, C. (2001) 'Voices from the front line: state social workers and New Labour', *British Journal of Social Work*, 31, 4, 547–62.

Kenny, C. (2004) 'Councils pushing patients through hospitals' revolving doors', *Community Care*, 28 October–3 November, 18–19.

Kestenbaum, A. (1999) *What Price Independence? Independent Living and People with High Support Needs*. Bristol: Policy Press.

Keywood, K. (2003) 'Gatekeepers, proxies, advocates? The evolving role of carers under mental health and mental incapacity law reforms', *Journal of Social Welfare and Family Law*, 25, 4, 355–68.

King, M. and Trowell, J. (1992) *Children's Welfare and the Law: The Limits of Legal Intervention*. London: Sage.

Kohli, R. and Mitchell, F. (eds) (2007) *Working with Unaccompanied Asylum Seeking Children: Issues for Policy and Practice*. Basingstoke: Palgrave Macmillan.

Laing, J. (2003) 'Reforming mental health law and the ECHR: will the rights of mentally vulnerable adults be protected?', *Journal of Social Welfare and Family Law*, 25, 4, 325–40.

Laming, Lord H. (2003) *The Victoria Climbié Inquiry: Report of an Inquiry by Lord Laming*. London: The Stationery Office.

Laming, Lord H. (2009) *The Protection of Children in England: A Progress Report*. London: The Stationery Office.

Law Commission (2008) *Adult Social Care: Scoping Report*. London: Law Commission.

Layton-Henry, Z. (1984) *The Politics of Race in Britain*. London: George Allen & Unwin.

Leece, D. and Leece, J. (2006) 'Direct payments: creating a two-tiered system in social care?', *British Journal of Social Work*, 36, 8, 1379–93.

Leece, J. (2002) 'Extending direct payments to informal carers: some issues for local authorities', *Practice*, 14, 2, 31–44.

Leece, J. (2007) 'Direct payments and user-controlled support: the challenges for social care commissioning', *Practice*, 19, 3, 185–98.

Lefevre, M. (2008) 'Being, doing and knowing: core qualities and skills for working with children and young people who are in care', in B. Luckcock and M. Lefevre (eds) *Direct Work: Social Work with Children and Young People in Care*. London: BAAF.

Lefevre, M., Tanner, K. and Luckcock, B. (2008) 'Developing social work students' communication skills with children and young people: a model for the qualifying level curriculum', *Child and Family Social Work*, 13, 166–76.

LGO (2002) *Report Summaries: Social Services*. London: Local Government Ombudsman.

LGO (2007) *Report Summaries: Social Services*. London: Local Government Ombudsman.

LGO (2008) *Injustice in Residential Care: A Joint Report by the Local Government Ombudsman and the Health Service Ombudsman for England. Investigations into Complaints against Buckinghamshire County Council and against Oxfordshire and Buckinghamshire Mental Health Partnership*. London: The Stationery Office.

Little, M. (1999) 'Prevention and early intervention with children in need: definitions, principles and examples of good practice', *Children and Society*, 13, 304–16.

Lloyd, L. (2006) 'A caring profession? The ethics of care and social work with older people', *British Journal of Social Work*, 36, 7, 1171–85.

London Borough of Greenwich (1987) *A Child in Mind. Report of the Commission of Inquiry into the Circumstances Surrounding the Death of Kimberley Carlile*. London Borough of Greenwich.

Lord, P., Kinder, K., Wilkin, A., Atkinson, M. and Harland, J. (2008) *Evaluating the Early Impact of Integrated Children's Services*. Slough: NFER.

Luckock, B. (2008) 'Adoption support and the negotiation of ambivalence in family policy and children's services', *Journal of Law and Society*, 35, 1, 3–27.

Luckock, B. and Hart, A. (2005) 'Adoptive family life and adoption support: policy ambivalence and the development of effective services', *Child and Family Social Work*, 10, 125.

Lumley, I. (1998) 'To you it's a job: to us it's our lives', *Professional Social Work*, July, 6–7.

Lymbery, M. (1998) 'Care management and professional autonomy: the impact of community care legislation on social work with older people', *British Journal of Social Work*, 28, 6, 863–78.

Lymbery, M. (2006) 'United we stand? Partnership working in health and social care and the role of social work in services for older people', *British Journal of Social Work*, 36, 7, 1119–34.

Lymbery, M. (2007) 'Social work in its organisational context', in M. Lymbery and K. Postle (eds) *Social Work: A Companion to Learning*. London: Sage.

Lyon, C. (2007) 'Children's participation and the promotion of their rights', *Journal of Social Welfare and Family Law*, 29, 2, 99–115.

Lyons, K. and Manion, H. (2004) 'Goodbye DipSW: trends in student satisfaction and employment outcomes. Some implications for the new social work award', *Social Work Education*, 23, 2, 133–48.

MacDonald, S. (1991) *All Equal Under the Act?* London: Race Equality Unit/National Institute for Social Work.

Machin, S. (1998) 'Swimming against the tide: a social worker's experience of a secure hospital', in G. Hunt (ed.) *Whistleblowing in the Social Services. Public Accountability and Professional Practice*. London: Arnold.

MacPherson, W. (1999) *The Stephen Lawrence Enquiry: Report of an Enquiry by Sir William MacPherson of Cluny*. London: The Stationery Office.

Magill, M. (2006) 'The future of evidence in evidence-based practice: who will answer the call for clinical relevance?', *Journal of Social Work*, 6, 2, 101–15.

Manktelow, R. and Lewis, C. (2005) 'A study of the personality attributes of applicants for postgraduate social work training', *Social Work Education*, 24, 3, 297–309.

Marsh, P. and Triseliotis, J. (1996) *Ready to Practise? Social Workers and Probation Officers: Their Training and First Year in Work*. Aldershot: Avebury.

Masson, J. (2008) 'The state as parent: the reluctant parent? The problems of parents of last resort', *Journal of Law and Society*, 35, 1, 52–74.

Masson, J., Pearce, J. and Bader, K. (with Joyner, O., Marsden, J. and Westlake, D.) (2008) *Care Profiling Study*. London: Ministry of Justice.

Mathias-Williams, R. and Thomas, N. (2002) 'Great expectations? The career aspirations of social work students', *Social Work Education*, 21, 4, 421–35.

McConnell, D. and Llewellyn, G. (2002) 'Stereotypes, parents with intellectual disability and child protection', *Journal of Social Welfare and Family Law*, 24, 3, 297–317.

McDonald, A. (2001) 'The Human Rights Act and social work practice', *Practice*, 13, 3, 6–16.

McDonald, I. and Billings, P. (2007) 'The treatment of asylum seekers in the UK', *Journal of Social Welfare and Family Law*, 29, 1, 49–65.

McKeigue, B. and Beckett, C. (2004) 'Care proceedings under the 1989 Children Act: rhetoric and reality', *British Journal of Social Work*, 34, 6, 831–49.

Michael J. (2008) *Healthcare for All. Report of the Independent Inquiry into Access to Healthcare for People with Learning Disabilities.* London: The Stationery Office.

Millar, M. and Corby, B. (2006) 'The framework for the assessment of children in need and their families – a basis for a "therapeutic" encounter?', *British Journal of Social Work*, 36, 6, 887–99.

MoJ (2008a) *Mental Capacity Act 2005: Deprivation of Liberty Safeguards: Code of Practice to supplement the main Mental Capacity Act 2005 Code of Practice.* London: Ministry of Justice/The Stationery Office.

MoJ (2008b) *The Public Law Outline. Guide to Case Management in Public Law Proceedings.* London: The Stationery Office.

Morris, J. (2003) *The Right Support: Report of the Task Force on Supporting Disabled Adults in their Parenting Role.* York: Joseph Rowntree Foundation.

Morris, J. (2004) 'They deserve better', *Community Care*, 2–8 September, 32–3.

Morris, J. (2005) *Children on the Edge of Care. Human Rights and the Children Act.* York: Joseph Rowntree Foundation.

Morris, K. (2005) 'From "children in need" to "children at risk" – the changing policy context for prevention and participation', *Practice*, 17, 2, 67–77.

Munro, E. (1996) 'Avoidable and unavoidable mistakes in child protection work', *British Journal of Social Work*, 26, 6, 793–808.

Munro, E. (1998) 'Improving social workers' knowledge base in child protection work', *British Journal of Social Work*, 28, 1, 73–88.

Murphy, J. (2002) 'The recognition of same-sex families in Britain: the role of private international law', *International Journal of Law, Policy and the Family*, 16, 2, 181–201.

Musgrove, A. and Groves, N. (2007) 'The Domestic Violence, Crime and Victims Act 2004: relevant or "removed" legislation?', *Journal of Social Welfare and Family Law*, 29, 3–4, 233–44.

NACRO (2004) *The Mental Health of Children and Young People who Offend.* London: National Association for the Care and Resettlement of Offenders.

NACRO (2006) *Out of Court: Making the Most of Diversion for Young People (Recent Developments).* London: National Association for the Care and Resettlement of Offenders.

NACRO (2007a) *Mental Capacity and Related Crimes in the Youth Court.* London: National Association for the Care and Resettlement of Offenders.

NACRO (2007b) *Young Black People and the Criminal Justice System: The Home Affairs Committee Report.* London: National Association for the Care and Resettlement of Offenders.

NACRO (2008a) *Police Bail, Detention after Charge and the Duty to Transfer to Local Authority Accommodation*. London: National Association for the Care and Resettlement of Offenders.

NACRO (2008b) *Remands to Local Authority Accommodation: Secure and Non-Secure*. London: National Association for the Care and Resettlement of Offenders.

NACRO (2008c) *Children's Human Rights and the Youth Justice System*. London: National Association for the Care and Resettlement of Offenders.

NACRO (2008d) *The Dangerousness Provisions for Children and Young People Following Implementation of the Criminal Justice and Immigration Act 2008*. London: National Association for the Care and Resettlement of Offenders.

NCSC (2001) *Care Homes for Older People. National Minimum Standards*. London: The Stationery Office.

Newbiggin, K. and Lowe, J. (2005) *Direct Payments and Mental Health: New Directions*. Brighton: Pavilion Publishing.

Newton, J., Ryan, P., Carman, A., Clarke, K., Coombs, M., Walsh, K. and Muijen, M. (1996) *Care Management: Is It Working*? London: Sainsbury Centre for Mental Health.

NICE (2006) *Dementia. Supporting People with Dementia and their Carers in Health and Social Care*. London: National Institute for Health and Clinical Excellence and Social Care Institute for Excellence.

Ofsted (2005) *Every Child Matters. Framework for the Inspection of Children's Services*. Manchester: Ofsted.

Ofsted (2007) *Joint Area Review of Children's Services from April 2007*. Manchester: Ofsted.

ONS (2002) *Carers 2000*. London: Office for National Statistics.

Onyett, S., Standen, R. and Peck, E. (1997) 'The challenge of managing community mental health teams', *Health and Social Care in the Community*, 5, 1, 40–7.

Orme, J. and Rennie, G. (2006) 'The role of registration in ensuring ethical practice', *International Social Work*, 49, 3, 333–44.

Parmar, A., Sampson, A. and Diamond, A. (2005) *Tackling Domestic Violence: Providing Advocacy and Support to Survivors of Domestic Violence*. London: Home Office.

Peckover, S., Hall, C. and White, S. (2009) 'From policy to practice: the implementation and negotiation of technologies in everyday child welfare', *Children and Society*, 23, 2, 136–48.

Penna, S. (2005) 'The Children Act 2004: child protection and social surveillance', *Journal of Social Welfare and Family Law*, 27, 2, 143–57.

Petrie, S., Fiorelli, L. and O'Donnell, K. (2006) '"If we help you what will change?" – participatory research with young people', *Journal of Social Welfare and Family Law*, 28, 1, 31–45.

Pilgrim, D., Todhunter, C. and Pearson, M. (1997) 'Accounting for disability: customer feedback or citizen complaints?', *Disability and Society*, 12, 1, 3–15.

Pithouse, A. and Crowley, A. (2007) 'Adults rule? Children, advocacy and complaints to social services', *Children and Society*, 21, 201–13.

Platt, D. (2006) 'Investigation or initial assessment of child concerns? The impact of the refocusing initiative on social work practice', *British Journal of Social Work*, 36, 2, 267–81.

Plotnikoff, J. and Woolfson, R. (1996) *Reporting to Court under the Children Act. A Handbook for Social Services,* London: HMSO.

Postle, K. (2007) 'Value conflicts in practice', in M. Lymbery and K. Postle (eds) *Social Work: A Companion to Learning.* London: Sage.

Postle, K., Wright, P. and Beresford, P. (2005) 'Older people's participation in political activity – making their voice heard: a potential support role for welfare professionals in countering ageism and social exclusion', *Practice*, 17, 3, 173–89.

Preston-Shoot, M. (2000a) 'Making connections in the curriculum: law and professional practice', in R. Pierce and J. Weinstein (eds) *Innovative Education and Training for Care Professionals: A Providers' Guide.* London: Jessica Kingsley Publishers.

Preston-Shoot, M. (2000b) 'What if? Using the law to uphold practice values and standards', *Practice*, 12, 4, 49–63.

Preston-Shoot, M. (2001a) 'Regulating the road of good intentions: observations on the relationship between policy, regulations and practice in social work', *Practice*, 13, 4, 5–20.

Preston-Shoot, M. (2001b) 'Evaluating self-determination: an adult protection case study', *Journal of Adult Protection*, 3, 1, 4–14.

Preston-Shoot, M. (2001c) 'A triumph of hope over experience? Modernizing accountability: the case of complaints procedures in community care', *Social Policy and Administration*, 35, 6, 701–15.

Preston-Shoot, M. (2003a) 'Changing learning and learning change: making a difference in education, policy and practice', *Journal of Social Work Practice*, 17, 1, 9–23.

Preston-Shoot, M. (2003b) 'A matter of record?', *Practice*, 15, 3, 31–50.

Preston-Shoot, M. (2008) 'Things must only get better', *Professional Social Work*, March, 14–15.

Preston-Shoot, M. and Vernon, S. (2002) 'From mapping to travelling: negotiating the complex and confusing terrain of youth justice', *Youth and Policy*, 77, 47–65.

Preston-Shoot, M. and Wigley, V. (2002) 'Closing the circle: social workers' responses to multi-agency procedures on older age abuse', *British Journal of Social Work*, 32, 3, 299–320.

Preston-Shoot, M. and Wigley, V. (2004) 'Mapping older people's needs', *Research Policy and Planning*, 22, 3, 35–50.

Preston-Shoot, M. and Wigley, V. (2005) 'Mapping the needs of children in need', *British Journal of Social Work*, 35, 2, 255–75.

Preston-Shoot, M., Roberts, G. and Vernon, S. (1997) '"We work in isolation often and in ignorance occasionally." On the experiences of practice teachers teaching and assessing social work law', *Social Work Education*, 16, 4, 4–34.

Preston-Shoot, M., Roberts, G. and Vernon, S. (1998a) 'Social work law: from interaction to integration', *Journal of Social Welfare and Family Law*, 20, 1, 65–80.

Preston-Shoot, M., Roberts, G. and Vernon, S. (1998b) '"I am concerned at the possible level of legal input expected from practice teachers." Developing expertise in teaching and assessing social work law', *Social Work Education*, 17, 2, 219–31.

Preston-Shoot, M., Roberts, G. and Vernon, S. (1998c) 'Working together in social work law', *Journal of Social Welfare and Family Law*, 20, 2, 137–50.

Preston-Shoot, M., Roberts, G. and Vernon, S. (2001) 'Values in social work law: strained relations or sustaining relationships?', *Journal of Social Welfare and Family Law*, 23, 1, 1–22.

QAA (2004) *A Statement of Common Purpose for Subject Benchmarks for the Health and Social Care Professions*. Gloucester: Quality Assurance Agency for Higher Education.

QAA (2008) *Subject Benchmark Statements: Social Work*. Gloucester: Quality Assurance Agency for Higher Education.

Radford, L. and Hester, M. (2006) *Mothering Through Domestic Violence*. London: Jessica Kingsley Publishers.

Reder, P. and Duncan, S. (1999) *Lost Innocents: A Follow-up Study of Fatal Child Abuse*. London: Routledge.

Reder, P. and Duncan, S. (2003) 'Understanding communication in child protection networks', *Child Abuse Review*, 12, 82–100.

Reder, P. and Duncan, S. (2004) 'Making the most of the Victoria Climbié inquiry report', *Child Abuse Review*, 13, 95–114.

Reder, P., Duncan, S. and Gray, M. (1993) *Beyond Blame. Child Abuse Tragedies Revisited*. London: Routledge.

Richards, S. (2000) 'Bridging the divide: elders and the assessment process', *British Journal of Social Work*, 30, 1, 37–49.

Richardson, S. and Asthana, S. (2006) 'Inter-agency information sharing in health and social care services: the role of professional culture', *British Journal of Social Work*, 36, 4, 657–69.

Ritchie, J., Dick, D. and Lingham, R. (1994) *Report of the Inquiry into the Care and Treatment of Christopher Clunis*. London: HMSO.

Roberts, K. and Harris, J. (2002) *Disabled People in Refugee and Asylum Seeking Communities*. Bristol: Policy Press.

Robinson, C. and Williams, V. (2002) 'Carers of people with learning disabilities and their experience of the 1995 Carers Act', *British Journal of Social Work*, 32, 2, 169–83.

Robson, P., Begum, N. and Locke, M. (2003) *Developing User Involvement. Working Towards User-Centred Practice in Voluntary Organisations*. Bristol: Policy Press.

Roche, D. and Rankin, J. (2004) *Who Cares? Building the Social Care Workforce*. London: IPPR.

Rummery, K. and Glendinning, C. (1999) 'Negotiating needs, access and gate-keeping: developments in health and community care policies in the UK and the rights of disabled and older citizens', *Critical Social Policy*, 60, 335–51.

Sagar, T. and Hitchings, E. (2007) '"More adoptions, more quickly": a study of social workers' responses to the Adoption and Children Act 2002', *Journal of Social Welfare & Family Law*, 29, 3–4, 199–215.

Sashidharan, S. (1989) 'Schizophrenic – or just black?', *Community Care*, 783, 14–15.

Sashidharan, S. (2003) *Inside Out: Improving Mental Health Services for Black and Minority Ethnic Communities in England.* London: Department of Health/ National Institute for Mental Health in England.

Sawyer, C. (2006) 'The child is not a person: family law and other legal cultures', *Journal of Social Welfare and Family Law*, 28, 1, 1–14.

SCIE (2007) *Choice, Control and Individual Budgets: Emerging Themes.* Research Briefing 20. London: Social Care Institute for Excellence.

SCIE (2008) *Promoting Dignity with the Law.* London: Social Care Institute for Excellence.

Scourfield, P. (2007) 'Reviewing residential care reviews for older people', *Practice*, 19, 3, 199–209.

Selwyn, J., Frazer, L. and Quinton, D. (2006) 'Paved with good intentions: the pathway to adoption and the costs of delay', *British Journal of Social Work*, 36, 4, 561–76.

Sharland, E. (2006) 'Young people, risk taking and risk making: some thoughts for social work', *British Journal of Social Work*, 36, 247–65.

Sheppard, D. (1996) *Learning the Lessons*, 2nd edn. London: Zito Trust.

Sims, J. (2004) 'Putting up a fight', *Community Care*, 27 July–2 August, 24–5.

Sinclair, I. and Corden, J. (2005) *A Management Solution to Keeping Children Safe: Can Agencies on their Own Achieve What Lord Laming Wants?* York: Joseph Rowntree Foundation.

Sinclair, R. and Bullock, R. (2002) *Learning from Past Experience – A Review of Serious Case Reviews.* London: Department of Health.

Smith, C. (2005) 'Trust v law: promoting and safeguarding post-adoption contact', *Journal of Social Welfare and Family Law*, 27, 3 and 4, 315–32.

Smith, J. (1999) 'Prior criminality and employment of social workers with substantial access to children: a decision board analysis', *British Journal of Social Work*, 29, 1, 49–68.

Smith, R. (2002) 'The wrong end of the telescope: child protection or child safety?', *Journal of Social Welfare and Family Law*, 24, 3, 247–61.

Stalker, K., Duckett, P. and Downs, M. (1999) *Going with the Flow: Choice, Dementia and People with Learning Difficulties.* Brighton: Pavilion Publishing.

Stanley, N. (1999) 'User-practitioner transactions in the new culture of community care', *British Journal of Social Work*, 29, 3, 417–35.

Stanley, N. and Manthorpe, J. (eds) (2004) *The Age of the Inquiry.* London: Routledge.

Statham, J. and Aldgate, J. (2003) 'From legislation to practice: learning from the Children Act 1989 research programme', *Children and Society*, 17, 149–56.

Stein, M. (2005) *Resilience and Young People Leaving Care*. York: Joseph Rowntree Foundation.

Stepney, P. (2006) 'Mission impossible? Critical practice in social work', *British Journal of Social Work*, 36, 8, 1289–307.

Stevenson, O. (1988) 'Law and social work education: a commentary on the "Law Report"', *Issues in Social Work Education*, 8, 1, 37–45.

Suto, W., Clare, I. and Holland, A. (2002) 'Substitute financial decision-making in England and Wales: a study of the Court of Protection', *Journal of Social Welfare and Family Law*, 24, 1, 37–54.

Swain, P. (2002) *In the Shadow of the Law: The Legal Context of Social Work Practice*. Sydney: Federation Press.

SWIA (2005) *An Inspection into the Care and Protection of Children in Eilean Siar*. Edinburgh: Scottish Executive.

Syrett, V., Jones, M. and Sercombe, N. (1997) 'Implementing community care: the congruence of manager and practitioner cultures', *Social Work and Social Sciences Review*, 7, 3, 154–69.

Tanner, D. (1998) 'Empowerment and care management: swimming against the tide', *Health and Social Care in the Community*, 6, 6, 447–57.

Tanner, D. (2003) 'Older people and access to care', *British Journal of Social Work*, 33, 4, 499–515.

Tanner, D. (2005) 'Promoting the well-being of older people: messages for social workers', *Practice*, 17, 3, 191–205.

TOPSS (2002) *The National Occupational Standards for Social Work*. Leeds: Training Organisation for the Personal Social Services.

Trinder, L., Beek, M. and Connolly, J. (2002) *Making Contact: How Parents and Children Negotiate and Experience Contact After Divorce*. York: Joseph Rowntree Foundation.

UN (2008) *Convention on the Rights of the Child. Consideration of Reports Submitted by States Parties under Article 44 of the Convention: Concluding Observations – United Kingdom of Great Britain and Northern Ireland*. CRC/C/GBR/CO/4. UN Committee on the Rights of the Child.

UNICEF (2008) 'UK government withdraws reservations to UNCRC', http://www.unicef.org.uk/press/news_detail_full_story.asp?news_id=1198. Accessed 10 January 2009.

Utting, W. (1996) 'The case for reforming social services law', in T. Harding (ed.) *Social Services Law: The Case for Reform*. London: NISW.

Valentine, M. (1994) 'The social worker as "bad object"', *British Journal of Social Work*, 24, 1, 71–86.

Valios, N. (2006) 'An inspector in the family', *Community Care*, 7–13 December, 30–31.

Vernon, A. (2002) *User-defined Outcomes of Community Care for Asian Disabled People*. Bristol: Policy Press.

Vidler, E. and Clarke, J. (2005) 'Creating citizen-consumers: New Labour and the remaking of public services', *Public Policy and Administration*, 20, 19–37.

Wade, J., Mitchell, F. and Baylis, G. (2005) *Unaccompanied Asylum Seeking Children: The Response of Social Work Services*. London: British Association of Adoption and Fostering.

Walton, P. (2000) 'Reforming the Mental Health Act 1983: an approved social worker perspective', *Journal of Social Welfare and Family Law*, 22, 4, 401–14.

Ward, A. (1996) 'Never mind the theory, feel the guidelines. Practice theory and official guidance in residential child care: the case of the therapeutic communities', *Therapeutic Communities*, 17, 1, 19–29.

Warner, L., Bennett, S., Ford, R. and Thompson, K. (1997) *Home from Home: A Guide to Good Practice in the Provision of Housing and Support to People with Mental Health Problems*. London: Sainsbury Centre for Mental Health.

Waterhouse, R. (2000) *Lost in Care: Report of the Tribunal of Inquiry into the Abuse of Children in Care in the former Council Areas of Gwynedd and Clwyd*. London: The Stationery Office.

Wates, M. (2002) *Supporting Disabled Adults in their Parenting Role*. York: Joseph Rowntree Foundation.

Wellard, S. (1999) 'Inspection in a state of decay', *Community Care*, 7–13 October, 14–15.

Wells, J. (1997) 'Priorities, "street level bureaucracy" and the community mental health team', *Health and Social Care in the Community*, 5, 5, 333–42.

White, S. and Featherstone, B. (2005) 'Communicating misunderstandings: multi-agency work as social practice', *Child and Family Social Work*, 10, 207–16.

Williams, J. (2002) 'Public law protection of vulnerable adults: the debate continues, so does the abuse', *Journal of Social Work*, 2, 3, 293–316.

Williams, V. and Robinson, C. (2000) *In Their Own Right. The Carers Act and Carers of People with Learning Disabilities*. Bristol: Policy Press.

Willis, M. (2002) 'A case for training', *Community Care*, 17–23 January, 42.

Wilmot, S. (1997) *The Ethics of Community Care*. London: Cassell.

Wistow, G. (2005) *Developing Social Care: The Past, the Present and the Future*. London: Social Care Institute for Excellence.

Wyld, N. and Mendoza, L. (1998) 'Children's law review', *Legal Action*, April, 17–22.

Yarrow, S. (2005) *The Experiences of Young Black Men as Victims of Crime*. London: Criminal Justice System Race Unit/Home Office.

YJB (2004) *ASSET – Young Offender Assessment Profile: Introduction*. London: Youth Justice Board.

Author index

Subject index